Guide to North American
DIESEL
LOCOMOTIVES

Jeff Wilson

KALMBACH BOOKS

Kalmbach Books
21027 Crossroads Circle
Waukesha, Wisconsin 53186
www.KalmbachHobbyStore.com

Published in 2017
21 20 19 18 17   1 2 3 4 5

Manufactured in China

ISBN: 978-1-62700-455-8
EISBN: 978-1-62700-456-5

On the cover: BNSF 8411, an EMD SD70ACe built in 2014, leads an
eastbound train of empty grain hoppers on BNSF's Kootenai River
Subdivision near Fisher River, Montana, on February 7, 2016.
Tom Danneman

Library of Congress Control Number: 2016955351

C O N T E N T S

— INTRODUCTION —

Electro-Motive's GP7, introduced in 1949, wasn't the first road switcher. However, it proved to be among the most popular, with more than 2,700 built. These locomotives, with similar offerings from Alco and others, soon eliminated steam locomotives from railroads across North America. *EMD*

Whether you are a railfan, modeler, history buff, or any combination thereof, this book will take you through the history of diesel locomotive evolution and guide you through the hundreds of different models and variations that have been produced since the 1930s.

Starting in the 1920s, manufacturers realized that pairing an internal-combustion engine with a generator and electric motors on the axles had great promise for locomotives. Starting with small switching locomotives and progressing to ever-larger road locomotives, diesels eventually overtook steam locomotives. By the 1960s, steam was history, and diesel progression continued with the evolution of microprocessor control and AC traction motors. Today's 4,400-horsepower locomotives are powerful, fuel-efficient, reliable, technological marvels, but they still trace their roots to the pioneering locomotives of the 1930s and '40s.

Builders and models

By the 1940s, five major diesel locomotive builders had emerged: Electro-Motive (EMD), American Locomotive Co. (Alco), Baldwin, Fairbanks-Morse, and Lima. By the late 1950s this had dwindled to two—EMD and Alco—but then General Electric joined in, shortly relegating Alco to third place before Alco finally left the business in 1969. The market has belonged to EMD and GE since then.

Manufacturers offer a variety of models for different purposes, including switching, passenger, and freight service, with each often available in varying horsepower ratings. Most diesel locomotive models remain in production for several years, unlike automobiles, where a new model is introduced each year. Locomotive builders generally introduce new models for significant changes, such as a boost in horsepower or change in engine (prime mover).

Details and spotting features often change during each locomotive's production run. These changes can be large or small and reflect modifications to upgrade performance, replace troublesome components, cut manufacturing costs, or standardize components with other models. Examples include changes in grille, louver, and access door style or location, handrail style, window style or location, frame length, or cab and hood shape and style.

Other spotting features involve optional components. These usually vary by railroad preference, and can encompass multiple options offered by a builder. Examples include horn and bell (style and location), fuel tank size, headlight style and location, truck type, high or low nose (for first- and second-generation hood units), and

Long Island Rail Road No. 401, a 100-ton boxcab built by Alco/GE/Ingersoll-Rand, is often credited with being the first road diesel-electric in the U.S. *Long Island Rail Road*

whether a locomotive is equipped with dynamic brakes or a steam generator.

Locomotive model numbers or designations sometimes make sense, (often following the horsepower rating and number of axles), but often they don't—especially for EMD, long the dominant locomotive builder. The chapters on manufacturers include a description of each builder's nomenclature.

What's included

This book offers a summary of standard-gauge, heavy-duty diesel-electric models built by major manufacturers for use in the U.S., Canada, and Mexico. Builders covered include EMD, GE, Alco, Baldwin, Fairbanks-Morse, and Lima, along with their Canadian subsidiaries. It does not include small industrial switchers, electric locomotives, locomotives built for export, turbine locomotives, or experimental locomotives (or some locomotives where only a few were built).

Chapters 5 through 9 provide a model-by-model listing for each manufacturer, with basic spotting and identification features and information for each type. Summaries for each locomotive type list the major buyers for each model. If space allows, all initial buyers are included; some

include as-delivered road numbers (secondary owners are not included).

Tables in each of these chapters provide the total number built for each locomotive type, timelines of the period each was built (black lines), with an estimation of the years they remained in service (shaded gray lines). Use these as general guides, as with the thousands of locomotives built (and later rebuilt) it's impossible to verify the exact dates that all samples of a certain model are out of service.

Chapter 11 includes diesel rosters for more than 120 individual railroads, including road numbers (and changes) and dates built. Most are historical summaries of railroads that no longer exist (mainly through mergers, sales, or abandonment), but current summaries of current Class 1 railroads are included.

Railroads began rebuilding older locomotives in the 1950s. Several railroads embarked on major rebuilding programs from the 1960s onward, and many independent shops provide rebuilding services as well. Chapter 10 provides a summary of this, but the sheer number of rebuilds—not to mention the myriad new designations and model numbers given them—precludes providing spotting and roster information for all of them.

CHAPTER ONE

Diesel locomotive history

A matched A-B-B-A set of Electro-Motive FTs leads a Santa Fe train upgrade at Tehachapi, Calif., in the 1940s. The FT, introduced in 1939, proved that diesel-electric locomotives could perform well in heavy-haul mainline freight service—and do it economically—leading the way for the complete dieselization of American railroads. *Linn Westcott*

By the early 1900s, steam locomotives had become quite powerful. Many locomotives of the period were rated at 4,000 hp or higher, with tractive effort of 80,000 pounds and more. Larger and faster steam locomotives were being developed. Despite the widespread success and acceptance of the automobile, there were few applications of internal combustion in railroading. Other than gas-electric "doodlebug" motor cars, which began appearing around the turn of the century, and a few small experimental internal-combustion switchers, steam was the unquestioned champion of railroad power.

Gas-electric motor cars were the first successful applications of internal combustion on railroads. Chicago, Burlington & Quincy No. 9838 was an Electro-Motive product built by St. Louis Car Co. in 1927. It was powered by a 275-hp gasoline engine. *Gordon Lloyd*

By the 1920s, however, the diesel locomotive began making inroads as higher-horsepower boxcab diesel switchers began to appear. The 1930s saw diesels powering new, high-speed streamlined passenger trains. Finally, on the eve of World War II, the first heavy-duty diesel freight locomotive, the Electro-Motive FT, began its demonstration tour across the country. By the end of the war, the dieselization of North American railroads was well underway.

How did diesels replace steam—and do it so quickly? Simply put, economics. Even though diesel locomotives were more expensive and—in most cases—less powerful than a single steam locomotive, steam locomotives required an army of people to maintain them. Diesel locomotives could go farther between both routine and heavy maintenance stops. There were no ashes to dump or boiler tubes to clean. This also gave diesels a significantly higher availability percentage than steam, meaning fewer diesel locomotives were needed.

Mass production of diesels meant interchangeable parts, unlike steam locomotives, which had parts unique to that locomotive, or perhaps to a locomotive class.

Diesels proved to be flexible. A single road diesel model, by adding or removing units and changing gearing, was suitable for almost any application from pulling a fast freight train on the prairie to mountain helper service. Multiple diesels were controlled by one engineer. Running two

steam locomotives was called "double-heading," and required a crew for each locomotive. Also, each steam locomotive was of a type or class built for a specific task, and was usually unsuited for other duties.

Early internal combustion

Shortly after the automobile began taking over for the horse and wagon, enterprising individuals and companies began experimenting with methods of applying internal-combustion engines to railroad locomotives.

A fundamental problem was that a typical steam locomotive in 1900, although small by "modern steam" standards, was still a powerful machine. Contemporary gasoline engines, on the other hand, were small and limited in power.

After a few abortive attempts, the consensus became that the best way to apply the technology was by not using the engine to directly drive the wheels. Instead, an internal-combustion engine (gas, distillate, or diesel-powered) would drive a generator, which provided power to electric traction motors mounted on the trucks and axles. Heavy-duty electric locomotives had been in service since the turn of the century, so this was not exactly a new technology.

Gas-electric railcars began appearing in the early 1900s, and by the 1920s had proven themselves economical for branch line passenger service. They were becoming more powerful, from early 200-hp models

to twin-engine 800-hp railcars. Railroads would use them for pulling trailing coaches and occasional freight cars, but their relatively low power and light weight kept them from hauling a standard full-length train.

The main obstacle to development was power. Gasoline engines were reaching their largest practical limits, and gasoline prices were increasing with the growing popularity of the automobile. The explosive properties of gasoline also made gas-powered locomotives (and their requisite large fuel tanks) less than attractive options.

Distillate engines were one alternative. Distillate—which covered a wide range of refined products ranging from kerosene to naptha or light oil—was inexpensive, and large distillate engines were practical to build. The main problem with these engines was that distillate didn't burn easily, and required a complex firing system with multiple spark plugs in each cylinder head. The heavy nature of the fuel also tended to foul spark plugs quickly, meaning frequent replacement and high maintenance costs.

Practical diesels

The most promising technology was the diesel engine. Diesels offered several advantages over gasoline and distillate engines: Diesel fuel was cheaper than gasoline and presented less of a fire/explosion hazard. Diesel engines are more efficient than gas engines, delivering more power

Two eight-cylinder, 600-hp Winton 201 diesel engines were on display at the World's Fair in Chicago in 1933 and 1934. They provided power for the General Motors building at the Century of Progress exhibit. *EMD*

for the equivalent amount of fuel burned. Diesel engines last longer than gasoline engines, and diesels don't use spark plugs to ignite fuel as do gasoline and distillate engines.

Developed by Rudolf Diesel in the early 1890s, the diesel engine takes advantage of the heat created by high compression of air in a piston cylinder—rather than a spark—to ignite fuel in the combustion chamber. By the 1920s, diesel technology was no longer new, and diesel engines had been used successfully in many applications. However, diesels of that era were heavy, large, and slow. They were well suited to constant-speed stationary applications (such as power plants) or large moving platforms, such as ships.

Adapting a diesel engine to a locomotive platform by reducing its weight and physical size and making it durable enough to withstand the rigors of motion, changes in weather, and constant changes in power output presented a formidable challenge to engineers. The biggest advance was the injector that fed diesel fuel into the cylinder at extremely high pressure, eliminating the long (and large and heavy) fuel lines

that made earlier diesel engines cumbersome.

The American Locomotive Co. (Alco) partnered with General Electric and Ingersoll-Rand to produce several 300- and 600-hp diesel boxcab switchers in the mid-1920s. These were the first commercially available diesel locomotives, followed by Alco end-cab switchers in the early 1930s.

In 1932 the Winton Engine Co. (by then a subsidiary of General Motors) developed its model 201 diesel engine. The eight-cylinder, 600-hp engine was notable because it was a two-cycle engine, as opposed to earlier diesels, which were all four-cycle designs. The 201 had been designed as a power plant for Navy submarines, but would soon find its way into railroad applications.

Two of these engines were displayed at the Century of Progress exhibition in Chicago in 1933 and 1934. At the same time, the Chicago, Burlington & Quincy and the Edward G. Budd Manufacturing Co. were designing the railroad's lightweight streamlined *Zephyr* passenger train and were looking for a suitable engine to power it. After seeing the Winton diesel at the

Century of Progress, Burlington president Ralph Budd opted for a 201A diesel to power his train.

In spite of some teething problems, the diesel performed well. The train received a tremendous amount of publicity as it toured the country before going into service in 1934. Most notable was the *Zephyr's* non-stop run from Denver to Chicago on May 26, 1934. The 13-hour, 5-minute trip received extensive coverage from newspapers and radio throughout the country. The streamliner era had begun, and with it the diesel-electric locomotive. In short order the diesel became the new, fashionable trend to the general public.

The 201A would soon find its way into other Burlington passenger trains, Electro-Motive Corp. switching engines, and a variety of custom-built passenger power cars and locomotives, including the Illinois Central's *Green Diamond*, Boston & Maine's *Flying Yankee*, and others.

Heavy freight service
Through the mid- to late 1930s, diesel switchers became quite popular. Even die-hard steam supporters acknowledged that

The Chicago, Burlington & Quincy's *Zephyr* was the first diesel streamliner, entering service in 1934. The locomotive, which was articulated with the train set, was powered by a 660-hp Winton 201A diesel engine. *David P. Morgan Library collection*

diesel-electrics had their place as switchers, where low speed and high tractive effort rather than high horsepower were the important attributes. The diesels' short downtime for refueling and basic maintenance and their lower smoke output helped them bump steam from switching duties.

High-speed, lightweight passenger trains were another success area for diesels, proven by the *Zephyr* and other streamliners as well as stand-alone streamlined carbody diesels from Alco and EMC.

Heavy-duty freight service, however, was ruled by steam locomotives. Contemporary steam locomotives were powerful machines, with 2-8-4s, 4-8-4s, and 4-6-6-4s capable of pulling mile-long freight trains at high speeds. Few at the time thought that a diesel locomotive could be powerful enough or withstand the rigors of heavy-haul service well enough to displace steam.

The diesel that changed everything was EMC's pioneering FT of 1939. Electro-Motive took lessons learned from its earlier switchers and passenger locomotives and applied that knowledge—with a new, more powerful engine (the 567)—to a four-axle freight locomotive.

The streamlined FT was actually two units—an "A unit" with a cab and a cabless "B unit" booster, connected by a drawbar to form a single locomotive. Each was powered by a single 1,350-hp, 16-cylinder 567, driving four axles, with a traction motor on each. Two A-B sets could then be coupled back to back to form an A-B-B-A set with a combined horsepower of 5,400, putting it on a par with contemporary steam locomotives.

The initial FT demonstrator set went on a nationwide tour in 1939, where it proved itself in a variety of operating environments and situations, including mountain grades and prairies, drag freights, and high-speed time freights. Although the FT had a high price tag compared to an equivalent steam locomotive, the demonstrators showed the diesel had several advantages. General operating availability was much higher, as diesels didn't have to stop for coal or water or to dump ashes. Routine maintenance took less time as well, and—other than refueling—a diesel rarely had to pause.

Railroads liked the idea of a single freight locomotive that could be used in several types of service. By adding or subtracting units, a train could receive as much power as needed, and those multiple units were all controlled by a single engineer.

The biggest cost advantage of the diesel was maintenance: The army of men and extensive forge and shop equipment required to maintain steam locomotives were no longer needed for diesel locomotives.

World War II interrupted a lot of diesel locomotive production, but the War Production Board allowed Electro-Motive to continue building FTs for the duration of the war. The other diesel builders were limited to building switchers, again as allocated by the WPB. The hundreds of FTs built during WWII both proved the viability of the diesel and gave EMD a huge lead over its competitors in the learning curve in road-unit diesel production.

Dieselization began on a grand scale following the war, with railroads ordering thousands of diesels from several builders. By the late 1940s it was obvious to most railroaders that full dieselization was just a

An Electro-Motive Corporation FT A and B—half of the original demonstrator set No. 103—pose for the company photographer in 1939. The locomotives were about to embark on a nationwide journey to demonstrate the diesels' capabilities. *EMD*

Several switching locomotives are under construction at EMC's LaGrange factory shortly after opening in 1936. Also visible are a n early power unit for a Union Pacific streamliner (middle) and a boxcab passenger unit (in the distance at right). *EMC*

matter of time, and by the mid-1950s, even avowed coal railroads such as the Norfolk & Western, which built new steam locomotives as late as 1953, were phasing out steam.

Streamlined freight cab units began giving way to utilitarian road switchers by the 1950s. Alco had pioneered the idea with its RS-1 in 1941 and improved it with the 1,500-p RS-2 in 1946, but it was EMD that popularized the hood-unit concept with its GP7 (1949) and later GP9. Road switchers weren't as attractive but were easier to maintain and provided better visibility for switching duties on the main line.

Bigger engines, more horsepower

Once diesel locomotives had established their dominance in the field, the next goal was increasing power and other features. What has become known as the "second generation" of diesel locomotives appeared around 1960, defined as locomotives

Richmond, Fredericksburg & Potomac 52 is an Alco S-2 switcher, built in 1942. The War Production Board limited Alco to switcher production throughout most of World War II, with only EMD allowed to build road freight locomotives. *Alco*

Alco was first on the market with the road-switcher concept, but it was EMD that capitalized with its "Geeps," such as this Northern Pacific GP9. EMD sold more than 6,800 of its early Geeps (GP7s and GP9s). *EMD*

purchased not to replace steam, but to replace the first diesels. Electro-Motive's 2,000-hp GP20 of 1960 and GE's 2,500-hp U25B (1961) are generally credited as the first offerings of the second generation.

Advancements through the second-generation era included larger engines, higher-capacity traction motors and generators, and upgraded electrical and auxiliary control equipment. Horsepower continued to increase, with 3,000- and 3,600-hp locomotives common by the late 1960s.

By the late 1960s, railroads were routinely using six-axle diesels in heavy-haul as well as fast-freight service. This was a significant change in applications, as six-axle locomotives were originally designed for heavy, slow drag-freight and transfer runs (where high tractive effort was needed) or for improved axle loading on lightweight branchline rail.

By that time, EMD and GE were left as the only major diesel locomotive builders. Baldwin and Lima left the business in

the 1950s, followed by Fairbanks-Morse in 1963 and Alco in 1969. Although Montreal Locomotive Works continued building locomotives under Alco licenses for a few more years, the company was never a major player in the market.

The third generation of diesels, appearing in the 1980s, brought another round of technological advancements. Microprocessor control was applied in many ways, including improved engine performance, wheel-slip controls, and locomotive control

Alco was the country's second-largest steam builder and also became the second-largest diesel builder behind EMD. However, the new Century locomotive line of the 1960s, represented here by a 2,800-hp C-628, didn't halt dwindling sales. *Louis A. Marre collection*

Baldwin was the largest steam builder but was late in switching to diesel production. The company's switchers were reasonably well received, but its road switchers, such as this circa-1952 AS-616, never found a consistent market. *Louis A. Marre collection*

devices. Horsepower again increased, with typical road locomotives now at 4,400 hp per unit.

Since the early 1990s, locomotives with AC traction motors became practical and began selling in significant numbers. Although AC locomotives are more expensive, AC traction motors offer several advantages over their DC cousins. The motors are simpler, as they don't have the brushes and commutators used in DC motors. This makes them tougher, as they eliminate the risk of damage from

overheating under a heavy load. In addition, AC traction motors outperform DC motors, with AC versions achieving adhesion percentages of 36 percent and higher, compared to about 30 percent for a DC motor. The last DC-motor locomotive was built in 2012.

Diesel locomotives of today are high-tech, microprocessor-controlled, multimillion-dollar machines. However, even though a current-production EMD SD70ACe-T4 is more than three times as powerful and far more technologically advanced than the FT

of 1940, it can still trace its heritage to that and other pioneering diesels.

Let's take a quick look at the history of the major locomotive builders (each has a dedicated chapter later in the book, including lists of models built with dates and total production).

Electro-Motive

The Electro-Motive Corporation began by contracting construction of gas-electric motor cars (doodlebugs) by other companies. General Motors purchased both

Fairbanks-Morse switchers like this Milwaukee Road H-10-44 were distinctive, with tall hoods to hold the company's opposed-piston engines. F-M switchers were well regarded for their pulling power, but the company's road locomotives didn't fare as well, and the company couldn't make enough sales to remain in the locomotive business. *Fairbanks-Morse*

General Electric entered the heavy road freight market with its 2,500-hp U25B (500 more horsepower than EMD's contemporary GP20), introduced in 1960. By the mid-1960s, GE had eclipsed Alco for the No. 2 spot among builders. *J. David Ingles*

EMC and the Winton Engine Co. in 1930, but kept them as separate entities. The companies helped develop power cars for several high-speed passenger trains, notably the Burlington Route's *Zephyr* and Union Pacific's M-10000 in 1934. Switch engines and stand-alone passenger locomotives followed. After having its first locomotives assembled by outside contractors, EMC completed its own plant in LaGrange, Ill., in 1936.

General Motors merged Winton and EMC in 1941, and EMC became the Electro-Motive Division of GM (EMD). By the end of World War II, EMD—the only manufacturer allowed to build road freight diesels during the war—had a huge competitive advantage in mainline diesel production. The company would hold the top spot in North American locomotive sales into the 1980s.

In 1950, GM opened a plant in London, Ontario. General Motors Diesel, Ltd. (GMD; later General Motors Diesel Division, GMDD) built locomotives for Canadian and other export buyers.

General Motors shifted all assembly operations to the London plant in 1988, although many locomotives were also built at other independent and railroad-owned shops on a contract basis. At the same time, EMD and GMDD officially became General Motors Locomotive Group (GMLG).

In 2005, GM sold its locomotive business to Greenbriar Equity Group and Berkshire Partners. The new owners created a new company, Electro-Motive Diesel. In 2010, the new EMD was sold to

Lima was a well-regarded steam builder but its first production diesel switcher didn't appear until 1949. Although Lima diesels had some revolutionary features (involving throttles and control), the company's entry was too late to earn many sales. *Lima-Hamilton*

Progress Rail Services, a subsidiary of Caterpillar.

Electro-Motive Diesel now has its headquarters, as well as engineering and parts manufacturing facilities, at McCook, Ill., with locomotive assembly in Muncie, Ind.

American Locomotive Company (Alco)

The country's second-largest steam locomotive builder, the American Locomotive Co. (Alco), was also an early builder of electric and internal-combustion locomotives. In the 1920s, Alco partnered with General Electric and Ingersoll-Rand in building a line of 60- and 100-ton boxcab diesel-electric switchers. Alco began building conventional-design switchers on its own in the 1930s, and in 1940 entered a marketing and production partnership with GE that would last until 1953.

The company's main plant was located in Schenectady, N.Y. Alco also had a Canadian subsidiary, Montreal Locomotive Works (MLW), which built locomotives in Montreal, Quebec.

Although Alco was the second-largest diesel locomotive builder (and briefly led diesel sales in the mid-1930s), sales of Alco road diesels always trailed EMD. Alco's market share continued to fall throughout the 1950s. The company officially became Alco Products in 1956.

The release of Alco's new Century line of locomotives in the early 1960s didn't slow the drop in business. Former partner GE, which entered the domestic road-

switcher market with its U25B in 1959, soon eclipsed Alco in sales. Alco left the locomotive business in 1969. At that time, MLW acquired Alco's design patents and continued building its own locomotives. Bombardier acquired a major interest in MLW in 1975, eventually merging MLW. Bombardier continued building locomotives until 1985.

General Electric

General Electric was a pioneer in electric railway equipment, building traction motors, generators, and control equipment for streetcars and electric railways in the late 1800s. The company began supplying electrical equipment to gas-electric manufacturers in the 1920s. GE was an early partner with locomotive builder Alco and diesel engine maker Ingersoll-Rand, building heavy electric locomotives with Alco and diesel-electric boxcab switchers with Alco/I-R in the 1920s and providing equipment—and doing assembly—for Electro-Motive and others in the 1930s.

General Electric built several small- to medium-size switching and industrial diesel locomotives (notably its 44-ton and 70-ton models) beginning in the 1930s, and from 1940 to 1953 partnered with Alco to produce road freight and passenger locomotives,.

The company entered the domestic heavy-duty locomotive market on its own in 1959 when it introduced the Universal (U) series of locomotives, starting with the 2,500-hp U25B. The first production models appeared in 1961, and within three years GE

had bumped Alco from the No. 2 locomotive builder spot in the country. By 1968, GE's market share was 33 percent. Numerous improvements to GE's line led to increased sales, and by the mid-1980s, GE became the country's largest locomotive builder. Erie, Pa., is the home of production for GE locomotives.

Baldwin Locomotive Works, Lima-Hamilton

Baldwin was the country's largest steam locomotive builder. The company also partnered with Westinghouse to build several large electric locomotives in the early 1900s (in competition with the rival GE/Alco partnership). Baldwin also built several small gas-mechanical industrial locomotives from the 1910s through the 1920s, and although the company built a few experimental diesel-electric switchers in the 1930s, it didn't introduce a standard line of switchers until 1939.

Baldwin was only allowed to build diesel switchers during World War II, and, like Alco, was at a disadvantage to EMD when wartime restrictions ended in 1945. The company's switchers were well regarded for their pulling qualities, but problems with several early road diesels—particularly the Centipede passenger cab units—led to slow sales of road locomotives.

With sales declining and EMD's market share increasing, Baldwin merged with Lima-Hamilton in 1950. Lima, the third-largest steam builder, didn't start building

General Electric's 4,400-hp ES44AC is one of the most successful modern locomotives, with more than 2,300 built from 2005-2015. It features AC traction motors and computer/microprocessor control and diagnostic equipment. *Jeff Wilson*

Canadian National No. 3045 represents the latest in diesel locomotive technology. Built in 2016, the ET44AC features AC traction motors and is Tier 4 compliant for emissions. *Cody Grivno*

production-model diesel locomotives until 1949, two years after it had merged with diesel engine maker Hamilton. By that time the market simply couldn't support another diesel manufacturer.

Following the Baldwin-Lima-Hamilton merger, the Lima-Hamilton line of switchers and road switchers was discontinued, and the company focused its attention on Baldwin's models. The company's sales and market share continued to fall, and Baldwin built its last diesel locomotive in 1956—just seven years after building its last steam locomotive.

Baldwin's plant was at Eddystone, Pa., a suburb of Philadelphia. Baldwin partnered briefly in the 1940s with the Canadian Locomotive Co. (CLC) in Kingston,

Ontario, with limited success; CLC later became a licensee of Fairbanks-Morse.

Fairbanks-Morse

Fairbanks-Morse was a late entrant to diesel locomotive manufacturing. The company's unique opposed-piston (OP) diesel engine, which has two pistons in each cylinder with no cylinder head, was first used in naval vessels in the early 1930s. Looking for other applications for the design, F-M turned to railroads. In 1939, the company's OP engines were used in six railcars built by St. Louis Car Co. for the Southern Railway.

The company's first diesel switchers appeared in 1944, with cab and hood road locomotives following shortly after World

War II. Although the OP engine offered more power compared to a similar-size conventional diesel, maintenance problems and costs countered the OP engine's power and efficiency gains. The company's locomotive sales slowed during the 1950s, with the last F-M domestic diesel built in 1958 and the last export order completed in 1963.

Locomotives were built at F-M's plant in Beloit, Wis., except for the company's big six-axle Erie-Built cab units, which were built at (and named after) General Electric's Erie, Pa., plant. (They were built before GE introduced its own line of heavy locomotives.) Fairbanks-Morse-design locomotives were also built at F-M's Canadian licensee, Canadian Locomotive Co.

Timeline to victory

How diesels won the battle vs. steam from 1905 to 1960

BY GREG McDONNELL

1905 GAS CARS SPARK THE REVOLUTION: Union Pacific's William R. McKeen spearheads development of a gasoline-powered, mechanically driven railcar. The "McKeen Car" is the first successful use of internal-combustion power on North American railroads. Prototype car M-1 makes its first run, Omaha-Valley, Nebr., and back, on March 7; some 150 McKeens are sold to 35 roads. UNION PACIFIC

1922 ENTER ELECTRO-MOTIVE: The Electro-Motive Engineering Corp. in Cleveland, Ohio, begins to market gas-electric railcars. With GE electricals, Winton engines, and carbodies from various builders, more than 700 EMC doodlebugs are sold by 1930. TRAINS COLLECTION

1923 THE DIESEL HITS THE ROAD: In December, the first GE/Ingersoll-Rand diesel-electric boxcab tests at I-R's plant in Phillipsburg, N.J. Numbered 8835, the locomotive embarks on 13-month tour in 1924. It hauls a passenger train Jersey City-Harrisburg, Pa., making 8835 the first diesel-electric to be used in U.S. road service. GENERAL ELECTRIC

1925 BALDWIN BUILDS ITS FIRST: In June, Baldwin completes its first diesel locomotive, 1,000-hp A1A+A1A-trucked box-cab 58501. Powered by a Knudsen Motor Corp. V-12 and equipped with Westinghouse electrical gear, the 58501 tests throughout summer and fall on the Reading Co., but fails to meet expectations. It is returned to Eddystone, serves as Baldwin's plant switcher, and is scrapped in 1941. BALDWIN

1905 DAWN OF THE DIESEL: International Power Co. in April outfits an Alco box-cab carbody with GE electrical equipment and two four-cylinder diesel engines built by the Corliss Steam Engine Co. to create an experimental locomotive for Southern Pacific. This is thought to be the first diesel locomotive built.

1906 GE GETS THE BUG: GE builds its first gas-electric railcar, or "doodlebug," Delaware & Hudson 1000, a baggage-coach powered by a 140-hp, six-cylinder Wolsley engine from Britain. The car operates in test and regular service on D&H for several months.

1914 HARNESSING THE POWER: GE's Lemp control system, named for inventor Hermann Lemp, is patented. Tested in gas-electric GE plant switcher *Bumble Bee* and perfected by 1922, this is a key achievement in the development of practical gas-electric cars and diesel-electric locomotives.

1917 GE'S OWN DIESEL: GE tests its 200-hp, twin-cylinder GM-50 diesel engine in the carbody of GE motor car No. 4 on March 8. In fall 1918, GE completes three GM-50-powered steeple-cabs for Jay Street Connecting, City of Baltimore, and the U.S. Army.

1924 ALCO/GE/I-R GET IT RIGHT: The consortium of Alco, GE, and Ingersoll-Rand produces North America's first standardized diesel locomotive models, five 300-hp boxcabs built as stock; one becomes CNJ 1000.

1925 CLASS 1 LOCOMOTIVE COUNT: 1 diesel, 63,612 steam

1925 NO SMOKING: New York City bans the operation of steam locomotives within its city limits. Chicago soon follows suit with restrictions on steam operation within its downtown area.

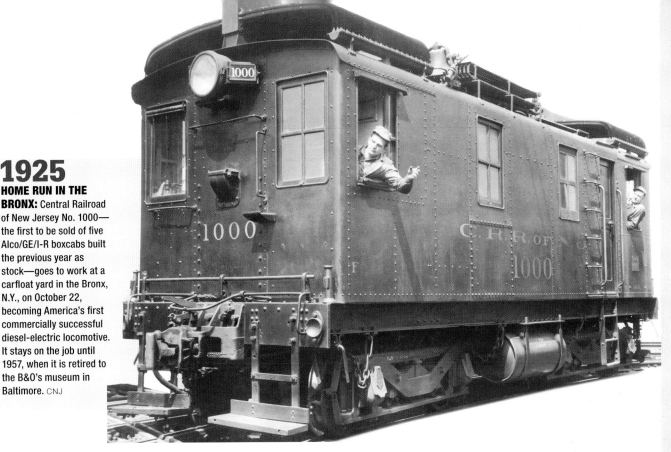

1925
HOME RUN IN THE BRONX: Central Railroad of New Jersey No. 1000—the first to be sold of five Alco/GE/I-R boxcabs built the previous year as stock—goes to work at a carfloat yard in the Bronx, N.Y., on October 22, becoming America's first commercially successful diesel-electric locomotive. It stays on the job until 1957, when it is retired to the B&O's museum in Baltimore. CNJ

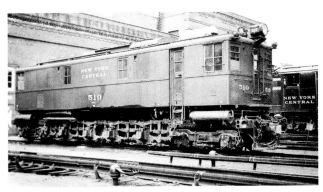

1928 ROADWORTHY:
Alco completes New York Central 1550 (later renumbered 510), a 750-hp Ingersoll-Rand-powered 2-D-2 freight boxcab in October for service in the New York area. This locomotive is considered the first successful road diesel in the U.S.
HAROLD L. GOLDSMITH

1929 MOTOR CARS TO LOCOMOTIVES:
Following a 1927 installation of Winton gas engines in two former mail cars, Rock Island converts three more to locomotive-baggage cars and orders seven all-new units from EMC with bodies by St. Louis Car Co. TRAINS MAGAZINE COLLECTION

1925 TRANSCONTINENTAL TRIUMPH:
Canadian National railcar 15820 completes a 2,937-mile Montreal-Vancouver trip in 67 hours, arriving on the Pacific coast November 4. The car averages 44 mph overall and reaches speeds of 60 mph, and its 185-hp Beardmore diesel is never once shut down.

1925 LONG ISLAND-BOUND:
Long Island Rail Road 401, an Alco/GE/I-R boxcab built at GE's Erie, Pa., plant (as were the rest of her kin), departs December 15 under her own power for delivery via the Pennsylvania Railroad to the carfloat slips at Greenville, N.J.

1928 WESTINGHOUSE WEIGHS IN:
Having acquired U.S. sales and production rights for the diesel engine designs of the William Beardmore Co. of Glasgow, Scotland, in 1926, Westinghouse completes its first diesel locomotive, an articulated two-unit, 600-hp, boxcab delivered as Long Island 403A and 403B.

1929 MAKING IT BIG:
CN 9000, a two-unit Canadian Locomotive Co.-Westinghouse locomotive powered by 1,330-hp Beardmores, makes its first run on the Montreal-Toronto *International Limited* on August 26. This is the first large road diesel in North America.

1929 EDDYSTONE TRIES AGAIN:
Baldwin's second diesel-electric locomotive, a 1,000-hp B-B "oil-electric" boxcab switcher numbered 61000, is outshopped in May and dispatched from Baldwin's Eddystone, Pa., plant on a demonstration tour covering at least seven Class 1 roads and lasting until 1931. The Depression derails further development.

1930 DETROIT GOES RAILROADING:
General Motors purchases Electro-Motive Co. and its gas-engine supplier, Winton Engine Co. GM backing fuels the development of a Winton diesel and the growth of EMC.

1931
SWITCHERS IN BROOKLYN: GE builds seven Ingersoll-Rand-powered, all-welded, hood-type switchers for Bush Terminal in Brooklyn, N.Y. The carbody design and configuration of the 300-hp, 60-ton units—internally similar to CNJ 1000—foreshadow the road-switcher, still a decade away. GE PHOTO; KEVIN HOLLAND COLLECTION

1933-34
DEPRESSION DIESELS: For two Depression years, Alco does not deliver a single steam locomotive. But during the same period, the Schenectady plant turns out nine "high-hood" switchers powered by 531-series engines: demonstrator 602 and eight units for the Lackawanna. LOUIS A. MARRE COLLECTION

1934
THE DIESEL GOES MAIN-LINE: In April, two months after UP's M-10000 streamliner debuts with a Winton distillate engine, GM unveils its first diesel-locomotive power plant, the Winton 201A, in Burlington Route's *Zephyr*. On May 26, America's first high-speed diesel-powered train makes a record run from Denver to Chicago in 13 hours 5 minutes, pulling the diesel out of the shadows of yard duty and into the spotlight. CB&Q

1930
SHAPE OF THINGS TO COME: CN receives CLC-Westinghouse switcher 7700. The first "visibility cab" locomotive, it heralds a trend that will lead to the standard switcher design and, ultimately, the road-switcher.

1930
CLASS 1 LOCOMOTIVE COUNT: 74 diesel, 55,875 steam

1931
A DIESEL BUILDER FOR BALDWIN: Baldwin purchases I. P. Morris & De La Vergne, Inc., whose experience with diesel engines is a key element of the Baldwin plan to design and build a line of diesel locomotives.

1931
FIRST STANDARD SWITCHER: Alco outshops 600-hp switcher No. 600 for demonstration on the New Haven, which numbers it 0900. Powered by the new 531-series engine from McIntosh & Seymour (which Alco bought in 1929), it is the first full-size locomotive with the hood-type, end-cab switcher layout. It is also Alco's first solo foray into the diesel field.

1935
DIESELS FOR THE SUPER: Santa Fe takes delivery in August of St. Louis Car-EMC box-cabs 1 and 1A for use on the all-Pullman *Super Chief*, which enters service behind 1 and 1A at Chicago on May 12, 1936.

1935
CLASS 1 LOCOMOTIVE COUNT: 113 diesel, 45,614 steam

1936
HOME OF THE DIESEL LOCOMOTIVE: EMC opens a 200,000-square-foot assembly plant in the Chicago suburb of McCook, Ill. Better known by its La Grange mailing address, the plant completes its first locomotive, Santa Fe SC switcher 2301, in May.

1936
ALCO UPS THE ANTE: Alco beefs up its 531 engine, adding a turbocharger—the first applied to a railroad diesel—to boost horsepower from 600 to 900.

1935 ELECTRO-MOTIVE'S LOCOMOTIVES: EMC's first true diesel locomotives are outshopped from General Electric's Erie plant: two 600-hp switchers for the Lackawanna (Nos. 425-426, above) and three twin-engined, 1,800-hp passenger boxcabs: EMC demonstrators 511 and 512 and Baltimore & Ohio 50. All are powered by GM's new Winton 201A diesel engine and equipped with GE electrical gear. EMC

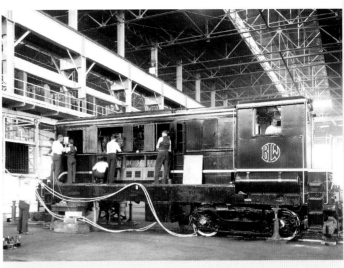

1936 UNVEILING THE VO: Baldwin outshops its first end-cab diesel switcher, demonstrator No. 62000, in the fall. The first locomotive powered by the 660-hp De La Vergne VO engine, the unit is later sold to the Santa Fe as No. 2200. Three 900-hp versions are delivered to New Orleans Public Belt in December 1937. BALDWIN

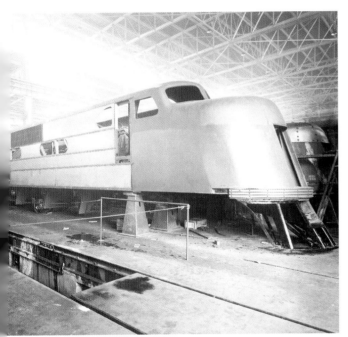

1937 A STAR IS BORN: EMC completes B&O model EA No. 51, launching a long line of streamlined, twin-engined units that will dominate the passenger-locomotive market for decades and evolve over 1,314 units from the slant-nosed, 1,800-hp, Winton-engined EA to the bulldog-nosed 2,400-hp, 567-powered E9. EMC

1939 GOING SOLO: Rock Island commissions Davenport Locomotive Works to construct a 44-ton diesel switcher whose size and weight allows one-man operation under the "90,000-pound" rule of the 1937 National Diesel Agreement with the railroad unions. Other small builders, like Whitcomb, a Baldwin subsidiary, offer similar models, but GE's 44-tonner, introduced in 1940, enjoys the most success, selling to industrial, shortline, and Class 1 customers worldwide. Above is St. Paul Union Depot 441, built by GE in 1941. TRAINS MAGAZINE COLLECTION

1930-1939

1937 EXIT INGERSOLL-RAND: Diesel pioneer Ingersoll-Rand leaves the locomotive business.

1937 SWITCHERS AND STREAMLINERS FOR THE ROCK: Chicago, Rock Island & Pacific, an early user of internal-combustion power, embraces the diesel with orders for two types of Winton-engined Electro-Motive B-B units: 600-hp switchers and six 1,200-hp model TA cab units that look like pocket-sized EAs for its new Budd-built *Rocket* streamliners.

1938 MORE MUSCLE FOR ELECTRO-MOTIVE: EMC introduces its 567 engine, the prime mover that, in 6-, 12-, and 16-cylinder versions, will quickly propel the builder to the top position in North America and be EMD's standard for a quarter-century. EMD also begins production of its own electrical equipment, based on designs previously supplied by GE.

1939 ALCO BEEFS UP: The Schenectady builder unveils the McIntosh & Seymour 539 engine, an in-line 6-cylinder diesel available in 660-hp normally aspirated and 1,000-hp turbocharged versions.

1939 EDDYSTONE ENHANCES ITS ENGINE: Baldwin introduces a redesigned VO engine and switcher line with VO660 demonstrator 299. The design will sire VO660 and VO1000 lines as well as later DS and S models that will be Baldwin standards.

1939 FM ENTERS THE FRAY: The first railroad application of Fairbanks-Morse's opposed-piston diesel engine, developed for U.S. Navy submarines, enters service in August, as power plants in six St. Louis Car Co. railcars for Southern Railway (Nos. 1-4) and subsidiary Alabama Great Southern (40-41).

1939 NO LOOKING BACK: Electro-Motive FT No. 103—a 5,400-hp, A-B-B-A demo set seen here at Denver on April 28, 1940—departs La Grange in November on an 83,764-mile, 35-state tour that will change railroading forever by showing that diesels can handle heavy-haul freight service. RICHARD H. KINDIG

1940 ALCO ANSWERS THE E UNIT: Alco introduces its first standard road diesel, the twin-engined, 2,000-hp, Otto Kuhler-styled DL-109. Rock Island gets the first, New Haven the most. The first true dual-service diesels, New Haven's 60 DL-109s work passenger trains by day and freights by night. Schenectady, N.Y., neighbors American Locomotive Co. and General Electric partner to market Alco-built diesels with GE electricals under the "Alco-GE" brand.

1943 EDDYSTONE THINKS BIG: Baldwin tests prototype locomotive No. 6000 on a 32-mile run over the B&O from Eddystone to Elsmere Jct., on June 16. Begun in 1941 but delayed by World War II, the immense cab unit is powered by four of an intended *eight* crossways-mounted 750-hp De La Vergne 408-series V8 diesels and has a 2-D+D-2 wheel arrangement more in line with electric-locomotive practice. Designed for passenger service, the giant proves unsatisfactory, but its running gear is later used for Seaboard Air Line DR-12-8-3000 No. 4500; SAL will get 14 total "Centipedes," National of Mexico 14, and Pennsy 24. BALDWIN

1939 FIRST ALL-DIESEL CLASS 1: Texas-Mexican, a 161-mile Corpus Christi-Laredo line, in November receives the last of seven "0-8-0" 660-hp boxcabs from Baldwin with De La Vergne VO engines and Westinghouse electricals, to completely dieselize—the first Class 1 railroad to do so.

1940 CLASS 1 LOCOMOTIVE COUNT: 797 diesel, 40,041 steam

1941 SUITED FOR THE DESERT: Santa Fe FT A-B-B-A set No. 100, first FT in revenue service, hits the road February 4.

1941 PERFECT RECORD: B&O EA 56 and EB 56x complete their 365th consecutive trip on the Washington-Chicago *Capitol Limited* on February 25, achieving 100 percent availability and logging more than 280,000 miles.

1941 DRAFTED YOUNG: Alco elongates the frame of the 1,000 h.p. S-2 switcher, adds a short hood for a steam generator behind the cab, puts the locomotive on road trucks, and the RS-1, granddaddy of all road-switchers, is born. The first, Rock Island 746-749, along with those sold to several other roads, are drafted by the U.S. Army and dispatched overseas.

1945 ERIE-BUILT: The first of FM's Loewy-styled A1A-A1A "Erie-built" cabs emerge in December from GE's northwest Pennsylvania plant as a Union Pacific A-B-A set. A total of 82 Erie-built cabs and 29 boosters will come from the GE facility before expansion of FM's Beloit, Wis., plant in 1948 allows the builder to construct all its locomotives there.

1945 BIRTH OF A BEST-SELLER: As the war winds down, EMD introduces the E7 and F3. Best-selling of all Es, the E7 will total 510 units, while sales of 1,807 F3s will pave the way for the even better-selling F7.

POWERED WITH THE O.P. DIESEL

FAIRBANKS-MORSE DIESEL
Switching Locomotives

1944 ANOTHER BUILDER: Fairbanks-Morse goes from supplier to builder on August 8 when its first locomotive—Milwaukee Road 1,000-hp switcher No. 1802—breaks through a ceremonial banner at FM's Beloit, Wis., plant.

1946 ALCO FIGHTS BACK: In January, Alco delivers to Gulf, Mobile & Ohio the first production units powered by its new 12-cylinder, 1,500-hp 244 power plant. In the streamlined freight locomotives that will later be labeled FA (for cabs) and FB (boosters), Alco finally has an answer to EMD's F unit. A 16-cylinder, 2,000-hp passenger version (the PA and PB) follows in September, amid publicity that includes designation of the first set, Santa Fe A-B-A No. 51, as the builder's 75,000th locomotive. Crankshaft, turbocharger, manifold, and other infirmities plague early examples of the 244 engine; most bugs are remedied, but not before Alco's reputation is sullied and its market-share diminished. ALCO

1945 BRIEF FLING FOR BLACK MARIA: Alco obtains War Production Board permission to finish a 241-powered prototype, an A-B-A test-bed cab-unit trio numbered 1500-ABC and dubbed "Black Maria." The precursor of the FA, the 1500 runs on NYC, D&H, and New Haven (above, at New Bedford, Mass.), but is scrapped in September 1947. NORTON D. CLARK

1945 CLASS 1 LOCOMOTIVE COUNT: 3,816 diesel, 38,853 steam

1946 EDDYSTONE SCORES: Baldwin beats RS-1 innovator Alco to the the first higher-horsepower, and also the first six-axle, road-switcher as Columbus & Greenville DRS-6-4-1500 No. 601 enters service October 8, weeks ahead of Alco's first 1,500-hp RS-2s and RSC-2s.

1947 LIMA GIVES IN: In October, steam stalwart Lima merges with General Machinery of Hamilton, Ohio, to form Lima-Hamilton and enter the diesel-locomotive business.

1947 PENNSY SPENDS BIG: The Pennsylvania, America's largest railroad and, until recently, a strong advocate of advanced steam designs, signals its motive-power future with diesel orders totaling $15 million.

1947 RARE MISSTEP AT LA GRANGE: EMD stumbles in responding to Alco's new road-switcher design with BL1 demonstrator 499, a semi-streamlined 1,500-hp B-B, aptly described by TRAINS magazine editor David P. Morgan as looking "like a cross between a cab unit and a Borden milk car." Only 58 more (designated BL2) will be built, for nine customers.

1948 BACK TO CLEVELAND: With the postwar diesel boom at full tilt and La Grange booked beyond its capacity, EMD returns to the place of its birth, opening a plant in Cleveland, Ohio, to assemble switch engines . . . and soon, Geeps.

1948 ALCO ABANDONS STEAM: The American Locomotive Co. delivers its last steam locomotive, Pittsburgh & Lake Erie 2-8-4 9401, on June 16. The end of steam production is coincident with Alco's 100th year of building locomotives. In 1946, 75 percent of the builder's production was still steam.

1949
LIMA-COME-LATELY: Lima-Hamilton on May 12 completes its first diesel locomotive, a 1,000-hp switcher to demonstrate as No. 1000 (sister 1001 is seen at the plant with a disassembled mining shovel loaded on several flatcars). One day later, Lima delivers its last steam locomotive, Nickel Plate 2-8-4 Berkshire No. 779. LIMA-HAMILTON

1949
UNLOVELY, UNSTOPPABLE: Learning from the BL1/BL2 flop, not to mention the Alco RS-1 and RS-2, in October EMD gets it right when it introduces Chief Engineer Dick Dilworth's "un-lovely"—but unstoppable—road-switcher creation, the 1,500-hp General Purpose GP7. The "Geep" (that's Texas & Pacific GP7 1113 greeting an F7 set) is born, and multiplies fast. LINN H. WESTCOTT

1949
DOODLEBUG REDUX: In September, the Budd Co. introduces its modern twin-underfloor-engined doodlebug, the Rail Diesel Car, as RDC1 demonstrator 2960 embarks on an 18,000-mile nationwide tour. In 13 years, Budd will deliver 398 RDCs to 26 railroads and 4 overseas operations. BUDD

1949
BALDWIN QUITS STEAM: BLW's last domestic steam locomotive, C&O H6 2-6-6-2 1309, is built in September.

1949
BIG-TIME VICTORY: Gulf, Mobile & Ohio announces complete dieselization on October 15, at Columbus, Miss., to become the first large U.S. road to kill steam. The event rates national news coverage, including a spread in *Life* magazine.

1950
DOMINION DIESELS: EMD expands into Canada, opening the General Motors Diesel Ltd. locomotive assembly plant at London, Ontario, on August 8.

1950
LOCOMOTIVE FLOOD TIDE: U.S. railroads put more new locomotives into service in the first 10 months of 1950 than in any corresponding period in the past 27 years: 1,915 diesel, 9 steam, and 8 electric. Another 1,496 diesels, 19 steam, and 8 electric locomotives remain on the order books. A total of 4,027 diesel locomotives, worth more than a half-billion dollars, are ordered by U.S. roads in 1950, with EMD holding 65 percent of the market.

1950
SURPRISE MERGER: Baldwin Locomotive Works and Lima-Hamilton merge to form Baldwin-Lima-Hamilton on November 30. Baldwin wants Lima not for its locomotive line but for non-rail assets such as its shovel and crane division. Lima completes its last locomotive, 2,500-hp center-cab transfer diesel Pennsylvania 5683, on September 11, 1951.

1950
CLASS 1 LOCOMOTIVE COUNT: 14,047 diesel, 25,640 steam

1951
CENTRAL SETS A RECORD: The New York Central in March announces orders for 387 new diesels from EMD, Alco, FM, and BLH, the largest-ever locomotive-buying binge by a U.S. railroad, eclipsing the previous record set just a year earlier by rival Pennsylvania for 226 units.

1950 **ILLINOIS CENTRAL SAYS NO:** IC President Wayne A. Johnston tells the *Chicago Journal of Commerce* that his coal-hauling road "will not dieselize its freight services for a long time, if ever." A decade later, IC finally is among the last carriers to abandon steam. TRAINS MAGAZINE COLLECTION

1950 **BELOIT'S BID FOR THE BIG-TIME:** Fairbanks-Morse introduces its "Consolidation Line" of freight and passenger diesels. Available in cab and booster versions rated at 1,600, 2,000, and 2,400-hp, the C-Line is cataloged in 14 models. Two CPA24-5 demonstrators tour nationwide, but it's late in the cab-unit era, and sales are slim. ROBERT M. STACY

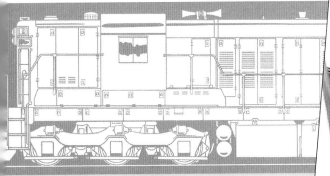

1952 **SIX MOTORS FOR LA GRANGE:** Late to the six-motor party, EMD in February expands its model lines with the introduction of the 1,500-hp SD7, heralded by demonstrator 990, direct ancestor of thousands of SD40s, SD70s, et al.

1953 **"MR. BIG" HITS THE ROAD:** Fairbanks-Morse introduces the 2,400-hp, six-motor Train Master, the "Mr. Big of road-switchers." Demonstrators TM-1 and TM-2 depart Beloit on May 16 for the Railway Supply Manufacturers' Association exposition in Atlantic City, N.J. Sister demos TM-3 and TM-4 are subsequently outshopped and embark on a sales tour. Lackawanna orders 10 TM's sight unseen, but the brute is ahead of its time, selling only 127 units to 10 railroads.

1951 **TURBINES, ELECTRICS . . .:** Union Pacific, after testing GE gas-turbine-electric No. 50 for nearly two years, orders 10 similar units, first of an eventual fleet of 55 UP turbines. Meanwhile, PRR orders 5 two-unit electrics from GE and Westinghouse, precursors of the road's 66 E44 freighters.

1951 **. . . AND STEAM:** With the builders out of the steam business and all other major railroads committed to diesels, Norfolk & Western stands out as steam's last great champion. In October, the coal road commissions its Roanoke, Va., shops to build 15 S-1a 0-8-0 switchers and six Y-6b 2-8-8-2s.

1951 **FADING FIRES:** The Lehigh Valley ends steam usage as 2-8-2 No. 432 arrives at Delano, Pa., on September 14 with a freight from Packerton, making the LV, once a major anthracite hauler, the first big Eastern road to fully dieselize. Texas & Pacific becomes the first major carrier in the Southwest to go all-diesel as 2-8-2 No. 800 works Shreveport-New Orleans train 28 for the last time on November 9.

1952 **N&W SAYS NO DICE:** In September, the Norfolk & Western tests an A-B-B-A set of Electro-Motive F7 freight units for 18 days. Apparently unimpressed, N&W sends the diesels packing without an order.

1953 **DIESEL-BUILDER DIVORCE:** General Electric goes its own way, dissolving the Alco-GE partnership formed in 1940. Alco still uses GE electricals for its diesels.

1953 **LAST NEW U.S. STEAM:** N&W's Roanoke Shops in December completes S-1a 0-8-0 No. 244—the last reciprocating steam locomotive constructed for a U.S. railroad. Hoping to stick with coal as a fuel, the following year N&W introduces experimental C-C+C-C 4,500-hp, Baldwin/Babcock-Wilcox/ Westinghouse steam-turbine-electric No. 2300. *Jawn Henry*, as the big fellow is known, proves no match for diesels, and dies an orphan.

1954 **MR. BIG GETS COMPANY:** Alco takes on FM's Train Master, introducing the six-motor, all-purpose 2,250-hp DL-600 (a.k.a. RSD-7) hood unit.

1953 **LOOKING AHEAD IN THE SOUTH:** Southern Railway officially says good-bye to steam on June 17 as 2-8-2 6330 arrives in Chattanooga with a freight from Oakdale, Tenn., pausing for the company photographer next to an A-B-B-A set of F units before yarding her train and dopping her fire for good. Steam will return to SR in 1964, but only for fun.

1956 **TOMORROW NEVER CAME:** GM's entry in the ultra-lightweight derby is the *Aerotrain*. Two sets, with cars based on bus bodies, are built, along with LWT12 locomotives to pull them (a third LWT12 goes to a Talgo consist). Far from trend-setting, all end up on Rock Island commuter runs.

1956 **ALCO TURNS UP THE HEAT:** Alco in February introduces a new model line of road-switchers powered by the new 251 engine. First is the 12-cylinder, 1,800-hp B-B RS-11 (or DL-701, above), followed by a C-C version, the RSD-12 (DL-702). The big guy in the lineup, though, is the 16-cylinder, 2,400-hp C-C DL600b, or RSD-15. ALCO

1953 **OUT OF STEAM:** For the first time since 1828, not a single U.S. railroad or industry orders a new steam locomotive. Diesels, meanwhile, move 74 percent of railroad freight tonnage, 79 percent of all passenger trains, and do 83 percent of switching work. EMD holds 73 percent of the U.S. locomotive market, Alco 15 percent, F-M 7 percent, and BLH 5 percent.

1954 **THE BEST GETS BETTER:** Electro-Motive introduces the 1,750-hp GP9 powered with latest version of its redoubtable prime mover, the 567C. At 4,257 units, the GP9 is the best-selling of all first-generation models.

1955 **STEAM REVIVAL:** A surge in traffic revives stored steam on many roads that had previously gone all-diesel, including Santa Fe, Soo Line, Milwaukee Road, and C&O.

1955 **ROANOKE RELENTS:** N&W gets its first diesels in October, four GP9s and four RS-3s, to dieselize its lightly trafficked Lynchburg, Va.-Durham, N.C., line. "This does not mean we have changed our view that our modern roller-bearing coal-burning steam locomotives can handle the major part of our traffic economically, nor does it mean that our interest in new and better types of coal-burning locomotives has diminished in any way," says N&W

President R. H. Smith. By January 1956, though, N&W had ordered 83 more diesels, 58 GP9s and 25 RS-11s.

1955 **CLASS 1 LOCOMOTIVE COUNT:** 24,786 diesel, 5,982 steam

1956 **BALDWIN BOWS OUT:** Struggling to stay alive, Baldwin-Lima-Hamilton puts its faith in diesel-hydraulic technology. BLH builds locomotives powered by German-built Maybach engines and driven with Mechydro transmissions for "Train X" lightweights for New York Central and New Haven. NYC RP210 No. 20 emerges from Eddystone in May; NH 3000-3001 follow in October. The trains—

1958 **STEAM ON THE RUN:** Northern Pacific declares itself all-diesel on January 17; Baltimore & Ohio (above, F3s shown) officially dieselizes in April; and Nickel Plate's legendary Berkshires ride into the sunset as S-2 746 makes a Bellevue-Conneaut (Ohio) run in July. WALTER G. MINNICH JR.

1959 **TRADE-INS, AND A NEW LOOK:** Boston & Maine, Milwaukee, and Minneapolis & St. Louis trade in FTs—steam-killers of the 1940s—on new GP9s, and SP gets a few '9s (above) with a "low nose," which will become universal. Also in '59, EMD introduces a souped-up Geep, the 1,800-hp GP18. ALAN MILLER; J. DAVID INGLES COLLECTION

1960 **VICTORY COMPLETE:** Regular steam operation ends on Grand Trunk Western, Illinois Central, Norfolk & Western (above, at Iaeger, W.Va., in 1959), and Missabe, leaving a handful of steam pockets that soon are abandoned or dieselized: Colorado & Southern's isolated Leadville, Colo., branch; Rio Grande's narrow gauge; Lake Superior & Ishpeming; and some short lines. Steam surrenders on the big Canadian roads as well. The '60s will belong to the diesel. BRUCE MEYER

Central's *Xplorer* and NH's *Dan'l Webster*—and their unique locomotives are withdrawn by spring 1960, though. BLH ships its last common-carrier-size diesel, Erie Mining S-12 403, on October 30; completed in '55, the unit had been held for use in testing the diesel-hydraulics. The last big diesel *finished* at Eddystone, Columbia Geneva Steel S-12 No. 35, is shipped August 6, along with sisters 33 and 34.

1956 **QUICK CHANGE:** C&NW dieselizes its Chicago commuter trains May 11 simply by reassigning existing locomotives.

1957 **THREE BIG DOMINOES FALL:** Eastern and Western giants New York Central, Pennsylvania, and Southern Pacific declare themselves fully dieselized.

1958 **SATURATION:** U.S. Class 1 roads take delivery of a mere 434 new diesels, compared with 1,316 in 1957—an indication that dieselization is nearly complete.

1959 **SUMMER OF DEFEAT:** Two more steam strongholds drop their last fires as Nickel Plate 0-8-0s, brought back to work at Conneaut, Ohio, during a traffic upswing, are put away

July 18 when a steel strike depresses rail traffic levels. Similarly, on July 23, 4-6-6-4 Challenger 3713 brings Union Pacific's last steam-powered revenue freight into Cheyenne, Wyo.

1959 **SECOND GENERATION DAWNING:** The second generation of diesel-electrics is here as EMD introduces the 2,400-hp, turbocharged SD24. It will sell just 224 units to five roads, but presages the big SDs of today. Also new for '59: the 2,000-hp turbocharged GP20.

1960 **CLASS 1 LOCOMOTIVE COUNT:** 28,278 diesel, 261 steam

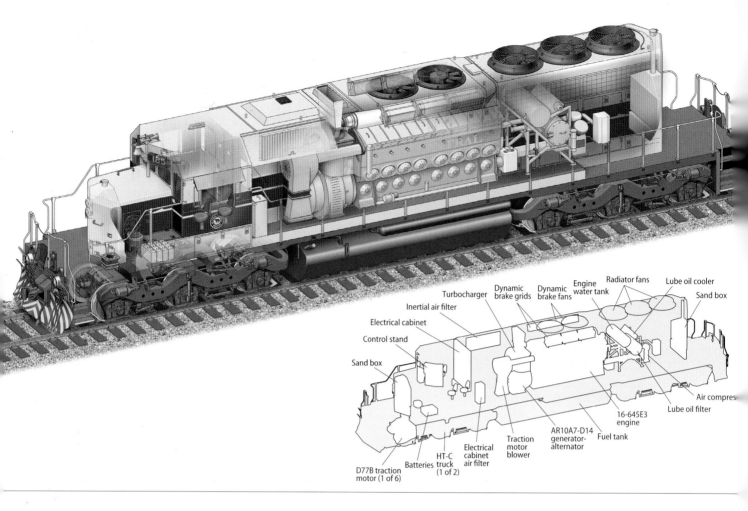

Turbocharger
Inertial air filter
Electrical cabinet
Control stand
Sand box
Dynamic brake grids
Dynamic brake fans
Engine water tank
Radiator fans
Lube oil cooler
Sand box
Air compres
Lube oil filter
16-645E3 engine
AR10A7-D14 generator-alternator
Fuel tank
Traction motor blower
Electrical cabinet air filter
HT-C truck (1 of 2)
Batteries
D77B traction motor (1 of 6)

— CHAPTER TWO —

How diesel locomotives work

This cutaway view of an EMD SD40 shows how the diesel engine and other components fit together on a locomotive platform. *Rick Johnson*

A diesel-electric locomotive is basically an electric locomotive that carries its own portable power plant driven by a large diesel engine. The engine turns a generator or alternator, which provides electricity for traction motors mounted on the axles. The specifics of how this is done vary by manufacturer and have evolved over time, but having a basic knowledge of how diesels work will help you understand why diesel locomotives are designed the way they are, what their strengths and limitations are, and what the differences are among the various models.

The diesel engine

Diesel engines are built to many different designs, but the principle of each is the same. A series of pistons, each in a cylinder, move up and down and in doing so rotate a crankshaft that runs through the engine. Unlike a gasoline engine, which uses a spark to ignite the fuel in each cylinder, a diesel engine fires by compression. This is done by compressing the intake air to 500 psi or higher, whereupon it reaches a temperature of about 1,000 degrees F. An atomized spray of diesel fuel is then injected and burns, propelling the piston.

Diesel engines are either four-cycle or two-cycle designs (see the following pages). A four-cycle engine completes four piston strokes (two up, two down, producing two driveshaft revolutions) to get one power stroke. The process starts with the intake stroke (the piston descends and clean air is drawn into the chamber), followed by the compression stroke (the piston moves upward and compresses the air), power stroke (fuel is admitted and burns from the high temperature gained by compression, forcing the piston downward), and exhaust stroke (the burned gases are discharged as the piston moves upward). Four-cycle engines are made practical by turbocharging, which we'll discuss in a bit.

A two-cycle engine accomplishes the same tasks with just two strokes and one revolution of the crankshaft, requiring the above steps to be accomplished in much less time. To do this, the cylinder simultaneously takes in clean air and expels exhaust gas on the piston downstroke, so that on the upstroke the new air is being compressed and is ready for ignition when the piston reaches the top of the cylinder.

By 1920, the diesel engine had proven itself practical for many applications, but engines were big, heavy, and slow. The main design challenge in reducing the size and weight was that fuel has to be forced into the cylinder at extremely high pressure (to combat the pressure required for the combustion air in the cylinder). The resulting long fuel lines needed to build up the pressure took up a lot of space. The breakthrough came in the 1920s with the development of injectors that could force air into the cylinder at the required pressure, and do it at the cylinder.

Engines from several manufacturers powered early railroad locomotives and motor cars, including Ingersoll-Rand and

This 1949 view of the erecting floor at EMD shows a 567 diesel engine, generator (on the deck at the left end of the engine), and electrical cabinet (far left) in place on an F7 frame. An FP7 is taking shape in the background. *EMD*

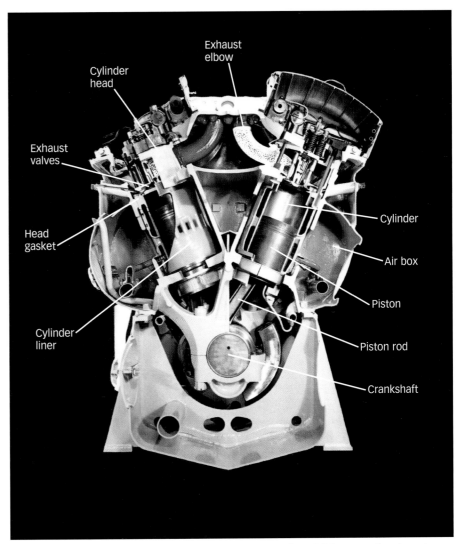

This cutaway cross-section view shows an Electro-Motive Division 567 diesel engine, a V-style design with cylinders at a 45-degree angle. *EMD*

FOUR-CYCLE DIESEL

Exhaust

Exhaust

First Upstroke

Crankshaft centerline

Exhaust valve lifts and piston pushes out spent gases

Intake

Air

First Downstroke

Air valve lifts and air is sucked and blown in

Compression

Second Upstroke

Valves are closed, air is heated by compression

Power

Fuel

Second Downstroke

Fuel is injected and burned, driving piston down

Alco's 244 diesel is a V-style, four-cycle, turbocharged engine (a 12-cylinder version is shown). The turbocharger is at upper right. *Alco*

TWO-CYCLE DIESEL

Scavenging and Charging Cylinder

Exhaust

Blower-propelled or turbocharged air intake

Blower-propelled or turbocharged air intake

Compression

Injection

Fuel

Power

Crankshaft centerline

Upstroke

Downstroke

Exhaust and intake are effected while power stroke is coming to bottom

Air is heated by compression

Fuel is injected and burned, driving piston down

Exhaust valve begins to open near bottom of power stroke

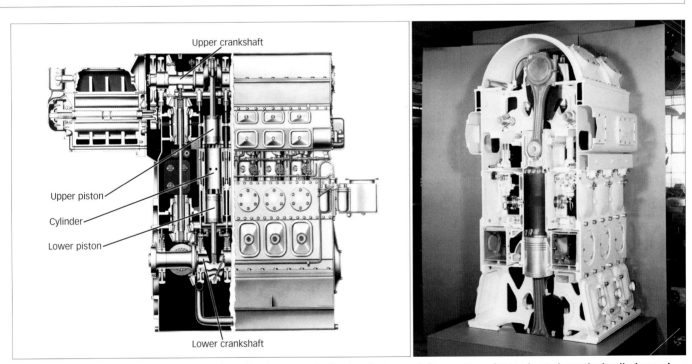

Upper crankshaft

Upper piston

Cylinder

Lower piston

Lower crankshaft

The Fairbanks-Morse opposed-piston (OP) engine has no cylinder heads. Instead, it uses two pistons in each vertical cylinder and has an upper and lower crankshaft. *Fairbanks-Morse*

McIntosh & Seymour engines in early Alco-GE-Ingersoll-Rand boxcab switchers of the 1920s and Alco locomotives of the 1930s; the Winton 201 engine of the early 1930s, used by Electro-Motive; Baldwin's DeLaVerne VO engine; and the Fairbanks-Morse opposed-piston (OP) diesel.

Electro-Motive chose the two-cycle Winton 201, introduced in 1932, to power its early passenger diesels and switchers, and designed a more-advanced, more-powerful two-cycle engine, the 567 (named

for the cubic-inch displacement of each cylinder), to power its FT freight locomotive in 1939. Most other diesel builders stuck with four-cycle designs.

Most diesel engines used in locomotives are V-style, with paired banks of cylinders at a 45-degree angle. Some early (and some smaller) engines used a straight (in-line) design, with all cylinders positioned vertically in a straight line over the crankshaft. Baldwin's VO and 600-series engines and Alco's 539 are examples.

Fairbanks-Morse locomotives were noted for that company's unique opposed-piston two-cycle diesel engines. In an OP engine, two pistons share a common vertical cylinder, so there's no cylinder head. Each bank of cylinders (one on top, one bottom), drives a crankshaft.

In theory the opposed-piston design offers several advantages: increased efficiency, more power for a given engine size, and no cylinder head to maintain. However, maintenance headaches—chiefly the

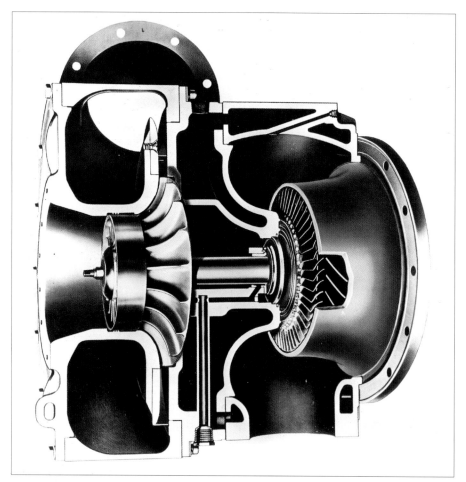

This cutaway view of an Alco turbocharger shows how the pressure of the exhaust gases (passing through the chamber at left) drive a turbine (right), which is used to pump air into the engine at high pressure. *Alco*

need to remove the upper crankshaft when doing any cylinder or piston maintenance—along with the engines' increased cooling needs (both water and oil) and their high requirements for air, which could be problematic at high altitudes, offset these advantages. These engines were successful on ships, submarines, and stationary platforms, but didn't receive as much day-to-day upkeep in railroad use.

Turbocharging

Turbocharging is a method of increasing an engine's power output without increasing its size. This is done by forcing more air into each cylinder, which allows more fuel to be injected and burned, resulting in more power.

The turbocharger is powered by a turbine driven by expelled exhaust gases. The turbine, turning at 10,000 or more rpm, drives an impeller, which forces air at high pressure into the engine.

Electro-Motive did not turbocharge its two-cycle 567 engine until the late 1950s, instead using a Roots blower, a less-complex (non-turbine) device powered by the crankshaft. The blower forces air into the combustion chamber at a lower pressure than a turbo. Starting with the GP20 and SD24 through the Dash-2 engines of the 1980s, EMD offered both turbocharged

Diesel locomotives have huge crankshafts, and this one for EMD's 20-cylinder SD45 is among the largest. *EMD*

and non-turbocharged versions of most of its locomotives. Most other manufacturers turbocharged their four-cycle engines, with the exception of some switchers and other low-power locomotives.

The advantage of turbocharging is more power for a given engine size, making the engine more efficient. However, higher maintenance costs, especially on early diesels, reduced some of the gains from the efficiency, which is why several railroads continued to opt for non-turbocharged locomotives into the 1980s.

Modern diesels from GE (GEVO) and EMD (1010) are four-cycle engines that use multi-stage turbos, advanced cooling systems, and exhaust recirculating systems to meet stringent (EPA Tier 4) pollution limit requirements.

Electrical and control systems

To produce electricity, the engine's crankshaft turns a generator (DC transmission) or alternator (AC transmission). Generators were used into the 1960s, but the growing size of locomotives and increased power output meant larger generators, and manufacturers were having a difficult time fitting generators into locomotives.

The solution was substituting an alternator, which is smaller and lighter than a generator for a given power output. The resulting AC power is sent through rectifiers, which convert it to DC. For DC-traction-motor locomotives (all locomotives through the 1980s), the DC then passes through the control system and to the traction motors. More on that in a bit.

The throttle is controlled by a sliding lever that on most road locomotives has eight notches, or control settings, plus idle. Idle is the position farthest away (to the right); pulling the lever toward you (to the left) increases the throttle.

The throttle is linked electrically (pneumatically in some early diesels) with the engine governor. Increasing the throttle each notch increases the fuel flow and engine speed, which increases the power coming from the generator or alternator, increasing the power supplied to the traction motors. Some switchers have "swipe" throttles without notches, allowing engineers quicker response and more-precise control; early GE road diesels had 16 control notches. The throttle position is indicated by the notch setting: for example, full throttle is "run 8" or "notch 8."

A worker installs silicon diodes in a new EMD AR-10 alternator in 1965. The diodes (rectifiers) convert AC generated by the alternator into DC for the traction motors. *EMD*

Throttle and air brake control stands were similar from early diesel road units through the 1980s. This is a Norfolk Southern EMD SD40. *Jeff Wilson*

— 31 —

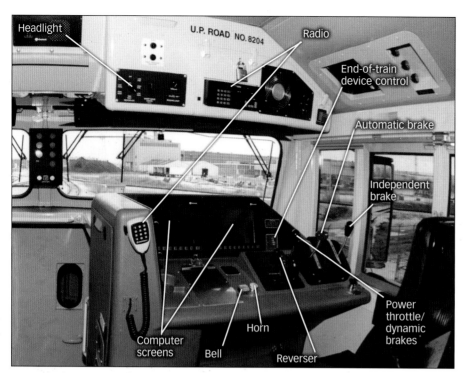

Labels on image: Headlight, U.P. ROAD NO. 8204, Radio, End-of-train device control, Automatic brake, Independent brake, Power throttle/dynamic brakes, Computer screens, Bell, Horn, Reverser

Many modern locomotives, like this Union Pacific SD9043MAC, have desk-style console controls with computer screens providing performance and operating information. Desktop consoles on earlier locomotives had gauges in place of the computer screens.
Union Pacific

A reverser lever on the control stand has forward, neutral, and reverse settings; removing the lever locks it in neutral. Unlike an auto or truck, a diesel locomotive has no forward or reverse gears. It doesn't matter which direction a locomotive is pointing. Instead, the reverser changes the direction of current flow in the field windings of the traction motors. (It's a different process on modern AC traction-motor diesels.)

Electrical control gave diesels a huge advantage over steam locomotives because two or more diesel locomotives can be joined (known as multiple-unit, or MU operation) under the control of a single engineer. Electrical control connections are made between locomotives with a jumper cable, with air hoses to control brakes and (on early diesels) sanders. This was the foundation of the building-block principle, in that a single diesel locomotive didn't have to be as powerful as a steam locomotive. Instead, as many diesels as needed can be combined to match what is required for each train.

Trucks and traction motors

With few exceptions, locomotive trucks have four or six wheels. Four-wheel (two-axle) trucks have both axles powered. Most six-wheel (three-axle) trucks have three powered axles, but early passenger diesels and some early (and some more recent) freight locomotives have the center axle unpowered, using it as an idler to better spread the weight of the locomotive.

Diesel locomotives are known by wheel arrangements, just as steam locomotives. Powered axles on each truck are indicated by letters: "A" for one powered axle, "B" for two, "C" for three, and "D" for four. Numbers indicate unpowered (idler) axles. Thus a six-axle diesel with all axles powered is a C-C; a six-axle diesel with the center axle of each truck unpowered is an A1A-A1A.

The AAR (American Association of Railroads) developed standard designs for road and switcher trucks, and most manufacturers developed their own designs as well. The locomotive sits on a bolster, which is supported on each side by a side-frame. A combination of coil and leaf springs, drop hangers, struts, and other accessories are used to distribute weight and provide a smooth ride.

In the 1960s, as locomotive size and power increased, many high-horsepower locomotives fought problems with being "slippery." Manufacturers worked to develop new truck designs to improve wheel-to-rail adhesion. The result was a series of new high-adhesion trucks from the major builders. All worked to reduce and control wheel slip, distribute weight evenly, and provide a smooth ride at high speed.

Many modern six-axle diesels (since the early 1990s) from EMD and GE feature radial or "self-steering" trucks. Older trucks have all three axles parallel with each other, meaning that when a three-axle truck is in a curve, only the middle axle follows the actual radius of the curve. The leading and trailing axles can't align properly, which causes wheel and rail wear, lowers adhesion, and can cause a rough ride. The axles on self-steering trucks pivot independently, reducing wear while increasing adhesion and ride quality.

Each powered axle is driven by a traction motor, which is supported by both the axle and the truck frame. A small pinion gear on the traction motor armature turns a larger gear mounted on the axle. The number of teeth on each gear determines the gear ratio, which varies depending upon the locomotive service. Each manufacturer offered its locomotives with a range of gear ratios. A low-speed freight or switching locomotive will have a high gear ratio, such as 65:12, while a high-speed passenger locomotive would be equipped with a low gear ratio, such as 58:25. This allows the freight locomotive greater torque and tractive effort at low speeds, but limits its top speed; the passenger locomotive can cruise easily at high speed, but doesn't have as much pulling power at low speeds.

The AC revolution

Through the 1980s, traction motors were all powered by direct current. The coming of the AC traction motor was one of the most radical innovations in diesel locomotive technology since the end of the steam era. The AC traction motor, after years of predictions and testing, finally proved to have practical mass market applications in 1991 with EMD's SD60MAC.

An AC traction motor offers several advantages over a DC motor. The AC motor is simpler, as it doesn't have the brushes and commutators needed in DC motors. This makes them much tougher, virtually eliminating the risk of damage from overheating under a heavy load. All DC motors have "short-time ratings"—the time a motor can withstand a specific high

An electrical multiple-unit (MU) cable and several air hoses connect diesel locomotives, allowing control of several units by one engineer. *Louis A. Marre collection*

current load before overheating and damage occurs. The higher the amperage, the shorter the time allowed for the motor to operate at that level.

The better torque of AC traction motors improves wheel-to-rail adhesion, with AC motors achieving adhesion above 35 percent, compared to about 30 percent for a DC motor.

The main reason AC traction motors were not used earlier was not the motor itself, but the challenge of controlling the AC power used for traction. Electrical engineers will understand this much better than the rest of us, but the bottom line is that the one-way flow of direct current makes it much easier to control multiple speeds on a DC motor than an AC motor. The advent of computers and microprocessor technology made the AC control process easier (and less expensive) to put into practice.

As with a DC locomotive, the diesel engine on an AC diesel turns an alternator, producing AC. However, the AC power directly from the alternator cannot be used by the traction motors. Rectifiers convert the AC to DC, which is then converted back to AC by a series of inverters that "chop" the current for use by the traction motors. Microprocessors control the process, which involves turning the power on and off rapidly (up to 500 times per second).

General Electric and EMD each offer their current road locomotives in both AC and DC versions, although the last DC locomotive was built in 2012. Some railroads continued to buy DC versions even after AC became popular as an economy decision, as the price tag on an AC locomotive is significantly higher ($1 million or more per locomotive). Other railroads bought both, assigning AC locomotives to heavy-haul service, which makes the best use of AC's advantages.

Braking systems

Stopping a moving train (as well as controlling speed on a downgrade) requires a great deal of energy. Diesel locomotives use three braking systems to accomplish this: the independent (locomotive) air brake, automatic (train) air brakes, and dynamic brakes.

The independent brake controls the brakes on the locomotive itself. The independent brake can be applied and released separately from the train brakes. A lever on the brake stand allows the engineer to vary this brake application from light to full.

The automatic brake system controls the air brakes on all cars of a train. The train line (brake line) runs the length of the train, with hoses connecting the locomotive and cars. Once a train is assembled and all brake hoses are connected, the train line is charged with air, usually to 90 pounds of pressure. A control valve on each car draws air from the train line for that car's air reservoir.

To apply the automatic brakes, the engineer moves the brake valve, a handle that allows air to escape from the train line, reducing the pressure. The drop in

Locomotive trucks have a combination of leaf and coil springs and other appliances to provide a smooth ride, even weight distribution, and maximum tractive effort. This is a four-wheel EMD GP ("Blomberg") truck. *Trains magazine collection*

pressure triggers the control valve on each car to apply the brakes. The percentage of air reduced determines the amount of air transferred from each car's reservoir to the brake cylinder, which regulates the amount of braking force.

To release the brakes, the engineer closes the brake valve. The train line begins recharging, which signals the control valves to release the brakes (by releasing air from the cylinders) throughout the train.

Dynamic brakes are an optional feature, but are found on almost all modern road locomotives. Dynamic brakes use the locomotive's traction motors as generators to provide resistance to a rolling train. Dynamics are employed mainly to keep a train's speed in check on a downhill grade, as opposed to bringing a train to a complete stop.

To apply the dynamic brakes, the engineer moves the throttle to idle and sets the dynamic brake lever to "setup." This energizes the traction motor fields, which turns the traction motors into generators. Energizing the motor fields provides a great

deal of turning resistance on the axles. The engineer then adjusts the amount of braking force by increasing the notches on the dynamic brake lever.

Dynamics provide significant rolling resistance, and dynamic brakes alone are sufficient to hold train speed in check in many downgrade braking situations. This saves a great deal of wear and tear on brake shoes and provides a measure of safety beyond the train air brakes. On locomotives built through the 1970s, dynamics were typically effective from about 18 to 25 miles per hour. In the 1970s extended-range dynamics became an option, allowing effective braking down to 8 mph; the dynamic brakes on many of today's AC traction-motor locomotives are effective down to 1 mph.

The electricity generated by the traction motors is dissipated as heat in large banks or grids of resistors—much like a giant toaster—with fans to cool them. The resistor grids are located in various locations depending upon locomotive type. Older EMD hood diesels had a flared blister

(housing) atop the middle of the long hood. Older GE diesels had grids in the screened radiator intake opening at the rear of each side, while tall-hood Alco road diesels had dynamics mounted in the long hood at roof level, with screened openings on each side. Modern GE and EMD locomotives have the dynamics directly behind the cab or at the extreme rear of the hood, respectively.

Ancillary systems

Many additional systems work to keep a diesel-electric locomotive running. Diesel engines are liquid-cooled, using 250 to 350 gallons of water. The radiator is usually located at roof level at the rear of the locomotive. Cooling air is pulled in through grilles or screens on the sides by thermostatically controlled fans on the roof (sometimes mounted below a protective grille or screen). The fans draw air through the radiator and expel the hot air upward.

Antifreeze is generally not used in locomotives because of the cost, the risk of contaminating lubricating oil, and the risk

This traction motor has yet to be mounted on its axle and truck. The pinion gear on the motor will turn the large gear on the axle inboard of the wheel. The axle will pass through the opening to the left of the pinion gear. *W.A. Akin*

of long-term damage to metal surfaces in the engine. In cold weather, locomotives are generally allowed to idle to stay warm. Some modern engines do indeed use anti-freeze; others have automatic start/stop features that sense when a stopped engine needs to be running.

The lubrication needs of a modern diesel are also quite significant, requiring up to 400 gallons of oil. An oil pan under the engine holds the oil, which is piped throughout the engine's moving parts for both lubrication and cooling.

The fuel tank on most diesels is suspended from the underframe between the trucks. Some early diesels (including the Alco RS-2 and several Baldwin road switchers) had a fuel tank under the cab or in the short hood. The tank on a modern road locomotive holds about 5,000 gallons of No. 2 diesel fuel, and the engine will burn between 1 and 5 gallons of fuel per mile depending upon throttle setting and load.

Diesel engines require a great deal of air, both for combustion and cooling. The louvers on the sides of early diesels covered oil-bath filters used for cleaning combustion air. Later engines often used paper filters (usually marked by a housing on the roof behind the cab). Inertial filters are used on locomotives with pressurized engine compartments. This is an active filter, essentially a small rotating cyclone, that suspends dust and particles from intake air and then expels them from the system.

Passenger diesels—and many dual-purpose freight diesels—were equipped with steam generators to provide heat and power for passenger cars. These were located at the rear of the locomotive for cab units and in the tall nose, directly behind the cab, or at the rear of the carbody of hood units. A steam generator consists of a diesel-fired boiler with a vent, stack, and safety valve above it on the roof. The water tank for the steam generator could be located inside the body (common for cab units) or located next to the fuel tank under the frame.

In the 1970s, head-end-power (HEP) units became more common, supplying electricity to cars for air conditioning, lighting, and heat. A separate small diesel engine and generator were often housed in the rear of the locomotive body. Some passenger diesels use power from the main generator for supplying train power.

Air reservoirs (long, narrow tanks with rounded ends) hold compressed air for the brake system and other accessories, such as the bell, horn, and sanders. The reservoirs can be located below the frame, either running lengthwise under the running board or transversely next to the fuel tank, or atop the roof.

A locomotive requires a lot of battery power (actually a set of batteries) compared to an automobile or truck. A set of locomotive batteries can weigh up to 3,000 pounds. The batteries can be located in cabinets atop the running boards next to the cab (hood units) or under the frame (hood or cab units).

Locomotive spotting

All of the above features are keys to look for when trying to identify a locomotive.

Looking under the rear hood of a GE U25B reveals the radiator as well as the dynamic brake grids (the staggered panels on the left). The larger the engine, the larger the radiator needs to be. *GE*

Start with the basic shape of the cab, nose, and hood to determine the builder, then the wheel arrangement to determine the class. Figuring out the specific model is a matter of looking at details such as grille, window, porthole, and louver locations; the number and location of hood doors; and the number and style of exhaust stacks and rooftop fans. Chapter 3 will provide more information on locomotive external details and options.

Locomotives are often modified over time, with their appearance changed. Grab irons are added and moved; louvers and grilles are added, removed, or modified; and side panels can be changed or swapped among locomotives. Locomotives are sometimes given new engines or completely rebuilt, which can drastically change their appearance. (Because of this, the photos and notes throughout this book apply mainly to locomotives as built.)

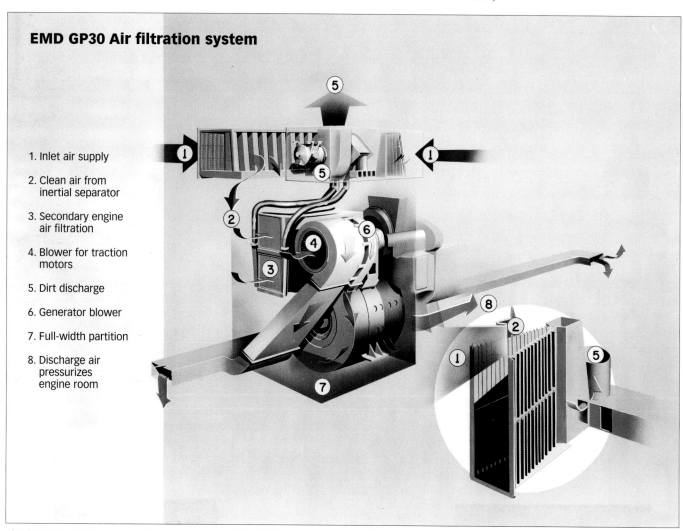

EMD GP30 Air filtration system

1. Inlet air supply

2. Clean air from inertial separator

3. Secondary engine air filtration

4. Blower for traction motors

5. Dirt discharge

6. Generator blower

7. Full-width partition

8. Discharge air pressurizes engine room

The inertial air filter, shown here as first used by EMD on its GP30, uses fans and centrifugal force instead of paper or cloth filters to clean the intake air for the engine and accessories. *EMD*

Air conditioner
Beacon
Wind deflector
Cab sunshade
Dynamic brake grid
Radiator air intake
Radiator fans
Anticlimber
Uncoupling lever
Plow
Hand brake
Bell
Fuel tank filler and gauge
Air reservoir

CHAPTER THREE

Details and options

Like a new automobile, every basic locomotive model has a number of optional accessories, mandated components, and variations of standard equipment. Being able to identify the many exterior components and details on a locomotive will help you to identify builders and specific models.

Diesel locomotives have a variety of standard and optional accessories. Many vary among manufacturers and models, but others are standard across most locomotives. This is a brand-new Santa Fe EMD GP50 in 1981. *Santa Fe*

This Southern Pacific Alco has a single (red) Pyle Gyralight mounted above a horizontal twin sealed-beam headlight. *Southern Pacific*

Chapter 2 covered many of the mechanical and internal features of a locomotive, so let's look at external accessories, details, and options.

Today's modern road locomotives are heavily standardized, and the number of railroads buying them is relatively few compared to the first two generations of locomotives. The hundreds of railroads that initially bought new diesel locomotives from the 1940s into the 1970s provided a tremendous variety in locomotive appearance, even within the same model.

Lighting

Lights are one option. Headlights can be located on the nose or above the windshield on hood units, and on the upper nose or lower in the nose door on cab units. Headlights are usually mounted in pairs, although many cab units had single-bulb headlights with large reflectors. Several types and styles of lights have been used. Some railroads opted for lights in multiple locations, using one position for a red signal light or for a moving light, such

as a moving Mars light or Pyle Gyralite.

Modern locomotives have front ditch lights (auxiliary lights) located outboard at pilot level. In use since the 1990s and mandated on road diesels since 1997, these lights can flash when approaching grade crossings. Older locomotives had these lights retrofitted to the pilot or edge of the platform.

Classification lights are lamps on the nose (above the cab windows on some hood units) that, in the era of timetable-and-train-order operations, indicated the class of a train: white for an extra and green to indicate that additional sections of a scheduled train were following. Red was used as a marker light, required at the end of a train (for example, when a locomotive is used as a pusher). Class lights were phased out by the 1970s. Some railroads plated over their openings; others (notably Conrail) left the red lights in for use as marker lights.

Rooftop beacons in various styles have been in use since the 1960s and although they were not mandated many railroads

used them. Most early ones were amber housings with rotating internal lights, although some had multiple lights that alternated blinking. Strobe lights are now more common.

Horns and bells

Horns are mandatory, but many types were and are available. Many early diesels had single-note horns, usually in pairs. For cab units this meant on the cab roof with one facing forward and one to the rear. Hood units could have them this way or mounted on either the side of the nose or hood.

Multiple-chime horns became popular in the 1950s and '60s in clusters of three or five bells tuned to a musical chord. The bells sometimes all face the same direction; one or two bells may be reversed to face the rear. Nathan and Leslie are the two main horn manufacturers, and most railroads standardized on a specific type and style of horn. Location varied; most railroads mounted them atop the cab roof, but some mounted them farther back on the hood roof.

Radiator — Exhaust stack — Dynamic brake housing — Dome covering antennas — Sand hatches — Ditch lights

MU socket

8413

5427

5427

5427

Air reservoirs — Fuel tank — Fuel filler and gauge — Plow

This modern GE ES44AC shares many of the same features as earlier diesels. Note the twin auxiliary (ditch) lights. *Jeff Wilson*

6332

6332

This Penn Central Alco C-636 has class lights above the number boards and a three-chime horn mounted to the cab front wall. The housing atop the nose is a sand-filler hatch. The visors under the headlights limit glare reflected back into the cab. *Penn Central*

Hancock air whistle

Headlight

Classification lights

1000

1000

Drop step

Light

MU socket

Uncoupling lever

MU hoses

Air line hose

Footboards

This Louisville & Nashville GP30 is equipped with a Hancock air whistle instead of a standard chime horn.

Northern Pacific equipped its Alco RS-3s with steam-style bells, classification lamps, and angled number boxes. *Jeff Wilson collection*

A variation was the air whistle, notably by Hancock (a prominent supplier of steam locomotive whistles). These were designed to mimic a steam whistle, and were usually placed in a shroud to direct the sound forward.

Bells fall into the same category. Many early diesels had bells of the same style as steam locomotives, mounted in brackets atop the hood or nose. These were relocated to the side of the hood on many locomotives, then the typical location became under the frame next to the fuel tank (hood units) or hidden behind the pilot (cab units). Some railroads (notably Chicago & North Western) used "gong" style bells (shaped like a typical school-style alarm bell).

Fuel, water, and air tanks

Fuel tank size varies widely, from about 600 gallons on small early switchers and road switchers to 5,000 gallons on modern road locomotives. Most locomotives have been offered with tanks of various sizes, which can be spotted by differences in length, width, and shape.

Fuel tank fittings vary by manufacturer and model, but you'll find a filler pipe with red cap, vertical fuel sight glass, and often a standard fuel gauge. There will also be a red switch labeled "EMERGENCY FUEL CUT-OFF" near the filler.

Passenger locomotives through the 1970s had water tanks to supply the steam generator. These were often next to or wrapped around the fuel tank under the chassis—look for separate filler hardware.

Air tanks or reservoirs are required to supply the train brake line. These are long, rounded-end cylindrical tanks. On modern diesels they're generally located alongside the fuel tank. Some early diesels had them mounted transversely under the frame aft of the fuel tank. On some early steam-generator-equipped hood units, this space was occupied by a water tank, so the air tanks were mounted longitudinally on the roof. These were sometimes called "torpedo-tube" tanks.

Pilots

Pilots—the lower part of the front and rear—are another source of variety. Many locomotives have unadorned pilots, but railroads operating in the north mount snowplows on pilots. Plows come in many styles and sizes, and railroads tended to standardize on one (or a limited selection).

Footboards were typical on switchers and many road switchers into the 1960s, but railroads by that time were restricting or banning their use for safety reasons. Their installation was eventually banned in the mid-1970s.

Anticlimbers are large, heavy horizontal extensions of the frame at the top of the pilot. They're designed to keep struck objects from traveling upward into the cab, and to keep other locomotives or cars from telescoping over the frame in a collision.

Air hoses are located on the pilot on each end. The largest-diameter hose (immediately to the right of the coupler as you're standing on the ground looking at it) is the train-line (reservoir) brake hose.

Northern Pacific no. 220 is an example of a "torpedo tube" GP9, with air reservoirs mounted longitudinally atop the long hood. The locomotive also has a canvas sunshade above the cab window and a firecracker-style antenna atop the cab. *Jeff Wilson collection*

A heavy, multi-connector cable plugs into the MU socket on adjoining locomotives to connect them electrically. *Jeff Wilson*

If a locomotive is not equipped for multiple-unit (MU) operation, this will be the only hose.

If a locomotive is equipped for MU, it will have additional hoses on the pilot on each side of the coupler—generally three, four, or five hoses depending upon the brake system used.

The MU socket is the receptacle for the heavy cable that electrically connects locomotives. It can be mounted atop the pilot or on an elevated stand or post. On cab unit noses the MU receptacle is usually behind a hatch located next to the nose headlight. Not all MU-equipped cab units had MU capabilities on the front end, especially when built, although many were later retrofitted for versatility.

Other pilot and nose details include an uncoupling lever and, on road switchers, a drop step that folds down to make it easier for crew members to pass between coupled locomotives. On engines with drop steps, a chain connects the middle two handrail stanchions. Some railroads did not use drop steps; on these engines the handrail

Two SD9s are set up for MU operation with air hose and MU cable connected and drop steps lowered into position. *Keith R. Tygum*

was usually solid between the middle stanchions.

Cab, nose, and roof details

Number boards are typically located above cab windows (hood units) or on the nose (cab units). Some early switchers and road switchers with tall noses had them mounted on the corners of the hood. These illuminated boards usually carry the loco-motive number, but through the 1960s some railroads used them to display the train number (namely Southern Pacific and Union Pacific), and they called them train indicator boards.

Atop the end of the nose (on hood units) you'll find a sand filler hatch, used for adding traction sand. You'll also find a hatch atop the roof at the end of the long hood. On cab units, the hatches are on the sides of the nose above the truck, with the rear hatches on the sides above the rear truck. The side of the nose often sports a hand brake (either a wheel or lever style).

Side cab windows often have sunshades. This is typically a large metal piece that

This Burlington F unit has a "wagon-wheel" antenna atop the cab. The sand filler hatch is at left under the wide red stripe. *Hol Wagner*

can be folded up or down; some early diesels used folding canvas shades. All-weather windows—boxy protrusions that extended outward—were common on diesels in northern climes.

Air conditioners are a railroad option, most often found in desert areas (and more common on modern locomotives). These are identfied by a box atop the cab.

The increased use of radios for communications from the 1950s onward led to antennas atop cab roofs of most diesels. These come in a variety of styles, with the most common being the firecracker (which resembles an upside-down firecracker), Sinclair (a long, narrow blade that lays flat), and can (a small cylinder on end). "Wagon-wheel" antennas, found on some

early diesels, featured a round spoked wheel on a post. Some modern locomotives have multiple antennas covered by a small dome.

On the roof you'll find fans in a variety of sizes and styles. Some are flush with the roof, while others are in protruding shrouds or housings. Radiator fans are generally at the rear. They draw in air through grille- or screen-covered openings in the sides through the radiator and upward through the fans. Dynamic brake fans can be in the middle or forward, depending upon locomotive model, again drawing air upward through the banks of resistors.

Exhaust stacks are also found on the roof. Turbocharged engines generally have a single stack, while normally aspirated engines typically have two to four stacks.

Locomotives that operate in cold-weather areas sometimes have a radiator fan covered by a winterization hatch. This is a box-like housing located above the fan. Shutters on the hatch allow redirecting warm air into the engine compartment in cold weather.

The roof of this Cotton Belt GP40-2 shows, from left, an amber beacon, cab air conditioner, firecracker antenna atop a mounting plate, and exhaust stack. *Jeff Wilson*

This EMD GP35 has a pair of 48" fans around a 36" fan at the radiator, with a single 48" fan above the dynamic brake grid. All are shrouded. *Don Dover; J. David Ingles collection*

The boxlike structure over a radiator fan on this GP7 is a winterization hatch. Shutters allow redirecting warm air back into the engine compartment. *EMD*

CHAPTER FOUR

Locomotive types

Diesel locomotive design has evolved significantly since the 1930s. Although diesels have been built in many shapes and sizes, they can all be divided into three basic styles or types: switchers, cab units, and road switchers. Each is distinctive and was designed for a specific type of service.

Modern road switchers, like this Montana Rail Link EMD SD70ACe, are high-horsepower, high-speed locomotives that trace their basic designs back to the first hood units of the 1940s. *Tom Danneman*

Diesel switchers had a common look that remained consistent from the 1930s to the 1980s. This 1,200-hp EMD SW9 was built for New York Central in 1951. *EMD*

Switchers

Diesel-electric switching locomotives began appearing in large numbers in the mid-1930s. Even ardent steam supporters of that period acknowledged that diesels were well-suited for yard, terminal, transfer, and other switching duties that required low speeds and high tractive effort. Diesels could run constantly, with no breaks needed for water, coal, or dumping ashes—just periodic refueling. Smoke ordinances in many cities also hastened the arrival of diesel switchers.

The first successful commercial diesel-electric switchers were boxcab locomotives. A 300-hp design built by an Alco-GE-Ingersoll-Rand partnership in 1925 is credited as the first successful diesel-electric switcher, with similar locomotives sold to Central of New Jersey, Baltimore & Ohio, and Lehigh Valley. Many other similar locomotives were built over the next 10 years.

The mid-1930s saw a trend toward more-powerful locomotives (600 to 1,000 hp), and manufacturers began assembling them in what would become the common body style for switchers: a cab at one end, a hood enclosing the engine and electrical components, and walkways (running boards) on either side and at the front of the hood.

Several features distinguish a switch engine from a road locomotive. Most switchers have smaller engines and lower horsepower, since speed isn't a critical factor—most have maximum speeds of 30 to 35 mph. Because of this, trucks on most switchers have a shorter wheelbase and less shock-absorption qualities compared to road diesels.

Switchers usually have swipe throttles or additional speed "notches" compared to the usual eight notches on a road locomotive, allowing greater control when switching cars in a yard.

The end-cab design usually features lots of window and windshield area, allowing crew members good visibility in all directions. Since they don't venture out of yards, switchers typically don't have classification lights or additional headlights like their railroads' road locomotives.

There are exceptions, but most switchers aren't equipped with multiple-unit connections, dynamic brakes, or steam generators.

Most manufacturers offered switchers with multiple horsepower options, ranging from 600 to 1,200 and finally (in the 1960s) 1,500 hp.

Switchers typically have long service lives compared to road diesels, and many switchers built in the 1930s and '40s (even from minority builders) were still going

strong in the 1970s and even later.

Alco and EMC were both offering standard switchers by the mid-1930s, with Baldwin joining in 1939. Fairbanks-Morse was a late entrant in the market, selling its first one in 1944 but earning a reputation for switchers with excellent lugging capabilities. Lima didn't build its first diesel switcher until 1949, and never made an impact in the market. General Electric stayed out of the switcher market, other than its 44- and 70-ton diesels, concentrating on road locomotives from the 1960s onward.

Basic switcher designs remained relatively unchanged through the 1960s, when the number of classification yards began dropping and railroads wanted more flexibility from switching locomotives. The answer was switchers with road trucks and higher horsepower, such as EMD's SW1500 and MP15.

By the 1980s, railroads were adapting older four-axle (and later six-axle) road switchers (often with slugs) as yard units. Sales of new switchers dwindled, with the last of them (EMD MP15Ts) rolling out in 1987.

Cab units

When diesels began powering passenger trains in the 1930s, railroads wanted the

By the time Missouri-Kansas-Texas MP15AC No. 58 was built in 1980, few diesel switchers were being produced. *Lee Langum*

The first diesel passenger units were articulated with their trains. Later engines, like Burlington No. 9905 (with one of the original *Twin Zephyrs*) were separate locomotives but retained their trains' unique styling. *Jim Seacrest collection*

Passenger cab units, like this twin-engine New York Central EMD E8, rode on six-wheel trucks with the center axle unpowered (A1A-A1A). This is a late-production E8, with stamped-metal Far-Air grill along the upper sides. *EMD*

power units in streamlined bodies to match their new, sleek trains. The first ones—Burlington's first *Zephyrs*, Union Pacific's M-10000, Boston & Maine's *Flying Yankee*, Illinois Central's *Green Diamond*—were articulated with their train sets. By the late 1930s, railroads were finding that the benefits of articulation (mainly lighter weight) were outweighed by a lack of flexibility: If a single car or the power unit had a problem or needed repairs, the whole train had to be removed from service.

Separate locomotives became the norm by the late 1930s. Many retained the styling of the earlier articulated power units and were still designed for specific trains, including several *Zephyrs*, UP's M-10002 to 10006, Gulf, Mobile & Ohio's Alco-powered *Rebels*, and Southern's Fairbanks-Morse-powered OP-800 units.

Electro-Motive built several four-axle (all wheels powered) passenger locomotives for Santa Fe and Baltimore & Ohio in 1935 and 1936. These were boxy and blunt-ended, but built for speed. They were the predecessors of the cab unit diesels to come.

Electro-Motive built its first E units (EA, E1, and E2) in 1937, establishing the basic styling for passenger cab diesels for the next 25 years. Unlike earlier

"shovel-nose" or custom-design locomotives, the E had a protruding nose (similar to an auto or truck) ahead of the cab.

The E (for Eighteen-hundred horsepower) had two engines and rode on a pair of three-axle trucks with the center axle unpowered (A1A). Other manufacturers followed suit, with each having distinctive nose and cab stylings that made them fairly easy to identify. These included Alco with its DL and later PA models, Fairbanks-Morse with its Erie-Built, and Baldwin with its "baby-face" and later "sharknose" models.

This streamlined look carried over to the first road freight diesels as well, as Electro-Motive's revolutionary FT of 1939 followed the same basic design as the manufacturer's sleek E units, albeit shorter with a less-slanted nose. Other manufacturers followed with freight cabs, including Alco's FAs, F-M's C-Liners, and Baldwin's DR-4-4-15 and RF-16. Over the years this style became known as cab, carbody, or covered-wagon diesels.

Cab unit designs

There's no doubt that appearance had a lot to do with early passenger and road freight cab-unit design. Carbody-style diesels provided railroads with a broad canvas on

which to splash their often-lavish multi-color paint schemes.

Cab diesels were designed so the truss framing of the body sides worked with the underframe to provide structural strength—similar to the design of a truss bridge. This is unlike switchers and hood-type diesels, which have much heavier underframes that are solely responsible for strength.

Carbody diesels with cabs including throttles and control equipment are known as "A units" and cabless locomotives are "B units" or boosters. For any given model, A and B units are mechanically identical except for the lack of an operating cab on B units. Early FTs were the exception—they were designed as an A-B set, and the B lacked batteries and a hostler control, so it was dependent upon its A unit.

The purpose of this was the building-block concept, with the idea that railroads would have an A unit leading, followed by one or more B units, with an A unit trailing the consist (known as an A-B-A or A-B-B-A consist). Matched sets looked good, and having an A unit at each end avoided the need to turn locomotives at the end of a run. Most early A units were delivered with multiple-unit (MU) connections only on the rear, as manufacturers planned that A units would always lead or trail a consist.

Freight cab units had single engines, were built in cab-equipped (A) and cabless booster (B) versions, and rode on four-wheel (B-B) trucks. This is Baldwin's A-B-B-A shark-nosed DR-4-4-15 demonstrator set in 1949. *Baldwin*

The truss bracing in the sides of cab units helped support the locomotive's weight, so cab units required a thinner underframe compared to switchers and road switchers. This is an F unit being assembled at EMD's LaGrange, Ill., plant. *EMD*

After a few years of experience, practical operation began outweighing aesthetics. Many A units not built with nose MU were modified by adding MU connections on their noses, enabling them to be mixed within a consist.

Many maintenance chores were difficult on cab units, with no easy side access to the engine and other major components. This became more critical as locomotives aged and more-extensive repairs became frequent. Railroads also found that

switching maneuvers were difficult with cab units because of the lack of rear visibility. As a result, cab-unit sales began shrinking in the early 1950s as railroads increasingly selected the utilitarian design of hood-style diesels. The last freight cabs

Alco's 1,000-hp RS-1, introduced in 1941, was the first true road switcher. It was basically an S-2 switcher on a longer frame with road trucks and a nose. Great Northern 183 was built in 1944. *Alco*

(F9s) rolled out in 1956, and a few passenger cabs came after that—the last one, Union Pacific E9A No. 914, was delivered in January 1964.

Many EMD freight Fs remained in service into the 1970s, but most Alco (and other minority builder) cabs were retired by the end of the 1960s. Amtrak kept many E units rolling through the 1970s, but by the 1980s cabs were hard to find in all but excursion and short-line service.

The cab design saw a renaissance in the 1990s, as Amtrak received new streamlined Genesis-series passenger locomotives from GE. Although they look radically different compared to traditional cab units, the bodies feature a monocoque design that provides structural strength, so a traditional heavy underframe isn't needed.

Hood units

Even though the first road freight diesels were streamlined cab-type locomotives, it didn't take long to figure out that crews on mainline freight trains had different needs than those working in passenger service. En route switching could be challenging due to poor rearward visibility, with the engineer often having to lean out of the window to see signals from brakemen. This wasn't good under normal circumstances, and could be downright miserable—not to mention dangerous—in darkness or bad weather.

Alco's RS-1, first built in March 1941, gets credit for being the first true road switcher. Alco took its popular 1,000-hp S-2 switcher, placed it on a longer frame,

added AAR type B road trucks in place of the short-wheelbase type A switcher trucks, and added a short hood on the other end of the cab. The result was the road switcher, also called a "hood unit."

The key design difference compared to a cab unit is that a hood unit relies on a heavy frame to support the engine, generator, and other components. Unlike a cab unit, the hood is there just to shelter components, not to provide structural support.

Doors along each side of the hood provide easier access to engine components compared to cabs, and the entire hood can be removed if necessary.

The RS-1 served many roles, especially in branch line, local, and light road-freight services, but it wasn't quite powerful enough for heavy mainline freight service. Alco's solution to that was the RS-2, introduced in 1946, which brought the horsepower to 1,500. This rivaled contemporary road cab diesels in mainline service. By 1946 and 1947, Baldwin and Fairbanks-Morse were also offering road switchers with similar designs.

Electro-Motive, in spite of being a pioneer in freight diesels, was slow to develop a road switcher. EMD offered beefier versions of its switchers (as the NW3, NW4, and NW5) with road trucks for use as transfer, terminal, and branchline freight locomotives, but didn't aggressively market them. It wasn't until the introduction of the BL2 in 1948 that EMD had anything resembling a true road switcher—albeit a light-duty one (the "BL" stood for "branch line").

The semi-streamlined BL2 was difficult and expensive to fabricate. It was a hybrid between a cab and hood unit, and although it allowed better rear visibility, access to the engine and internal components was just as cumbersome as on an F unit. It wasn't until 1949 that EMD finally built a true road switcher, the GP7—and even then, EMD didn't think of it as a mainline locomotive until railroads started treating it as such.

Although it appeared much later than other road switchers, the GP7 gets credit for popularizing the road-switcher concept, and more than 2,700 were sold. The GP7 featured the same proven 567 engine and mechanical and electrical equipment of its cab-unit sister, the popular F7.

The road switcher wasn't streamlined and few consider it pretty—but railroads soon became sold on the concept because of cost, operational benefits, and ease of maintenance. Cab unit sales began dropping in the early 1950s.

Six-axle road switchers began appearing in the mid-1940s. These were originally designed to spread the weight of a locomotive over two more axles, making them suitable for lightweight rail, and most early versions (such as Alco's RSC-2) had center idler (unpowered) axles. Railroads soon found the A1A-A1A design not well-suited for freight locomotives where high tractive effort (as opposed to high speed, as on passenger units) was needed, as the idler axles didn't contribute to tractive effort and also took weight off of powered axles.

Electro-Motive's 1,500-hp GP7 wasn't introduced until 1949, but it (and 1,750-hp successor GP9) quickly dominated the road-switcher market. They became known as "Geeps." This is GP7 demonstrator No. 100. *EMD*

A combination of swing and folding doors on hood-unit sides allows easy access to the engine and other components compared to cab units. This is a Southern Pacific GP9 showing off its 16-cylinder 567C engine. *EMD*

Milwaukee Road 2150 is a 1,600-hp Alco RSD-5, one of the first popular six-axle (C-C) road switchers. It was built in 1953. *Alco*

Alco built a six-powered-axle version of the RS-1 (the RSD-1) in 1946, but only turned out six examples. However, others soon followed, by Baldwin (DRS-6-6-15, 1948), Alco (RSD-4, 1950), Fairbanks-Morse (H-16-66, 1950), and EMD (SD7, 1951). Through the 1950s, six-axle diesel sales increased, and they began finding their niche in heavy-duty drag service, especially at low speeds where high tractive effort was needed. Four-axle diesels were the speedsters on priority freight trains.

That began to change in the late 1960s, as EMD's SD40 and SD45 (and later Dash-2 versions) proved themselves capable of hauling high-speed freight trains as well as lugging drag freights. By the mid-1970s, six-axle diesels were outselling four-axle diesels; by the 1990s, EMD and GE no longer built four-axle road switchers.

Twin-engine hood units

The 1960s saw a flurry of super-sized, twin-engine locomotives from the three remaining builders. Designed and built mainly at the request of the Union Pacific and Southern Pacific, these locomotives amounted to two standard locomotives joined together on a longer frame. These included EMD's DD35 and DDA40X, GE's U50 and U50C, and Alco's C-855 (although only three Alcos were built).

Twin-engine hood diesels actually date back to the late 1940s, such as Baldwin's 2,000-hp DT-6-6-20, but those were designed for low-speed operation and marketed as transfer locomotives. The new, big diesels of the 1960s were intended for high-speed

freight service.

The loss in flexibility of these high-horsepower units and the unique maintenance issues they presented doomed most of them to short careers, although the DDA40X "Centennial" proved quite successful on the UP and enjoyed a normal diesel-electric life span.

Cowl units

Cowl units, although they are streamlined, are classified as road switchers. Although they lack the side walkways of hood units, their sheathing provides no additional structural support to the frame (unlike cab units), and internally and mechanically they are essentially identical to a hood unit.

Examples include EMD's F45, FP45, SDP40F, F40PH, and SD40-2F and GE's U30CG and P30CH. The cowl provides a streamlined look (important to some passenger operators) and provides more protection to crew members having to move between units on moving trains.

Second-generation hood units

The second generation of diesels is broadly defined as the diesel locomotives that began to replace the first diesels (as opposed to replacing steam). The second-generation era began around 1960 with the introduction of EMD's turbocharged 2,000-hp GP20, which was advertised to replace older diesels on a three-to-two ratio, and with GE's pioneering U25B, which at 2,500 hp offered more power than competing locomotives and had several innovative features.

The horsepower race picked up in the 1960s as builders tried to pack as much horsepower into a single-engine locomotive as possible. Sets of 1,750-hp GP9s were the typical road power of the late 1950s; less than 10 years later, sets of 3,600-hp SD45s could be found heading the same trains. However, the popular horsepower choice settled in at the 3,000-hp level from the late 1960s into the 1980s.

Although EMD's 3,600-hp SD45 sold in decent numbers, railroads often opted for a smaller (16- instead of 20-cylinder), more fuel-efficient (and lower-maintenance) engine. The SD40 (and later SD40-2) family of diesels became the most-popular fast-freight and heavy-haul locomotive from the late 1960s through the 1980s, with GE's U30C and C30-7 also finding their niche in heavy-haul service, especially on coal trains. High-horsepower four-axle diesels such as EMD's GP40 and GP40-2 and GE's U30B, U33B, B30-7, and B36-7 led lighter-weight, high-speed trains, such as piggyback and auto-parts hotshots.

Third-generation diesels

In the 1980s, EMD and GE again began trying to boost locomotive power. Increasing engine RPMs and getting additional horsepower into a locomotive was only part of the equation. As locomotives grew in size, the challenge became getting all of that power to the rail. Several earlier high-horsepower four-axle diesels had earned reputations for being "slippery," and even

Union Pacific's DDA40X Centennials were the most successful of the twin-engine 1960s road switchers. The 6,600-hp EMDs, delivered beginning in 1969, were the first wide-nose road switchers and ride on four-axle trucks. *Joe McMillan*

Great Northern No. 434 is an EMD F45, a cowl-covered version of the 3,600-hp SD45. A passenger version, the FP45, was also built. Unlike cab units, the cowl doesn't contribute to frame strength. *EMD*

Burlington Northern 7854 is an SD40-2. The 3,000-hp locomotive was among the most popular diesels of all time, with more than 4,400 built (including variations). The second-generation diesel made six-axle locomotives popular for fast freight. *F. Hol Wagner Jr.*

high-horsepower six-axle diesels suffered from tracking issues and were causing excessive rail wear, especially on curves.

The advent of microprocessor controls ushered in the third generation of diesel locomotives, namely EMD's SD60 line and GE's Dash 8 locomotives. Microprocessors allowed finer control of engine, fuel, and electrical settings, along with advanced wheel-slip controls that, together with a new generation of high-adhesion, self-steering trucks, greatly increased wheel-to-rail adhesion. The standard horsepower rating increased to 4,000 and eventually 4,400 hp, and the coming of the AC traction motor made even more powerful locomotives possible.

By the 1990s, road-switcher design from both EMD and GE had evolved with variations of the wide-nose North American safety cab. A Norfolk Southern order of Dash 9-40Cs in 1994 were the last conventional-cab hood units built.

During this time, the status of the two remaining locomotive builders was changing. General Electric, after more than 20 years as the No. 2 locomotive builder, surpassed EMD in 1983 to take the lead in North American production, a spot that it continues to hold.

EMD officially became part of General Motors Locomotive Group, and in 1988 shut down assembly operations at its LaGrange, Ill., plant, moving assembly to London, Ontario (and also contracted with other plants to assemble locomotives, including Bombardier-Concarril in Mexico, the Conrail [later Norfolk Southern] Juniata Shops in Altoona, Pa., and Super Steel Schenectady in Glenville, N.Y.). In 2005 EMD was sold to Greenbriar and renamed Electro-Motive Diesel, and since 2010 has been owned by Progress Rail (owned by Caterpillar). Its engineering and parts division is located in McCook, Ill., with assembly done at Muncie, Ind.

Heavier trains, especially the emergence of double-stack container trains, meant six-axle power began replacing four-axle locomotives. The last four-axle road freight locomotives—GP60s for Southern Pacific—were delivered in 1994.

A brief foray into 6,000-hp locomotives in the late 1990s had mixed results. Problems with new prime movers on EMD's SD90MAC and GE's AC6000CW slowed railroads' interest. Putting so much power on a single platform also limits flexibility in multiple-locomotive applications and makes engine failure on single-locomotive

trains a problem. The horsepower race settled back down, with EMD and GE both standardizing their lines on six-axle, 4,400-hp locomotives.

Fourth-generation diesels

The latest evolution in locomotive design is the result of EPA emissions regulations. These were stepped in gradually more-restrictive levels, beginning with Tier 0 in 2000 and advancing to Tier 4 in 2015. Existing locomotives met Tier 1 specs in the early 2000s, but tougher Tier 2 regulations, which took effect Jan. 1, 2005, forced both GE and EMD to redesign locomotives to be both more fuel efficient and cleaner to operate. The results (GE's Evolution-series GEVO locomotives and EMD's SD70ACe and SD70M-2) featured advanced electronic engine controls, diagnostics, automatic shutdown and startup, and even more advanced microprocessor systems.

Tier 4 also required a major revision of locomotive designs, including the engine itself, increased cooling capacity, and multi-stage turbochargers. GE met the regulations with its ET44AC and ET44C4, and EMD with its SD70ACe-T4.

— CHAPTER FIVE —

Electro-Motive

Electro-Motive's first two diesel switchers, Delaware, Lackawanna & Western Nos. 425 and 426 (above), were built at General Electric's Erie, Pa., plant prior to the opening of EMC's own assembly plant at LaGrange, Ill. The pioneering locomotives, built in 1935, have distinctive cab, hood, and truck designs that wouldn't be repeated on later EMC or EMD switchers. *EMD*

The company that came to dominate locomotive construction from the 1940s through the 1970s had humble beginnings, contracting the construction of motor cars at other companies' plants in the 1920s. As Chapter 1 explained, the Electro-Motive Corporation was purchased by General Motors in 1930, followed shortly by GM's purchase of the Winton Engine Company.

The company—then EMC—worked to develop diesel switching locomotives as well as power plants for several of the new passenger streamliners of the 1930s, notably Burlington's *Zephyr*. Electro-Motive finally opened its own manufacturing and assembly plant at LaGrange, Ill., in 1936.

In 1941 GM merged both Winton and EMC, with EMC becoming the Electro-Motive Division (EMD) of General Motors. The company would continue to develop locomotives of all types, including switchers, passenger and freight cab units, road switchers, and cowl-style passenger and freight locomotives.

Switchers

Electro-Motive's first Winton-engine switchers were offered in 600- and 900-hp versions ("S"ix or "N"ine) with cast or welded (C or W) frames: the SC, SW, NC, and NW. Cast-steel frames were expensive to produce, hence the quick transition to fabricated (welded) frames. Upgraded models received number suffixes (SW7, SW8, SW9), which didn't correspond to horsepower until the 1950s, with the SW600 through SW1500 models matching their power output.

Cow-and-calf versions were offered of several switchers. These sets included a standard cab-equipped switcher ("cow") semipermanently coupled to a cabless "calf." These received the designation "TR" for transfer. They were built following the lines of basic switcher models, but often without the lower windows in the rear of the cab.

The switcher roster below doesn't include the first two EMC switchers, built as Delaware, Lackawanna & Western 425 and 426 (page 55). Built in February and March 1935, these 600-hp switchers had cast frames. As with EMC's passenger units of the era, the new

switchers were not built at LaGrange, but by General Electric at Erie, Pa.

EMD switchers had a fairly common look from the 1930s into the 1960s, with similar cab and hood designs. All EMD switchers through the SW1200 shared the same frame length. Early switchers were built with short exhaust stacks, but these were often lengthened by railroads, and have a different appearance with straight or tapered sides. Spotting features include the number and placement of exhaust stacks and louvers and the size and location of radiator openings.

Early passenger units

Electro-Motive Corp. partnered with several passenger car builders in the design of the first streamlined diesel-powered passenger trains of the 1930s, including the Burlington *Zephyr*, Union Pacific M-10000 (which used a distillate engine) and later trains, and Illinois Central *Green Diamond*. Each of these early power units was custom-built for a specific train, so each was a specialized locomotive.

As these locomotives became larger to pull bigger trains, it became common to build them as separate units. The first E units (named because they were rated at *E*ighteen-hundred horsepower) were a major step toward a standardized locomotive that could be ordered essentially off-the-shelf for use by any railroad on any train.

Among the first stand-alone passenger locomotives were five twin-engine, 1,000-hp experimental locomotives with boxy bodies riding on four-wheel trucks. They proved the worthiness of the design, and were built before EMC's own LaGrange assembly plant was finished in 1936. Related to these are the exclusive-to-Rock Island TAs. These four-axle, single-engine locomotives

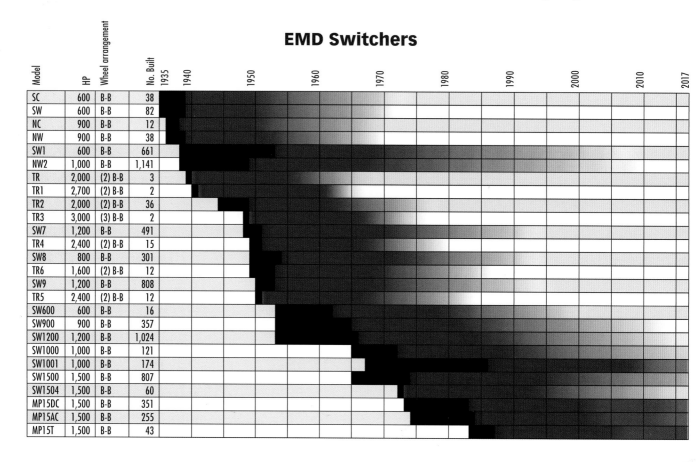

EMD Switchers

Model	HP	Wheel arrangement	No. Built
SC	600	B-B	38
SW	600	B-B	82
NC	900	B-B	12
NW	900	B-B	38
SW1	600	B-B	661
NW2	1,000	B-B	1,141
TR	2,000	(2) B-B	3
TR1	2,700	(2) B-B	2
TR2	2,000	(2) B-B	36
TR3	3,000	(3) B-B	2
SW7	1,200	B-B	491
TR4	2,400	(2) B-B	15
SW8	800	B-B	301
TR6	1,600	(2) B-B	12
SW9	1,200	B-B	808
TR5	2,400	(2) B-B	12
SW600	600	B-B	16
SW900	900	B-B	357
SW1200	1,200	B-B	1,024
SW1000	1,000	B-B	121
SW1001	1,000	B-B	174
SW1500	1,500	B-B	807
SW1504	1,500	B-B	60
MP15DC	1,500	B-B	351
MP15AC	1,500	B-B	255
MP15T	1,500	B-B	43

resembled early Fs but with steeply slanted noses.

Beginning with the EA, all E units shared a common design. All were powered by a pair of 12-cylinder engines, starting with the Winton 201A and followed by various versions of the EMD 567. They rode on a pair of three-axle trucks with center idler axles (A1A-A1A configuration). The idler axles limited starting tractive effort, but spread the weight of the engines, steam generator, and other internal equipment, and provided a smooth ride and good tracking at high speeds.

Starting with the E3 and continuing through the E6, E units were built with a long, slanted nose at a shallower angle than F units. From the E7 through E9, E units adopted the same steeper-angle "bulldog" nose as on F units.

Horsepower increased to 2,000 with the E3, 2,250 with the E8, and 2,500 with the E9. Spotting features include the nose, side openings (portholes or square windows), style of side grilles, and rooftop fans and louvers.

Freight cab units

Electro-Motive's FT was the first heavy-duty road freight diesel, proving that diesels could do the job better and more efficiently than steam. From the FT of 1939 through the last F9s of the late 1950s, EMD F units maintained a consistent appearance. Most significant changes were internal, with some external variation in details such as rooftop fan housings, louvers, and portholes.

Although designed as freight locomotives, several major railroads bought F units specifically for passenger service (including Great Northern, Santa Fe, and Northern Pacific). These were usually geared for higher speeds than freight versions. They can be spotted by a steam-generator stack and vents on the rear roof panel. The FP7 and FP9 versions had longer bodies (by four feet) to accommodate a larger water tank for the steam generator.

All F units used various non-turbocharged versions of EMD's 16-cylinder 567 engine. Traction motors, generators, and other mechanical and electrical equipment were improved and upgraded through F unit production. Horsepower rose from 1,350 for the FT to 1,500 for the F3 and F7 and finally 1,750 for the F9.

Common options and variations on all F units included optional nose-door headlights—which some railroads used as the main light, and others as a signal light or rotating (Mars or Pyle) light. Most Fs were delivered with a pair of single-note air horns, with the right-hand horn facing forward. Some railroads opted for

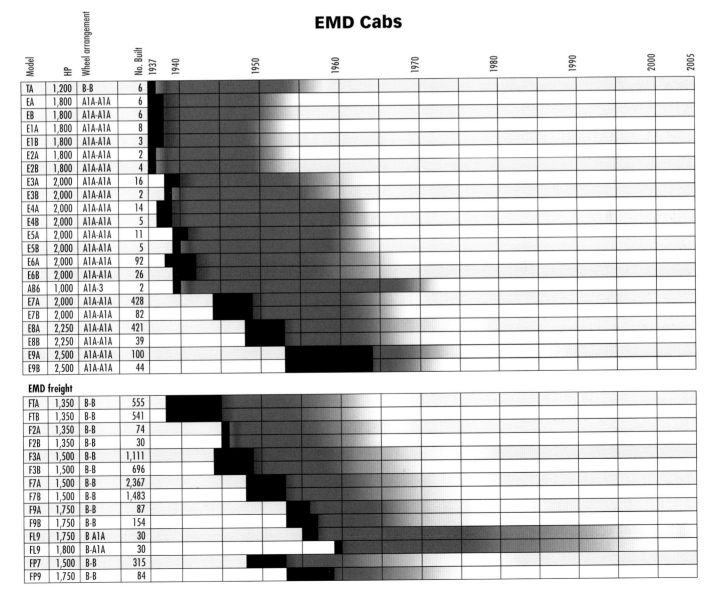

EMD Cabs

Model	HP	Wheel arrangement	No. Built
TA	1,200	B-B	6
EA	1,800	A1A-A1A	6
EB	1,800	A1A-A1A	6
E1A	1,800	A1A-A1A	8
E1B	1,800	A1A-A1A	3
E2A	1,800	A1A-A1A	2
E2B	1,800	A1A-A1A	4
E3A	2,000	A1A-A1A	16
E3B	2,000	A1A-A1A	2
E4A	2,000	A1A-A1A	14
E4B	2,000	A1A-A1A	5
E5A	2,000	A1A-A1A	11
E5B	2,000	A1A-A1A	5
E6A	2,000	A1A-A1A	92
E6B	2,000	A1A-A1A	26
AB6	1,000	A1A-3	2
E7A	2,000	A1A-A1A	428
E7B	2,000	A1A-A1A	82
E8A	2,250	A1A-A1A	421
E8B	2,250	A1A-A1A	39
E9A	2,500	A1A-A1A	100
E9B	2,500	A1A-A1A	44

EMD freight

Model	HP	Wheel arrangement	No. Built
FTA	1,350	B-B	555
FTB	1,350	B-B	541
F2A	1,350	B-B	74
F2B	1,350	B-B	30
F3A	1,500	B-B	1,111
F3B	1,500	B-B	696
F7A	1,500	B-B	2,367
F7B	1,500	B-B	1,483
F9A	1,750	B-B	87
F9B	1,750	B-B	154
FL9	1,750	B A1A	30
FL9	1,800	B-A1A	30
FP7	1,500	B-B	315
FP9	1,750	B-B	84

multi-note horns. Nose-mounted MU connections were often added to F units after delivery, as were nose-mounted grab irons and ladder holders. Another option was the pilot. Most railroads opted for the open ("freight") pilot, but some chose the closed ("passenger") pilot with retractable coupler, which was more common on E units.

Early road switchers

Although a latecomer to the hood unit market, EMD became the dominant builder of road switchers with the GP7. The six-axle

SD7 followed soon after. Although the cab shape and overall size changed over the years, EMD road switchers through the Dash-2 series share many common spotting features.

Dynamic brakes are indicated by a protruding housing ("blister") with grids atop the middle of the long hood, with rooftop cooling fans above it. The radiators are at the end of the hood, with an intake grille or louvers on each side and fans (varying in size and number) on the roof above it.

Four-axle road switchers ride on versions of the distinctive GP truck, which is popularly known as the "Blomberg" (named after

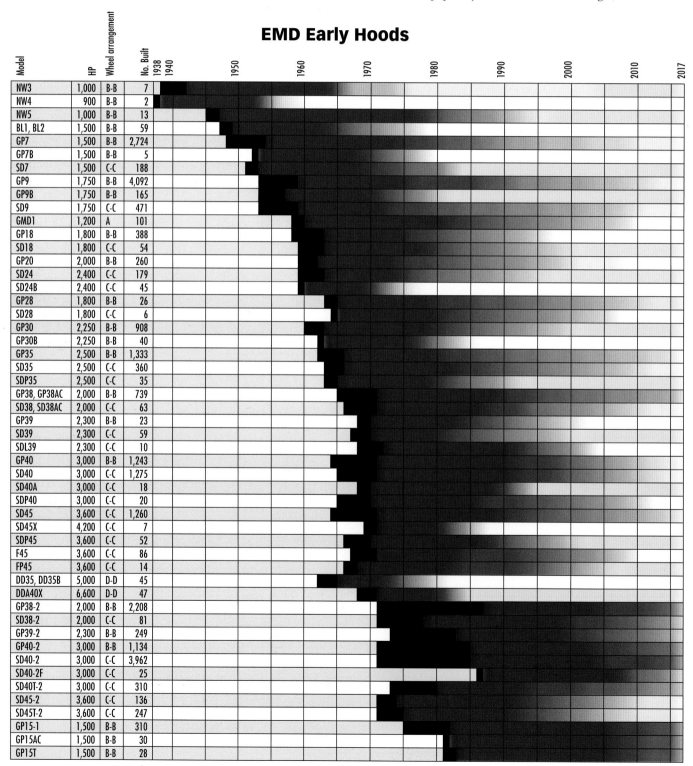

EMD Early Hoods

Model	HP	Wheel arrangement	No. Built
NW3	1,000	B-B	7
NW4	900	B-B	2
NW5	1,000	B-B	13
BL1, BL2	1,500	B-B	59
GP7	1,500	B-B	2,724
GP7B	1,500	B-B	5
SD7	1,500	C-C	188
GP9	1,750	B-B	4,092
GP9B	1,750	B-B	165
SD9	1,750	C-C	471
GMD1	1,200	A	101
GP18	1,800	B-B	388
SD18	1,800	C-C	54
GP20	2,000	B-B	260
SD24	2,400	C-C	179
SD24B	2,400	C-C	45
GP28	1,800	B-B	26
SD28	1,800	C-C	6
GP30	2,250	B-B	908
GP30B	2,250	B-B	40
GP35	2,500	B-B	1,333
SD35	2,500	C-C	360
SDP35	2,500	C-C	35
GP38, GP38AC	2,000	B-B	739
SD38, SD38AC	2,000	C-C	63
GP39	2,300	B-B	23
SD39	2,300	C-C	59
SDL39	2,300	C-C	10
GP40	3,000	B-B	1,243
SD40	3,000	C-C	1,275
SD40A	3,000	C-C	18
SDP40	3,000	C-C	20
SD45	3,600	C-C	1,260
SD45X	4,200	C-C	7
SDP45	3,600	C-C	52
F45	3,600	C-C	86
FP45	3,600	C-C	14
DD35, DD35B	5,000	D-D	45
DDA40X	6,600	D-D	47
GP38-2	2,000	B-B	2,208
SD38-2	2,000	C-C	81
GP39-2	2,300	B-B	249
GP40-2	3,000	B-B	1,134
SD40-2	3,000	C-C	3,962
SD40-2F	3,000	C-C	25
SD40T-2	3,000	C-C	310
SD45-2	3,600	C-C	136
SD45T-2	3,600	C-C	247
GP15-1	1,500	B-B	310
GP15AC	1,500	B-B	30
GP15T	1,500	B-B	28

the designer, Martin Blomberg). The Blomberg B truck, used into the 1970s, is characterized by having two brake cylinders on each sideframe, with two brakeshoes on each wheel. In 1972, with the introduction of the Dash 2 line, the truck was modified with a vertical snubber on the right-hand bearing and only one brake cylinder with a single brake shoe on each wheel. This variation is often called the Blomberg M (for "modified") truck. Many Dash-2 locomotives were still delivered with the older style trucks, often from traded-in locomotives.

Starting with the SD7, six-axle EMD road switchers use the Flexicoil truck, which—unlike other three-axle, all-powered trucks of the era—has even axle spacing. An improved design, the HT-C, first appeared on EMD demonstrators in 1970 and became standard in 1972. It's longer, and is marked by three holes in the sideframe on either side of the center axle, a snubber on the center axle, and distinctive sideframe ends which wrap around the ends of the trucks.

Many early Geeps were built with steam generators, which were located in the high nose. Other buyer options included a variety of headlight and horn options as well as fuel tank sizes.

Electro-Motive model designations have always been rather vague. Four-axle road switchers are GPs (for "general purpose"), and were eventually nicknamed "Geeps." Six-axle road switchers are SDs (which originally stood for "special duty"). The numbers briefly corresponded with horsepower for GP18s, GP20s, SD18s, and SD24s, but went out of sync again with the 2,250-hp GP30.

Many early EMD road switchers are still in service, thanks in large part to their strong frames, solid construction, and the ease of rebuilding the 567 engine. Some resemble their as-built appearance, but most have been rebuilt and many have been heavily modified with low noses or new cabs and hoods.

The Dash-2 line

By the late 1960s, the horsepower race had quieted, with 3,000-hp locomotives becoming the norm for fast freight (EMD's GP40 and SD40, GE's U30B and U30C) and 2,000 for local service (EMD's GP38). EMD had successfully introduced a new, larger engine, the 645, to power these locomotives. Entering the 1970s, EMD looked to upgrade its line of locomotives, but instead of

EMD Modern

Model	HP	Wheel arrangement	No. Built	1976	1980	1990	2000	2010	2017
GP39X	2,600	B-B	6						
GP40X	3,600	B-B	23						
SD40X	3,500	C-C	4						
GP49	2,900	B-B	9						
GP50	3,500	B-B	278						
SD50S	3,500	C-C	6						
SD50	3,500	C-C	361						
SD50F	3,600	C-C	60						
GP59	3,000	B-B	36						
GP60	3,800	B-B	380						
GP60M	3,800	B-B	63						
GP60B	3,800	B-B	23						
SD60	3,800	C-C	537						
SD60M	3,800	C-C	461						
SD60I	3,800	C-C	81						
SD60F	3,800	C-C	64						
SD70	4,000	C-C	120						
SD70M	4,000	C-C	1,646						
SD70I	4,000	C-C	26						
SD70MAC	4,000	C-C	1,124						
SD75M	4,300	C-C	76						
SD75I	4,300	C-C	207						
SD80MAC	5,000	C-C	30						
SD90MAC	4,300	C-C	410						
SD90MAC-H	6,000	C-C	22						
SD90MAC-H II	6,000	C-C	46						
SD70ACe	4,300	C-C	1,628						
SD70M-2	4,300	C-C	240						
SD70ACe-T4 *	4,400	C-C	105*						
Passenger locomotives									
F40PH	3,000	B-B	325						
F40PH-2	3,200	B-B	90						
F40PH-2D	3,000	B-B	59						
F40PH-2C	3,000	B-B	26						
F40PHM-2	3,200	B-B	30						
F59PH	3,000	B-B	83						
F59PHI	3,000	B-B	74						
DE30AC	3,000	B-B	23						
DM30AC	3,000	B-B	23						

*Currently in production

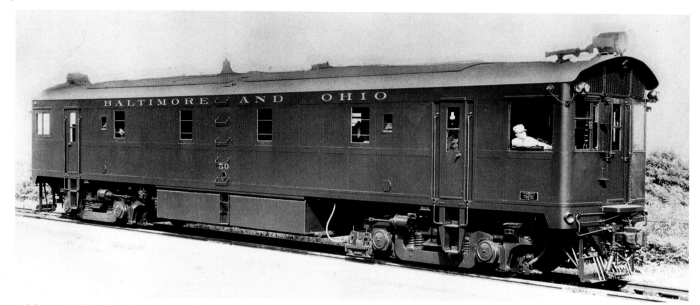

Baltimore & Ohio No. 50 was one of several Electro-Motive Corp. twin-engine, four-axle passenger units. It was assembled at General Electric's plant in Erie, Pa. *General Electric*

introducing all-new locomotive models the company chose to revise and improve its existing locomotives.

The result was the "Dash-2" line, indicated by adding "-2" to the existing model designation. Introduced in 1972, the new locomotives looked much like their predecessors and maintained the same horsepower ratings, but featured new modular electrical and electronic assemblies, upgraded radiators and engines, new HT-C trucks for six-axle engines, and Blomberg M trucks for four-axle models. AC transmission became standard.

The Dash-2 line was successful, and models remained in production through the mid-1980s. The SD40-2 became the most-popular second-generation diesel, with more than 4,000 built (including variations). The GP38-2 became railroading's standard low-horsepower engine, with more than 2,200 built.

Spotting features across all models included a small oval-shaped sight glass (for engine water) on the right side of the long hood, a slight overhang at the rear of the cab roof, battery-box covers bolted in place (instead of hinged), and the left battery box cover jutting under the cab.

New noise regulations in 1979 resulted in component changes. Rooftop fans changed from standard grid-covered to a "Q-fan" (for "quiet"). These have a staggered blade pattern and a central housing. Exhaust stacks became thicker at the base with the addition of a silencer/muffler. A cab modification in 1977 resulted in noses on most Dash-2s going from 81" long to 88" long. Also during production, side radiator intakes changed from wire-grid-covered grilles to vertically corrugated two- and one-piece screens.

Modern hood locomotives

By the early 1980s EMD's basic locomotive models had been in production for almost 15 years. The 3,600-hp, 20-cylinder SD45-2 and the new-generation SD50, its high-horsepower replacement, were pushing the power limits of EMD's existing 645 engine. The SD50 suffered from numerous mechanical and electrical problems. In response, EMD designed a new, larger engine, the 710 (710 cubic inches per cylinder). The new engine would require new locomotive frames/platforms, and with improvements in electrical

equipment and microprocessor control, new locomotive models were needed.

The 710 would become EMD's engine of choice through its 60-series GP and SD locomotives into the 2000s, which also featured microprocessor control, aside from a brief 1990s foray with the 6,000-hp SD90MAC, which used EMD's first four-cycle diesel engine, the 265H.

A push for tougher emissions standards led to the implementation of the EPA's Tier 2 emissions standards, effective Jan. 1, 2005. When EMD designed new locomotives to meet the standards, the company chose to stick with the 710 engine for the new SD70ACe and SD70M-2 (DC traction motor) locomotives, modifying it to match the Tier 2 standards.

This period also saw GM's sale of EMD to Greenbriar Equity/Berkshire Partners (2005), and EMD became Electro-Motive Diesel. In 2010, the new EMD was sold to Caterpillar subsidiary Progress Rail Services (see Chapter 1).

As EPA standards progressed through Tier 3 and then Tier 4 standards (2015), EMD redesigned the 265 into the four-cycle, 12-cylinder 1010 prime mover for its current-production SD70ACe-T4.

Modern passenger power

By the 1960s the few railroads needing new passenger diesels opted for steam-generator-equipped versions of standard six-axle diesels such as the SDP35 and SDP40. The Santa Fe and Milwaukee both opted for FP45s, basically SD45s with steam generators wrapped in a cowl body.

The coming of Amtrak created a need for new power, and EMD's answer was the SDP40F. This was a cowl-style SD40 with two steam generators. Amtrak bought 150 of them in 1973-74, but a series of derailments led to Amtrak trading them in for new four-axle F40PHs starting in 1976. The F40PH was very successful, with more than 500 built (including variations) into the 1990s. Next were orders of F59s, DM30ACs, and DE30ACs in the mid-1990s. The latest passenger model, the 4,700-hp F125, began rolling off the line in 2016.

SC, SW

Boston & Maine SC No. 1103 has a cast frame. The pair of offset stacks and short hood with sandbox in front indicate a 600-hp engine. *EMD*

Electro-Motive's first mass-produced diesels were the 600-hp SC and SW, built from May 1936 through January 1939. Both were powered by the eight-cylinder in-line Winton 201A engine. They can be identified by the three screened openings at the top of each side (found on all Winton-engine switchers), the large sandbox in front of the hood, and two stacks offset to the left side (because of the in-line engine). The frame on the SC has a lip where it overlaps the trim at the corner step; on the SW this seam is flush.

SC: AT&SF, B&M, Canton, CGW, CNJ, M&StL, MP, NYC, P&BR, PB&NE

SW: B&OCT, BCK, C&NW, C&EI, CB&Q, CRI&P, CV, EJ&E, LV, M&StL, P&BR, PB&NE, PRR, RDG

NC (NC1, NC2), NW (NW1, NW1A)

Soo Line NW1A No. 2100 shows the features of 900-hp switchers: a longer hood, no sandbox in front of the hood, and stacks centered instead of offset. It has a welded frame. *EMD*

The NC and NW were the 900-hp ("N") companions of the SC and SW, the difference being the cast or welded frames. These engines used the 12-cylinder (V-style) 201A engine, which required a longer hood than the SC and SW. The N engines had exhaust stacks centered on the hood (because of the V-style engine). Externally, the locomotives are identical other than the frames, with the designation numbers indicating electrical equipment supplier differences.

NC: GN 5101; NC1: BS 71-75; NC2: MP 4100, 4101

NW: AT&SF 2350-2352; KCT 60, 61; NP 100; PB&NE 210, 211

NW1: C&NW 901; CB&Q 9200, 9201; CRI&P 700-707; EJ&E 400, 401; GN 5102; IV 120-130; M&StL D538, D738; Soo 2100-2102 (NW1A)

SW1

New York Central No. 617 is an early SW1, with curved cab windows and a double step where the hood meets the cab. *New York Central*

One of the most-popular early diesel switchers, the SW1 remained in production for 15 years. It used a six-cylinder version of the 567 engine, rated at 600 hp. The locomotive can be spotted by its short hood with sandbox in front and its single stack compared to two on the earlier SW. In 1949 the hood taper in front of the cab changed from a stepped design to a continuous angle from the hood to the cab. The tops of the front cab windows, which were originally curved to match the cab roof, became straight in 1950.

Major buyers: B&O, B&M, CG, CNJ, C&EI, C&NW, CB&Q, CRI&P, DL&W, DT&I, EJ&E, GLS, GN, IC, LV, L&N, MILW, MP, MON, NC&StL, NYC, PRR, PM, PB&NE, RDG, RS, SAL, Soo, SP, TRRA, URR, WAB, WP

NW2, TR, TR1, TR2, TR3

Rock Island NW2 No. 767 has two tall stacks and six louvered doors with a space (letterboard gap) between the top and bottom louver sets. *Rock Island*

The 1,000-hp NW2 was EMD's all-time best-selling switcher. It used the 12-cylinder 567 engine, and it didn't have the screened side openings like the earlier Winton-engine locomotives. The switch to tall exhaust stacks occurred during NW2 production, but many early NW2s had their original short stacks extended. As with the SW1, the hood roof on early NW2s had a double taper where it met the cab; later engines had a single taper. Late NW2s had six louvered doors on the cab end of each side, which were eventually modified with a letterboard gap between top and bottom louver sets. The TR and TR2 are cow/calf versions of the NW2 (page 161), and the TR3 is a three-unit (cow/calf/calf) set. The TR1 was a larger cow/calf version of the TR, with an extended body and cab, Blomberg road trucks, and larger (16-cylinder, 1,350-hp 567) engine.

NW2 major buyers: AT&SF, ACL, B&O, B&M, CN, C&EI, CGW, CB&Q, CRI&P, DT, DT&I, EJ&E, Erie, GRR, GTW, GN, IC, IHB, KCS, LV, MILW, MON, NYC, NKP, NYO&W, PRR, PM, SOU, SP, SLSF, TRRA, T&P, UP, URR

TR: IC 9203-9205

TR1: IC 9250, 9251

TR2: BRC 500, 501; C&NW 2000, 2001; CB&Q 9400-9413; CGW 58-66; IC 9206-9208; MILW 2000; SOU 2400-2404

TR3: C&O 6500, 6501

SW7, TR4

Union Pacific No. 1800 is a late SW7, indicated by the straight-top cab windows. The hood has the single taper at the cab of later SW-series locomotives. *EMD*

The TR4 is a cow/calf version of the SW7. Chesapeake & Ohio No. 6000 was one of 13 sets built. *EMD*

The 1,200-hp SW7 has two exhaust stacks centered on the hood roof, a large front grille that extends to the bottom of the hood, and six rows of louvers along the hood sides with a gap between the top and bottom sets. Early SW7s have cab windows with curved tops; these became rectangular after April 1950. Early SW7s had louvered rooftop radiator openings; in mid-1950 this changed to a wire-covered opening. The TR4 is a cow/calf version of the SW7.

SW7 major owners: ACL, CNJ, C&O, C&EI, C&IW, CB&Q, CRR, DT&I, Erie, GN, IC, IHB, KCS, LV, L&N, MEC, MP, NC&StL, NYC, NKP, NP, PRR, SSW, SLSF, SOU, T&P, UP, WAB

TR4: AT&SF 2418, 2419; BRC 502-506; C&O 6000, 6001; MILW 2001-2006

SW8, TR6

Rock Island No. 817 is an SW8, with a single stack and eight louvered doors on the hood. *EMD*

An eight-cylinder 567 engine bumped the SW8's horsepower to 800 from the 600 of the SW1. The locomotive shared the same body as the later SW600 and SW900, but had six battery-box louvers behind the cab (as did some early units of the later models). The TR6 is a cow/calf version of the SW8.

SW8 major buyers: ACL, B&M, CN, CP, CStPM&O, CRI&P, C&W, DL&W, GN, LV, NYC, NKP, SP, T&P, US Army, WAB

TR6: SP 4600-4603; OM 1207-1213, 1216

SW9, TR5

The SW9 has two exhaust stacks and eight louvered hood doors, but lacks the upper set of louvers found on the SW7. *EMD*

The SW9 was an upgraded version of the SW7. Both were rated at 1,200 hp, but the SW9 had the improved 12-cylinder 567B engine. Its appearance is similar to the SW7, but the SW9 lacks the upper set of louvers along the side. The SW9 also has a straight edge on the trim piece at the stairwell (the SW7's is curved), a fifth lift ring on each side, and new engine-door latches of the same style as the GP7. The TR5 is a cow/calf version of the SW9.

SW9 major buyers: AN, AT&SF, ACL, B&O, B&M, CN, CG, CNJ, C&O, C&NW, CRI&P, DL&W, DM&IR, Erie, FEC, GTW, HB&T, IC, LV, L&N, MP, MKT, NYC, NKP, PRR, Soo, SLSF, TRRA, T&P, UP, URR, WAB

TR5: UP 1870-1877; Union 701, 702, 703C, 704C (C units are extra calves)

SW600, SW900

Weyerhaeuser No. 1 is an SW600. It has five slits on the battery-box louver behind the cab—but early models had six slits, like the SW8. *Stan Mailer*

The 600-hp SW600 and 900-hp SW900 shared the same body, but had six- and eight-cylinder 567C engines, respectively. Features include a single exhaust stack and tall front grille. Early bodies were identical to the SW8; later bodies had battery-box louvers with five slits instead of six. Few SW600s were built, mostly for industrial users, as train sizes were growing and common-carrier railroads were looking for more powerful switching locomotives.

 SW600: C&NW and 13 industrial owners
 SW900 major buyers: AT&SF, B&O, BS, CN, CP, C&NW, CRI&P, GTW, LV, NYC, RR, RDG

SW1000

The SW1000 introduced a new cab design and higher-level running boards. *EMD*

When EMD introduced the 645 engine, the 1,000-hp SW1000 became the company's low-horsepower switcher, using an eight-cylinder version of the engine. The 645 required a taller hood than the 567 (and the hood was a foot narrower as well), changing the appearance significantly. The running boards were located noticeably higher than on earlier switchers, and the locomotive had a taller cab with a shallower roof radius. Options included standard AAR type A switcher trucks or Flexicoil trucks, which allowed higher speed for road use.

 SW1000: BS, CB&Q, D&RGW, D&NE, HB&T, several industrial owners

SW1001

The SW1001 has lower running boards than the SW1000, but retains the taller hood. EJ&E No. 445 rides on AAR type A trucks. *Tom Healey*

The SW1001 was built at the request of industrial users who wanted a lower-profile switcher for clearance reasons. The SW1001 is internally the same as the SW1000, but had a shorter cab, low-level running boards, a cab profile like the SW1200, and two side cab windows (the SW1000 has four). The hood is still tall. Options included AAR type A or Flexicoil trucks.

 SW1001: BS, EJ&E, GW, G&W, KCS, LIRR, RDG, several industrial users

SW1200

Rock Island SW1200 No. 930 rides on Flexicoil trucks instead of the standard AAR type A trucks. *EMD*

The SW1200 was almost identical to the earlier 1,200-hp SW9, but had an upgraded 567C engine. About the only way to differentiate an SW1200 is by the five louvers in its battery box (behind the cab). The SW9 has six louvers, but so do SW1200s built until March 1955. Some SW1200s rode on Flexicoil trucks. These locomotives had notches cut in the frame at the corner steps to clear the trucks.

 Major buyers: AT&SF, B&O, BRC, CN, CP, C&IM, C&NW, CB&Q, CRI&P, DL&W, D&RGW, EJ&E, FEC, GTW, GN, IT, KCT, L&N, MILW, MN&S, MP, MKT, NYNH&H, NP, P&BR, PRR, RDG, RF&P, SSW, Soo, SP, TRRA, WAB

SW1500, SW1504

CSX No. 1113 is an SW1500, marked by its two stacks and long radiator compared to the SW1000. It rides on Flexi-coil trucks. *John C. Benson*

The 1,500-hp SW1500 was EMD's high-horsepower switcher of the late 1960s and early 1970s, powered by a 12-cylinder 645E engine. As with the SW1000, the SW1500 has tall running boards and a tall cab with a shallow roof curve, and it was available with Type A or Flexicoil trucks. The SW1500 can be spotted by its longer radiator and two exhaust stacks, compared to one for the SW1000 and SW1001. The SW1504, built for National of Mexico only, featured Blomberg trucks and was essentially a prototype for the slightly longer MP15DC. It also has a large air-filter box in front of the cab.

   SW1500 major buyers: AN, A&S, BRC, BN, C&I, CRI&P, GN, HBT, IHB, IT, KCS, L&N, MKT, MN&S, MP, MT, NOPB, PC, P&LE, RDG, RF&P, SLSF, SOU, SP, SSW, TP&W, TRRA, Union, WP

   SW1504: NdeM 8800-8859

MP15 (MP15DC)

Union Pacific MP15 No. 1278 is a former Pittsburgh & Lake Erie engine. Blomberg trucks are the best spotting feature. *George Cockle*

The 1,500-hp MP15 (renamed the MP15DC after the AC-transmission version was introduced) replaced the SW1500 in EMD's catalog in 1973. It resembles the SW1500, but the MP15's frame is three feet longer to accommodate Blomberg road trucks. The MP stands for "multi purpose"—sales for switchers were declining by the time the MP15 was introduced, as railroads were looking for locomotives that could also be used in road service. Locomotives built after 1980 have a muffler housing atop the hood at the stacks.

   Major buyers: A&S, BRC, BS, C&NW, G&W, HB&T, KCS, LEF&C, L&N, MRS, MP, NL&G, P&LE, PC&N, RDG, SLSF, StM, SOU, SP, Union

MP15AC

The MP15AC has a pair of exhaust stacks and a radiator intake at running board level on each side. *John C. Benson*

The MP15AC followed the trend of using an alternator and rectifiers as with contemporary EMD road switchers. The AC has low-level radiator intakes on each side at the front, instead of on the nose as on the DC version.

   Major buyers: LIRR, L&N, MILW, NdeM, MKT, SCL, SP

MP15T

Seaboard System No. 1201 has the single rectangular stack that marks it as a turbocharged MP15T.
Glen P. Koshiol

The MP15T uses a turbocharged eight-cylinder engine (hence the "T") instead of the non-turbo 12-cylinder 645E of earlier MP15s. These locomotives have a single turbo stack and a blower duct ahead of the cab on the right side. Seaboard System bought all but one.

   MP15T: Dow 957; SBD 1200-1241

TA

The Rock Island's TAs appear at first glance like early E units, but they are shorter and ride on four-wheel trucks. *CRI&P*

Rock Island owned the only six TAs, which were built for the railroad's *Rocket* passenger trains. Although E units were already being built, Rock Island didn't require locomotives with that much power. Each TA had a single 16-cylinder 201A engine rated at 1,200 hp and rode on four-wheel trucks with all axles powered. They had slanted noses, similar to early Es, and bodies designed to match the Rock's passenger cars. The TAs were built with single headlights, but soon received lower headlights as well. New (larger) number boxes were added in the early 1950s.

    TA: CRI&P 601-606

EA

Baltimore & Ohio EA No. 52 pauses in Washington, D.C., in July 1937. Note the height of the windows compared to the E1. *Trains magazine collection*

The EA and cabless EB were built exclusively for the Baltimore & Ohio. The 1,800-hp locomotives were powered by a pair of Winton 12-cylinder 201A engines and can be identified from later E units by their recessed headlights (a trait shared with E1s) and by their side windows with rounded ends, which aren't as tall as those of the E1 (which were built concurrently).

    EA: B&O 51-56
    EB: B&O 51X-56X

E1

Santa Fe No. 2 displays the taller side windows of the E1 and the recessed headlight common to EAs and E1s. *Santa Fe*

Santa Fe owned the only E1s, which were built at the same time as—and share internal machinery with—EAs and E2s. Distinctions include a recessed headlight and small recessed notches for locomotive numbers in the corners of the nose on either side of the headlight. The E1's side windows were taller than those on the EA.

    E1A: AT&SF 2-9
    E1B: AT&SF 2A-4A

E2

Electro-Motive E2 No. LA-1, co-owned by Union Pacific and Chicago & North Western, has the bulbous nose unique to that model. *Trains magazine collection*

Two A-B-B sets of E2s were built for service on the *City of San Francisco* and *City of Los Angeles*, trains at the time operated jointly by the Union Pacific, Chicago & North Western, and (for the *COLA*) Southern Pacific. The A units had bulbous, rounded noses unique to this model, and As and Bs both had round portholes along their sides. Internally they matched the EA and E1. They were the last Winton-engine passenger diesels built.

    E2A: SF-1, LA-1
    E2B: SF-2, -3; LA-2, -3

E3, AA

The E3 introduced the slanted nose used through the E6. This is Chicago & North Western No. 5002. *EMD*

The E3 was the first passenger diesel to receive Electro-Motive's new 567 engine, with a pair of them boosting the horsepower to 2,000. To the E3 goes the credit for being the first truly mass-produced passenger diesel, with orders from multiple railroads. The E3 introduced the body that would remain standard through the E6, with a long slanted nose with protruding headlight at the top, square side windows in pairs, and rectangular screened air intakes atop each side. Mechanically the E3 through E6 were basically the same; in fact, the last E3 rolled out of LaGrange in June 1940, when the E6 had been in production for seven months. A variation was the AA, a single locomotive built for Missouri Pacific with only one engine and a baggage compartment in the rear.

E3A: AT&SF 11; ACL 50; CRI&P 625, 626; C&NW 5001A, B-5002A, B; KCS 21; MP 7000, 7001; UP 5M1
E3B: ATSF 11A; UP 5M2
AA: MP 7100

E4

Seaboard's E4s had pull-out doors in their noses, as well as a unique screen over the side air intakes. *EMD*

The E4, built exclusively for Seaboard Air Line, was mechanically an E3 but with nose multiple-unit connections. This gave the A unit a unique nose door which, when used, pulled out from the slanted nose to a vertical position before opening. The door enabled crew members to pass between units if needed. Nose doors became standard on later E units (E7 through E9) with the less-slanted "bulldog" nose.

E4A: SAL 3000-3013
E4B: SAL 3100-3104

E5

The E5, unique to the Burlington, had stainless-steel sheathing with corrugated fluting on the lower sides. *EMD*

The E5 was the last of the customized E units, built exclusively for the Chicago, Burlington & Quincy and its Colorado & Southern and Fort Worth & Denver subsidiaries. The E5 was sheathed in fluted stainless steel to match those lines' *Zephyr* passenger cars. The locomotives had short side windows to allow a letterboard between the window tops and air intake screens on each side. They also had shrouds above the trucks, which were removed fairly soon after delivery (as they interfered with routine maintenance) Internally, the E5 was mechanically identical to the E3 and E6. The E5s were built in two lots, and early and late E5s differed in their roof grilles, steam generator vents, and pilots/anticlimbers.

E5A: CB&Q 9909A-9915A, 9914B, 9915B; C&S 9950A; FW&D 9980A
E5B: 9910B-9912B; C&S 9950B; FW&D 9980B

E6

Santa Fe No. 14 is an E6, the last of Electro-Motive's slant-nosed passenger diesels. *Trains magazine collection*

The most popular of the early passenger diesels, the E6 sold in significant numbers before production was halted by the War Production Board in mid-1942. The body was almost identical to the E3, but with some minor variations in the roof louvers and the side batten strip locations between models and individual orders. The Union Pacific's E6s differed in that they had round side portholes (similar to those on the E2) instead of rectangular windows.

E6: AT&SF, ACL, B&O, C&NW, CRI&P, FEC, IC, KCS, L&N, MILW, MP, SAL, SOU, UP

AB6

The AB6 looks like an E6 B unit, but has a blunt-end operators cab. *Trains magazine collection*

The AB6, built exclusively for the Rock Island, was essentially an E6 B unit with a single 1,000-hp engine and a baggage compartment where the other engine would normally go. It had a full operating cab, but a flat face. It was used on the *Rocky Mountain Rocket* to haul a separate section of the train when it was split at Limon, Colo. (separate sections operated to Colorado Springs and Denver). When the trains combined, the other train's A unit could then couple to the front of the AB6, which would appear to be a standard B unit.

AB6: CRI&P 750, 751

E7

Southern Pacific No. 6003A, built in 1947, displays the blunt F-unit-style nose used on the E7 and later E units. *EMD*

The E7, EMD's best-selling passenger diesel, ushered in a significant new look, with a shorter, less-sharply angled nose (the same as the FT). Although rated at 2,000 hp like the E3 to E6, the E7 was much improved, with new electrical equipment and improved 567A engines. Variations included an optional lower headlight. Early E7s (built before March 1947) had small side-mounted number boards; later locomotives received the large 45-degree-angle boxes common to F units. Other variations included access panels behind the cab door in louvered, screened, or plain versions, and (on late versions) air intake openings between the rectangular side windows. Missouri Pacific and Texas & Pacific E7s had round portholes instead of the standard rectangular side windows.

E7: ACL, BAR, B&O, B&M, CG, C&EI, C&NW, C&O, CB&Q, CRI&P, FEC, GN, GM&O, IC, KCS, L&N, MEC, MKT, MILW, MP, NYC, PRR, SAL, SLSF, SP&S, SOU, SP, T&P, UP, WAB

E8

Early E8s, such as Southern No. 2928, had a fabricated stainless-steel grille running the length of the upper side and round-knob sand hatches (left of the cab door and next to the last porthole). Winterization hatches were standard on the E8 and E9. *EMD*

Upgraded 567B engines gave the 2,250-hp E8 a 250-hp boost over the E7, and that—with new traction motors—gave them better acceleration and longer short-time ratings than earlier E units. The E8 had a new look, with four portholes on each side and a long stainless-steel grille covering the air intakes atop each side. These were originally EMD's standard fabricated grilles with horizontal slits, but starting in November 1951 these were replaced with stamped Far-Air grilles, which had three rows of vertical slits (page 48). The sand hatches also changed during production, from round-knob type to pull-handle (starting in May 1953). On the roof, four 36"-diameter radiator fans replaced the louver-covered openings of earlier E units.

E8: AT&SF, ACL, B&O, C&O, CP, CG, C&EI, C&NW, CB&Q, CRI&P, DL&W, Erie, GM&O, IC, KCS, L&N, MKT, MP, NYC, PRR, RF&P, SAL, SLSF, SP, SOU, T&P, UP, WAB

E9

The flush-mounted headlight lens is the only way to tell an E9 from a late E8. Southern Pacific No. 6051, built in 1954, has nose MU connections. *EMD*

Although in production almost 10 years, only 144 E9s were built until the last E unit (Union Pacific E9A No. 914) rolled out of LaGrange in December 1963. The 567C engine boosted the horsepower to 2,400, with other internal improvements as well. Externally about the only way to tell an E9 from a late E8 is that the E9 nose headlight lens is flush-mounted; E8s have this glass recessed, with a gasket on top of it. Exceptions are the first two E9s built (Illinois Central 4034 and 4035).

E9A: B&O 1454-1457; C&EI 1102; CB&Q 9985A, B-9989A, B, 9990-9995; FEC 1031-1035; IC 4034-4043; KCS 25; MILW 30A, C-38A, C; SAL 3060; SP 6046-6054; UP 900-914

E9B: IC 4106B-4109B; MILW 30B-35B; UP 900B-904B, 910B-913B; 950B-974B

FT

The FT can be identified by its four side portholes. New York, Ontario & Western No. 804 has dynamic brakes, evidenced by the boxy housing on the roof. *S.K. Bolton*

The 1,350-hp FT was the first EMD diesel with the "bulldog" nose, which is shorter with a steeper angle compared to early Es. The FT has four closely spaced portholes on each side. When delivered, FTs had drawbars semipermanently coupling them together in sets (A-B or A-B-A). The B units in A-B-A sets were shorter than the B units of A-B sets, which had a long overhang beyond the rear truck. These short B units were designated "FTSB." Some FTs remained this way until retirement; others were separated and equipped with couplers. The drawbar ends lacked stirrups and vertical grab irons. The FT roof had four exhaust stacks and four recessed radiator fans, and units equipped with dynamic brakes had a square housing (with either straight or angled sides) atop the roof around the exhaust stacks. Some FTs had large illuminated number panels at the bottom of each side.

FT: AT&SF, ACL, B&O, B&M, C&NW, CB&Q, CRI&P, DL&W, D&RGW, Erie, GN, LV, MILW, M&StL, MP, NYC, NYO&W, NP, RDG, SOU, SSW, SAL, WP

F2

Burlington Route No. 153 is an F2, which uses the same body as early (Phase I) F3s. *EMD*

The F2 was only in production for five months. It was a transitional locomotive, having the same 1,350 hp of the FT, but featuring an upgraded engine (567B). The body had three evenly spaced portholes on each side and four tall (shrouded) radiator fans on the roof, a style that would continue through the first F3s. Locomotives with dynamic brakes have a pair of screened rectangular openings on the roof just behind the cab (as on F3s as well).

F2A: A&EC 400, 401; ACL 324-335; B&M 4224A-4226A, 4250-4264; CB&Q 150-154A, 155-159C; CRI&P 38-49; M&StL 147A, C; NdeM 6200-6213; NYC 1604,1605; SOU 6700, 6701

F2B: ACL 324B-335B; B&M 4224B-4226B; M&StL 147B; NdeM 6200B-6213B

F3

Gulf, Mobile & Ohio is an early Phase II F3, with screen between the portholes and four tall radiator fans. *EMD*

This Baltimore & Ohio late Phase II F3 has screen between portholes but low-profile fans. *R.H. Payne*

Frisco No. 5014 is a Phase III F3. Solid panels cover the area between portholes, with louvers covering the air intakes. *St. Louis-San Francisco*

The 1,500-hp F3 went through several body variations as EMD improved the engine air intake systems and other components. These body variations have become known as "Phases." The first F3s (Phase I) were identical to F2s, with three widely spaced side portholes, screened and louvered openings across the top of each side, and four shrouded rooftop radiator fans. On Phase IIa F3As, the center porthole disappeared, replaced by four vent openings, with the area between portholes covered by screen (often called "chicken wire"). Phase IIb F3s received non-shrouded (low) radiator fans. On Phase III F3s, standard side panels replaced the screened area between portholes, with the four air intakes covered by louvers. The last (Phase IV) F3s received a stainless-steel grille covering the openings across the top of each side. They look like early F7s from the side, but have screen-covered dynamic brake openings in the roof (F7s have a roof-mounted fan). Starting in August 1948, some EMD correspondence indicated that a model designation of F5 would be used for these locomotives, but this was not widely used, and later EMD reference data books state that "all F5 locomotives were delivered as F3 units."

F3: AT&SF, A&StAB, A&RF, ACL, BAR, B&M, B&O, CG, CN, CNJ, C&EI, C&NW, CB&Q, CGW, CRR, D&RGW, DL&W, Erie, FEC, GTW, GM&O, GN, Georgia, KCS, L&A, L&N, LV, M&StL, MEC, MON, MP, NC&StL, NYO&W, NYC, NP, PRR, RDG, SAL, SLSF, SP, SP&S, Soo, SOU, TP&W, UP, WofA, WM, WP

F7

The dynamic brake fan (on the roof above the lead porthole) marks Burlington No. 167 as an F7. The grille is the early fabricated style with horizontal slits. *CB&Q*

Chesapeake & Ohio No. 7076 is a late-production unit, with Far-Air grille, vertical-slit louvers, and rounded cab door and side window. Most Fs received nose grab irons in the 1960s.

Jack Emerick

With more than 3,700 delivered in just under five years, EMD built more F7s than any other cab diesel. The F7 remained at 1,500 hp like the F3, but the new D27 traction motor was a significant improvement over its predecessor, allowing the F7 a longer short-term rating. Other internal improvements increased reliability and operating efficiency. The appearance was almost the same as the Phase IV F3, with two side portholes on the A unit and a fabricated side grille with horizontal openings. The difference was the dynamic brakes, which now used a 36" fan identical to the radiator fans. Changes during production included a larger windshield (October 1949), rounded corners on cab doors (March 1950) and windows (June 1951), a Far-Air grille with stamped vertical slits replacing the fabricated grille (October 1951), and a larger (48") dynamic brake fan (October 1952). Also, the slight rear roof overhang was eliminated in February 1952 and the final F7s had a new louver style with vertical openings (seen on the Chesapeake & Ohio F7 above).

F7: Alaska, AT&SF, ACL, B&M, B&O, B&LE, CN, C&NW, C&O, CB&Q, CGW, CRI&P, CRR, D&RGW, DL&W, Erie, GM&O, GN, KCS, L&A, L&N, LV, MKT, MILW, MP, NdeM, NC&StL, NYC, NP, PRR, RDG, RF&P, SP, SP&S, SLSF, Soo, SOU, SSW, T&P, T-M, UP, WAB, WM, WP

FP7

The extra length of the FP7 is seen in the additional space between the forward porthole and louver. Reading No. 901 has the early fabricated grille. *EMD*

The dual-purpose (freight/passenger), 1,500-hp FP7 looks like an F7—and, for all practical purposes, is an F7—but is four feet longer to provide additional water tank capacity for the steam generator. This appears as a longer space between the lead porthole and first air-intake louvers. These were A units only; there's no such thing as an FP7B. Changes during production were the switch from a fabricated (horizontal-slit) side grille to the stamped (vertical-slit) Far-Air grille and a larger (48"-diameter) dynamic brake fan in November 1951. Other spotting features also follow those of F7s.

FP7: Alaska, ACL, A&WP, C&O, C&EI, CGW, CRI&P, CRR, CP, FEC, Georgia, L&N, MILW, MKT, NdeM, NP, ON, PRR, RF&P, RDG, SLSF, SSW, SP, SOU, Soo, SCOP, UP, WofA, WP

F9

The louver in front of the forward porthole identifies Northern Pacific No. 6701A as an F9. The nose lift rings were an NP option. *Jeff Wilson collection*

By the time the 1,750-hp F9 made its debut, railroads were opting for hood units in large numbers, and the GP9 outsold the F9 by a ratio of 17 to 1. The F9 used the 567C engine and upgraded traction motors for the bump in horsepower over the F7. The F9A can be spotted by its forward porthole being moved back compared to the F7, with an extra (fifth) air-intake louver located in front of the porthole. The NP F9 above also shows the hatch next to the headlight for the nose MU cable socket. Far more F9 B units were sold than A units; F9Bs had the same external appearance as late F7Bs, with three portholes, a Far-Air grille and 48" dynamic brake fan.

F9: AT&SF, CRR (B only), CN (B only), CP (B only), D&RGW, Erie Mining, L&N, MILW, NdeM, NP, SLSF (B only), GN (B only), MKT (B only)

FP9

Canadian Pacific FP9 No. 1415 displays the framed grilles unique to the Canadian-built model. GMD-built Fs retained conventional louvers after EMD switched to the vertical-slit style. *GMD*

The dual-purpose FP9 was a stretched version of the F9, and as with the FP7, the extra four feet of length provided space for a larger water tank for the steam generator. As with the F9, the FP9 has an added louver in front of the forward porthole. Only four were built for service in the U.S. (rebuilt from FTs for the Chicago & North Western). The remainder went to Canada (54 units) and Mexico (25).

FP9: C&NW 4051A-4054A; CN 6500-6542; CP 1405-1415; NdeM 7010-7034

FL9

The dual-service FL9 rode on Flexicoil trucks, with a three-axle truck (with a center idler axle) at the rear. *New Haven*

The FL9 was a dual-service (electric/diesel-electric) locomotive built for the New York, New Haven & Hartford. Diesels were not allowed to operate into either Grand Central or Penn Station, so the railroad wanted diesels that could also use the outside-third-rail power at the stations. The steam-generator-equipped FL9 looks like an elongated FP9, but rides on Flexicoil trucks instead of the GP ("Blomberg") trucks of F units. The first 30 engines (Nos. 2000-2029) had 567C engines and were rated at 1,750 hp. They also had small pantographs on their roofs. The last 30 FL9s (Nos. 2030-2059) had the improved 567D1 engine and were rated at 1,800 hp. The FL9s were the last F units built by EMD.

FL9: NYNH&H 2000-2059

NW3

The NW3 is powered by a 12-cylinder 567 engine. Note the stretched frame and Blomberg road trucks. The steam generator is between the cab and engine. *EMD*

A locomotive that looks like a switcher that's been stretched, the 1,000-hp NW3 was powered by a 12-cylinder 567 engine. It rides on road trucks—the same GP Blomberg B as the then-new FT freight diesel—and has a steam generator, an elongated cab, and larger tanks. It was designed for transfer work in passenger terminals. The Great Northern was the only buyer.

NW3: GN 5400-5406

NW4

The tall stack between the cab windows on MoPac's NW4 is for the steam generator, located in the hood next to the cab. *EMD*

The NW4 (which was actually built before the NW3) is a transfer engine that looks much like other EMC switch engines of the period, but it's longer and many classify it as a light road switcher because it rides on AAR type B road trucks (the only Electro-Motive locomotives to do so, as EMD's own GP Blomberg B road trucks would soon appear). The 900-hp NW4 was powered by a Winton 201A engine and was also equipped with a steam generator. Missouri Pacific bought the only two.

NW4: MP 4102, 4103

NW5

The NW5 was the first EMD locomotive that resembled a road switcher, looking a bit like an Alco RS-1. It's powered by a 1,000-hp, 12-cylinder 567 engine. *EMD*

The NW5 follows the same general mechanical specifications as the NW3, but looks more like a road switcher in that it has a short hood behind the cab to house its steam generator. It rides on Blomberg trucks.

NW5: GN 186-195; SOU 2100; Union Belt of Detroit 1, 2

BL1, BL2

The semi-streamlined BL2 was expensive to produce, and access to the engine was difficult. *EMD*

Electro-Motive's first real attempt at a light-duty road switcher was the BL1. The locomotive had the mechanical specs of an F3 atop a light-frame (truss-sided like F units), semi-streamlined body. Tapered cutaways along each long hood allowed crew members to see to the rear. No other locomotive looks like a BL2 (the lone demonstrator BL1 had an air throttle and other minor mechanical differences; it was soon rebuilt to BL2 standards). The BL1 and early BL2s had openings on the hood covered with screen; later engines used louvers (and most early ones eventually had their screens replaced). The BL2 was not a good seller. Its funky hood design was expensive to produce, access to the engine and generator were difficult, and its lightweight frame kept it from heavy-duty service.

BL2: BAR 550-557; B&M 1550-1553; C&O 1840-1847; C&EI 1600; 1601 (renumbered shortly after delivery to 200, 201), 202 (BL1); CRI&P 425-429; FEC 601-606; MP 4104-4111; MON 30-38; PM (delivered to C&O) 80-85; WM 80, 81

GP7

The winterization hatch (the boxy housing on the roof above the radiator fans) and extra headlights on this Burlington GP7 were buyer options. This Geep does not have dynamic brakes. *CB&Q*

Missouri Pacific GP7 No. 4257 has air reservoirs moved to its roof because of its large fuel tank. These were called "torpedo-tube" Geeps. *EMD*

The GP7 introduced the basic road-switcher design that would be followed by EMD diesels into the early 1960s. The EMD cab has a shallower curve than an Alco, with tall hoods that have angled ends (unlike Baldwin's blunt ends). The GP7 had F7 mechanical components in a hood-unit body, with the same 567B engine and 1,500-hp rating. The GP7 can be identified from the later GP9 and GP18 by its three sets of louvers below the cab and on the adjacent battery box; the two rows of louvers under the radiator opening on each side at the end of the long hood; and by its use of T-shaped castings that joined the handrails and stanchions. Dynamic brakes were an option after late 1950, identified by a housing (often called a "blister") with a grid in the middle of the hood (see GP9 photos on page 72). A 36" dynamic brake fan was used through August 1952, with a 48" fan after that. Pilots with sloped plates were used until mid-1952; flat plates with boxes for MU hoses appeared after that. All GP7s had a full skirt that angled down from the frame over the top of the fuel tank sides. These skirts were later cut back on many locomotives. Some early GP7s lacked the box/step on the walkway behind the left side of the cab. Steam-generator-equipped engines can be spotted by a stack and vents atop the high nose. Some Geeps had their air reservoirs moved to the roof to make room for a larger fuel tank or for the added steam-generator water tank located under the frame. All GP7s were delivered with high noses. Five cabless B units were built, all for the Santa Fe.

Major buyers: AC, AT&SF, ACL, BAR, BRC, B&M, CN, CG, CNJ, C&O, CB&Q, C&EI, C&NW, CRI&P, CRR, DL&W, D&RGW, DT&I, D&TSL, Erie, FEC, GRR, GN, IC, L&N, MEC, MILW, MKT, MP, NC&StL, NYC, NKP, P&LE, PRR, QNS&L, RDG, SAL, SOU, SLSF, T&P, UP, WAB, WP

GP9

The GP9 has a different arrangement of louvers compared to a GP7. Dynamic-brake-equipped Norfolk & Western No. 651 is a late GP9 as indicated by the single 48"-diameter fans above the radiator and air intake. *EMD*

Union Pacific ordered 125 GP9Bs. The cast T stanchion tops, double sets of 36" fans (one rear fan covered by a winterization hatch), and full fuel-tank skirt mark this as an early GP9. *EMD*

The improved 567C engine gave the GP9 a boost of 250 hp over its predecessor. The spotting features between GP7s and GP9s are subtle, and many GP9 details changed during production. The first GP9s have a single louver on the battery box cover (above the walkway just ahead of the cab), compared to three on the GP7, and rows of louvers on the first two tall engine-room doors behind the cab (a third row was added during production). The stanchion style changed from castings to a stamped fitting by June 1954. Late GP9s (after October 1957) used single 48"-diameter fans fore and aft, replacing the pairs of 36" fans on earlier units. Late GP9s have the single battery-box louver replaced by two small louver sets. The side skirting above the top of the fuel tank, which was perforated on early GP9s, changed to a cut-down style during production (see the N&W GP9 above). This was often done retroactively to early GP9s and GP7s, so it's not a reliable spotting feature—but it's a characteristic to be aware of when detailing a model. Most GP9s were delivered with high noses, but the low nose became an option late in production. A GP9 was the first low-nose EMD diesel, built for Southern Pacific in 1959. Other options included dynamic brakes, steam generator (located in the nose), and fuel tanks (several sizes were available). Some fuel/water tank options required the air reservoirs to be moved to the roof, which, as with GP7s, became known as "torpedo tube" units. Only the Pennsylvania and Union Pacific purchased GP9Bs.

Major buyers: AT&SF, B&O, B&M, CN, CP, CG, C&O, C&NW, CB&Q, CRI&P, CV, D&RGW, DT&I, FEC, GN, GTW, IC, L&N, MILW, M&StL, MP, NdeM, NYNH&H, NYC, NKP, N&W, NP, PRR, QNS&L, SAL, Soo, SOU, SP, SSW, T&P, UP, WAB, WM

SD7

Chicago, Burlington & Quincy SD7 No. 316 has dynamic brakes (the blister on the long hood), a steam generator (stack visible atop the nose), and separate water and fuel tanks under the frame. *CB&Q*

Introduced in 1952, the SD7 was EMD's first six-axle freight diesel. Unlike passenger diesels, the SD series had all six axles powered. The SD stands for "special duty," and SD7s were initially intended for branchline service, where the six axles would spread the locomotive's weight over light track. The SD7 had twin exhaust stacks and four 36" radiator fans in a group at the rear of the roof. They can be identified from later SD9s by their T-shaped castings atop the handrail stanchions and by their classification lights, which are set in from the sides and attached to access doors. Options included dynamic brakes (most had them) and steam generators (look for vents and stacks atop the nose). Most had two fuel tanks; several railroads opted for single tanks to save weight.

SD7: B&O, B&LE, CB&Q (C&S, FW&D), CG, C&NW, D&RGW, GN, KC, MILW, NN, PRR, SP, UP

SD9

Formed handrail stanchions and outward-positioned class lights (above the number boards) mark Atlanta & St. Andrews Bay No. 505 as an SD9. It does not have dynamic brakes. *EMD*

The SD9 proved more popular than the earlier SD7, as railroads began finding more uses for six-axle power. As with concurrent Geeps, the SD9 bumped horsepower to 1,750 from 1,500. You can spot an SD9 from an SD7 by its class lights, which are near the edge of the hood (the SD7's are set in). Early SD9s have the same cast-T handrail fittings as SD7s, but this quickly evolved to formed stanchions that wrap over the handrail. The side radiator louvers are covered by diagonal-pattern wire (often called "chicken wire"), compared to horizontal formed-wire screens on later SDs. Late SD9s have a taller cab and nose, which was continued on the high-nose version of the SD24. Options included dynamic brakes (most were so equipped), steam generators, and several fuel/water tank sizes.

SD9: A&StAB, B&O, CB&Q, C&NW, CG, C&IM, DM&IR, D&RGW, EJ&E, GN, MILW, NKP, PRR, RM, Soo, SP

GMD1

The GMD1 was built specifically for light-rail branchline service. Canadian National No. 1900 has B-B trucks and a steam generator. *GMD*

The GMD1 was built by GMD in Canada. The lightweight, 1,200-hp locomotive was powered by a 12-cylinder, non-turbocharged 567 engine, and it was designed for branchline service. It rode on Flexicoil B-B or A1A trucks: Canadian National Nos. 1900-1917 had four-axle (B-B) trucks, while the other CN engines and all Northern Alberta engines had A1A-A1A trucks. Several CN engines were later rebuilt with four-axle trucks.
   GMD1: CN 1000-1077, 1900-1917; NAR 300-305

SD18

This low-nose SD has horizontal-wire screen over the radiator louvers, marking it as an SD18. It lacks the hood blower bulge of the SD24. The Chesapeake & Ohio's SD18s ride on traded-in Alco tri-mount trucks. *EMD*

The SD18 is the non-turbocharged version of the SD24, putting out 1,800 hp instead of the SD24's 2,400 hp. As with its four-axle partner, the GP18, sales were slow with the SD18. All but the Duluth, Missabe & Iron Range engines (the first ones built) had low noses and dynamic brakes. The SD18 can be identified from the SD24 by its two exhaust stacks and lack of a rounded blower bulge on the left side of the hood. The DM&IR SD18s look like late SD9s. The Chesapeake & Ohio's SD18s (above) rode on tri-mount trucks from traded-in Alco RSD-5s.
   SD18: B&LE 851-857; C&O 1800-1818; C&IM 60, 61; DM&IR 175-193; Reserve Mining 1226-1232

GP18

New York, Susquehanna & Western No. 1800 is a GP18. It has two exhaust stacks and lacks the bump in the hood behind the cab of the GP20. *EMD*

The GP18 continued the evolution from the GP9, with a slight upgrade in horsepower (to 1,800) from the non-turbocharged 567D1 engine, and introduced EMD's use of horsepower in the model number. The locomotive was marketed concurrently with the turbocharged GP20. The GP18 looks like a late GP9, but the air intakes at the top of each side have barred grilles. Late GP18s had notched skirts and flat-top roof fans. Railroads were beginning to show a preference for low-nose diesels at this time, and just over half (201) of GP18s were built with high noses. Other options included dynamic brakes (131 units) and steam generators (Grand Trunk Western and National of Mexico).
   GP18: A&R, B&O, B&M, CG, C&NW, CRI&P, GTW, IC, LV, L&N, MP, NdeM, NYS&W, NKP, NS, N&W, NP, PD, SAL, TA&G, T&P, TM, TP&W

GP20

Union Pacific No. 714 shows the single large turbo stack (just behind the forward roof fan) of a GP20. *Union Pacific*

The GP20 was EMD's first turbocharged four-axle locomotive, providing a boost of 200 horsepower compared to the GP18. The GP20's introduction followed Union Pacific's experiments at turbocharging EMD's 567 engine. The UP added turbos to several GP9s, which were dubbed "Omaha GP20s." With the GP20, EMD began offering concurrent turbocharged and non-turbocharged locomotives. The GP20 has a single exhaust stack (a hallmark of turbo diesels) compared to the two stacks of earlier Geeps. The GP20 can be spotted from the GP18 by its single stack and by bulges on the hood sides just behind the cab. Most GP20s had low noses, with the nose sloping slightly downward from the base of a one-piece windshield (as on the GP18 and SD24). Western Pacific and Great Northern ordered high-nose versions. All but the New York Central's GP20s had dynamic brakes. Radiator fans varied, with 48" shrouded flared-top fans early, then "pan-top" fans after that, although the Santa Fe engines had 36" pan-top fans.
   GP20: AT&SF 1100-1174; CB&Q 900-935; GN 2000-2035; NYC 6100-6114; SP 7200-7237; SSW 800-819; UP 700-729; WP 2001-2010

SD24

The blower-housing bulge behind the cab identifies Chicago, Burlington & Quincy No. 503 as an SD24. The nose is slightly taller than the hood behind the cab. *CB&Q*

The 2,400-hp SD24 was EMD's first turbocharged diesel (the GP20 would soon follow) and its highest-horsepower locomotive at the time. The SD24 resembles earlier SDs, but can be spotted by its single turbo stack atop the roof, the air reservoirs mounted on the right side of the roof just behind the cab (except for the lone Kennecott Copper unit), and the rounded bulge on the left side of the hood (to clear two internal blower housings). Most had low noses, with large one-piece windshields and sloping noses like GP18s and GP20s. High-hood versions went to the Burlington and Southern; on these the nose is slightly taller than the long hood. All were equipped with dynamic brakes. EMD also built 45 cabless B units; all went to Union Pacific. There was no matching 2,400-hp four-axle diesel from EMD.

SD24: AT&SF 900-979; CB&Q 500-515; KC 904; SOU 2502-2524, 6305-6325, 6950-6953; UP 400-429, 445-558, 400B-444B (B units)

GP28

At first glance the GP28 looks like a GP35, but the GP28 has two standard exhaust stacks on the roof. This is Illinois Central No. 9430. *EMD*

The non-turbocharged 1,800-hp GP28 shared the same body style as—and was built concurrently with—the turbocharged 2,500-hp GP35. The GP28 can be identified by its twin exhaust stacks and two 48" rear radiator fans, as opposed to the GP35's single turbo stack and three fans (two 48" and one 36"). It's also 3 feet shorter than the similar-appearing GP38. Chihuahua Pacific's locomotives had dynamic brakes, and three had high noses. Sales were slow, as most railroads opted for the higher horsepower of the GP35.

GP28: ChP 801-810; IC 9429-9440; KO&G 700, 701; MC 211; TM 856

GP30

The housing above the cab roof to the hood is unique to the GP30. Soo Line 717 doesn't have dynamic brakes (no grille on the mid-roof housing). Soo's GP30s ride on trucks from Alco trade-ins. *Jim Hediger*

The beetle-browed GP30 was EMD's answer to GE's revolutionary U25B as the horsepower race of the 1960s began heating up. At 2,250 hp, the GP30 didn't quite match the 2,500 hp of the U25B (and EMD model numbers no longer matched horsepower), but the GP30 featured a pressurized engine compartment and other electrical improvements first used on the U25. The GP30 was built for speed but had a reputation as a "slippery" engine, as getting the additional horsepower to the rails could lead to wheels slipping at low speeds with heavy loads. The GP30 has a unique body, with a housing above the cab that continued rearward through the dynamic brake blister. Non-dynamic units still possess this fairing, but without the grille openings. Three railroads (Gulf, Mobile & Ohio, Milwaukee Road, and Soo Line) specified the use of AAR type B trucks from traded-in Alco diesels on their GP30s (above). The Union Pacific bought 40 cabless B versions; eight were equipped with steam generators. High-hood versions were purchased by Norfolk & Western and Southern.

GP30: Alaska, AT&SF, ACL, B&O, CP, C&O, CB&Q, CGW, C&EI, C&NW, D&RGW, GN, GM&O, KCS, L&N, MILW, NYC, N&W, NKP, PRR, P-D, RDG, SAL, SSW, Soo, SOU, SP, TP&W, UP

SD28

Columbus & Greenville No. 702 is one of six SD28s built. It has two exhaust stacks compared to the single turbo stack of the SD35. *EMD*

The 1,800-hp SD28 uses the non-turbocharged version of the 567D1 engine. It looks like a stretched version of the GP28, with two rear radiator fans and two exhaust stacks. Unlike the earlier SD18, the SD28 has an angled cab roof and blower bulge on the left side of the hood. Only six were built, as most railroads opted for the higher-horsepower, turbocharged SD35. Reserve Mining's engines have dynamic brakes.

SD28: C&G 701, 702; RM 1233-1236

GP35

Erie-Lackawanna No. 2562 has the two large and one small radiator fans that mark it as a GP35.

Louis A. Marre collection

With the 1963 introduction of the GP35, EMD finally matched the 2,500 hp of GE's U25B. The GP35 introduced the basic cab, nose, and body style that would be used on EMD diesels through the 1980s, with an angled cab roof and two-piece windshield above the low nose. The GP35 can be spotted by its two large (48") radiator fans bracketing one small exhaust (36") fan at the rear of the roof, and by its single turbo exhaust stack. As with the GP30, some GP35s were equipped with AAR type B trucks from traded-in Alcos (Ann Arbor and Southern). One option was a large (3,000-gallon) fuel tank; these locomotives (Chicago & North Western and St. Louis-San Francisco) had their air reservoirs on the roof. High-nose versions were purchased by National of Mexico (also the only GP35s with steam generators), Norfolk & Western, and Southern.

GP35: Alaska, AA, AT&SF, B&O, CN, CP, C&O, C&EI, C&NW, CB&Q, CRI&P, D&RGW, DT&I, EL, GN, GM&O, L&N, MILW, MP, NdeM, NYC, N&W, NKP, PRR, RDG, RF&P, SCL, Soo, SP, SSW, SOU, SLSF, T&P, TP&W, UP, WAB, WM, WP

SD38, SD38AC

Elgin, Joliet & Eastern No. 651 is an SD38, with two large radiator fans and fairly large platforms at each end. The paper air filter box projects from the roof ahead of the dynamic brake blister. *EMD*

The non-turbocharged 2,000-hp SD38 sold just 63 copies, less than 5 percent of sales for the turbocharged (3,000-hp) SD40. The SD38 is longer than the SD28—the SD38 shared the same frame as the SD45, which had a longer body. Because of this, the SD38 and SD40 both have large open areas on their end platforms, often called "porches." The SD38 can be identified by its two large radiator fans and twin exhaust stacks. As with the GP38, an AC transmission became an option in 1971 with the SD38AC (15 were sold), but there's no visual difference between AC and DC models.

SD38, SD38AC: B&LE 861-869; BC Hydro 381; DT&I 250-254; DM&IR 201-208; EJ&E 650-655; MCR 36-38; PC 6925-6959

SD35

The single turbo stack and three-fan (large/small/large) radiator arrangement identify Atlantic Coast Line No. 1000 as an SD35. *EMD*

The 2,500-hp SD35 looks like an elongated GP35, with the same radiator arrangement of two 48" fans separated by a 36" fan. Norfolk & Western and Southern SD35s had high noses. High-horsepower six-axle diesels had yet to become popular, but EMD sold 360 SD35s during the model's relatively short (20-month) production run.

SD35: ACL, CNJ, B&O, C&O, L&N, N&W, PRR, SAL, SOU, SP, UP, WM

GP38, GP38AC

The GP38, like GM&O No. 726, has a pair of 48" radiator fans. *J. David Ingles*

The GP38 was the non-turbocharged (2,000-hp) version of (and built concurrently with) the turbocharged GP40, with both using 16-cylinder versions of the new 645 engine. Although it offered 1,000 less horsepower, many railroads opted for the GP38 for the lower maintenance costs. It found its niche as a low-speed road switcher, leaving fast-freight service to the GP40. The GP38 shares the GP40's body, but has two 48" radiator fans at the rear of the roof compared to three on the GP40, and the GP38 is 36" longer than the similar-looking GP28 (count handrail stanchions: The GP38 has 10 and the GP28 has 9). Some GP38s have a longer cab, with the front wall moved forward to accommodate dual control stands. Paper air filters were an option; these were located in a box just behind the forward air intake. Several fuel tank sizes were offered. Southern's and TA&G's GP38s have high noses. EMD began offering AC transmission as an option (the GP38AC) in 1971; there's no external difference between the two models (the AC models used an alternator with rectifiers instead of a generator)—261 units were the AC version.

GP38, GP38AC: A&R, AT&SF, AHdeM, B&O, BAR, BN, CP, C&O, CRR, DT&I, EM, FdelS, GM&O, L&N, MEC, MKT, MP, MGA, NS, PC, PRSL, P-D, SOU, TA&G, TM

GP39

Chesapeake & Ohio No. 3909 is a GP39. It looks like a GP38, but has a single turbo stack in front of the dynamic brake fan. *J. David Ingles*

The GP39 was an "in-between" locomotive, using a smaller (12-cylinder) turbocharged 645 engine rated at 2,300 hp, putting it between the GP38 and GP40. It never became popular, as most railroads opted for 16-cylinder locomotives. The GP39 has just two rear radiator fans like a GP38, but has the single exhaust stack of a turbocharged engine.

   GP39: A&StAB 507; C&O 3900-3919; KC 1, 2

SD39

The SD39 has a single turbo stack and two radiator fans. Santa Fe No. 4007 is at Las Cruces, N.M., in 1970.
Chris Raught

The SD39 was a six-axle version of the GP39, using the same 12-cylinder turbocharged engine. It can be identified by its single turbo stack (compared to the two stacks of the non-turbocharged SD38). Only 59 were built.
   SD39: AT&SF 4000-4019; IT 2301-2306; MN&S 40, 41; SP 5300-5325

SDL39

The SDL39, designed for the Milwaukee Road, was intended for service on light-rail branch lines. It's shorter and has different trucks than the SD39. *EMD*

The Milwaukee Road custom-ordered the lightweight SDL39 specifically for use on its light-rail branch lines. The railroad bought five of the locomotives in 1969 and followed with an order for another five in 1972. Mechanically, the 2,300-hp locomotive is an SD39, with a 12-cylinder 645E3 engine, but on a shorter (lighter) frame with a small (1,200-gallon) fuel tank and short-wheelbase trucks commonly used on EMD export locomotives.
   SDL39: MILW 581-590

GP40

Chesapeake & Ohio No. 4069's three radiator fans mark it as a GP40. *George W. Hamlin*

EMD introduced its new, larger 645 engine in the 3,000-hp GP40, and the locomotive would prove popular for fast-freight service. The GP40 can be identified by its three large (48") radiator fans at the rear of the roof. Early units had "button-top" fans, with circular plates in the middle; later engines had all-open fans. Three fuel tank options were available. Early models had screen-covered radiator openings, and later units had wire grids. Very late GP40s had the option of extended-range dynamic brakes, which allow braking at lower speeds than standard dynamics. These are marked by a small door at the front of the dynamic brake housing. Late GP40s have an electrical cabinet air filter box on the walkway behind the left side of the cab. Norfolk & Western GP40s have high noses.
   GP40: A&WP, ACL, B&O, C&O, CB&Q, CRI&P, ChP, CN, D&E, D&RGW, DT&I, FEC, GRR, IC, L&N, MILW, MKT, NdeM, N&W, NYC, PC, RF&P, SAL, Soo, SSW, TO&E, WofA, WM, WP

SD40

The SD40 has three radiator fans and is about three feet shorter than the later SD40-2. Southern Pacific No. 8431 was built in 1966. *EMD*

The 3,000-hp SD40 popularized the use of high-horsepower, six-axle units on fast freight trains as well as heavy-haul drag freights. As with the SD38, the SD40 was built on the long underframe of the SD45. The resulting open areas on the end platforms, although not as large as on the later SD40-2, give the engine a distinct look. The SD40 has three radiator fans at the end of the roof, with fan changes during production as with the GP40. Most were equipped with dynamic brakes, with extended-range versions marked with an access door on the blister. Norfolk & Western and Southern models have high noses.

    SD40: AC, A&SAB, AT&SF, BN, B&O, CN, CP, CGW, C&NW, C&O, C&S, CRR, DE, GM&O, GTW, IC, KCS, L&N, MP, NdeM, N&W, PC, PRR, QNS&L, Soo, SOU, SP, UP, WM

SD40A

The extra-long frame and fuel tank is quite noticeable on Illinois Central SD40A No. 6017. The hood is also extended behind the dynamic brake blister. *B.L. Bulgrin*

EMD built 18 SD40A locomotives exclusively for the Illinois Central in 1969 and 1970. Mechanically, the SD40A is an SD40, getting 3,000 hp from its 16-cylinder engine. However, the SD40A has a stretched hood and is placed atop a longer SDP45 frame. The extended space between trucks allowed for a larger (5,000-gallon) fuel tank. These locomotives have dynamic brakes and L-shaped cab windshields.
    SD40A: IC 6006-6023

SD45

The flared radiator grilles, combined with three radiator fans, identify Rio Grande No. 5340 as an SD45. *Jim Hediger*

To make the SD45, EMD built a 20-cylinder version of the 645 engine and turbocharged it, providing 3,600 horsepower, the most powerful single-engine C-C locomotive when introduced in 1966. Produced concurrently with the SD40, the SD45 has a longer body but rides on the same frame. The SD45 is distinguished by its flared (outwardly tapering) radiator grilles at the rear of each side, needed to make room for the larger radiator core and extra cooling capacity required by the bigger engine. Several SD45s were delivered with an optional L-shaped windshield on the engineer's side. Norfolk & Western (see page 255) and Southern engines have high noses. Frisco's SD45s have smaller (3,600-gallon) fuel tanks than all others (4,000-gallon).

    SD45: AT&SF, ACL, BN, C&NW, CB&Q, C&S, D&RGW, EL, GN, MILW, NP, N&W, PC, PRR, RDG, SCL, SLSF, SOU, SSW, SP, UP

SD45X

At first glance the SD45X looks like an SD45, but the SD45X has a longer radiator section with four rooftop fans. *R.T. Sharp*

The SD45X was an experiment to get more power (4,200 hp compared to 3,600) from the 20-cylinder 645 engine. Built in 1970-71, they were the first locomotives to use the new EMD HT-C truck, which would become standard on six-axle Dash-2s. Only seven were built, all for Southern Pacific. The locomotive can be spotted by its longer radiator section with four radiator fans, compared to three fans on an SD45.
    SD45X: SP 9500-9506

F45

The cowl-body F45, including Great Northern No. 429, had radiator grilles extending almost to the rear of the body.
Edward L. Kanak

Take an SD45 and enclose it with a cowl-style body and the result is the F45. Built at the request of the Santa Fe, the 3,600-hp F45 is about five feet shorter than the passenger-service FP45, with the radiator at the end of the body. The ATSF wanted a streamlined locomotive; the Great Northern and Burlington Northern wanted protection from the elements for crew members performing basic maintenance while a locomotive was in motion.
  F45: AT&SF 1900-1939; BN 6600-6613; GN 427-440

FP45

The FP45 is longer than the F45, with the steam generator located behind the radiator. The front platform distinguishes it from the later SDP40F. *J. David Ingles*

Known as cowl units for their enclosed bodies, the passenger-service FP45 was an SD45 with an enclosed body and a steam generator. The FP45 is about five feet longer than the similar freight-version F45, with the steam generator behind the the radiator. The FP45's front platform sets it apart from the later SDP40Fs ordered by Amtrak in the 1970s.
  FP45: AT&SF 100-108; MILW 1-5

SDP35, SDP40, SDP45

Great Northern No. 322 is an SDP40, with a steam generator at the rear of the extended body behind the radiator.
EMD

The SDP45 can be spotted by its flared radiator grilles like the standard SD45. *Earl Thiel collection*

In the early to mid-1960s, railroads were faced with the dilemma of declining passenger service and old locomotives that needed to be replaced. The 2,500-hp SDP35 was an attractive solution. It's an SD35 with an extension on the rear hood to house a steam generator, meaning it could be used in either passenger service or fast freight service. The SDP has a squared-off rear hood with steam generator vents atop the roof. The 3,000-hp SDP40 followed, then the 3,600-hp SDP45, all with the rear housing behind the radiator. Other body details matched standard SD35s, SD40s, and SD45s. The flared radiator housing differentiates the 3,600-hp SDP45 from earlier SDPs. The hood extension for the steam generator required a longer frame than the standard SD45. The Erie Lackawanna bought SDP45s without steam generators—the railroad wanted them for their extra-large fuel tanks, enabled by the long space between trucks.
  SDP35: ACL 550; L&N 1700-1703; SAL 1100-1119; UP 1400-1409
  SDP40: GN 320-325; NdeM 8522-8535
  SDP45: EL 3635-3668; GN 326-333; SP 3200-3209

DD35, DD35A

The DD35A has a standard EMD cab and nose, with a pair of flared radiator housings at the center of the body. *EMD*

EMD's first large double-engine diesel, the 5,000-hp DD35, amounted to a pair of GP35s placed on a single long frame atop a pair of four-axle trucks. It's powered by two 567D3A engines. The DD35 was originally offered strictly as a cabless B unit; the A unit version was built at Union Pacific's request. The B version has a radiator profile similar to the GP35, while the A has flared radiator housings like the SD45. The A unit version has a conventional cab, unlike the later wide-nose DDA40X.

DD35: SP 8400-8402; UP 72B-98B
DD35A: UP 70-84

DDA40X

Union Pacific's DDA40X can be spotted by its full-width nose and four-wheel trucks. *Jeffrey L. Torretta*

Nicknamed "Centennials" for the 100th anniversary of the Golden Spike ceremony, the big DDA40X is hard to confuse with anything else. Built exclusively for the Union Pacific, the 6,600-hp diesel rode on four-axle trucks and sported a wide nose like those used on cowl units. The two 645E3A engines bumped up the horsepower by 1,600 hp compared to the DD35, and the DDA40X debuted many of the electrical equipment upgrades that would become standard in EMD's Dash-2 line in 1972. The DDA40X was by far the most successful of UP's twin-engine freight diesels of the 1960s, and Centennials remained in service through the mid-1980s.

DDA40X: UP 6900-6946

GP38-2

Union Pacific GP38-2 No. 2025 has the upgraded GP trucks with snubbers. It's an early unit, with screened radiator intake and square paper-filter box. *Jeffrey L. Torretta*

CSX No. 2697 is a late GP38-2, built in 1979 for SCL. It has a one-piece corrugated radiator grille and an air-filter housing with beveled sides. *Dwight Jones*

The 2,000-hp GP38-2 proved to be EMD's most popular second-generation four-axle road locomotive, with more than 2,200 sold. The GP38-2 has the common Dash-2 spotting features found across all models: A water-sight glass on the right side of the hood, slight overhang at the rear of the cab roof, and bolted-on battery-box cover (instead of hinged). Most have the new Blomberg "M" trucks, with a snubber on the sideframe at the right axle. All but extremely early GP38-2s have a shorter radiator section with the two radiator fans closer together (7" apart) than the standard GP38 (21" apart). Early side radiator intakes had single screen-grid-covered panels, but these were changed to a split design on mid-production models, then corrugated grilles in mid-1976. Paper air filters were an option, marked by a raised box on the hood between the central air intake and dynamic brake blisters. After 1975 this box had beveled side corners. The cab design changed in 1977, including a change in nose length from 81" to 88", with a new fan style (Q-fans) in 1979. GP38-2s built after 1982 (mainly for CP Rail) have the new free-flow blower duct (used on later GPs) on the right side. Other variations include 20 steam-generator-equipped locomotives for National of Mexico and high-nose versions for Norfolk & Western and Southern. Canadian National received 51 wide-nose GP38-2Ws, dubbed "comfort cabs," Nos. 4760-4810, in 1973 and 1974 (also see the GP40-2 listing on page 80).

Major buyers: AC, A&StAB, BRC, B&M, BN, BA&P, CN, CP, C&NW, CRI&P, CSS&SB, ChP, CRR, C&W, CR, DT&I, D&S, EJ&E, FdelM, FEC, GRR, GTW, GM&O, ICG, IT, KCS, LV, LIRR, L&N, MILW, MKT, MP, ON, PC, P-D, P&LE, P&W, SCL, Soo, SOU, SP, SLSF, TM, TP&W, UP, VTR

SD38-2

Built in 1973, Southern Pacific SD38-2 No. 2975 shows the twin exhaust stacks, two radiator fans, and large "porches" of that model. *Trains magazine collection*

The non-turbocharged 2,000-hp SD38-2 rides on the same platform as the SD40-2, and has the same large open end platforms, but can be differentiated by its two rear radiator fans and two exhaust stacks, compared with three fans and one turbo stack on the '40-2. Other spotting features evolved as with the GP38-2, including radiator and central air intake grilles and paper air filters. Not as popular as its big brother SD40-2, the SD38-2 was designed for slow-speed drag-freight and transfer service.

SD38-2: BC Hydro 382-384; B&LE 870-892; C&IM 70-75; C&NW 6650-6659; DM&IR 209-213; EJ&E 656-668; L&N 4500-4504; MCR 39; NAR 401-404; RM 1237-1245; SLSF 296-299; SP 2971-2975; USS 1; YD 20-22

GP39-2

Santa Fe No. 3668 is a mid-production GP39-2, built in April 1975. It has a corrugated-pattern, two-piece radiator grille and Blomberg M trucks. *Andy Sperandeo*

The GP39-2 got 2,300 hp from a 12-cylinder turbocharged 645 engine. Its appearance was similar to the GP38-2, but the GP39-2 has a single turbo stack compared to the twin stacks of the GP38-2. Units built after 1977 have an extra three-foot blank hood section between the back of the cab and the air intake grille. Kennecott Copper's units have a tall cab and nose and higher under-body clearance, giving them a distinctive appearance. MKT's GP39-2s came in GP49 carbodies.

GP39-2: AT&SF 3600-3705; BN 2700-2739; D&H 7601-7620; KC 1-3, 705-711, 779-799, 905; MKT 360-379; P-D 33; RDG 3401-3420

GP40-2

Baltimore & Ohio No. 4125 is an early GP40-2, built in 1972. It has screened radiator intakes and an 81" nose. *Jim Hediger.*

Canadian National 9542 is a GP40-2L(W), a wide-nose version with larger fuel tanks built by GMD. *Jim Hediger.*

Southern Pacific No. 3198 is a GP40P-2, with a steam generator behind the radiator at the end of the hood. These also have flared radiator grilles. *Robert Del Grosso*

The 3,000-hp GP40-2 is identified by its three radiator fans and the standard Dash-2 spotting features. Radiator and air intake grilles evolved from a grid to a corrugated pattern as on the GP38-2, and the nose length changed from 81" to 88" in 1977. Models built in 1983 and later have the redesigned free-flow blower duct, giving them an appearance somewhat like a GP50 (but without the '50's large radiators). Canadian National and GO Transit together had 279 wide-nose "comfort cab" versions of the GP40-2, built by GMD in Canada as GP40-2L(W) with lighter frames and larger fuel tanks and GP40-2W with standard frames and tanks. Three GP40P-2s for Southern Pacific have steam generators at the rear. These have flared radiators.

GP40-2: Alaska, A&WP, B&M, B&O, C&O, CR, D&RGW, DT&I, FEC, Georgia, KCS, L&N, RDG, RF&P, SCL, SP, SSW, SLSF, TO&E, USDOT, WM, WP, WofA
GP40-2W: CN 9633-9667; GO 700-710
GP40-2L(W): CN 9400-9632
GP40P-2: SP 3197-3199

SD40-2

Chicago & North Western No. 6816 is an early-production SD40-2, with screened radiator openings. The nose-mounted bell was a C&NW option. *J. David Ingles*

Union Pacific SD40-2 No. 3415 has the long "snoot" nose. It also has the corrugated radiator screen found on post-1976 engines. *Jim Hediger*

The 3,000-hp SD40-2 became the most popular locomotive of the second-generation era, with more than 4,000 sold (including variations) as railroads continued converting to six-axle diesels for fast-freight as well as heavy-haul service. The SD40-2 has a unique appearance: Its frame is about three feet longer than the earlier SD40 (it shares the same frame as the SD45-2 and SD38-2) to accommodate the new HT-C trucks used on each. This gives the SD40-2 larger, distinctive open areas ("porches") at each end. It maintains the 40-series' three radiator fans and single turbo stack, as opposed to the SD38-2's twin fans and stacks. Variations during production included a large anticlimber on many locomotives and a switch from grid-covered to corrugated radiator openings in 1976. Additional spotting features matched other Dash-2 bodies, including the water sight glass, cab roof overhang, and bolted battery box covers. Other variations included long (116") nose versions (to house radio equipment), nicknamed "snoots," on some Union Pacific, Kansas City Southern, and Southern Pacific units, wide-nose comfort-cab locomotives for Canadian National (SD40-2W), and high-nose versions for Norfolk & Western and Southern. The N&W also received some low-nose engines. Conrail's SD40-2s were delivered with Flexicoil trucks instead of the new Dash-2 standard HT-C trucks. The final six SD40-2s built (for Soo Line) received the free-flow blower duct.

SD40-2: AC, AT&SF, B&O, BC Rail, BN, CP, C&NW, CRI&P, CRR, CR, ICG, KC, KCS, L&N, MILW, MKT, MP, N&W, ON, O&W, QNS&L, SCL, SLSF, Soo, SOU, UP

SD40-2W: CN 5241-5363

SD40-2F

The SD40-2F has an enclosed cowl body and the "Draper Taper" beveled side to allow rear visibility from the cab. *CP Rail*

A special version of the SD40-2—and the last of the type to be built—was the SD40-2F, a full-cowl locomotive built specially for Canadian Pacific in 1988. Nicknamed "red barns," the locomotives have a notch behind the cab that tapers out to full body width. Called the "Draper Taper" for its developer, the feature improved rear visibility over earlier cowl units, such as the F45. The same feature was used on CN and CP cowl locomotives from other builders.

SD40-2F: CP 9000-9024

SD45-2

Santa Fe 5708 is an SD45-2, with a longer body, longer radiator, and wider fan spacing than the SD40-2. *Jim Hediger*

By the time the Dash-2 line entered production, most railroads had begun opting for the SD40 series, which—although 600 less horsepower—was less maintenance-intensive and more fuel efficient than the 20-cylinder, 3,600-hp SD45. Only 136 SD45-2s were built, none after 1974. They don't have the flared radiators of standard SD45s, but can be identified from SD40-2s by their longer bodies and—since they ride on the same frames—the resulting lack of large end platforms. The SD45-2 also has longer side radiator grilles, and its three radiator fans are more widely spaced than on the SD40-2.

SD45-2: AT&SF 5625-5714; CRR 3607-3624; EL 3669-3681; SCL 2045-2059

SD40T-2, SD45T-2

Tunnel-motor locomotives, such as Rio Grande SD40T-2 No. 5369, have radiator openings at running-board level.
Andy Sperandeo

Southern Pacific SD45T-2 No. 9169 shows the three access doors above the radiator opening of that model; SD40T-2s have two doors. *EMD*

The SD40T-2 and SD45T-2 are known as "tunnel motors," and can be distinguished by their low-mounted radiator intake grilles on the rear of each side. These are distinctive, as the internal area behind is open, allow viewers to see through the hood. The radiator fans are also recessed under the rooftop screen, and can't be seen from the side. This gives the hood a very smooth, clean appearance compared to a standard SD40-2 or SD45-2. Built for Southern Pacific, St. Louis Southwestern, and Rio Grande, these locomotives pulled in cooler air from a lower level in tunnels and snowsheds, improving engine performance by limiting overheating. Other than their radiator openings, the locomotives are mechanically the same as standard SD40-2s and SD45-2s. Their bodies are nearly identical, but the 3,000-hp SD40T-2 has a pair of access doors above the radiator grille, whereas the 3,600-hp SD45T-2 has three access doors. The SSW and some SP SD40T-2s had long "snoot" noses. SP and SSW tunnel motors had L-shaped windshields on the engineer's side.

SD40T-2: D&RGW 5341-5413; SSW 8322-8326, 8372-8376; SP 8230-8321, 8327-8341, 8350-8371, 8377-8391, 8489-8573

SD45T-2: SSW 9157-9165, 9261-9301, 9371-9404; SP 9166-9260, 9302-9370

GP15-1, GP15AC, GP15T

The GP15-1 can be spotted by its short body and low-level radiator intake at the rear of the hood.
Louis A. Marre collection

The 1,500-hp GP15-1 was EMD's late-1970s attempt to grab a share of the market for rebuilt Geeps. Although a rebuild, the GP15-1 was sold as a new locomotive with a 12-cylinder 645E engine, with remanufactured components from trade-ins, including the generator—giving it a DC transmission when contemporary Dash-2s all featured AC. The GP15AC used an alternator instead of a generator. The GP15T used a turbocharged eight-cylinder engine. All GP15s had four exhaust stacks except the GP15T, which had a single turbo stack. MoPac's first 20 GP15-1s rode on Blomberg M trucks; all other GP15s had Blomberg B trucks. C&O's GP15Ts had dynamic brakes.

GP15-1: C&NW 4400-4424; CR 1600-1699; MP 1555-1714; SLSF 100-124

GP15AC: MP 1715-1744

GP15T: AN 720-722; C&O 1500-1524

SDP40F

Amtrak No. 583 is an SDP40F. It has a different side panel arrangement and lacks the front platform of the FP45.
Jim Hediger

The 3,000-hp SDP40F was the first passenger locomotive built for Amtrak. It was basically a fully cowled SD40-2 on a long frame, with two steam generators in the rear (designed to be easily replaced with a head-end power unit). Several accidents led to them being removed from service in the late 1970s. Most were then scrapped (technically traded in to EMD for new F40PHs), but Santa Fe acquired 18 of them and regeared them for freight service. The first 40 had noses that came to a point; the remainder, like no. 583 above, had a flat area at the end of the nose. The SDP40F doesn't have a front platform with railing as on the F45 and FP45.

SDP40F: Amtrak 500-649

F40C

The F40C has a cowl body and large corrugated side grilles not found on other locomotives.

Louis A. Marre collection

The six-axle, 3,200-hp F40C was built for Chicago-area Metra commuter service. It had a cowl body similar to the SDP40F, but used an alternator to supply train power, and was shorter than the SDP40F. The F40C has distinctive corrugated side panels.
  F40C: Metra 600-614

GP40TC, GP40P

The head-end-power equipment occupies the body extension at the rear of GO Transit GP40TC No. 9806. *GO Transit*

The GP40TC (built in late 1966) and GP40P (December 1968) were passenger versions of the GP40 built for commuter service. The eight GP40TCs, built by GMD for GO Transit (Ontario), had stretched bodies and frames to house a small engine that powered an alternator for train lighting, heat, and air conditioning. The 13 GP40Ps (all for Central of New Jersey) were similar, but with a steam generator at the rear of the hood. See the CNJ roster on page 179 for a photo.
  GP40TC: GO Transit 600-607
  GP40P: CNJ 3671-3683

F40PH, F40PH-2

The F40PH was the mainstay of Amtrak's fleet from the mid-1970s through the 1980s. *Andy Sperandeo*

Amtrak adopted the four-axle, 3,000-hp F40PH after tracking problems plagued its SDP40F fleet. Mechanically identical to the GP40-2, the F40PH featured a cowl body, an alternator for passenger-car power, and faster gearing (57:20 for a 103 mph maximum). The first 30 Amtrak F40s had their fuel tanks mounted toward the rear truck; later models had larger tanks mounted behind the lead truck. Locomotives built from 1980 on had Q-style radiator fans and exhaust silencers. Many later units are technically F40PHRs, using rebuilt components from traded-in SDP40Fs, but there is no difference in appearance. The F40PH-2 reflects a boost in horsepower to 3,200, but body details remain the same.
  F40PH: Amtrak 200-409, GO Transit 510-515; MBTA 1000-1017; Metra 100-127;
  F40PH-2: CalTrain 900-919, Metra 128-184

F40PHM-2

Nicknamed "Winnebagos," Metra's F40PHMs have a radically different nose compared to a standard F40.

M.W. Blaszak

The 3,200-hp F40PHM-2 has a dramatically different appearance than other F40s, with the cab moved farther forward and the nose eliminated.
  F40PHM-2: Metra 185-214

F40PH-2D, F40PH-2C

The F40PH-2D has special equipment for Canadian use, including ditch lights. *Peter Jobe*

MBTA's F40PH-2C is longer than a standard F40 to house the HEP unit. Note also the screens on the windshields.

Tom Nelligan

The F40PH-2C, built for MBTA, is eight feet longer than a standard F40PH. It houses a separate head-end-power diesel engine and generator at the rear of the body. The F40PH-2D, built for VIA, looks like a standard F40PH-2 but is equipped with ditch lights (required in Canada before the U.S.), special headlight, and plow pilot, and the fuel tank is mounted toward the rear truck.

    F40PH-2C: MBTA 1050-1075
    F40PH-2D: VIA 6400-6458

GP40X

The GP40X has an SD45-style flared rear radiator housing.
John C. Benson

The GP40X, built in 1977-78, was a prototype for EMD's coming 50-series locomotives. The GP40X used a 16-cylinder 645F engine, boosting the horsepower to 3,600—600 more than the GP40-2 with the same number of cylinders. Its key spotting feature is flared radiator grilles like the SD45, with three radiator fans. A distinctive new truck, the HT-B, was optional and chosen by Southern Pacific and Union Pacific. Southern's had high noses.

    GP40X: AT&SF 3800-3809; SOU 7000-7002; SP 7200, 7201, 7230, 7231; UP 9000-9005

GP39X, GP49

Alaska Railroad No. 2801 is a GP49. One of its two radiator fans is covered by a winterization hatch, and the air intake has a snow hood. *Louis A. Marre collection*

The 2,600-hp GP39X was a prototype for an intermediate-horsepower locomotive using a 12-cylinder turbocharged 645 engine. Only six were built, and they were shortly rebuilt to GP49 standards. The GP49 was an upgrade to 2,800 hp, but only found one buyer (Alaska Railroad) and nine total sales. Both had large radiator grilles but only two rooftop fans. The GP39X had a standard blower housing and the GP49 has a free-flow blower. The Alaska units also had a winterization hatch and a hood over the central air intake.

    GP39X: SOU 4600-4605
    GP49: Alaska 2801-2809

SD40X, SD50S

Kansas City Southern SD40X No. 703 looks like an SD50, but on a shorter frame. *C.W. McDonald*

The revised 645F engine meant an upgrade to the SD40-2 line. The 3,500-hp SD40X (not to be confused with the 1960s test-bed SD40X) and identical SD50S (the S is for "short") featured the new engine and components, which resulted in a longer body, but placed on an SD40-2 frame. Starting with this locomotive, the dynamic brake on six-axle diesels was moved directly behind the cab. There's no more overhanging blister or housing, instead just a grille behind the cab below roof level. The SD40X and SD50S are shorter (by 28") than the SD50.

   SD40X: KCS 700-703
   SD50S: N&W 6500-6505

GP50

Burlington Northern No. 3160 shows the taller radiator grille used on the GP50, and it's equipped with a free-flow blower duct (on the hood just behind the cab). *Jeff Wilson*

The 3,500-hp GP50 replaced the GP40-2 as EMD's high-horsepower four-axle diesel (even though some GP40-2s were built after GP50 production started). Like the SD50, the GP50 used the upgraded 16-cylinder 645F engine. The main spotting feature is its larger side radiator grilles compared to the Dash-2. Early models (through 1981) had standard blower ducts; free-flow ducts (as on the Burlington Northern engine above), with a distinct angled shape, were used after that. BN received the last five GP50s, which had extended cabs with additional seating (and shorter noses). Southern received high-nose versions.

   GP50: AT&SF 3810-3854; BN 3110-3162; C&NW 5050-5099; MP 3500-3529; SLSF 790-799; SOU 7003-7092

SD50

The SD50 has a free-flow blower duct on the left side, with dynamic brakes relocated immediately behind the cab (marked by a small grille). *Jeff Wilson*

The SD50 used a frame 28" longer than the SD40-2, the better to contain the upgraded 16-cylinder 645F engine and electrical components. This eliminated the "porches" of the SD40-2. The SD50 has a larger radiator than its predecessor, and the dynamic brake grilles are relocated behind the cab, just in front of the air intake. The SD50 has six door panels with four latched doors below the radiator. Most SD50s (built through July 1984) were rated at 3,500 hp; those built later were 3,600 hp. The SD50 series had many operational problems related to the 645F engine, which was being pushed to its limits, as well as with electrical equipment.

   SD50: B&O, C&O, C&NW, CR, D&RGW, KCS, MP, N&W, SBD, SOU

SD50F, SD60F

Canadian National SD50F No. 5409 has a four-piece windshield, hood taper behind the cab, and a porthole in the access door in front of the radiator. *B.P. Curry*

The SD50F and SD60F are comfort cab (wide-nose), cowl-body locomotives built specially for Canadian National. The hood behind the cab has the Draper Taper notch behind the cab to improve rearward visibility. The two are externally identical; mechanically they are standard SD50s and SD60s. The SD50Fs were the last SD50-class locomotives built.

   SD50F: CN 5400-5459
   SD60F: CN 9900-9903, 5504-5563

GP59

Norfolk Southern No. 4608 shows the boxy dynamic brake housing and seven handrail stanchions of the GP59. *EMD*

Designed to be the successor to the GP49 and the low-horsepower option to the GP60, the GP59 used a 12-cylinder turbocharged 710 engine to develop 3,000 horsepower. Sales were slow, with Norfolk Southern taking the only 36 built. The locomotives have a boxy dynamic brake housing, large radiator screens, and free-flow blower duct. The GP59 has six tall engine access doors and seven handrail stanchions on each side, compared with eight doors and 10 stanchions on the GP60.

   GP59: NS 4606-4641

GP60

Early GP60s, such as Santa Fe No. 4000, were nearly identical to GP50s. *James Drennan*

The introduction of the more-powerful (and more-reliable) 710 engine, coupled with microprocessor controls, resulted in a new model, the 3,800-hp GP60, which replaced the GP50. Externally, the GP60 is nearly identical to the GP50. Late GP60s (after mid-1989) have a much more boxy dynamic brake housing than earlier engines (see the photo of the BNSF GP60M). Sales of four-axle engines were on the downslide, with railroads opting for six-axle locomotives instead. The last GP60, SP 9794, was the last four-axle road locomotive built by EMD.

   GP60: AT&SF 4000-4039; DOE 106; D&RGW 3154-3156; NS 7100-7150; SP 9600-9619, 9715-9794; SSW 9620-9714; TexMex 869, 870

GP60M

Former Santa Fe GP60M No. 140 was repainted orange and green following the railroad's merger into Burlington Northern Santa Fe. *Jeff Wilson*

The wide-nose, comfort-cab GP60M and cabless GP60B were both built exclusively for Santa Fe, which initially placed them in charge of its priority intermodal trains. They have the later, boxy style dynamic-brake housing. Internally, both are standard GP60s; the B units have their dynamic-brake housings moved to the cab end of the locomotive.

   GP60M: AT&SF 100-162
   GP60B: AT&SF 325-347

SD60

The six latched doors under the radiator help identify Oakway Leasing No. 9061 as an SD60. *Jeff Wilson*

The 3,800-hp SD60 was the first six-axle locomotive to use EMD's new, larger 16-cylinder 710G engine. Along with the new engine, the SD60 featured microprocessor controls. The main spotting feature differentiating the SD60 from the SD50 is under the radiator grilles: The SD60 has eight door panels with six latched doors, while the SD50 only has six doors. The SD60 series proved to be very successful, overcoming the problems that plagued SD50s.

   SD60: BN, C&NW, CR, CSX, KCS, NS, OAK, Soo, UP

SD60MAC

Number 9500 is one of four SD60MACs built. Note how the handrail is attached to an equipment cabinet directly behind the cab. *EMD*

The SD60MAC is an AC-traction-motor version of the SD60M. Four were built to test the AC control equipment, traction motors, and a new radial (self-steering) truck. The SD60MAC has an equipment box on the walkway directly behind the cab on the left side, and the dynamic brake grille is pushed back adjacent to the central air intake. Although owned by EMD, they were painted in Burlington Northern colors and run on BN.
  SD60MAC: EMD/BN 9500-9503

SD70

The SD70, like Illinois Central No. 1010, has an air-intake screen below the radiator opening on the left side.

John C. Benson

An upgrade to the 710 engine (the 710G3B) and improved traction motors led to the 4,000-hp SD70. The popularity of the safety cab that debuted with the SD60M continued in the SD70 series, with only 120 conventional-cab models built. Spotting features include a bulge on the right side of the nose and an air-intake screen below the radiator screen on the left side of the hood. All ride on EMD's HTCR-II radial trucks.
  SD70: CR 2557-2580; IC 1000-1039; NS 2501-2556

SD60M, SD60I

Union Pacific No. 2431 is an SD60M. It looks like a standard SD60, but with a wide-nose North American Safety Cab. The two-piece windshield and tapered nose sides mark it as a late-production unit. *Jeff Wilson*

Number 6745 is an SD60I, evidenced by the gasket line running up the side of and across its nose. The former Conrail engine has been renumbered by new owner Norfolk Southern. *Jeff Wilson*

Union Pacific No. 6087 is an early production SD60M, with a three-piece windshield and straight nose sides. *EMD*

First built for the Union Pacific, the SD60M has a full-width nose and a redesigned cab (North American Safety Cab) that features console-style controls. The design soon became the standard for the SD60 line. The nose was redesigned in 1981, receiving a distinctive taper, and a two-piece windshield replaced the original three-piece design. The SD60I, ordered by Conrail, is an SD60M with an isolated cab, designed to insulate the cab from engine and other noise. It's marked by a visible gasket line on the nose, running up the sides and across the top.
  SD60M: BN 1991, 9200-9298; CR 5500-5574; Soo 6058-6062; UP 6085-6365
  SD60I: CR 5544, 5575-5653

SD70M, SD70I

Early SD70Ms, like Union Pacific No. 4656, built in May 2001, had standard flat radiator grilles. They can be spotted from SD60Ms by their HTCR trucks. *Jeff Wilson*

Later SD70Ms have flared (angled) radiator grilles at the rear of the hood. *Jeff Wilson*

The safety-cab version of the SD70, the 4,000-hp SD70M, looked much like the earlier SD60M, but the SD70M was equipped with HTCR radial trucks. A major body change came in 2002 with the switch to flared (angled) radiator grilles (similar to those on the SD45). These radiators initially had two panels on each side; later engines have four panels per side. The SD70I, like the SD60I, features an isolated cab and can be spotted by its gasket seam on each side of the nose. All SD70Is went to Canadian National.

SD70M: CSX 4675-4699; NYS&W 4050, 4052, 4054; NS 2581-2648, SP 9800-9824, UP 3779-3984, 3986-4689, 4692-5231

SD70I: CN 5600-5625

SD70MAC

The nose gasket seam marks BNSF SD70MAC No. 8948 as having an isolated cab. The small grilles behind the cab and below the radiator grille differentiate it from the SD70M. *Jeff Wilson*

The AC-traction-motor version of the SD70, the 4,000-hp SD70MAC quickly became the best seller in the SD70 line. It can be spotted from the SD70M by its having two small vertical grilled openings in each side: one just behind the cab and the other below the radiator grille. SD70MACs built after mid-2000 are rated at 4,300 hp and have flared radiators. The isolated cab (as on the SD60I and SD70I) was an option; locomotives so equipped are not separated as a separate model.

SD70MAC: Alaska 4001-4328; BN 9400-9499; BNSF 8800-8989; CR 4130-4144; CSX 4500-4589; TFM/KCS 1600-1674

SD75M, SD75I

The hood bulge below the intake grille identifies Santa Fe No. 222 as an SD75M. *John C. Benson*

The SD75M and SD75I used the same engine as SD70 series locomotives, but bumped up the engine's maximum RPMs from 900 to 950 to get 4,300 horsepower compared to 4,000-hp for the SD70M. The body is nearly identical to the SD70M, but the SD75M and SD75I have a bulge on the right side of the hood below the air filter intake grille. The SD75I has an isolated cab, marked by a gasket around the front of the nose and directly behind the cab (as with the SD70I).

SD75M: ATSF 200-250; BNSF 8251-8275

SD75I: BNSF 8276-8301; CN 5626-5800; ON 2100-2105

SD80MAC

Conrail SD80MAC No. 4120 displays the model's huge flared radiator and the dynamic brake compartment at the rear of the body. *John C. Benson*

The AC-traction-motor SD80MAC marked a return to a 20-cylinder power, using EMD's current 710G3 engine. This size resulted in a boost in horsepower to 5,000. The 80-foot-long SD80MAC body is distinctive, shared with the SD90MAC shown below, with large flared radiator grilles toward the rear. The dynamic brake grids and grilles are moved to the rear of the locomotive, housed in a squared-off area behind the radiator. All have isolated cabs, and all 30 went to Conrail.
   SD80MAC: CR 4100-4129

SD90MAC-H, SD90MAC-H II

The redesigned nose and beveled edges atop the hood in front of the radiator are visible on Union Pacific SD90MAC-H II No. 8548. *John C. Benson*

The "-H" designation indicates SD90MACs that were delivered with the 6,000-hp 16V265H engine (the H-engine). The body is similar to the SD90MAC and SD80MAC, but the MAC-H has two exhaust stacks atop the hood (the 265H uses two turbochargers) and the hood in front of the radiator has beveled edges. The first 22 locomotives built had noses the same as the '90MAC, and locomotives built after that (the "II" designation) had redesigned noses with rectangular windshields and a full-height nose door. Continued reliability problems with the 265H engine, combined with questionable viability of a 6,000-hp locomotive, limited sales.
   SD90MAC-H: UP 8500-8521
   SD90MAC-H II: CP 9300-9393, UP 8522-8561

SD90MAC (SD9043MAC)

The SD90MAC, as shown by Union Pacific No. 8177, shares the same massive body as the SD80MAC. *Jeff Wilson*

The SD90MAC was intended to be a 6,000-hp locomotive powered by a new 16-cylinder, four-cycle engine—the 265H, sometimes simply called the "H-engine." However, reliability problems with the 265 led EMD to substitute the 4,300-hp, 16-cylinder 710G3B engine, with the intention of swapping engines when the new 265H was ready. Because of this, these locomotives (delivered through 1995) are often informally called "convertibles," SD9043MACs, or SD90/43MACs. Because of delays and continued problems with the 265H engine, neither owner (Canadian Pacific or Union Pacific) opted for conversions to be done. The SD9043MAC body was identical to the '80MAC, with the dynamic brake housing and grille at the extreme rear of the body behind the radiator.
   SD90MAC: CP 9100-9160, UP 8000-8308

SD70ACe

The cabinet behind the conductor's (left) side of the cab is apparent in this view of Montana Rail Link SD70ACe No. 4300. *Tom Danneman*

The SD70ACe is shorter than an SD90MAC, with an exposed area between the body and the trucks. *Jeff Wilson*

The 4,300-hp SD70ACe is EMD's AC-traction-motor answer to the Environmental Protection Agency's Tier 2 emissions standards, which took effect Jan. 1, 2005. The locomotive uses a modified 710 engine to cut emissions. The SD70ACe resembles a late SD90MAC, but the ACe is shorter, with a shorter dynamic brake area (at the rear of the hood) and has a lot of exposed piping and wiring under the walkway and cab, making it appear to ride tall. The ACe has an electrical cabinet behind the cab on the left side, a different pattern of air intake grilles on each side compared to the '90MAC, and a single exhaust stack.

SD70ACe: BNSF 8800-8989, 9130-9499, 9504-9999; CSX 4831-4850; FMex 4000-4014; KCS 3997-4129; MRL 4300-4315; TFM; UP 1982, 1983, 1987, 1988, 1995, 1996, 4141, 8309-8670

SD70M-2

This view of Norfolk Southern No. 2777 highlights the rear (dynamic brake) area of the SD70M-2. *Rick Selby*

The 4,300-hp SD70M-2 was EMD's DC-traction-motor locomotive alternative to the SD70ACe that was also introduced in 2005 to meet EPA Tier 2 emission standards. It is nearly identical in appearance to the SD70ACe, as both EMD and GE moved to standardize body styles between their AC and DC offerings. The SD70M-2 didn't sell as well as the AC version, with 331 built through a final order for Canadian National in late 2010.

SD70M-2: CITX 140-142; CN 8000-8024, 8800-8964, FEC 100-107; NS 2649-2778

SD70ACe-T4

The SD70ACe-T4 has a different cab design and trucks compared to the SD70ACe. *Chris Guss*

The SD70ACe-T4, introduced in 2015, is EMD's answer to Tier 4 emissions requirements. The locomotive uses a new engine—the four-cycle, 12-cylinder 1010, redesigned and improved from the old 265H—which has a two-stage turbocharger system (three separate turbos). The 4,400-hp locomotive has new fabricated trucks, three (instead of two) radiator fans, an updated cab design with "teardrop" windows that drop down at the outside corners), and a new style of louvered opening at the dynamic brake area (behind the radiator). The locomotive is also longer (76'-8") than its predecessor (74'-3").

SD70ACe-T4 (currently in production): UP 3000-3099

F59PH

The F59PH has a nose that resembles a GP60M more closely than an F40PH. It is powered by the 710G engine.
Brian Griebenow; Louis A. Marre collection

The 3,000-hp F59PH, ordered by two commuter agencies, was a successor to the F40PH family of passenger locomotives. It has a 12-cylinder version of the 710G engine. The body features a nose and cab similar to other contemporary safety cab locomotives.

F59PH: Metrolink 851-873; GO Transit 520-568

F59PHI

The F59PHI features radically different streamlined styling compared to the earlier F59PH. *EMD*

EMD streamlined the F59 in 1994, giving it a new, sloped fiberglass nose, large fuel tank skirt, and roof covering, designating it the F59PHI. Internally, the locomotive is basically the same as the earlier F59PH, but with an updated version of the 710 engine.

F59PHI: Amtrak 450-470, Amtrak Montreal 1320-1330; BC Transit 901-905; Coaster 3000, 3001; Metrolink 874-881, 884-887; California DOT 2001-2015; Sound Transit 901-911; State of North Carolina 1755, 1797; Trinity Rail Express 569, 570

DE30AC, DM30AC

Long Island Rail Road's DE30AC features European styling and all-new trucks. *EMD*

These distinctive AC-traction-motor locomotives received newly designed four-wheel trucks with 44" wheels. Both use a 12-cylinder 710G engine to produce 3,000 hp; the difference is that the DM30AC also has a shoe for collecting current from an outside third rail for service into Penn Station.

DE30AC: LIRR 400-422
DM30AC: LIRR 500-522

F125

The F125 has a streamlined body and tapered nose, but a different body shape than the F59PHI. *EMD*

The F125 is a 4,700-hp passenger diesel powered by a 20-cylinder, four-cycle Caterpillar C175 engine—the first EMD locomotive to feature a Cat engine. The Tier-4-compliant locomotive uses AC traction motors and is geared for a top speed of 125 mph. The streamlined, monocoque body was designed by a Spanish company, Vossloh Rail Vehicles. Metrolink ordered the first 20, which were all to be delivered by 2017.

F125: Metrolink

— CHAPTER SIX —

General Electric

Four U25B demonstrators climb upgrade on the Northern Pacific near Blossburg, Mont., in 1961. The U25B brought GE into the heavy diesel market, and within a few years the company had eclipsed Alco for the No. 2 spot among loco-motive builders. *General Electric*

Geneneral Electric has a long relationship with railroad motive power. The company began building heavy electric locomotives in the 1890s, furnished traction motors and electrical equipment to other builders through the 1950s, and eventually become the dominant diesel-electric locomotive manufacturer in North America.

Along with switchers, the GE-Alco-Ingersoll-Rand partnership placed the first road diesel-electrics in service, including this 1928-built 800-hp passenger unit powered by a McIntosh & Seymour diesel. *General Electric*

GE Early Hoods

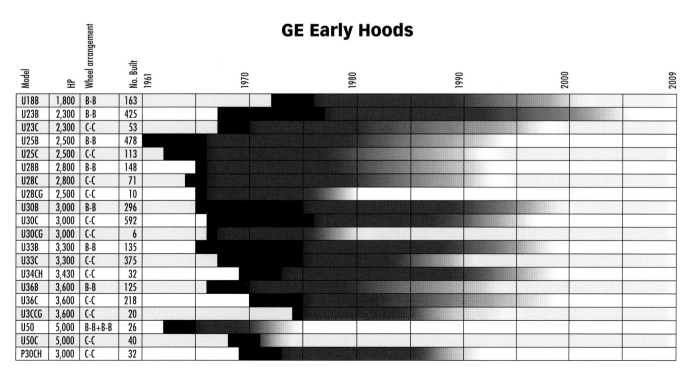

Model	HP	Wheel arrangement	No. Built
U18B	1,800	B-B	163
U23B	2,300	B-B	425
U23C	2,300	C-C	53
U25B	2,500	B-B	478
U25C	2,500	C-C	113
U28B	2,800	B-B	148
U28C	2,800	C-C	71
U28CG	2,500	C-C	10
U30B	3,000	B-B	296
U30C	3,000	C-C	592
U30CG	3,000	C-C	6
U33B	3,300	B-B	135
U33C	3,300	C-C	375
U34CH	3,430	C-C	32
U36B	3,600	B-B	125
U36C	3,600	C-C	218
U3CCG	3,600	C-C	20
U50	5,000	B-B+B-B	26
U50C	5,000	C-C	40
P30CH	3,000	C-C	32

Many don't think of GE as being a pioneer in diesel-electric locomotives, but the company was an early partner with Alco and Ingersoll-Rand starting in 1925. The group produced several gas-, oil-, and diesel-electric locomotives—mainly switchers, but some early road units as well.

After Alco dropped out of the consortium in 1929, GE developed its own line of industrial locomotives and light switchers. A series of GE boxcabs in 1930 used small constant-speed diesel engines to charge storage batteries. GE built seven center-cab, twin-engine 600-hp switchers from 1933 to 1935, then followed with ten custom-built single-engine, 98-ton, 600-hp locomotives for the New Haven. These had cabs toward the end, with a short nose that held the radiator.

During this time, GE supplied components to other builders, including Alco, Baldwin, and Fairbanks-Morse (and even to Electro-Motive until 1938). The company provided additional services as well: GE assembled EMC's first two diesel switchers and several boxcab passenger engines in 1935, and built F-M's big six-axle passenger units in 1945, which were nicknamed "Erie Builts" for their construction location.

The best-known and most-popular early GE locomotives are its 44-ton and 70-ton switching locomotives, both of which found favor among large Class I railroads as well as short lines and industrial users. The 44-ton locomotive was significant, as it was the heaviest locomotive that, by operating rules, could be run by an engineer alone without a fireman.

The 44-tonner was distinctive and easy to spot, with a center cab and a small diesel engine in each hood. More than 370 were built from 1939 through 1956.

The 70- through 95-ton models shared a common body (and were built in a wide range of weights), with an end cab and long hood. Both were rated at 600 hp and powered by a single diesel engine. More than 280 were built starting in 1945, and they could be found in use as light switchers or as road power on short lines and branch lines.

The "switchers" chart lists significant and well-known locomotives; small industrial switchers, single units, and small orders are not listed (GE built many small industrial switchers, as well as single larger engines and small orders of larger locomotives up to 128 tons and 1,500 hp).

GE Modern

Model	HP	Wheel arrangement	No. Built
B23-7	2,250	B-B	536
BQ23-7	2,250	B-B	10
B30-7	3,000	B-B	199
B30-7A	3,000	B-B	78
B30-7A(B)	3,000	B-B	120
C30-7	3,000	C-C	1,137
C30-7A	3,000	C-C	50
B36-7	3,600	B-B	222
C36-7	3,600	C-C	169
B32-8	3,150	B-B	3
Dash 8-32B	3,200	B-B	46
C32-8	3,150	C-C	10
B39-8	3,900	B-B	145
C39-8	3,900	C-C	161
Dash 8-40B	4,000	B-B	151
Dash 8-40BW	4,000	B-B	83
Dash 8-40C	4,000	C-C	581
Dash 8-40CW	4,000	C-C	756
Dash 8-41CW	4,100	C-C	154
Dash 8-40CM	4,000	C-C	84
Dash 8-44CW	4,400	C-C	53
Dash 9-40C	4,000	C-C	125
Dash 9-40CW	4,000	C-C	1,090
Dash 9-44CW	4,400	C-C	2,296
Dash 9-44CWL	4,400	C-C	27
AC4400CW	4,400	C-C	3,078
AC4000/6000CW	4,400	C-C	106
AC6000	6,000	C-C	199
ES44AC	4,400	C-C	2,537
ES44C4	4,400	**	589
ES40DC	4,000	C-C	220
ES44DC	4,400	C-C	1,240
ET44AC	4,400	C-C	582*
ET44C4	4,400	**	236*

Passenger locomotives

Model	HP	Wheel arrangement	No. Built
Dash 8-32BWH	3,200	B-B	20
P40	4,000	B-B	46
P42DC	4,200	B-B	228
P32AC-DM	3,200	B-B	53

In 1954, following GE's breakup with Alco, GE built an experimental four-unit set of cab diesels. The UM20Bs tested on Erie for several years, wearing Erie lettering, before being rebuilt and sent to Union Pacific. No production models were built. *General Electric*

Road diesels

From 1940 to 1953 GE was a partner in producing and marketing road diesels with Alco, with GE supplying the traction motors, generators, and other electrical equipment. GE dissolved the partnership in 1953 (although GE continued to supply Alco with electrical gear, just not on an exclusive basis).

As a long-time heavy electric builder, GE had the manufacturing space and knowledge to build larger diesels (and it had just turned out several large turbine locomotives for Union Pacific), and the company was eyeing the heavy road diesel market. In 1954 GE built an A-B-B-A set of cab units as a test bed. Dubbed UM20Bs, they had a unique nose and corrugated sides. All were powered by 12-cylinder diesels, with the locomotives of one A-B set each rated at 1,200 hp and the others at 1,800 hp. No orders were taken for them, and no other cab units were built. The locomotives tested on the

Erie for several years (wearing Erie paint and lettering), and in 1959 GE rebuilt all of them with 2,000-hp engines. They went to Union Pacific in 1960 and were retired by 1963.

U-Boats

The locomotive trend in the 1950s was turning heavily toward road switchers, so GE focused its design efforts that direction and introduced its Universal (U) series of road switchers in 1959 (the company had successfully sold export versions starting in 1956). After successful tours of the demonstrator U25B locomotives, the first production locomotives were delivered in 1961.

The U25B marked GE's entry into the domestic road diesel market, and it featured several innovations. It was powered by GE's 16-cylinder FDL engine rated at 2,500 hp, 500-hp higher than EMD's competing GP20 (and 100 more hp

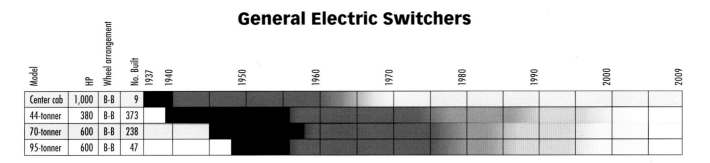

General Electric Switchers

Model	HP	Wheel arrangement	No. Built	1937	1940	1950	1960	1970	1980	1990	2000	2009
Center cab	1,000	B-B	9									
44-tonner	380	B-B	373									
70-tonner	600	B-B	238									
95-tonner	600	B-B	47									

than Alco's slow-selling RS-27). The U25B had a pressurized engine compartment to help keep out dirt and dust, a new air filtration system, and simplified mechanical equipment. The locomotives (and future GE U-series locomotives) became known as U-boats. A six-axle version, the U25C, followed in 1963.

GE's nomenclature featured a U for Universal series, followed by the first two numerals of the horsepower rating, then by a B for two-axle and C for three-axle trucks. Later combination freight/passenger units received a G suffix if equipped with steam generators or an H for head-end-power generators, and a P prefix for dedicated passenger locomotives.

The horsepower progression gradually increased, with the U28, U30, U33, and U36 models, with the 1,800-hp U18B and 2,300-hp U23B eventually offered as low-horsepower alternatives. As with EMD, beginning in the late 1960s GE offered locomotives with high- and low-horsepower options at the same time, but all were turbocharged. As with EMD and Alco, GE dabbled in large twin-engine diesels in the 1960s at the request of Union Pacific, offering the 5,000-hp, twin-engine U50 and U50C.

GE road switchers had a common look through the 1970s, with a distinctive cab and hood design and a flat-sided fuel tank that tapered at an angle toward the bottom. Dynamic brakes, when installed, are evident as grids just inside the rear air intake screen on the sides of the hood.

Most four-axle U-boats rode on AAR type B road trucks, and in 1972 GE's FB-2 (floating bolster) trucks became an option. Until 1966, six-axle GEs were delivered with trimount trucks with uneven axle spacing (similar to Alco's design). In 1966 GE adopted a design with equal axle spacing that eliminated the outside drop equalizers.

Modern hood units

General Electric's first major upgrade to its road switchers came in the late 1970s with the introduction of its Dash 7 line. As with EMD's Dash-2 locomotives, GE's Dash 7s used the basic specifications of its existing U-boats, but with upgraded components.

The Dash 7s paved the way for the more-significant improvements in GE's Dash 8 line, which were the first of that company's locomotives to feature microprocessor controls. General Electric changed its nomenclature in 1988, spelling out the word "Dash" before the locomotive designation, as in Dash 8-40B. Be aware that many railroads, however, continued using the old style of classification (i.e. B40-8).

The early 1990s saw the introduction of the Dash 9 line. Improvements included new bolsterless HiAd (self-steering) trucks, an upgraded 7FDL engine, improved cooling system, and advanced microprocessor controls. As with EMD, GE began offering AC-traction-motor versions of its six-axle locomotives as the AC4400CW, which would sell more than 3,000 copies.

General Electric's response to the EPA Tier 2 emissions standards of the early 2000s was an all-new diesel engine, the GEVO, to power its 4,400-hp ES44AC and ES44DC. These models were upgraded in the 2010s to meet current EPA Tier 4 regulations, with the ET44AC and ET44C4 the current models in the GE catalog.

44-tonner

Baltimore & Ohio No. 190 is a Phase II 44-tonner, with the grilles at the ends and steps added at the corners.
General Electric

This New Haven 44-tonner is a Phase I engine, with single side steps and radiator louvers on the sides of the hood.
General Electric

The 44-tonner was popular with both industrial users and common carriers, as it skirted just under the rule that a fireman must be used on any diesel 90,000 pounds and heavier. It used a pair of Caterpillar diesel engines and was rated at 380 or 400 hp. Phase I bodies (through October 1942) had side radiator louvers and a single set of steps on each side—set in from the end—illustrated by the Baltimore & Ohio locomotive above. On Phase II models (through May 1943) the louvers moved to the ends, with ladders added at each corner. Phase III (through June 1945) versions have multi-panel access doors on the hoods. Phase IV (through September 1951) engines have small rectangular air intakes at the top of each hood side. Phase V models (through 1956) have ridges in the hood doors and a rectangular headlight (instead of round).

Major buyers: A&A, AT&SF, B&O, B&M, CN, CB&Q, D&RGW, DL&W, GN, IC, LV, MEC, M&StL, MILW, MP, NC&StL, NYNH&H, NYO&W, NKP, NP, PE, PRR, SN, SLSF, Soo, SOU, SP, Union, WM

70-tonner, 95-tonner

Southern Pacific 70-tonner No. 5113 has the nose louver location and rectangular headlight housing marking it as a Phase II locomotive. *James Belden*

The 70- and 95-ton end-cab locomotives shared the same body and used single Cooper-Bessemer engines rated from 600 to 660 hp. Phase I versions had side radiator louvers; Phase II models (above) had the louvers moved to the front, and also had rectangular headlights. In spite of their names, the weights of these locomotives varied a great deal—often more than the name implied.

Major buyers: AD&N, B&C, B&ML, CN, FDDM&S, KC, MEx, MKT, PGE, StJ&LC, SP

1,000-hp center-cab

Ford's center-cab GEs, built in 1937, featured streamlined styling to match Ford automobiles. *General Electric*

The best known of these twin-engine, 1,000-hp center-cabs were the eight owned by Ford and used as plant switchers. They had streamlined bodies, chrome trim, and curved nose grilles resembling those found on Ford automobiles. The Ford locomotives weighed 125 tons; the non-streamlined version owned by Monongahela Connecting weighed 115 tons.

1,000-hp: Ford 1000-1007; MC 150

600-hp, 98-ton

GE built a series of 600-hp switchers exclusively for New Haven. *General Electric*

GE built 10 98-ton, 600-hp switchers for New Haven in 1936-37. The locomotives had single Cooper-Bessemer engines in the long hood, with the radiator in a short hood or nose on the opposite side of the cab.

600-hp: NH 0901-0910

U25B

The U25B has a longer nose than later U-boats and has an elevated walkway at the rear. New York Central No. 2501 has dynamic brakes—note the grids behind the radiator screen at rear. *General Electric*

GE broke into the road locomotive market in 1959 with the revolutionary U25B, which, at 2,500 hp, was the highest-horsepower single-engine road diesel on the market. By the end of its production run, GE had become the second-largest locomotive builder. The U25B had an elevated portion of the walkway at the rear of each side, and had a longer nose than later U-boat models. The demonstrator locomotives and four early units each from Frisco and Union Pacific had high noses, but the remainder had low noses. Low-nose U25Bs initially had large one-piece windshields; this changed to a two-piece design in 1965.

U25B: AT&SF, CB&Q, C&O, CRI&P, EL, GN, L&N, MILW, NYC, NYNH&H, PRR, SLSF, SP, UP, WAB

U25C

The U25C, as on Atlantic Coast Line No. 3001, shares spotting features with the U25B but has a shorter nose. It has GE's original tri-mount trucks. *General Electric*

The six-axle version of the U-boat didn't appear until three years after the U25B debuted. The 2,500-hp U25C rode on a longer frame than the U25B, but had a shorter nose. Otherwise, spotting features were much the same, with an elevated walkway and corresponding jog in the handrail at the rear. Ten late U25Cs were rated at 2,750 hp. The first U25Cs had air reservoirs on either end of the fuel tank; later engines had larger fuel tanks, with air reservoirs moved inside the hood. Late U25Cs had screen-covered openings behind the cab; early units lacked this feature.

U25C: ACL 3000-3020; CB&Q 550-561; LS&I 2500, 2501; L&N 1500-1517; NP 2500-2529; Oro Dam 8010-8019; PRR 6500-6519

U28B

The U28B has a shorter nose and a small step outward at the radiator housing. Milwaukee No. 130 has dynamic brakes and a plow. *General Electric*

The first 2,800-hp U28Bs had the same body as late U25Bs, including all P&LE and SP engines and some Milwaukee and Rock Island units. After that, the cab was moved forward, resulting in a shorter nose. The box atop the walkway was moved, so there was no longer a jog in the walkway along the long hood.

U28B: CB&Q 106-115, 140-149; CRI&P 240-281; GN 2524-2529; L&N 2500-2505; MILW 130-135, 137-140, 380, 393-398; N&W 1900-1929; NYC 2822, 2823; P&LE 2800-2821; SP 7025-7028

U28C

Union Pacific U28C No. 2804 rides on GE's new trucks that were introduced in 1966. *Union Pacific*

As with the four-axle U28B, early (Burlington and Northern Pacific) U28Cs shared the same bodies as late U25Cs. After that, the step-up in the walkway was eliminated (as seen the the above photo). The trucks also changed during production, with the drop-equalizer style with uneven axle spacing that had been used since the introduction of the U25C replaced by a truck with even axle spacing.

U28C: CB&Q 562-577; L&N 1525-1532; NP 2800-2811; PRR 6520-6534; SP 7150-7159; UP 2800-2809

U28CG

Santa Fe's U28CGs were delivered in the red-and-silver warbonnet passenger scheme. *W.A. Gibson Jr.*

General Electric built ten steam-generator-equipped U28Cs for the Santa Fe, designating them U28CGs ("G" = steam generator). The steam generator was located behind the cab, with a vent and stack on the roof above it. Other than that, they looked like standard U28Cs. As with EMD's SDP diesels, the U28CG was a locomotive that could easily operate in fast freight service as passenger service declined.

U30CG: AT&SF 7900-7909

U30B

Western Pacific U30B No. 754 displays the model's larger radiator area compared to the U28B. This engine rides on EMD Blomberg trucks. *General Electric*

With the U30B, GE increased the horsepower to 3,000 to match EMD's GP40. Visually, early U30Bs are identical to late U28Bs. On later models the radiator opening wasn't as long, and two extra vertical openings appeared forward of the radiator opening. The Norfolk & Western's units had high noses; Seaboard Air Line and Western Pacific U30Bs (above) rode on EMD GP trucks from traded-in locomotives.

U30B: ACL, C&O, CB&Q, IC, L&N, MILW, NYC, N&W, SAL, SLSF, WP

U30C

The U30C has eight tall engine access doors and a step up in the hood sides and roof at the front of the radiator.
Jim Hediger

The six-axle version of the U30 proved more popular than the four-axle version, as the 3,000-hp U30C earned a reputation as a good-pulling locomotive in heavy-haul freight service, especially coal trains. Spotting features are the same as the U30B, with eight tall engine-room doors on each side. A change in radiator design during production added an angled fillet between the radiator roof bulge and the body. The side radiator intake screen was initially the full-width of the radiator. It was later shortened, with a pair of smaller vertical openings in front of it.

U30C: ACL, BN, CB&Q, C&O, C&NW, CRI&P, D&H, DOT, DE, KS, L&N, MILW, MP, N&W, FdelP, PRR, RDG, SOU, SP, Soo, T&P, UP

U30CG

The cowl body on the U30CG featured corrugated sides, a rounded nose, and a front platform. *Joe McMillan*

The Santa Fe again requested a custom locomotive with a steam generator, and in a departure from the U28CG, the U30CG featured a streamlined, corrugated cowl body with a rounded nose. These distinctive diesels are difficult to confuse with anything else. Other than the cowling and steam generator, they were standard U30Cs.

U30CG: AT&SF 8000-8005

U23B

Milwaukee Road No. 4802 is a U23B, with six tall engine-access doors on the long hood. It rides on GE FB-2 trucks.
Ronald A. Plazzotta

General Electric brought out the 2,250-hp U23B in 1968 as a medium-horsepower general freight locomotive, similar to EMD's GP38. It uses a 12-cylinder version of GE's FDL engine. The locomotive was built on the same frame as its higher-horsepower brethren, but the body looks like a shortened version of the U30B. The U23B only has six tall engine access doors on each side (one for each pair of cylinders) compared to eight tall doors on the U30B. Most ride on AAR type B trucks, but some (like the Milwaukee engine above) have GE's FB-2 trucks or EMD trucks from traded-in units. Southern's have high noses (see page 278).

U23B: AT&SF, C&O, CR, D&H, FdelP, LV, L&N, MILW, MKT, MP, MON, NdeM, PC, SOU, Texas Utilities, WP

U23C

Lake Superior & Ishpeming U23C No. 2301 was built in 1968. It's longer than the U23B, but has the same six tall hood access doors. *General Electric*

Demand wasn't as strong for the six-axle version of the U23, with just four railroads buying 53 units. It was intended for low-speed drag-freight service. Spotting features are the same as on U23Bs, with six tall engine compartment doors on each side.

U23C: AT&SF 7500-7519; CB&Q 460-468; LS&I 2300-2304; PC 6700-6718.

U33B

The U33B has a wider radiator roof housing than the U30B. Seaboard Coast Line U33Bs, including No. 1734, ride on traded-in EMD trucks. *General Electric*

Produced at the same time as the U30B and U36B, the U33B offered 3,300 horsepower. The locomotive has a larger radiator bulge on the rear roof compared to the U30B, and a step on the body sides (increase in width) at the start of the radiator area. A tapered front housing was used on the radiator (seen on the photo of SCL 1734 above) into 1968. Seaboard Coast Line's U33Bs rode on EMD trucks from trade-ins.

U33B: CRI&P 190-199, 285-299; NYC 2858, 2859; PC 2890-2970; SCL 1719-1747

U33C

Southern Pacific U33C No. 8775 has a large L-shaped windshield on the engineer's side of the cab. It's a late-production unit without the angled fairing on the radiator housing. *General Electric*

The six-axle U33C shares the same spotting characteristics as the U33B, with a bigger radiator housing than the U30C. Hood openings varied during production. SP had the biggest fleet (212); all of its units had large L-shaped windshields on the engineer's side. Southern's had high noses.

U33C: AT&SF 8500-8524; BN 5725-5763; D&H 754-762; EL 3300-3315; GN 2530-2544; IC 5050-5059; MILW 8000-8003; NP 3300-3309; PC 6540-6563; SOU 3805-3814; SP 8585-8796

U36B

The U36B has a wide wing at the radiator. Auto-Train's engines were built to SCL specs. *Jim Hediger*

The highest-horsepower four-axle U-boat, the 3,600-hp U36B, shares an identical body with the U33B, with the only differences internal. The Auto-Train and Seaboard Coast Line engines rode on traded-in EMD GP trucks. The four Conrail engines were built for Auto-Train (as Nos. 4013-4016), but because of A-T's financial woes they were never delivered. The locomotives were stored for several years and had their EMD trucks replaced by AAR B trucks when they were bought by CR in 1976.

U36B: Auto-Train 4000-4012; CR 2971-2974; SCL 1748-1855

U36C

Erie Lackawanna No. 3321 is a U36C, which shares the same body as the U33C. *Louis A. Marre collection*

The 3,600-hp U36C shares the same body as the U33C, with internal changes to increase the horsepower by 300. It was the highest-horsepower single-engine locomotive (with the U36B) in the Universal line, not to be topped until the Dash 8s appeared.

U36C: AT&SF 8700-8799; CRR 3600-3606; EL 3316-3328; FdelP 409-418; MILW 8500-8503; NdeM 8900-8937, 8958-8986, 9300-9316

U36CG

National of Mexico bought 20 steam-generator-equipped U36CGs. *W.D. Volkmer*

The U36CG is a U36C equipped with a steam generator. It's visually identical to a U36C, but with roof vents for the generator directly behind the cab. The only 20 built went to National of Mexico.

U36CG: NdeM 8938-8957

U34CH

The U34CH is a U36C modified to supply head-end power for commuter train cars. *J. David Ingles*

A passenger version of the U36C, the U34CH was built for the New Jersey Department of Transportation (operated by Erie Lackawanna) as a commuter locomotive. Instead of a steam generator as on NdeM's U36CGs, the U34CH used part of the engine's output to provide power for train heat, lighting, and air conditioning (the "H" is for "head-end" power), with 3,430 hp left for propulsion—hence the "34" designation. Its external appearance is almost identical to a U36C, but the hood lacks the air intake screens behind the cab on the sides.

U34CH: EL/NJDOT 3351-3382

U18B

The four tall access doors (between the middle of the C and X) identify CSX No. 1989 as a U18B. This unit rides on EMD trucks. *John C. Benson*

The 1,800-hp U18B was GE's low-horsepower locomotive of the early 1970s, competing with EMD's GP15-1. The U18 was powered by an eight-cylinder FDL engine. The U18B body is about six feet shorter than the U23B, with just four tall engine access doors on each hood side in front of the radiator. Trucks varied: some rode on AAR B trucks, others on GE's FB-2, and some on EMD Blomberg trucks from trade-ins.

U18B: MEC 400-409; NdeM 9000-9044; P&W 1801; SCL 250-261, 300-392; Texas Utilities 101, 102

U50, U50C

The U50C has paired radiators in the middle of its body and a longer space between trucks compared to the U50.
Louis A. Marre collection

The U50 has prominent see-through screened openings behind the cab and at the rear. It rides on a pair of two-axle trucks at each end. *GE*

The U50 (built 1963-65) and U50C (built 1969-71) were both twin-engine, 5,000-hp, stub-nose diesels, both built primarily at the request of Union Pacific, which was sampling twin-engine locomotives from all builders in the 1960s. At first glance the two locomotives appear similar, but they have key differences. The earlier U50 (sometimes incorrectly called a U50D) was essentially two U25Bs on a single platform. It was powered by two 16-cylinder engines and rode on pairs of two-axle trucks (connected by span bolsters) at each end (B+B-B+B wheel arrangement)—the trucks and bolsters were re-used from retired UP turbine locomotives. The radiators for each engine were at opposite ends, with one just behind the cab and the other at the rear of the hood, and had distinctive, see-through screens. The later U50C rode on a pair of three-axle trucks and had two 12-cylinder FDL engines, with the radiators for each in the middle of the locomotive. The U50s were fairly successful, but wiring and engine problems plagued the U50Cs. All were retired by the late 1970s.

U50: SP 8500-8502; UP 31-53
U50C: UP 5000-5039

P30CH

The P30CH can be identified by its cowl body and squared-off nose. *GE*

General Electric built 25 P30CH passenger locomotives for Amtrak in 1974. The 3,000-hp locomotive—nicknamed "Pooch"—was a U30C with a cowl body and an auxiliary engine and generator (head-end power) to provide train lighting, heat, and air conditioning. The Pooch can be spotted from the contemporary EMD SDP40F by its blunt, squared-off nose.

P30CH: Amtrak 700-724

B23-7

The step in the hood (between the O and N) on Conrail B23-7 No. 1983 is characteristic of all Dash 7 locomotives. The locomotive has AAR trucks. *Conrail*

The 2,250-hp B23-7 replaced the U23B as the medium-horsepower four-axle locomotive in General Electric's line, and it would become the best-selling four-axle Dash 7 locomotive. It's powered by a 12-cylinder FDL engine. The B23-7 is two feet longer than the U23B and can be identified by the jog or step in the side of the hood just forward of the radiator, along with its six tall door panels (one for each pair of engine cylinders) in front of the radiator. Many of these locomotives rode on GE's own FB-2 trucks, although some have AAR B trucks. Southern's B23-7s had high noses.

B23-7: ATSF, CR, FSRR, L&N, MP, NdeM, P&W, SCL, SOU, SP, TU

BQ23-7

Seaboard Coast Line No. 5132 displays the distinctive blunt-faced crew-quarters cab unique to the BQ23-7.
Paul T. Maciulewicz

The BQ23-7, built in 1978-79, was a B23-7 with a large ("crew quarters") cab. The appearance is unique, with the cab front pushed forward and the nose eliminated. The intent was to provide room for additional crew members that would be displaced with the elimination of cabooses. Reductions in crew sizes soon made the additional cab space unnecessary, and only ten were built. Ironically, these locomotives ended their careers as B units, with their controls removed and windows plated over.
BQ23-7: SCL 5130-5139

B30-7

The B30-7 has eight tall hood doors and the characteristic step in the hood of Dash-7s (between the "S" and "C" in "Frisco." *Louis A. Marre collection*

The 3,000-hp B30-7 replaced the U30B, and the key spotting feature is the same as other Dash 7 locomotives: A step in the hood forward of the radiator. The B30-7 has eight tall door panels in front of the radiator, distinguishing it from the B23-7, and is powered by a 16-cylinder engine as opposed to the 12-cylinder B30-7A. Trucks can be FB-2, AAR type B, or EMD Blomberg.
B30-7: C&O 8235-8298; SLSF 863-870; SSW 7774-7799; SCL 5500-5516; SP 7800-7883

B30-7A, B30-7A(B)

The B30-7A shares the same body as the B23-7, with six tall engine access doors. Missouri Pacific No. 4848 rides on GE's FB-2 trucks. *Jim Hediger*

Burlington Northern No. 4000 is an early B30-7A(B), with dynamic brakes in the rear of the hood under the radiator. The second order of B30-7A(B) locomotives have dynamics toward the plain end. *General Electric*

The B30-7A differs from the standard B30-7 by using a turbocharged 12-cylinder engine instead of a 16-cylinder engine, while still producing 3,000 horsepower. Externally they have the same appearance as B23-7s. Variations included the B30-7A1, built for Southern after April 1982, which had grilles for the equipment blower located directly behind the cab (these also had high noses), and the cabless B30-7A(B) for Burlington Northern. The first group of these B units have plain hoods; units from a later order (No. 4053 onward) have grilles mounted toward what would have been the cab end, with dynamic brakes in a box protruding from the roof.
B30-7A: MP 4800-4854, SOU 3500-3521
B30-7A(B): BN 4000-4119

C30-7

Burlington Northern No. 5522 is a C30-7. The step in the hood is between the 5 and 2 in the number.

Andy Sperandeo

The C30-7 was an upgrade of the U30C. It has the same spotting features as other Dash-7 locomotives, namely the stepped widening of the hood just in front of the radiator area. The 3,000-hp C30-7 competed directly with EMD's SD40-2, and it proved popular with coal-hauling railroads and in other heavy-haul applications. It was GE's best-selling Dash-7 locomotive by far, with more than 1,100 built.

    C30-7: AT&SF, BN, CR, FdelP, L&N, NdeM, N&W, SCL, UP

C30-7A

The C30-7A has six tall power assembly doors on the hood (starting at the "A" in Conrail). *Conrail*

As with its four-axle little brother, the six-axle C30-7A used a smaller (12-cylinder) turbocharged engine to get the same horsepower as a standard C30-7. It can be spotted by its six (instead of eight) tall engine access doors in front of the step on the side. All 50 C30-7As went to Conrail.

    C30-7A: CR 6550-6599

B36-7

The plates over the radiator intakes on Santa Fe B36-7 No. 7485 are sound baffles, designed to quiet noise from the radiator fans. *C.W. McDonald*

The 3,600-hp B36-7 shares the same body and details as the B30-7. Southern's B36-7s have high noses. The blank headlight box in the nose is only found on the first B36-7s (Santa Fe's). All ride on FB-2 trucks.

    B36-7: AT&SF 7484-7499; CR 5000-5059; SSW 7770-7773; SBD 5806-5925; SP 7754-7769; SOU 3815-3820

C36-7

The housing atop the roof behind the cab of Norfolk Southern C36-7 No. 8542 is for the dynamic brakes.

Jeff Wilson

The 3,600-hp C36-7 used the same 16-cylinder engine as the C30-7 and shared the same body. Look for an exhaust silencer at the exhaust stack to identify them. Late ones built for NS and MP had a dynamic brake housing on the roof behind the cab (like early Dash 8s); the final 85 domestic models were rated at 3,750 hp.

    C36-7: CR 6620-6644; FdelP 419-433; MP 9000-9059; NdeM 9317-9341; N&W 8500-8530; NS 8531-8542

B32-8, Dash 8-32B

GE demonstrator B32-8 No. 5497 was painted in Burlington Northern colors. The nose and cab represent significant design changes from earlier GE diesels. *Trains magazine collection*

The cab roof is at the same level as the hood roof on Norfolk Southern Dash 8-32B No. 3557. *John C. Benson*

Microprocessor controls marked the introduction of General Electric's Dash 8 line. A 12-cylinder engine gave the test-bed B32-8 (top photo, three were built) a rating of 3,150 hp. The model introduced a new tapered nose and cab shape, with the cab roof below the level of the dynamic brake and blower boxes, which were located atop the hood just behind the cab. The large radiator housing was also redesigned, with a boxier, more squared-off appearance compared to Dash 7 locomotives. The B32-8 is three feet shorter than the B36 and B39, with six engine access doors (one for every pair of cylinders). The production 3,200-hp Dash 8-32B, only purchased by Norfolk Southern, shares the B32-8 body, but has the cab roof at the same level as the hood behind it.
   B32-8: BN 5497-5499
   Dash 8-32B: NS 3522-3566

Dash 8-32BWH

Nicknamed "Pepsi cans," the Dash 8-32BWH passenger diesels look like Dash 8-40BWs but have six tall power assembly doors. *Brian Griebenow; Louis A. Marre collection*

The Dash 8-32BWH ("W" for wide nose, "H" for head-end power) was built specifically for Amtrak. It's a Dash 8-40BW with a smaller (12-cylinder, 3,200-hp) engine and a second alternator to provide head-end power. The Dash 8-32BWH has six engine-access door panels, compared to eight on a B40.
   Dash 8-32BWH: Amtrak 500-519

C32-8

Conrail C32-8 No. 6610 has the new GE cab and nose styling, with the cab roof below the level of the rooftop housings behind it. *John C. Benson*

The C32-8 follows the same nose, cab, and hood spotting features as the B32-8. The C32 has six tall access doors like the B32, but is about four feet longer. Only 10 were built, all for Conrail.
   C32-8: CR 6610-6619

B36-8, B39-8

LMX Leasing No. 8541 shows the angled radiator grilles and eight power-assembly doors common to the B39-8.
Trains magazine collection

GE used a 16-cylinder engine good for 3,800 hp on the lone B36-8 demonstrator and 3,900 hp for the B39-8. (The demonstrator B36-8 was later rebuilt to a B39-8). The B39-8 can be distinguished from the B32 by its side radiator grilles, which are slightly angled, and by its eight engine access doors, compared with six on the B32. The first three B39-8s (ATSF 7400-7402) had a cab roof lower than the dynamic brake housing; the remainder had cabs that matched the housing.

    B36-8: GE 606
    B39-8: AT&SF 7400-7402, LMX 8500-8599; SP 8000-8039

C36-8, C39-8

Norfolk Southern 8551 is an early C39-8, with a cab lower than the roof-mounted housings behind it. *Rick Johnson*

The 3,900-hp C39-8 is just over three feet longer than the C32-8. It also has eight tall doors in front of the radiator instead of the six of the C32. The last 25 C39-8s, built for Norfolk Southern, ushered in the body that would be used on the following Dash 8-40C, with a taller cab and redesigned grille openings. The C36-8 was a 3,600 demonstrator locomotive; GE later rebuilt it to C39-8 standards.

    C36-8: GE 607
    C39-8: CR 6000-6021; NS 8550-8688

Dash 8-40B

The Dash 8-40B featured the new General Electric cab and nose style as well as tapered radiator grilles. *Lon Coone*

The Dash 8-40B was the first GE locomotive to officially use the new spelled-out "Dash" prefix designation. At 4,000 hp it represented a slight boost in horsepower over the B39-8, with several internal improvements. Externally it was almost identical to the late B39-8; the B39-8 has its rear sand filler hatch on the roof behind the radiators instead of in a notch below the rear headlight as on the '40.

    Dash 8-40B: AT&SF 7410-7449; CR 5060-5089; DoE 107; NYS&W 4002-4048 (even); SSW 8040-8093

Dash 8-40BW

GE built the safety-cab Dash 8-40BW at the request of the Santa Fe, which used them on its hotshot transcontinental intermodal trains. *Jeff Wilson*

The Dash 8-40BW was the wide-nose ("W") version of the Dash 8-40B. It shared the same spotting features as the standard Dash 8-40B, but with the North American safety cab. They were built at special request for the Santa Fe, and were GE's last four-axle road freight diesels. The last order, Nos. 560-582, had notches in the cab corners (known as "gull-wing" cabs), also found on Santa Fe's six-axle Dash 8s.

    Dash 8-40BW: AT&SF 500-582

Dash 8-40C

The cab roof on the Dash 8-40C matches the roof and housings behind it. This is a former C&NW unit. *Jeff Wilson*

The 4,000-hp Dash 8-40C has a standard cab and shares the same body as the final C39-8s. The cab roof is the same height as the dynamic brake housing on the hood behind it. A spotting feature distinguishing it from the C39 is on the right side, where two air reservoirs are located in a notch at the top of the fuel tank. Starting in August 1990, the dynamic brake grilles were relocated to the sides of the hood directly behind the cab.

 Dash 8-40C: C&NW 8501-8577; CR 6025-6049; CSX 7500-7646; NS 8689-8763; UP 9100-9355

Dash 8-40CM

The Dash 8-40CM is a full-cowl version of the Dash 8, with the Draper Taper behind the cab. *John C. Benson*

The Dash 8-40CM is a Canadian-only version of the Dash 8-40, featuring a full-cowl body with the same behind-cab taper found on earlier Canadian Electro-Motive/GMD and Alco/MLW locomotives. These 4,000-hp locomotives ride on MLW-designed Dofasco trucks, which have a distinctively tighter axle spacing than GE's standard trucks.

 Dash 8-40CM: BC Rail 4601-4626; CN 2400-2454; QNS&L 401-403

Dash 8-40CW, Dash 8-41CW

Conrail No. 6161 is a Dash 8-40CW, with a wide-nose cab and the brakewheel at the rear of the left side.

General Electric

The North American safety cab became the norm for most diesels by the early 1990s, and more Dash 8-40CWs were built than the standard-cab version. Behind the cab the body was the same as the standard Dash 8-40C, except for the brake wheel, which was relocated to the rear of the left side. Santa Fe's have the "gull-wing" tapers in the cab roof. The Dash 8-41CW represented a horsepower boost to 4,150. The first of these were externally identical to Dash 8-40CWs; later '41s had five steps (instead of four) at the corners of the locomotive.

 Dash 8-40CW: AT&SF 800-926; CR 6050-6265 (and LMS Leasing 700-759); CSX 7650-7929; UP 9356-9405
 Dash 8-41CW: AT&SF 927-951; UP 9406-9559

Dash 8-44CW

The Dash 8-44CW has a thicker radiator section than the Dash 8-40CW. CSX classifies them as C44-9Ws.

John C. Benson

CSX received all 53 Dash 8-44CWs built (but classifies them as C44-9Ws). The 4,400-hp locomotives were actually delivered after the first Dash 9s. The Dash 8-44CW looks like a Dash 8-40CW, but has a thicker radiator section to house the split cooling system that was first introduced on late Dash 8-40CWs.

 Dash 8-44CW: CSX 9000-9052

Dash 9-44CW

You can see the tapered "gull-wing" cab roof on BNSF Dash 9-44CW No. 5320. It was first used on Santa Fe Dash 8s. *Jeff Wilson*

The first Dash 9 locomotive introduced by GE was the extremely successful 4,400-hp Dash 9-44CW. Continued improvements in the 16-cylinder 7FDL engine, advanced microprocessor controls for wheel slip control and other functions, an improved cooling system, and new bolsterless HiAd trucks marked the Dash 9 series. The Dash 9-44CW is 30" longer than the Dash 8-44CW. Options include number boards mounted on either the nose or above the windshield. CN's have a teardrop taper at the outside corner of each windshield. Santa Fe and BNSF units have the gull-wing cab roofs also used on Dash 8s.

Dash 9-44CW: AT&SF 600-699; BC Rail 4645-4654; BNSF 700-799, 960-1123, 4000-4199, 4300-5529, 5370-5499; CN 2200-2205, 2523-2726; C&NW 8601-8730; QNS&L 404-414; SP 8100-8200; UP 9700-9739

Dash 9-44CWL

BC Rail No. 4642 is one of four Dash 9-44CWL locomotives on the railroad. *John C. Benson*

Built for Canadian lines only, the Dash 9-44CWL is 6" longer than a standard Dash 9 and has a distinctive Canadian cab with a four-piece windshield and a different nose shape. In other respects it looks like a Dash 9-44CW.

Dash 9-44CWL: BC Rail 4641-4644; CN 2500-2522

Dash 9-40C

Norfolk Southern was the only railroad to order the standard-cab Dash 9-40C. *John C. Benson*

GE built the 4,000-hp Dash 9-40C, which came out two years after the Dash 9-44CW made its debut, for the Norfolk Southern, which preferred locomotives with a lower horsepower rating. The locomotives were the last domestic conventional-cab locomotives built. Other than the cab, the Dash 9-40C looks like a Dash 9-44CW and rides on GE's bolsterless HiAd trucks. The locomotives are known as "top hats" for the air conditioner atop the cab.

Dash 9-40C: NS 8764-8888

Dash 9-40CW

Norfolk Southern's Dash 9-40CWs, such as No. 9455, are externally the same as the Dash 9-44CW. *Jeff Wilson*

Norfolk Southern finally opted for North American cabs beginning in 1996, ordering 4,000-hp versions of the otherwise identical Dash 9-44CW. The Dash 9-40CW uses the same engine and mechanical equipment as the '44, but the lower horsepower rating saves fuel and engine wear, and NS felt the higher horsepower wasn't needed for its heavy-haul operations. The locomotives were made to be convertible to higher horsepower, and beginning in 2013 the locomotives were converted to 4,400 hp operation.

Dash 9-40CW: NS 8889-9978

AC4400CW

The large inverter cabinet behind the left side of the cab, as on Union Pacific No. 6724, is the key in spotting the AC4400CW. *John C. Benson*

General Electric began offering an AC-traction-motor version of the Dash 9-44C in 1994. The key spotting feature is a large cabinet on the running board behind the left side of the cab. The cabinet houses the inverters and circuitry that "chop" the DC power to three-phase AC for the traction motors. New on the right side are louvers under the cab for the air conditioner. GE's new steerable trucks were an option from 1996 on, marked by inverted V-shaped brackets around the middle axle on each sideframe, but HiAd trucks were used on most locomotives.

AC4400CW: BNSF 5600-5717, 5838-5840; CP 8500-8580, 8600-8655, 9500-9683, 9700-9740, 9750-9784, 9800-9840; Cartier 18-29; C&NW 8801-8835; CEFX 1001-1059; CSX 1-599, 5101-5122, 9100-9120; FMex 4500-4574; FerO 1058, 1059; FSRR 4400-4437; FvrM 2600-2674; GECX 4000-4009; KCS 2000-2049; QNS&L 415-421; SP 100-378; UP 5554-5694, 5700-6081, 6430-6699, 6738-6887, 6995-6999, 7080-7297, 9997-9999

ES44AC, ES44C4

UP ES44AC has six tall power assembly doors (at the flag) and a larger radiator than the AC4400CW. *Jeff Wilson*

The ES44—known as the Evolution series, or GEVO—was designed to meet EPA Tier 2 emissions limits using a new (GEVO) 12-cylinder engine. The ES44AC looks like an AC4400CW (and rides on the same frame), but the GEVO has a wider, longer, stepped radiator housing. It only has six tall hood doors (for the 12-cylinder engine) compared to eight on the AC4400, and a different arrangement of side air-intake openings. GE's Hi-Ad trucks are standard, but steerable trucks are an option. Other options include nose- or high-mounted lights and number boards. Variations include the ES44C4, which only has four traction motors (A1A-A1A). On these locomotives, microprocessors control air cylinders on the truck to adjust the weight on drive axles. Another variation is the ES44CH (for "heavy"), has additional crontrols to provide more tractive effort at low speeds.

ES44AC: BNSF 5718-6438; Cartier 301, 302; CN 2800-2983; CP 8700-8960, 9350-9379; Cemex 81; CREX 1201-1215, 1301-1350, 1401-1435, 1501-1525; FMex 4600-4699; Ferrosur 4700-4722; IAIS 500-516; KCS 4680-4709, 4765-4869; KCSdeM 4650-4679, 4710-4764, 4870-4894; NS 8000-8168; SVTX 1912, 1982, 1986; UP 5248-5352, 5353-5553, 7345-7529, 7600-8051
ES44C4: BNSF 6500-7199, 7921-8399; FEC 800-823
ES44AH: CSX 700-799, 3000-3249; UP 8052-8267

AC6000CW, AC4000/6000CW

The AC6000CW has a massive rear radiator overhanging the sides and a large cabinet for the AC inverters on the left side behind the cab. *General Electric*

Union Pacific No. 7316 is a convertible AC4000/6000CW, identifiable by its single exhaust stack. *Jeff Wilson*

The 6,000-hp AC6000 gets its additional power from GE's new 7HDL engine, which was developed specifically for this locomotive. The AC6000CW is distinguished by its massive rear radiator wings that overhang the rear platform and by the running board on the right side, which is elevated to clear the relocated air reservoirs. The AC6000CW is also almost three feet longer than the AC4400CW. After initial problems with the new engine, the Union Pacific received a group of AC4000/6000CWs ("convertibles") delivered with 4,400-hp engines designed to be swapped out later for the 6,000-hp engine. This was never done, however. The AC6000CW can be spotted by its twin square exhaust stacks (convertibles have a single stack). All ride on GE steerable trucks.

AC6000CW: CSX 600-699, 5000-5016; UP 7000-7009 (later 7500-7509), 7510-7579
AC4000/6000CW: UP 7010-7079, 7300-7335

ES44DC, ES40DC

BNSF No. 7451 is an ES44DC. *Keith Thompson*

The ES44DC is the DC-traction-motor version of the Evolution series. The lower price tag compared to the AC version appealed to some railroads, especially for fast freight and general service. The ES44DC is nearly identical in appearance to the AC version, even keeping the inverter cabinets on the left side (but the panel arrangement is different). CN's ES44DCs have "teardrop" windows that angle down at the outside edges, with a matching cutaway in the nose. As with previous generations of GE diesels, Norfolk Southern ordered their ES locomotives rated at 4,000 hp, hence the ES40DC (they're visually identical); these were converted to 4,400 hp in 2014. CSX also has the '40 version.

    ES44DC: BNSF 7200-7920; CN 2220-2344; CSX 5200-5501
    ES40DC: CSX 5200-5501; NS 7500-7719

P40DC (Genesis 1, AMD-103)

The P40 introduced a monocoque, streamlined body to Amtrak's passenger locomotive fleet. *General Electric*

The distinctive P40DC (also called Genesis 1, AMD-103, or Dash 8-40BWH), features a monocoque body that eliminates the need for a traditional frame and lowers the locomotive weight. It has a low profile (14" shorter than the F40PH), important for clearance in the Northeast. The P40 has a slanted front with no conventional nose, giving it a very European appearance. The model also introduced new bolsterless trucks with hydraulic shock absorbers. Mechanically, the 4,000-hp locomotive followed the designs of GE's contemporary Dash 8-40 line.

    P40DC: Amtrak 800-845

ET44AC, ET44C4

Canadian National ET44AC No. 3045 shows the "hump" above the exhaust manifold ahead of the radiator.

Cody Grivno

GE introduced its Tier-4-compliant ET44AC in 2012, and it is GE's current-production model. It's 16" longer than the previous ES44AC, and has a larger radiator and a pronounced elevated area ("hump") on the roof above the exhaust manifold directly in front of the radiator. The air intake grilles are also arranged differently. As with the earlier ES locomotives, the ET is also available with A1A-A1A trucks as the ET44C4 and in a heavy version as the ET44AH.

    ET44AC: CN 3000-3126; CSX 3250-3424; NS 3600-3646
    ET44C4: BNSF 3764-3999
    ET44AH: UP 2570-2769

P42DC, P32AC-DM

Amtrak No. 141 is a P42DC, with most differences internal compared to the earlier P40. *Jeff Wilson*

Almost identical externally to the P40DC, the P42 is missing the rear hostler's window. It represents an increase to 4,200 hp, and also includes more advanced microprocessor and diagnostic controls. The similar P32AC-DM is rated at 3,200 hp, has AC traction motors, and can operate either by its diesel engine or drawing power from an outside third rail—similar to EMD's FL9 of 1960.

    P42DC: Amtrak 1-207; VIA 900-920
    P32AC-DM: Amtrak 700-717; ConnDOT 228-231; Metro North 201-231

— CHAPTER SEVEN —

The American Locomotive Co. was North America's second-largest manufacturer of steam locomotives. The company began making the transition to internal combustion early, building diesel locomotives in the 1920s while continuing to build steam locomotives (which it did until 1948).

The 1,600-hp RS-3 was Alco's all-time best-selling road switcher, with more than 1,200 built from 1949 to 1956. Rock Island No. 492, built in 1951, operated in commuter service. *Rock Island*

Alco had more success with diesels than other steam builders, and also sold more early switchers than other builders. However, after the late 1930s Alco never seriously challenged Electro-Motive's No. 1 ranking, and after years of struggles the company ceased building locomotives in 1969.

Early diesels

By 1929, Alco had moved all locomotive production to its Schenectady, N.Y. plant. Alco also owned Canadian subsidiary Montreal Locomotive Works (MLW), which built locomotives under license to Alco.

Alco partnered with General Electric and Ingersoll-Rand in the early 1920s to build the first mass-produced diesel-electric locomotives. A 300-hp design built by Alco-GE-IR in 1925 is credited as the first successful diesel-electric switcher, with similar locomotives sold to Central of New Jersey, Baltimore & Ohio, and Lehigh Valley. Many other similar locomotives were built over the next 10 years.

After these early boxcabs, Alco acquired engine manufacturer McIntosh & Seymour in 1929 and began building its own line of switchers. These followed what would become the standard basic design for switchers, with an end cab, a long hood enclosing the engine and generator, and walkways on either side of the hood.

Early Alco switchers were known as high hoods (HH prefix), with the hood as tall as the cab roof to accommodate the McIntosh & Seymour model 531 engine. The introduction of the S-1 and S-2 switchers in 1939 refined the appearance, with a shorter hood (housing the newer 539 engine) with cab windows above it. Alco switchers have a distinctive appearance, with a steeply rounded cab roof and a hood that doesn't taper as it meets the cab. Model numbers on HH locomotives reflect horsepower; later S switchers have arbitrary numbers.

Passenger diesels

Electro-Motive got the jump on Alco with passenger-service diesels integrated with trains in the early and mid-1930s, but Alco answered with power cars for the Gulf, Mobile & Northern *Rebel*, which had a shovel-nose appearance similar to the Burlington's Winton-powered *Zephyr*.

Alco's first stand-alone passenger diesel was the DL-103b in January 1940, using twin 538 engines and riding on six-wheel trucks with unpowered center idler axles (A1A). A significant redesign resulted in the similar-appearing (but mechanically upgraded, with the newer 539 engine) DL-109 by 1941.

Alco's PA passenger diesels represented a major design change from the DL-109. Introduced in 1946, the PA-1 had a single 16-cylinder 244 engine but still rode on A1A-A1A trucks. The PAs had distinctive noses with grilled headlight casings, and the noses (and locomotives themselves) were longer than the four-axle freight FAs. Cabless boosters were classified PBs.

Alco's early (pre-World War II) passenger diesels were known simply by their Alco specification numbers (DL-) rather than a model designation (such as PA). The "PA" designations appeared after the locomotives were in production and were retroactively applied; the DL passenger units were never given model designations.

Freight cab units

Wartime production restrictions gave Alco a late start on its carbody freight designs. Alco's first experimental cab locomotive, nicknamed "Black Maria" (see page 21) was an A-B-A set built in late 1945 using the Alco 241 engine. Problems with the 241 led to Alco's shelving these units and adopting the 244-engined FAs, which had been in concurrent development.

The FA introduced Alco's distinctive blunt-faced nose with grilled headlight housing, with a nose shorter than Alco's passenger PAs. Each FA (and cabless FB booster) had a single 244 engine and rode on four-wheel trucks. Though FA sales didn't come close to matching EMD's F units, more than

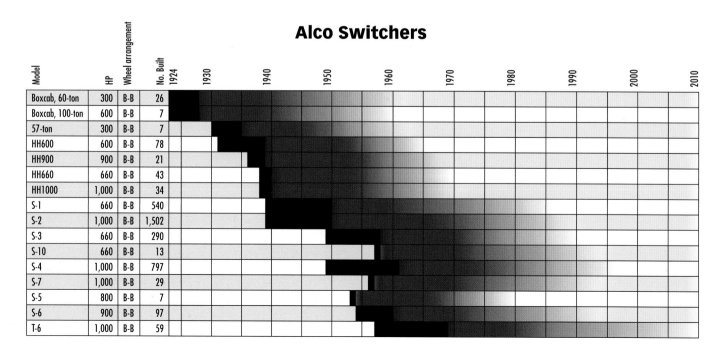

Alco Switchers

Model	HP	Wheel arrangement	No. Built	1924	1930	1940	1950	1960	1970	1980	1990	2000	2010
Boxcab, 60-ton	300	B-B	26										
Boxcab, 100-ton	600	B-B	7										
57-ton	300	B-B	7										
HH600	600	B-B	78										
HH900	900	B-B	21										
HH660	660	B-B	43										
HH1000	1,000	B-B	34										
S-1	660	B-B	540										
S-2	1,000	B-B	1,502										
S-3	660	B-B	290										
S-10	660	B-B	13										
S-4	1,000	B-B	797										
S-7	1,000	B-B	29										
S-5	800	B-B	7										
S-6	900	B-B	97										
T-6	1,000	B-B	59										

They weren't Alco's best sellers, but PAs were arguably Alco's most popular locomotives among railfans. *Fred Mathews*

1,100 FAs were built, making them a common sight on railroads across the country.

Although designed as freight units, FAs (as with EMD Fs) could be equipped with steam generators. These versions were classed "FPA" (or FPB).

Road switchers

Alco was a pioneer in hood unit road diesels, and its RS-1 of 1941 is credited as being the first true road switcher. It had a longer frame with a cab set inward between a high nose and long hood, and it rode on AAR type B road trucks. Even though the locomotive was designed for branchline and light road duty, the design set the pattern for heavier, more-powerful diesels to come.

A common spotting feature of early RS units is the exhaust stack. Early Alco road switchers were built with air-cooled turbochargers, indicated by the stack crosswise to the hood. Problems with this turbocharger led to the adoption of a water-cooled turbo, which required a stack placed lengthwise

on the hood. Most air-cooled turbos were eventually replaced with water-cooled versions.

Through 1966, four-axle Alcos rode on AAR type B road trucks. Freight six-axle A1A (center axle unpowered) Alcos used single-drop-equalizer trucks with a short wheelbase (10'-5") and even axle spacing; units with all axles powered used a trimount double-equalized truck with uneven spacing and a longer (12'-6") wheelbase. In 1967 Alco began offering as an option its own distinctive Hi-Ad (high-adhesion) trucks in two- and three-axle versions.

Early model numbers are ambiguous; RS locomotives are four-axle road switchers (B-B), RSD locomotives have six powered axles (C-C), and RSC engines have six axles but only four powered (A1A-A1A). Model numbers don't reflect horsepower, nor do they follow a progression in series. Many were applied after the fact, as Alco initially only used specification numbers (DL-) instead of model numbers.

Alco and GE partnered in marketing road diesels from

Alco Cabs

Model	HP	Wheel arrangement	No. Built	1940	1950	1960	1970	1980	1990	2000	2005
DL-103b	2,000	A1A-A1A	1								
DL-105	2,000	A1A-A1A	2								
DL-107	2,000	A1A-A1A	2								
DL-109	2,000	A1A-A1A	69								
DL-110	2,000	A1A-A1A	4								
PA-1	2,000	A1A-A1A	167								
PB-1	2,000	A1A-A1A	41								
PA-2	2,250	A1A-A1A	81								
PB-2	2,250	A1A-A1A	8								
FA-1	1,500	B-B	433								
FB-1	1,500	B-B	249								
FA-2	1,600	B-B	341								
FB-2	1,600	B-B	209								
FPA-2	1,600	B-B	73								
FPB-2	1,600	B-B	33								
FPA-4	1,800	B-B	36								
FPB-4	1,800	B-B	14								

1940 to 1953, when GE dissolved the partnership in preparation for launching its own line of road switchers (although GE continued to supply Alco with electrical components). By that time Alco's sales were dwindling and Baldwin and Fairbanks-Morse were building their last diesels.

Alco's 244 engine, used in all contemporary Alco locomotives except switchers and the RS-1 (which used the 539), was problematic and proving to be a factor in gaining new locomotive sales. A new, more-reliable, more-powerful engine, the 251, had undergone rigorous testing and was the focal point of the new RS-11, RSD-12, and RSD-15 diesels introduced in 1955. These adopted the body style first used on the RSD-7, with taller hoods, a new cab design with steep roof curve, and notches at the upper corners of the hood and nose.

Alco's last push to regain its dwindling market share was the introduction of the Century line of locomotives in 1963. Innovations included transistorized electrical controls, a pressurized engine compartment, improved cooling, and an upgraded 251 engine. Body appearance was revised: The cab front was modified, with the windshield area coming to a point in the middle, extending farther outward than the headlight above it. The hood and nose corners were revised, with smooth transitions replacing the notches.

Four- and six-axle Century locomotives had horsepower ratings from 1,500 to 3,600 hp. The model designations reflected the number of axles (first digit) followed by the first two numbers of the horsepower rating. Thus, the C-424 was a four-axle locomotive rated at 2,400 hp.

The Century line was not enough to save the company (which had officially become Alco Products in 1955). By the mid-1960s, GE had taken over second place in locomotive sales, leaving Alco at No. 3. The company ceased building locomotives in 1969. Alco's design patents went to MLW, which continued building locomotives. Subsequent locomotives received an "M" prefix, then an "HR" prefix (for "high reliability").

Bombardier acquired a major interest in MLW in 1975 (and eventually merged MLW), and continued building locomotives until 1985.

This summary includes Alco units as well as those Montreal Locomotive Works diesels manufactured under license after Alco left the locomotive market.

Alco Early Hoods

Model	HP	Wheel arrangement	No. Built
RS-1	1,000	B-B	353
RSD-1	1,000	C-C	6
RS-2	1,500	B-B	383
RSC-2	1,500	A1A-A1A	70
RS-3	1,600	B-B	1,265
RSC-3	1,600	A1A-A1A	19
RSD-4	1,600	C-C	36
RSD-5	1,600	C-C	167
RSD-7	2,250	C-C	17
RS-10	1,600	B-B	128
RS-11	1,800	B-B	426
RSD-12	1,800	C-C	161
RSD-15	2,400	C-C	87
RS-18	1,800	B-B	351
RSC-13	1,000	A1A-A1A	35
RSC-24	1,400	A1A-A1A	4
RS-23	1,000	B-B	40
RS-27	2,400	B-B	27
RS-32	2,000	B-B	35
RS-36	1,800	B-B	40
C-415	1,500	B-B	26
C-420	2,000	B-B	131
C-424	2,400	B-B	190
C-425	2,500	B-B	91
C-430	3,000	B-B	16
C-628	2,750	C-C	181
C-630	3,000	C-C	133
C-636	3,600	C-C	34
C-855	5,500	B-B+B-B	3
M-630	3,000	C-C	67
M-636	3,600	C-C	100
M-420	2,000	B-B	92
M-420B	2,000	B-B	8
M-420R	2,000	B-B	5
M-424	2,000	B-B	11
HR-412	2,000	B-B	72
HR-616	3,000	C-C	20

60-ton, 100-ton boxcabs

Baltimore & Ohio boxcab No. 1, built in 1925, weighed 60 tons and was rated at 300 hp. *General Electric*

These early boxcabs, produced by the conglomeration of Alco, General Electric, and Ingersoll-Rand, get the credit for being the first mass-produced diesel locomotives. Individual locomotives differed slightly in details, but they shared a common appearance. The 60-tonners were powered by a single six-cylinder diesel rated at 300 hp; the 100-ton models were longer and used a pair of 300-hp engines.

60-ton: CNJ 1000; B&O 1; LV 100; C&NW 1000-1002; Erie 19, 20; RDG 50, 51; DL&W 3001, 3002; (plus industrial users)

100-ton: LI 401, 402; GN 5100; Erie 21, 22; (plus industrial users)

HH600, HH900

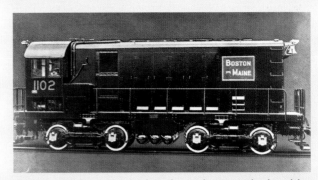

Boston & Maine No. 1102 has the early HH600 body, with sharp angles where the hood meets the nose.
Trains magazine collection

The HH600 (HH for "High Hood") used a six-cylinder, non-turbocharged 531 engine. Industrial designer Otto Kuhler restyled the locomotive in 1934, rounding the joint of the hood sides and nose with a sharp angle where the roof meets the front. This edge became rounded in 1938. The HH900 used a turbocharged 531 engine to increase the horsepower to 900. The HH900 had larger radiator openings in the sides of the hood and roof.

HH600 major buyers: AT&SF; BRC; B&A; B&M; CNJ; C&EI; C&IW; DL&W; EJ&E; IC; LV; NYNH&H; NYC; PT

HH900: BS 81-88; CRI&P 730; EJ&E 402; KCT 50; MT 90-92; PB&NE 207; RDG 40, 41; WRT 50, 51; Y&N 211, 212

HH660, HH1000

The HH660 has a smaller radiator opening (in front of the cab) than the HH1000. It rides on Blunt trucks.
James G. La Vake

Alco used its then-new 538 engine to boost horsepower in the upgraded HH660 and HH1000 switchers. The body styles matched that of late HH600s and HH1000s, with the higher-horsepower model having a slightly larger radiator opening.

HH660: B&M 1162; BC 43; DL&W 409-411; EJ&E 210-212; Erie 302-305; GB&W 101; LV 116; L&N 10; MEC 951, 952; M&StL D939; MILW 1600-1603; NYNH&H 0921-0930; NP 125-127; SP 1001-1003; TC 50; WAB 100, 150

HH1000: AT&SF 2310-2321; ACL 600; BS 89; MRy 201-203; M&StL D539; MILW 1670, 1671; MP 9102

S-1

New York Central No. 85 shows the new hood and cab style introduced on the S-1. *Alco*

The 660-hp S-1, together with the 1,000-hp S-2, replaced the HH line and introduced the basic look that Alco switchers would carry into the 1960s. The S-1 used a new engine, a six-cylinder, non-turbo version of the 539. The locomotives have a lower hood (allowing cab windows above it) compared to HHs and radiator grilles at the end of the hood rather than near the cab. The S-1 has a tall, narrow radiator grille compared to the S-2. Early S-1s have a round radiator fan housing atop the hood; later models have square housings. The S-1 rides on Blunt trucks.

Major buyers: AA, AT&SF, B&O BRC, BS, B&M, CG, CNJ, C&EI, C&NW, CGW, EJ&E, Erie, GM&O, LIRR, L&N, MEC, MP, NC&StL, NYNH&H, NYC, PRR, RDG, SOU, SP&S, TRRA, Union, WAB, WP

S-2

The S-2 has a larger radiator grille (wider than it is tall) compared to the S-1. Note also the cab overhang.
Trains magazine collection

The 1,000-hp S-2 proved to be Alco's most-popular diesel locomotive, with more than 1,500 built. It uses the same six-cylinder 539 engine as the S-1, but it's turbocharged. The locomotive shares the same basic body as the S-1, but the S-2 has a wider radiator opening. The S-2 is equipped with Blunt trucks.

Major buyers: Alton, ATSF, ACL, B&O, BRC, CN, CP, CG, C&O, C&NW, CB&Q, CRI&P, D&H, DL&W, D&RGW, EJ&E, Erie, GTW, GN, GM&O, HB&T, KCT, LV, LIRR, MILW, MP, MCon, NdeM, NYNH&H, NYC, NKP, NP, PRR, RDG, RF&P, SAL, SOU, SP, SP&S, TRRA, URR, UP, WAB, WM

S-3, S-10

The small radiator grille and AAR type A trucks help identify Boston & Maine No. 1184 as an S-3.
Louis A. Marre collection

The S-3 replaced the S-1 as Alco's 660-hp switcher in 1950. The only visual difference is the trucks: S-3s have AAR type A compared to the S-1's distinctive Blunt trucks. It has a non-turbocharged 539 engine. The S-10 is an MLW version of the S-3 built only for the Canadian Pacific. It has a squared-off joint where the roof meets the front, and angled front number boards.

S-3 major buyers: AA, B&M, CN, CP, C&NW, L&N, MEC, NYC, PRR, SP

S-10: CP 6601-6613

S-4, S-7

Delaware & Hudson No. 3048 has the large radiator and AAR trucks common to the S-4. *Philip Miller*

The S-4 took over for the S-2 as Alco's 1,000-hp switcher in 1950, and as with its predecessor it is powered by a turbocharged six-cylinder 539 engine. The key spotting feature is that the S-4 rides on AAR type A trucks, and has the same large shutter openings as the earlier S-2. The S-7 was a Canadian-only version of the S-4, built by MLW and identical in appearance. Canadian National was the only buyer.

S-4 major buyers: AT&SF, B&O, B&M, CN, CP, CV, C&O, C&NW, D&H, Erie, GTW, L&N, MEC, MILW, MT, MCon, NdeM, NYC, NKP, NP, PRR, P&LE, SAL, SP, UP

S-7: CN 8206-8234

S-5, S-6

Northern Pacific No. 750 is an S-6, indicated by the grille on the nose instead of the hood side. *Don Dover*

The 800-hp S-5 and 900-hp S-6 were powered by Alco's 251 engine instead of the 539 engine used on earlier switchers. The S-5 and S-6 were visually identical, and can be distinguished from other Alco switchers by their lack of radiator openings on the sides—the grille was on the front—and their forward-mounted exhaust stack. Alco built two cow/calf sets of S-6 switchers, both for Oliver Mining, and designated them as SSB-9s.

S-5: B&M 860-865; Island Creek Coal 909

S-6 major buyers: BRC, ChP, FdelP, NdeM, NP, SP, WM

T-6

The notched hood corners identify Norfolk & Western Alco switcher No. 29 as a T-6. *Alco*

The last Alco switcher, the T-6, was rated at 1,000 hp from its 251B engine. It had notched corners in the hood, similar to late RS-series road switchers. The locomotives were marketed as transfer locomotives (hence the "T"), and had a higher minimum speed than a standard switcher. The Newburgh & South Shore units were the last diesels built at Schenectady.

Major buyers: Kaiser Steel 1022, 1023; MCon 400; N&SS 1016, 1017; N&W 10-49; PTOr 46, 47; PRR 8424-8429

DL-103b

Rock Island DL-103b No. 624 was unique, with eight rectangular side windows and a combined radiator at the rear. *Louis A. Marre collection*

The 2,000-hp DL-103b, built for the Rock Island, was the first Alco passenger diesel and established the basic appearance of all of the company's Otto Kuhler-designed prewar passenger cabs. Compared to the later DL-109, the DL-103b was longer with wider truck spacing, four windows (instead of three) on either side of the side door, and a different pilot design and roof curvature. It used a pair of turbocharged 538T diesel engines with a combined radiator at the rear, marked by pair of large rectangular grilles at the rear of each side and a pair of fans above it on the roof.

DL-103b: CRI&P 624

DL-105, DL-107

Gulf, Mobile & Ohio No. 272 is a DL-105. *Elliott Kahn; Louis A. Marre collection*

The 2,000-hp DL-105 followed the basic lines of the DL-103b, but was mechanically more advanced, starting with a pair of 539T engines. The only two DL-105s went to the Gulf, Mobile & Ohio. The locomotive was shorter, had two large side radiator grilles (one in the middle, one at the rear), and three windows on each side of the center grille. This styling would continue through the rest of DL passenger production. The GM&O engines had a unique style of single headlights. The DL-107s were virtually identical, but also had an additional lower nose headlight.

DL-105: GM&O 270, 271
DL-107: CRI&P 622, 623

DL-109, DL-110

New Haven operated the largest fleet of DL-109s, using them in both passenger and freight service. *New Haven*

The DL-109 followed the same specifications as the earlier DL-105 and DL-107, but Alco chose not to change the specification number among orders for the locomotive's many buyers. The War Production Board allowed Alco to continue producing the DL-109 during World War II. Only four B units (DL-110s) were built.

DL-109: AT&SF 50; C&NW 5007A; MILW 14A, 14B; CRI&P 621; GM&O 272; NYNH&H 0700-0759; SOU 2904, 6400, 6401
DL-110: AT&SF 50A; SOU 2954, 6425, 6426

PA-1, PB-1

The PA-1 has a distinctive nose and headlight, with a curved trim piece directly behind the cab and screened side openings. *Alco*

Alco's PA-1 and cabless PB-1 booster locomotives represented a radical redesign from earlier DL passenger diesels. A single 16-cylinder 244 engine replaced the twin 539s, and it was housed in a new, shorter body with a distinctive blunt-faced nose. The PAs kept three-axle (A1A) trucks, and were longer (and had longer noses) than freight FAs. PAs earned a reputation for good pulling power even on grades, which was a weakness of Es and DLs. Problems with the 244 engine kept the PAs from more widespread acceptance.

PA-1, PB-1: AT&SF, D&RGW, Erie, GM&O, LV, MKT, MP, NYNH&H, NKP, NYC, PRR, SSW, SP, UP, WAB

PA-2, PB-2

Southern No. 6902 displays the appearance of most PA-2s, with a Far-Air grille and no curved grille trim.

Louis A. Marre collection

Externally the first PA-2s were identical to the PA-1; internally they featured a boost from 2,000 to 2,250 hp. By mid-1950 the curved trim piece behind the cab door was removed and the screened side openings were replaced by a Far-Air grille. Some sources list late PA-2s as PA-3s, but there never was an official PA-3 designation.

PA-2, PB-2: Erie, MKT, MP, NYC, SP, SOU

FA-1, FB-1

Union Pacific No. 1500A is an FA-1, with its radiator grille at the rear of the side. *Union Pacific*

The FA-1 and cabless FB-1 booster were direct competitors to EMD's F3. They used turbocharged 12-cylinder versions of Alco's new 244 diesel engine and were rated at 1,500 hp (the last 21 FA-1s and 16 FB-1s were rated at 1,600 hp). They were built with a rectangular exhaust stack oriented lengthwise on the roof, a characteristic of Alco's original air-cooled turbocharger. These were eventually rebuilt with water-cooled turbos, and the stack was relocated crosswise to the body. The first 36 FAs built had a curved trim strip over the air intake screens behind the cab and headlights mounted several inches down into the nose (see page 221). The trim was eliminated and the headlight made even with the top of the nose on later units. Canadian versions have large winterization hatches on the roof.

FA-1, FB-1: CN, CP, CRI&P, Erie, GN, GB&W, GM&O, LV, MKT, MP, NYNH&H, NYC, PRR, RDG, SLSF, SAL, Soo, SP&S, TC, UP, WAB

FA-2, FB-2

Western Maryland No. 302 shows the forward radiator placement that identifies it as an FA-2. *Western Maryland*

The 1,600-hp FA-2 is two feet longer than the FA-1, with the radiator area moved forward to provide space for an optional steam generator. This gives the FA-2 the spotting feature of the radiator openings on each side being set forward about six feet from the rear of the locomotive, as opposed to FA-1s, which have the opening at the rear. Most FAs built after mid-1951 received Far-Air side grilles; earlier units, above, had wire-covered openings.

FA-2, FB-2: AA, B&O, CN, CP, Erie, GN, L&N, LV, MKT, MP, NdeM, NYC, PRR, SP&S, WAB, WM

FPA-2, FPB-2

Canadian National FPA-2 No. 4084 has a Far-Air grille and the boxy winterization hatch and housings atop the roof found on Canadian versions. *Jim Shaughnessy*

The FPA-2 is an FA-2 equipped with a steam generator for passenger service. Externally the locomotive is identical to the FA-2 except for steam generator vents atop the rear of the roof.
    FPA-2: B&O, CN, CP, FdM, FdP, GN, LV, L&N, MP
    FPB-2: B&O, CN, CP, FdM, LV, MP

FPA-4, FPB-4

The FPA-4 had an additional grille below the usual radiator shutters at the rear of each side. This is Canadian National No. 6792. *Jim Shaughnessy*

The FPA-4 was a special order built by MLW for Canadian National, which wanted FAs for passenger service. Alco's 251B engine gave the FPA-4 1,800 hp, an extra 200 hp compared to the earlier FPA-2. The FPA-4s were built more than two years after the last standard FA order, and can be spotted by an extra radiator opening below the standard one on earlier FAs.
    FPA-4: CN 6760-6793
    FPB-4: CN 6860-6871

RS-1

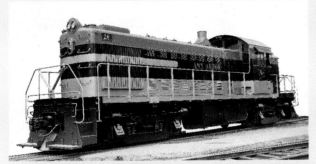

Alco's RS-1 can be identified by its cab roof overhang. Ann Arbor No. 20 has its original lengthwise turbo stack; these were eventually modified. *Alco*

Alco built the first true road switcher, the RS-1, by taking its 1,000-hp S-2 switcher, stretching the frame, putting AAR type B road trucks under it, and adding a short hood on the cab end. The versatile, 539-engined RS-1 remained in production for almost 20 years, the longest production run for a diesel-electric locomotive. It can be distinguished from later RS engines by the overhang on the cab roof fore and aft. Late RS-1s had open filters on the sides instead of louvers.
    Major buyers: AT&N, Alaska, Alton, AT&SF, A&StAB, CNJ, C&O, C&EI, C&WI, C&NW, CRI&P, DSS&A, G&W, GTW, GN, GM&O, IT, KCS, LS&I, LIRR, MILW, M&StL, NdeM, NYNH&H, NYC, NYS&W, NP, PRR, RUT, Soo, SI, SP&S

RSD-1

Number 5702 is one of six RSD-1s purchased by National Railways of Mexico. *C.W. Witbeck*

Alco offered the RS-1 on six-wheel trucks for lightweight branchline service. The locomotive body and frame are the same; in fact, although National of Mexico received the only original North American RSD-1s, several railroads later had standard RS-1s converted to RSD-1s. The total in the chart doesn't include 144 RSD-1s built for the U.S. Army that were exported to Russia during World War II. These locomotives had a different cab shape (sloped sides) than domestic RS-1s.
    RSD-1: NdeM 5700-5705

RS-2

The RS-2 lacked the cab overhang of the RS-1. The angled number boards on No. 209 were an option chosen by Great Northern. *Jeff Wilson collection*

The RS-2 used a 12-cylinder version of the 244 engine to boost horsepower to 1,500, making the RS-2 suitable for mainline service before EMD's Geeps hit the market. The RS-2 cab roof has no overhang as with the RS-1, and the RS-2 lacks the battery boxes atop the walkways (next to the cab) of the later RS-3. The RS-2 also has its fuel filler and gauge in recessed pockets at the bottom of each cab side (the tank was under the cab). All RS-2s were built with air-cooled turbochargers (lengthwise exhaust stack); these were later rebuilt with water-cooled turbos (crosswise stack). The last 31 RS-2s built were rated at 1,600 horsepower.

Major buyers: A&S, A&D, BRC, BS, B&M, CP, C&O, C&NW, CGW, CRI&P, D&H, D&M, EJ&E, Erie, GN, GB&W, GM&O, LS&I, L&NE, LV, MEC, MON, NYNH&H, NYC, OM, ON, SLSF, SAL, SOU, SP&S, T&P, TP&W, UP, Union, WM

RSC-2, RSC-3

Union Pacific D.S. 1187 is an RSC-2, riding on A1A trucks with even axle spacing. The body is identical to an RS-2. *Union Pacific*

The RSC-2 and RSC-3 are an RS-2 and RS-3 riding on three-axle trucks with a center idler axle (A1A-A1A). The locomotive was designed for lower axle loadings on light-rail branch lines. Alco's A1A trucks can be identified by their short wheelbase and even axle spacing compared to the uneven spacing on C-C trucks. Most RSCs were eventually converted to two-axle trucks, making them standard RS-2s and RS-3s. The last five RSC-2s (Seaboard Air Line 1532-1536) were 1,600 hp.

RSC-2: MILW 975-992; SAL 1500-1536; Soo 368-371; UP 1180-1190

RSC-3: PGE 561-568; SAL 1537-1543; Soo 372-374

RS-3

The RS-3, like Northern Pacific 852, had a battery box atop the walkway in front of the cab. This one still has its original air-cooled turbo (lengthwise stack). *Alco*

Five RS-3s, including Western Maryland 192, had both dynamic brakes and a steam generator, resulting in a cab-height short hood. *Louis A. Marre collection*

Alco's best-selling road switcher was the 1,600-hp RS-3, with more than 1,200 built. It can be distinguished from the RS-2 by the battery boxes mounted on the walkway on the short-hood end of the cab. Most late RS-3s (after late 1953) have openings with exposed filters in the sides, which replaced the louvered openings on early models. The most common variation had two vertical filter openings, but some units had a row of square filters even with the top of the radiator louvers. RS-3s built after September 1954 had water-cooled turbochargers, but most earlier units were later retrofitted. Options included dynamic brakes, marked by large vents on the sides of the short hood, and a steam generator, indicated by a rooftop stack and vent in the short hood. Five RS-3s had both, and received a taller (cab-roof-height) nose (four for Western Maryland, above, and one for Pennsy). Rock Island's (see page 111) were used in Chicago commuter service and had an extra box for signal equipment on the walkway.

Major buyers: A&S, B&M, CN, CP, CG, CNJ, CV, C&O, C&NW, CRI&P, CStPM&O, D&W, D&H, DL&W, D&RGW, Erie, FdelP, GTW, GN, GB&W, GM&O, IRR, LS&I, L&HR, LV, L&M, LIRR, L&N, MD&S, MEC, MILW, MP, MKT, NdeM, NYNH&H, NYC, NKP, N&W, NP, OM, ON, PGE, PRR, P&N, P&LE, QNS&L, RDG, RUT, SSW, SAL, Soo, SOU, SP&S, TC, TRRA, T&P, TP&W, WM

RSD-4, RSD-5

Alco's RSD-4 and RSD-5 shared similar bodies. Santa Fe No. 2159 is an RSD-5 built in late 1953. *Santa Fe*

Alco's RSD locomotives have six axles, but unlike RSCs, all axles are powered. The trucks are a drop-equalizer design with uneven axle spacing (needed to clear traction motors facing each other on neighboring axles). Both are rated at 1,600 hp, with the only difference between the two internal (generator). Three Chicago & North Western RSD-5s had steam generators and dynamic braking, resulting in a cab-height short hood. These locomotives were delivered in several hood louver (early) or open-filter (late) configurations.

 RSD-4: AT&SF 2100-2109; CNJ 1601-1614; C&NW 1619, 1620; Kennecott Copper 201; Utah 300-305

 RSD-5: AT&SF 2110-2162; BS 150; C&O 5570-5595; C&NW 1665-1667, 1684-1690; CNJ 1615; FdelP 801-835; MILW 570-575; NdeM 6900, 6901; PRR 8446-8451; SSW 270-272; SP 5294-5307, 5336-5339, 5445-5448, 5494-5507; T&NO 155-176, 185, 186; Utah 306

RSD-7

The RSD-7 was the first Alco road switcher with tall hoods and notched corners for the number boards. *Santa Fe*

The 16-cylinder, 244-engined RSD-7 introduced the tall hoods with notched corners that would be repeated two years later on the four-axle RS-11 and subsequent models. The RSD-7 has a distinctively long nose (all were built with high noses). The first two demonstrators built (later Santa Fe 600, 601) were rated at 2,250 hp, and later engines are 2,400 hp.

 RSD-7: AT&SF 600-611; PRR 8606-8610

RS-11

Norfolk & Western RS-11 No. 378 was built in 1959. The five square filter openings and rooftop housing indicate dynamic brakes. *Alco*

The 1,800-hp RS-11 followed the lead of the RSD-7 in adopting a tall hood. The RS-11 and concurrent RSD-12 and RSD-15 were the first hood units to use the 251 engine. It was also the first Alco hood offered with high or low nose options. Lehigh Valley (page 232), New York Central, and Southern Pacific opted for low noses. Dynamic-brake-equipped engines have five filter openings along the long hood with a hatch and housing on the roof; non-dynamic locomotives lack the housing and the two filters closest to the cab. Schenectady-built RS-11s have notches at the tall hood corners that are not found on MLW-built RS-11s.

 RS-11: D&H, DW&P, EM, FdelP, GB&W, LV, MEC, MP, MCon, NdeM, NYC, NKP, N&W, NP, SAL, SP, TP&W

RSD-12

Southern Pacific No. 7002 is a low-nose RSD-12 equipped with dynamic brakes. *G.W. Hockaday*

The RSD-12 was the low-horsepower partner offered concurrently with the RSD-15. The RSD-12 has a smaller engine (12-cylinder 251B) and is rated at 1,800 hp. Its nose is noticeably shorter than the RSD-7 or RSD-15, and the locomotive was available with a high or low nose.

 RSD-12: C&O 6700-6709; FdeP 509-520, 1502-1508; LS&I 1801-1804; NdeM 7400-7472; NKP 325-333; PRR 8655-8679; SP 7000-7020

RSD-15

The RSD-15 was known as the "alligator" for its long nose. Santa Fe No. 829 was one of 50 on the railroad. *J.J. Young Jr.*

The 2,400-hp RSD-15 is powered by a 16-cylinder 251B engine, and was Alco's answer to the 2,400-hp Fairbanks-Morse Train Master. The RSD-15 can be spotted by its very long nose, which gave them the nickname "alligators." Santa Fe, Southern Pacific, and Cotton Belt (SSW) had low-nose versions. The high-nose versions are identical in appearance to the RSD-7.

    RSD-15: AT&SF 800-849; B&LE 881-886; C&O 6800-6811; PRR 8611-8616; SP 250-252; SSW 5150-5159

RSC-13

The RSC-13 was built by MLW exclusively for Canadian National. *Louis A. Marre collection*

The body of the MLW-built, 1,000-hp RSC-13 resembled an RS-3, but with the hood and nose ends shaped like Century-series hoods. Designed for branch lines, the RSC-13 was powered by a turbocharged 539T engine and rode on A1A (center axle unpowered) trucks built by Dominion Foundries and Steel (DOFASCO), which were also used on the RSC-24. All went to Canadian National.

    RSC-13: CN 1700-1734

RS-10, RS-18

Canadian National No. 3643 is an RS-18. The RS-18 and RS-10 lacked the corner notches of U.S.-built tall-hood RS Alcos. *Canadian National*

The 1,600-hp RS-10 and later 1,800-hp RS-18 are Canadian-only locomotives built by MLW. Internally the RS-10 had the components of an RS-3, with a 244 engine, but it had a tall (cab-height) hood. The RS-18 used a 251B engine like its U.S. contemporary, the RS-11, but its body was identical to the RS-10.

    RS-10: CN 3058-3065, 3074-3093, 3800-3822; CP 8462-8482, 8557-8600; ON 1400-1403; PGE 579-586

    RS-18: Arnaud 901-911; CN 3100-3129, 3615-3745, 3830-3893; CP 8729-8800; Cartier 101-108; Int'l Nickel 208-2, -3, -4; PGE 587-599, 614-630; R&S 24, 25

RSC-24

The diminutive RSC-24 looks like a switcher, but with a stubby nose. *MLW*

Built by MLW only for Canadian National, the 1,400-hp, 251-engined RSC-24 rode on DOFASCO A1A trucks. It was designed for branchline use on light rail. The locomotive looked like a six-axle switcher, but with a stubby short hood/nose that housed an electrical cabinet.

    RSC-24: CN 1800-1803

RS-23

The MLW RS-23 has a taller hood than contemporary Alco switchers. *Greg McDonnell*

The 1,000-hp MLW RS-23 looks like a switcher, but it's designed as a light road switcher and transfer engine (hence the "RS" prefix). It has a taller hood than contemporary Alco switchers, with a pronounced step up on the walkway. It's powered by the 251D engine. Canadian Pacific was the major buyer.

RS-23: CP 8013-8046; S&L 200-202; Texas Gulf Sulphur 3457-01 to -03.

RS-32, RS-36

New York Central No. 8022 is an RS-32. It does not have dynamic brakes. *Alco*

The 2,000-hp RS-32 and 1,800-hp RS-36 shared the same body, with two groups of three filter openings on the hood (compared to five openings on the RS-11). The RS-32 has a 251C engine and the RS-36 a 251B (both 12-cylinder). All RS-32s had low noses; both models had longer noses than the RS-27.

RS-32: NYC 8020-8044; SP 7300-7309

RS-36: Apache 700, 800, 900; C&NW 904; D&H 5012-5023; TC 301-305; A&D 1, 2; NKP 407-412, 865-875

RS-27

The RS-27 has a stubby nose and a different pattern of air-intake filters compared to other RS locomotives. The two small openings in the middle of the hood are for the dynamic brakes. *Union Pacific*

The 2,400-hp RS-27 didn't prove popular, but it led the four-axle horsepower race until the GE U25B hit the market. The RS-27 used a 16-cylinder version of the 251B engine. The extra space needed for the engine pushed the cab forward, giving it a short nose compared to the RS-11, -32, and -36.

RS-27: C&NW 900-903; GB&W 310; PRR 2400-2414; Soo 415, 416; UP 675-678

C-415

Rock Island's Century 415 diesels had medium-height cabs and AAR type B trucks. *Alco*

Alco offered the distinctive tall-center-cab C-415 as a light road switcher/heavy-duty switch engine. It was powered by an eight-cylinder 251F engine. Three cab heights were offered: high, medium, and tight-clearance. Some were delivered with AAR type B trucks (above); others received Alco's Hi-Ad trucks.

C-415: C&C 701; CW 684; CRI&P 415-424; MCon 701; SP 2400-2409; SP&S 100, 101

C-420

The C-420 has a long nose with no notches, and has the new style of cab front found on Century locomotives. The three middle filters indicate dynamic brakes. *Alco*

The 2,000-hp Century 420 used a 12-cylinder, 251C engine and had a longer nose than any other Century locomotive. Locomotives with dynamic brakes have a series of screened openings across the top of each side. Early models had handrail stanchions mounted to the walkway, and those built in December 1965 and later had stanchions mounted to the side sill. Fuel tank sizes varied, with some rounded and some having flat sides. The Long Island and two Monon locomotives had high noses with steam generators; the Norfolk & Western's also had high noses. All had AAR type B trucks.

C-420: EM 600-602; L&HR 21-29; LIRR 200-229; L&N 1300-1315; LV 404-415; MEx 63; MON 501-518; NKP 578; N&W 413-420; P&N 2000, 2001; SAL 110-136; Mexico DOT 7123-10, -11; TC 400, 401

C-425

The only visual difference between the C-425 and C-424 is the protruding area on the hood above the radiator opening, shown here on Spokane, Portland & Seattle C-425 No. 315. *Alco*

The 2,500-hp C-425 differed from the C-424 by the use of a 16-cylinder 251C engine powering a larger main generator. The two are nearly identical, but the C-425 has a boxy protrusion in the hood between the radiator opening on the side and the rooftop radiator overhang. All rode on AAR type B trucks.

C-425: C&NW 401-404; EL 2451-2462; NYNH&H 2550-2559; N&W 1000-1016; PRR 2416-2446; SP&S 310-327

C-424

Canadian Pacific No. 4237 displays the short nose and slight radiator overhang of the C-424. *Jim Hediger*

The 2,400-hp C-424 used a larger (16-cylinder 251B) engine than the C-420. The resulting longer hood moved the cab forward, giving the C-424 a shorter nose than the C-420. The larger engine required a bigger radiator, which bulged out slightly from each side at the rear of the hood. Early C-424s had number boards that extended from the radiator over the end. By 1964 these had been replaced by notched corners. All rode on AAR trucks.

C-424: BRC 600-605; CN 3200-3240; CP 4200-4250; EL 2401-2415; EM 500; GB&W 311-314; NdeM 8100-8144; PRR 2415; RDG 5201-5210; SP&S 300-306; TP&W 800-801; WAB 8900-8906

C-430

A prominent aftercooler bulge just behind the cab is the key spotting feature on the C-430. Green Bay & Western No. 315 rides on Alco Hi-Ad trucks. *Stan Mailer*

The 3,000-hp C-430 resembles a C-425, but it has a distinctive aftercooler bulge (with grille sides) that protrudes upward from the roof immediately behind the cab. Internally the C-430 used a 16-cylinder 251E engine to drive an alternator (AC) instead of a generator, similar to high-horsepower locomotives from EMD and GE. All C-430s but the Reading's had Alco Hi-Ad trucks, as shown on the Green Bay & Western engine above.

C-430: GB&W 315; NYC 2050-2059; RDG 5211, 5212; SCL 1275-1277

C-628

Atlantic Coast Line C-628 No. 2000 displays the smooth hood lines common to the model. *Alco*

The 2,750-hp C-628 has a relatively smooth hood/roof line, distinguishing it from the C-630 and C-636. Ten National of Mexico locomotives were equipped with steam generators, which were located directly behind the cab. Norfolk & Western's engines have high noses. All rode on standard tri-mount trucks.

C-628: ACL 2000-2010; D&H 601-618; ChP 901-904; FdelP 601-610; LV 625-632; L&N 1400-1414; MON 400-408 NdeM 8300-8331; N&W 1100-1129; PRR 6300-6314; SP 4845-4873

C-630

A rooftop aftercooler box and small protrusion above the radiator intake mark Chesapeake & Ohio No. 2102 as a C-630. *Jim Shaughnessy*

The C-630 can be identified by an aftercooler housing that protrudes from the roof several feet behind the cab. The C-630 was the first locomotive built with an alternator instead of a generator. The Norfolk & Western ordered high-hood versions, and they rode atop trucks from traded-in Fairbanks-Morse H-24-66s. Hi-Ad trucks were used on C&O (above) and some Reading locomotives.

C-630: ACL 2011-2013; CN 2000-2043; CP 4500-4507; C&O 2100-2103; L&N 1425-1432; N&W 1130-1139; PGE 701-704; PRR 6315-6329; RDG 5300-5311; SP 7800-7814; UP 2900-2909

C-636

The C-636 has a step in the hood sides where the radiator area gets wider. Spokane, Portland & Seattle No. 335 rides on Alco's Hi-Ad trucks. *Alco*

The 3,600-hp C-636 resembles the C-630, with its prominent aftercooler box on the roof, but the C-636 has an additional boxy housing protruding from the roof in front of the radiator and a step out in the hood sides at the front of the radiator. It used a 16-cylinder 251F engine. All C-636 diesels were equipped with Hi-Ad trucks.

C-636: IC 1100-1105; M-K 5401-5403; PC 6330-6344; SP&S 330-335, 340-343

C-855, C-855B

The C-855 had a pair of 251C engines and rode on four two-axle trucks. Union Pacific No. 61 was one of only three built. *Alco*

The C-855 was Alco's answer to Union Pacific's early 1960s request for twin-engine locomotives. Only three were built: two standard-cab-equipped locomotives and one cabless C-855B. The 86-foot-long, 5,500-hp C-855 amounted to two C-425s mounted on a long frame, with two turbocharged 16-cylinder 251C engines. Each end rode on a pair of two-axle trucks connected by a span bolster, giving the C-855 a B+B-B+B wheel arrangement.

C-855: UP 60, 61; C-855B: UP 60B

M-420, M-420R, M-424, HR-412

The openings behind the central air intake on BC Rail M-420 No. 641 indicate that this locomotive has dynamic brakes. *John C. Benson*

Canadian National 2582 is a Bombardier HR-412. The radiator grille is taller compared to an M-420. CN was the only customer. *Trains magazine collection*

The 2,000-hp M-420 (often labeled M-420W because of the wide nose), built by MLW, had a 12-cylinder 251 engine. It features the wide-nose comfort cab and rides on high-adhesion (MLW called them ZWT, for "zero weight transfer") trucks. The BC Rail units have dynamic brakes, indicated by openings along the upper sides of each hood behind the central air intake. Eight cabless M-420Bs were built, all for BCR. The five M-420R locomotives built for Providence & Worcester are identical to standard M-420s except for their AAR type B trucks, which came from traded-in locomotives. The M-424, built after Bombardier acquired MLW, was a 2,400-hp unit that was externally nearly identical to the M-420 but with a different air intake behind the cab. All went to Mexico. The final version of this locomotive was the 2,400-hp Bombardier HR-412 (for "high reliability, 4 axles, 12 cylinders"). It had a taller side radiator grille than the M-420. Canadian National was the only buyer.

M-420: BCR 640-647, CN 2500-2579, FdelE M001, M002
M-420B: BCR 681-688
M-420R: P&W 2001-2005
M-424: NdeM, FCP
HR-412: CN 2580-2589

M-630, M-630W, M-636, M-640

Canadian Pacific No. 4559 is an MLW M-630 built in 1971. It rides on MLW-design trucks. *Louis A. Marre collection*

Montreal Locomotive Works continued to build these six-axle locomotives under license after Alco's demise. The 3,000-hp M-630 and 3,600-hp M-636 are similar to the earlier Alco C-630 and C-636, but the aftercooler housing behind the cab has beveled sides blended to the hood. Both used 16-cylinder versions of the 251E engine. The M-630 has a boxy structure on the roof from the radiator forward to the stack. A wide-nose version, the M-630W, was built for BC Rail. The lone experimental (4,000-hp) M-640 used an 18-cylinder 251F engine. It had thick, wide radiator "wings" at the rear and boxy air intakes on the roof behind the cab.

M-630: CP 4508-4512, 4550-4573; NdeM 8600-8619; PGE 705-722
M-630W: BCR 723-730
M-636: CN 2300-2339, CP 4700-4743; FdelP: 651-666; Cartier 71-76, 81-85
M-640: CP 4744

HR-616

Canadian National No. 2100 is an HR-616, featuring a cowl body and Draper Taper. Note the large radiator grilles at the rear of the side. *Canadian National*

Bombardier's version of the M-630 had a wide nose, MLW-design trucks, and cowl body with the "Draper Taper" found on other EMD, GE, and MLW locomotives. The 3,000-hp unit was powered by a 16-cylinder engine and had large radiator openings at the rear of each side. Canadian National was the lone customer.

HR-616: CN 2100-2119

CHAPTER EIGHT

Baldwin and Lima-Hamilton

Baldwin, the country's largest steam locomotive builder, was no stranger to electric and internal-combustion locomotives. It was, however, slow to offer a standard line of diesel road engines. Baldwin's late entry to the market and slow reactions to changing needs of railroads doomed the company to also-ran status as railroads began rapidly replacing steam with diesels in the 1940s.

Baldwin's best-known diesels are its sharknose cab units, in particular the DR-4-4-15 and RF-16 freight units that became favorites among railfans. Here DR-4-4-15 demonstrator 6001 and a booster pause at Des Moines, Iowa, on the Wabash in 1950. *Louis A. Marre collection*

Baldwin and Westinghouse had collaborated on building several large electric locomotives in the early 1900s, mainly for the New Haven (including the EP-1, EP-2, EF-1, EF-3, and several steeple-cab switchers) but also for Great Northern (Z-1 boxcabs) and others. These locomotives were built at Baldwin's Eddystone, Pa. (Philadelphia) plant, which, along with steam, would soon provide manufacturing space for internal-combustion locomotives as well.

Early locomotives and switchers

Baldwin built several small gas-mechanical industrial locomotives in the 1910s and '20s. The company then built a pair of experimental boxcab diesel-electric locomotives in 1925 and 1929, followed by a 660-hp and a 900-hp switcher in 1937 and another 660-hp switcher in 1939.

In 1939 Baldwin launched its line of switching locomotives, calling it the VO line (named after the De La Verne VO diesel engine used) for production models. The number corresponds to the horsepower, either 660 (powered by a six-cylinder engine) or 1000 (eight-cylinder). Starting in 1945, Baldwin abandoned the VO for its 606NA (six-cylinder) and 608NA

(eight-cylinder) engines. The resulting new line of switchers were labeled as DS (diesel switcher), followed by the number of powered axles, number of total axles, and a number to indicate horsepower.

Baldwin's final line of switchers used turbocharged versions of the 606 and 608 engines, and were designated by an S (for switcher) followed by a number indicating horsepower (the 800-hp S-8 and 1,200-hp S-12).

Baldwin's switchers shared a common appearance distinct from other builders. They had tall hoods with squared corners, radiator openings on the front (nose), and cabs with a shallow roof angle (all similar to the company's road-switchers as well).

Switchers and road diesels used Westinghouse traction motors and electrical equipment, which helped give Baldwins a reputation for being excellent lugging locomotives (albeit with temperamental engines). Westinghouse left the railroad electrical equipment market in 1953, and although Baldwin had stockpiled enough Westinghouse equipment to last for a year or two after that, the company had to redesign locomotive frames and other equipment to fit the new GE generators and traction motors used thereafter.

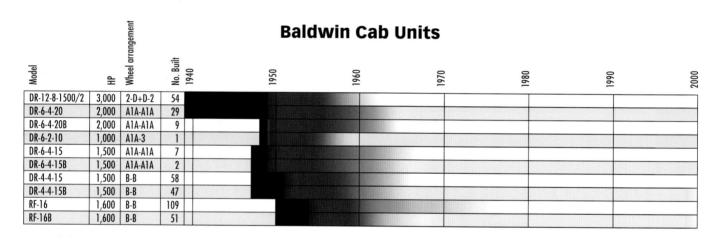

Baldwin Cab Units

Model	HP	Wheel arrangement	No. Built
DR-12-8-1500/2	3,000	2-D+D-2	54
DR-6-4-20	2,000	A1A-A1A	29
DR-6-4-20B	2,000	A1A-A1A	9
DR-6-2-10	1,000	A1A-3	1
DR-6-4-15	1,500	A1A-A1A	7
DR-6-4-15B	1,500	A1A-A1A	2
DR-4-4-15	1,500	B-B	58
DR-4-4-15B	1,500	B-B	47
RF-16	1,600	B-B	109
RF-16B	1,600	B-B	51

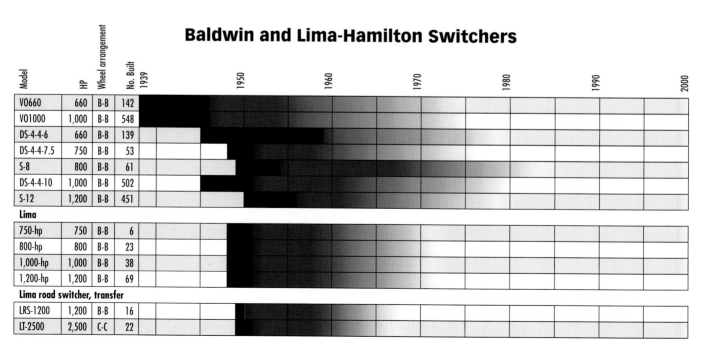

Baldwin and Lima-Hamilton Switchers

Model	HP	Wheel arrangement	No. Built
VO660	660	B-B	142
VO1000	1,000	B-B	548
DS-4-4-6	660	B-B	139
DS-4-4-7.5	750	B-B	53
S-8	800	B-B	61
DS-4-4-10	1,000	B-B	502
S-12	1,200	B-B	451
Lima			
750-hp	750	B-B	6
800-hp	800	B-B	23
1,000-hp	1,000	B-B	38
1,200-hp	1,200	B-B	69
Lima road switcher, transfer			
LRS-1200	1,200	B-B	16
LT-2500	2,500	C-C	22

Baldwin's first answer to EMD E units was a pair of 2,000-hp passenger demonstrators, Nos. 2000 and 2001. *Louis A. Marre collection*

Road diesels

Baldwin didn't produce any road diesels before World War II and, like Alco, was hampered by War Production Board restrictions that allowed only EMD to build road locomotives (Baldwin and Alco were limited to switchers). Baldwin's first attempt at a cab diesel came in 1943 with an experimental 6,000-hp unit (page 20). The 12-axle locomotive was designed to use eight V-8 diesel engines—one for each powered axle—but only four were initially installed, and the locomotive was stored shortly after leaving the factory. The similar-appearing Centipede locomotives followed two years later, and although several production models were built, they suffered from many mechanical problems (as well as difficult maintenance access).

A pair of demonstrator passenger cabs, Nos. 2000 and 2001, began touring the country in early 1945. Similar in design to

E units, they each had a pair of 8-cylinder engines, were rated at 2,000 hp, and rode on A1A trucks (center axle unpowered). They were streamlined with conventional noses, although no production models were built this way.

Early production cabs had low sloped noses, known as the "babyface" cab. Later cab engines (after 1948) had Baldwin's distinctive shark-nose styling, designed by Raymond Loewy.

Production passenger models included 2,000-hp twin-engine versions with shark noses (Pennsylvania) or babyface noses, and single-engine (1,500-hp) versions with babyface noses (Central of New Jersey's had cabs on both ends).

Freight cabs were single-engine, four-axle locomotives (like EMD Fs and Alco FAs). Early versions had babyfaces, but production soon switched to shark noses. These included the DR-4-4-15 and later RF-16.

Baldwin Road Switchers

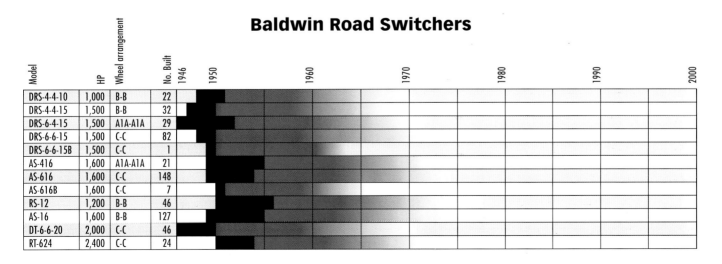

Model	HP	Wheel arrangement	No. Built	1946	1950	1960	1970	1980	1990	2000
DRS-4-4-10	1,000	B-B	22							
DRS-4-4-15	1,500	B-B	32							
DRS-6-4-15	1,500	A1A-A1A	29							
DRS-6-6-15	1,500	C-C	82							
DRS-6-6-15B	1,500	C-C	1							
AS-416	1,600	A1A-A1A	21							
AS-616	1,600	C-C	148							
AS-616B	1,600	C-C	7							
RS-12	1,200	B-B	46							
AS-16	1,600	B-B	127							
DT-6-6-20	2,000	C-C	46							
RT-624	2,400	C-C	24							

Cab units initially carried a DR prefix ("Diesel Road"), then the number of axles, the number of powered axles, and the first two numbers of the horsepower rating. This changed with the RF-16 freight diesels ("Road Freight").

Baldwin built its first road switchers in 1946. These initially had a DRS prefix, then AS and RS. The most successful of these were the six-axle, 1,600-hp AS-616 and its four-axle brother, the AS-16. Baldwin also built several twin-engine transfer locomotives (DT and RT). For six-axle units, trucks with even axle spacing indicated A1A-A1A (center axle unpowered) trucks; uneven spacing indicated all axles were powered (C-C).

As with switchers, Baldwin hood units had a distinctive appearance, with squared-off hood corners and cabs with shallow-curve roofs. The switch from Westinghouse to GE electrical equipment required lengthening hood-unit frames by 6" late in production.

Variations included number boards, which could be integral to the body or separate castings that protrude at the corners. Most had long-hood handrails mounted on the side of the hood, but some were delivered with handrails on stanchions mounted on the outside edge of the running boards. Four-axle diesels rode on the long version of AAR type B road trucks, required by the large Westinghouse traction motors.

The relatively low number of locomotives produced, combined with a number of features that changed during production (radiator opening placement, louver arrangement, cast and welded underframes, truck styles) means that it can be difficult to identify many models based on photos. Roster numbers are the best method.

Merger and decline

Faced with dwindling sales and declining market share, Baldwin merged with Lima-Hamilton in 1950. Lima (pronounced with a long "i" like the bean) had been the third-largest steam builder, but the company ignored the diesel market until merging with engine builder Hamilton in 1947. The combined Lima-Hamilton (often referred to just as Lima) didn't build a production-model diesel-electric locomotive until 1949, and the results were too little, too late. The company built just 174 diesels (mostly switchers) before the line was eliminated in favor of Baldwin's own designs in 1951.

Lima switchers were built with four horsepower ratings: 750, 800, 1,000, and 1,200. It wasn't an official designation, but they're typically referred to with an LS prefix ("Lima Switcher") followed by the horsepower. They shared a common body except for the LS-800, which had a shorter body.

Lima's only road switcher was a 1,200-hp model dubbed the LRS-1200, which looked like an Alco RS-1 with squared-off hood corners. New York Central was the only buyer. Lima also built an order of twin-engine, 2,500-hp transfer locomotives (LT-2500s) for the Pennsylvania—the only sales to what had been a major customer for its steam locomotives.

The Baldwin-Lima-Hamilton merger did nothing to boost sales, and Baldwin exited the locomotive manufacturing business in 1956. Most Baldwin road diesels were retired by the end of the 1960s, as components became difficult to obtain and reliability issues for older diesels became more pronounced. Many switchers lasted through the 1970s.

VO660

Denver & Rio Grande No. 67 is an early VO660, marked by its pointed nose, side grilles, and headlight mounted atop the hood. *Trains magazine collection*

The VO660 introduced the basic appearance that Baldwin switchers would maintain into the 1950s. The 660-hp locomotive was powered by a six-cylinder VO engine, and early models had a large, oval-shaped radiator fan opening in the nose, side radiator grilles, and a nose that was slightly pointed. Models built after 1940 had a smaller opening in the front, no side openings, and a lower-mounted headlight. The last VO660s lacked the curved fairings at the cab end of the running boards. All but the last few VO660s had two exhaust stacks (the last ones had four).

Major buyers: CG, CNJ, C&NW, D&RGW, EJ&E, L&N, MILW, MN&S, MP, NYC, NP, PRR, RDG, SP, TRRA, WM

VO1000

Northern Pacific VO1000 No. 172 has four low stacks, barely visible above the side. *R.V. Nixon*

The 1,000-hp VO1000 was powered by the eight-cylinder version of the VO engine. It was Baldwin's best-selling diesel locomotive, with more than 540 sold. It was slightly taller and longer (by three feet) compared to the VO660, and provided 340 more horsepower. Early VO1000s (39 of them) had angled noses with a large oval grille and radiator openings at the front of each side. In 1941 the side openings were eliminated and the grille revised. VO1000s can be found with one, two, or four stacks, which were often extended and added after manufacture.

Major buyers: ACL, AT&SF, BRC, CG, CNJ, C&NW, CB&Q, CRI&P, EJ&E, GN, LV, L&N, MILW, M&StL, MP, NC&StL, NYC, NP, OM, PRR, RDG, SAL, SLSF, SP, SP&S, SSW, TRRA, WAB, WM, WP

DS-4-4-6

Norfolk Southern No. 662 is a DS-4-4-6. It shares the same body as a late VO660. *Louis A. Marre collection*

The 660-hp DS-4-4-6 (also called the DS-4-4-660) replaced the VO660 in the catalog, but used the same body as the late VO660. A new six-cylinder 606NA engine replaced the VO. The DS-4-4-6 had a flat front and four exhaust stacks.

   Major buyers: C&NW, Erie, LIRR, NOPB, NS, P&BR, PRR, WAB

DS-4-4-10

Restored Seaboard Air Line DS-4-4-10 was on display at the Spencer, N.C., museum in 1992. *Jeff Wilson*

The DS-4-4-10 (also called a DS-4-4-1000) was built in two variations: Those built into 1948 were powered by a normally aspirated eight-cylinder 608 engine (spotted by its four stacks), and those built later (446 of them) had a smaller (six-cylinder 606) turbocharged engine, marked by a single fat exhaust stack. All had flat noses, distinguishing them from VO1000s.

   Major buyers: AT&SF, BRC, B&O, CP, CG, CNJ, C&NW, CGW, Erie, LV, MILW, MKT, MP, NKP, NS, OM, PRR, RDG, SLSF, SAL, Soo, SOU, SP, SSW, UP, WM

DS-4-4-7.5, S-8

La Salle & Bureau County DS-4-4-7.5 No. 8 shows the flat front and three exhaust stacks common to that model and the S-8. *Allen Rider*

The main difference between the 750-hp DS-4-4-7.5 (also known as the DS-4-4-750) and later 800-hp S-8 is internal—both can be identified by their three exhaust stacks and flat front. Both used Baldwin's normally aspirated, six-cylinder (606NA) engine. Baldwin built nine sets of S-8 cow/calf sets; all went to Oliver Mining.

   DS-4-4-7.5 major buyers: AT&SF, CW, Erie, PRR, TM, Weyerhaeuser, YS&T
   S-8 major buyers: CRI&P, OM, PRR, PRSL, YS&T

S-12

Southern Pacific No. 1442 is an S-12. It has a single exhaust stack and no cab windows above the hood.

David P. Morgan Library collection

Bumping the horsepower to 1,200 with the turbocharged 606A engine created the S-12. The S-12 is almost identical to the late DS-4-4-10, but all but a few early S-12s have an additional separate radiator section mounted within the large radiator opening in the nose. The single exhaust stack marks the turbo engine.

   Major buyers: B&O, C&NW, CRI&P, CG, CNJ, Erie, EM, GN, KCS, LC, MCR, MILW, MP, MKT, MGA, NYC, PRR, PRSL, SAL, Soo, SOU, SP, TRRA, WAB

DR-12-8-1500/2

The nickname "Centipede" becomes obvious when seeing the running gear of a DR-12-8-1500/2. Seaboard No. 4507 was one of 14 on the railroad. *Baldwin*

The 3,000-hp DR-12-8-1500/2 (or DR-12-8-3000) featured a pair of 1,500-hp engines (turbocharged 608SC) driving eight powered axles on a long, hinged frame with unpowered four-axle leading and trailing trucks. These complex locomotives had Baldwin's babyface cab and were nicknamed "Centipedes" for their long wheelbases. They were indeed massive—91 feet long, weighing 593 tons—a combination that was rough on track. Although designed for passenger service, they suffered from numerous maintenance and reliability issues and finished their careers in helper and hump-yard service.

    DR-12-8-1500/2: NdeM 6400-6413; SAL 4500-4513; PRR 5811-5834

DR-6-4-15, DR-6-2-10

New York Central No. 3200 is a DR-6-4-15. All of these locomotives had babyface cabs. *Baldwin*

The 1,500-hp babyface DR-6-4-15 (also called DR-6-4-1500) locomotives used single eight-cylinder engines, giving them 500 less horsepower compared to the DR-6-4-20. The locomotives were also shorter, but rode on six-wheel Commonwealth trucks with center idler axles. New York Central also received cabless B units. Chicago & North Western received the only DR-6-2-10. Designed for short passenger trains, the locomotive had a baggage compartment at the rear, and the rear six-wheel truck was unpowered. The single 1,000-hp forward engine powered two axles on the lead truck.

    DR-6-4-15: NYC 3200-3203 (B units 3210, 3211); SAL 2700-2702

    DR-6-2-10: C&NW 5000A

DR-6-4-20

The Pennsy's DR-6-4-20s debuted Baldwin's Loewy sharknose design. The six-axle diesels were designed for passenger service. *Pennsylvania RR*

The DR-6-4-20 (or DR-6-4-2000) and cabless DR-6-4-20B booster represented Baldwin's move toward the same A1A-A1A wheel arrangement as contemporary EMD and Alco passenger loco-motives. The DR-6-4-20 used two eight-cylinder VO or 608NA engines or six-cylinder 606SC engines. Because orders were so small for these, Baldwin essentially custom-built the bodies for each buyer, giving each railroad's locomotives a distinctive look. Pennsylvania's DRs debuted Baldwin's sharknose design and angled carbody; all others had babyface cabs. The Central of New Jersey locomotives had cabs at each end.

    DR-6-4-20: CNJ 2000-2005; GM&O 280, 281; NdeM 6000, 6001; PRR 5770A-5787A (B: 5770B-5786B, even numbers only)

DR-4-4-15

The DR-4-4-15 was the first freight shark. Note the louvered openings and narrow space between the bottom batten strip and the bottom of the body. *P.M. Rotzler*

The DR-4-4-15 had a 1,500-hp, eight-cylinder turbocharged engine, and a cabless B unit booster was also available. Early versions sported babyface noses; starting in 1948 they received the shark-nose design. The Missouri Pacific locomotives were three feet longer than other babyface engines to provide room for steam generators, which were never installed. A narrower portion of the frame is visible on each side compared to the later RF-16, except for the last order of DR-4-4-15s (Pennsy's 9700 series), which had the same body as the RF-16.

    DR-4-4-15: CNJ 70-79 (baby); EJ&E 700A, 701A (shark); MP 201A-208A (baby); NYC 3800-3803 (baby); PRR 9568A-9593A, 9700A-9707A (shark)

    DR-4-4-15B: CNJ K, L, M, R, S; EJ&E 700B, 701B; MP 201B-204B; NYC 3700-3701; PRR 9568B-9593B, 9700B-9707B

RF-16

Pennsy RF-16 No. 9721 shows the wider frame visible, as well as the model's exposed filters. *Bert Pennypacker*

The 608A engine gave the 1,600-hp RF-16 (and cabless RF-16B) a slight power boost over the earlier DR-4-4-15. All RF-16s were built with shark noses. They can be differentiated from the DRs by their exposed open filters on each side and by the wider portion of the frame visible below the bottom batten strip. The RF-16 was Baldwin's best-selling cab unit, but by the time it was introduced the days of the cab unit—and Baldwin—were numbered.

RF-16: B&O 4202-4220, NYC 1204-1221; PRR 2000A-2027A, 9594A-9599A, 9708A-9745A

RF-16B: B&O 5202-5214; NYC 3702-3709; PRR 9594B-9598B, 9708B-9714B, 9728B-9744B, 2000B-2026B (all even numbers only)

DRS-4-4-10

Tennessee Central No. 75 was the first DRS-4-4-10 built.
Louis A. Marre collection

The 1,000 hp DRS-4-4-10 (or DRS-4-4-1000) used a turbocharged six-cylinder 606SC engine. All had high noses. They lack the radiator openings at the ends of the long hoods and the bulges on the sides of the hoods found on higher-horsepower Baldwin road switchers. Visually they are identical to the later RS-12s, with a constant-thickness sideframe.

DRS-4-4-10: CP 8000-8012; PRR 5591-5594, 9276, 9277; TC 75-77

DRS-4-4-15

This Northern Pacific DRS-4-4-15 has a low-level radiator opening. Note the bulge on the hood and the single exhaust stack. *Baldwin*

The DRS-4-4-15 (or DRS-4-4-1500) used a turbocharged eight-cylinder engine to get an extra 500 hp compared to the DRS-4-4-10. Its appearance changed during production. It has a bulge on the hood behind the cab on the left side (long-hood front) and a single exhaust stack. Many early units had radiator openings at walkway level at the end of the long hood; on others this opening is higher. They were built with either cast underframes, which were stepped at the ends, or welded frames, which have a uniform straight profile for the length of the locomotive.

DRS-4-4-15: Erie 1100-1105; LV 200; Soo 360-367; MP 4112-4115; NYC 7300-7301; NP 500, 501; PRSL 6000-6005; WM 170-172

DRS-6-4-15, DRS-6-6-15

Duluth, South Shore & Atlantic No. 201 is a DRS-6-6-15, identified by the uneven axle spacing of the trucks. It has a raised radiator screen. *A.C. Kalmbach*

These were 1,500-hp, six-axle versions of the DRS-4-4-15. The DRS-6-4-15 had four axles powered, with A1A trucks (with even axle spacing). The DRS-6-6-15 (shown) had all axles powered and had trucks with unequal axle spacing (providing room for neighboring traction motors). One cabless DRS-6-6-15 was built; it went to Southern Pacific.

DRS-6-4-15: C&NW 1504; C&G 601-605; Kennecott Copper 901; NS 1501-1510; S&A 100-107; SP 5200-5202; UP 1250

DRS-6-6-15: B&LE 401-407; C&O 5530-5532; C&NW 1500-1502, 1505-1509; DSS&A 200-203; Erie 1150-1161; Kaiser Steel 1010A, B; MCR 28, 29; MN&S 15; NP 525; SP 187-190, 5203-5226, 5227 (B unit); TCI&RR 1500, 1501; URR 613-624

RS-12

The Seaboard Air Line owned ten Baldwin RS-12s. The RS-12 shares a body with the DRS-4-4-10. *Linn Westcott*

The 1,200-hp RS-12 replaced the DRS-4-4-10 as the light road switcher in the Baldwin catalog, and the two locomotives shared the same body. It was powered by a turbocharged 606A engine. The noses on some RS-12s were taller then the long hoods to house dynamic brakes (McCloud River) or a large steam generator. The RS-12 lacked the bulge in the side of the hood of the more-powerful AS-16.

RS-12: CNJ 1206-1209; MILW 970, 971; D&S 1200-1202; MCR 32, 33; NYC 6220-6236; PRR 8105-8110, 8776, 8975; SAL 1466-1475

AS-16

Reading No. 532 is an early AS-16, as it has a hood and nose slightly shorter than later-production models.

Ken Douglas; Louis A. Marre collection

The most-popular four-axle Baldwin road switcher, the 1,600-hp AS-16, has a turbocharged 608A engine. It has a uniform-thickness underframe for the length of the locomotive. On AS-16s after October 1953, the roof of the nose and hood were extended upward to just under the cab roofline. Many AS-16s and DRS-4-4-15s had fuel tanks under the cab and in the short hood—not under the frame.

AS-16: B&O 6200-6215; Erie 1106-1120, 1140; MP 4195, 4196, 4326-4331; Soo 379, 380; MKT 1571-1586, 1787, 1788; NKP 320-323; PRSL 6007-6016, 6022-6027; RDG 530-554; 560-563, 576-589; WM 173-176

AS-416, AS-616

The even axle spacing on the short-wheelbase trucks and the bulge in the side of the hood mark Norfolk Southern No. 1605 as an AS-416. *Baldwin*

The six-axle, 1,600-hp AS-416 and AS-616 shared common bodies with the four-axle AS-16. Those built after June 1951 have fabricated frames with notches to clear truck-mounted brake cylinders; earlier versions have a thicker frame without notches. AS-416s had trucks with even axle spacing and an unpowered center axle (A1A-A1A); AS-616s have all axles powered (C-C) and ride on longer-wheelbase trucks with uneven axle spacing (see the DRS-6-6-15 entry and page 12). Two styles of C trucks were used: cast and drop-equalizer. Cabless AS-616Bs went to Milwaukee Road and Southern Pacific.

AS-416: C&G 606; NS 1601-1617; S&A 108-110
AS-616: B&LE; C&O; C&NW; DSS&A; HB&T; Kaiser; MILW; NdeM; O&NW; PRR; P&WV; SP; TCI&RR; UP; URR; Trona
AS-616B: MILW 2100B, 2101B; SP 5501-5505

DT-6-6-20, RT-624

Santa Fe DT-6-6-20 has an engine on each end with a cab in the middle. *Baldwin*

Baldwin built several large (70-foot-long), twin-engine center-cab diesels for transfer service. The 2,000-hp DT-6-6-20 was designed for slow speeds and high tractive effort. The first one built (Elgin, Joliet & Eastern No. 100) had two non-turbocharged eight-cylinder engines; later locomotives had turbocharged six-cylinder engines. The RT-624 used upgraded engines to boost horsepower to 2,400. EJ&E No. 100 has four exhaust stacks; the remainder of these locomotives have the same appearance, with one stack per engine.

DT-6-6-20: AT&SF 2600-2606; EJ&E 100-126; MN&S 20-24; Trona 50, 51; SSW 260; DSS&A 300-303
RT-624: MN&S 25; PRR 8113, 8724-8731, 8952-8965

Lima LH-800

Rock Island No. 800 is a Lima 800-hp switcher built in 1950. Note the squared hood corners. *Lima-Hamilton*

Lima-Hamilton's 800-hp switcher (informally the LH-800) had a slightly shorter body than the company's other switchers—note the 11 hood doors/rows of louvers (compared to 13 on other models) and a side radiator grille (at the front) that's not as long as other models. General Lima switcher spotting features include a blunt nose (similar to Baldwin's) with a more-steeply curved cab roof similar to an Alco.

LH-800: CRI&P 800, 801; NYC 9800-9820

Lima LRS-1200

All 16 models of Lima's lone road-switcher design went to New York Central. *Lima-Hamilton*

Lima built 16 1,200-hp light road switchers in 1950. They were extended versions of the firm's 1,200-hp switchers, but on AAR type B road trucks. They resembled an Alco's RS-1 but with squared-off corners at the hood, roof, and nose. They were powered by a turbocharged Hamilton T89SA (in-line, eight-cylinder) engine.

LRS-1200: NYC 5800-5815

Lima LH-750, LH-1000, LH-1200

New York Central LH-1000 No. 8400 shows the body style shared with the LH-750 and LH-1200. *Lima-Hamilton*

Lima's 750-, 1,000-, and 1,200-hp switchers shared a common body that was longer than the 800-hp model. The LH-1000 and LH-1200 used eight-cylinder turbocharged Hamilton T89SA engines; the LH-750 and LH-800 used six-cylinder (T69SA) versions.

LH-750: CUT 20-25

LH-1000: Armco Steel 707-709; B&O 330-339; Erie 650-659; NYC 8400-8405; NKP 305-308; TP&W 300-302

LH-1200: Armco 710, E109, E110; B&O 320-329, 340-353; Erie 660-665; NYNH&H 630-639; NKP 309-312; NYC 8406-8411; TRA 1200-1205; WAB 401-406, 408-411

Lima LT-2500

Number 5676 is one of 22 twin-engine, 2,500-hp transfer locomotives Lima built for Pennsy in 1950 and 1951.

Louis A. Marre collection

Lima's 2,500-hp transfer locomotives used two T89SA engines, one under each hood. Compared to Baldwin's transfer locomotives, Lima's have a large grille on each side at each end, squared exhaust stacks placed farther toward the ends, a constant-thickness frame, louvers on hood doors, and a different cab design and trucks.

LT-2500: PRR 5671-5683, 8943-8951

— CHAPTER NINE —

Fairbanks-Morse

The H-24-66 Train Master is arguably Fairbanks-Morse's most famous locomotive, and at 2,400 hp was king of the horsepower leader board when it debuted in 1953. Wabash owned six of them, and No. 553 is one of 127 total Train Masters built through 1957.

Fairbanks-Morse

Even though Fairbanks-Morse built relatively few diesels compared to EMD or Alco, F-M locomotives have a solid following among railfans. They were known for being rugged, excellent-pulling locomotives, in spite of their temperamental opposed-piston engines.

Fairbanks-Morse was a latecomer to the diesel locomotive market. The company was looking for additional uses for its unique opposed-piston diesel engine, used successfully in ships and submarines before and during World War II. Its first railroad use came in power cars built by St. Louis Car Co. for the Southern Railway in 1939.

Fairbanks-Morse chose to develop and build its own line of locomotives, starting with switchers at its Beloit, Wis., plant in 1944. Cab units and road switchers followed. The Canadian Locomotive Company (CLC), located in Kingston, Ontario, built locomotives in Canada (primarily for Canadian railroads) under F-M licence. Switchers proved to be the most successful locomotives in the F-M line—they were regarded as tough, good-pulling locomotives. The OP engine proved problematic in many road freight applications (especially high-horsepower designs), due to its large cooling and oil needs, excessive wear in lower pistons, and the inaccessability of the lower crankshaft (see Chapter 2).

The company's switchers were distinctive, characterized by their tall (cab-roof-height) hoods, necessitated by the tall OP engine, and smooth, semi-streamlined styling (by industrial designer Raymond Loewy). The model numbers use an H (for "hood"), followed by the first two numerals of the horsepower rating, then the number of powered axles and total axles.

Fairbanks-Morse was a late entrant in the cab-unit market, starting with six-axle passenger locomotives dubbed "Erie-Builts" in 1945. These locomotives took their name from their construction at General Electric's Erie (Pa.) Works, as F-M didn't have sufficient space at Beloit at the time. As with later Alco PAs, Erie-Builts had a single engine (10-cylinder OP) and rode on A1A-A1A (center idler axle) trucks. At a glance they resemble PAs, which isn't a surprise considering the PAs were later built in the same shops.

The company began building cab units at its own Beloit factory in 1950 with its new Consolidation Line, and these locomotives became known as C-Liners. The idea was to use a common body that could serve a platform for several engine and horsepower configurations and options. The model numbers have a C, followed by the first two numerals of the horsepower rating, then the total number of axles. They were available with or without steam generators. Sales were not strong, as railroads were increasingly opting for road switchers by the early 1950s.

Fairbanks-Morse road switchers also have a distinctive appearance. All F-M road switchers had high noses, with the long-hood end usually designated as the front. As with switchers, the first letter indicates "H" for "hood," followed by horsepower, number of powered axles, and total axles.

Road switchers ranged from 1,500 hp up to the big 2,400-hp H-24-66, dubbed the Train Master. It was the highest-horsepower road locomotive on the market by far when first built in 1953, and it remains a favorite among railfans.

Increased horsepower and improvements in design and reliability weren't enough to boost sales, and F-M's share of the market—never strong—declined in the early 1950s. Fairbanks-Morse built its last U.S. diesel in 1958 and its last locomotive for Mexico in 1963. CLC was renamed Fairbanks-Morse Canada in 1965 and closed in 1969.

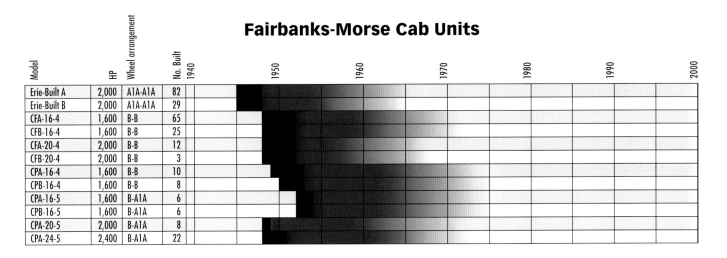

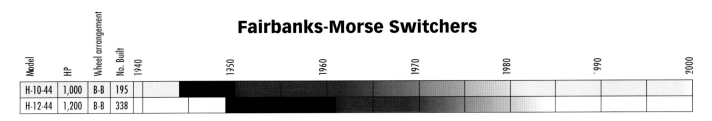

H-10-44

Chicago & North Western No. 1064 is an H-10-44. It has the rear cab overhang and slanted nose used into H-12-44 production. *J. David Ingles*

The H-10-44, designed by Raymond Loewy, was F-M's first production locomotive. It has graceful lines, a distinctive overhang behind the cab, a slightly slanted nose, and radiator grilles on the front of each side. The 1,000-hp locomotive used a six-cylinder OP engine. The tall profile of the engine dictated the tall (cab-roof-height) hoods of F-M switchers and road switchers. All rode on AAR type A switcher trucks. Many were later upgraded to 1,200 hp.

Major buyers: AT&SF, B&O, C&NW, D&RGW, IU, K&IT, MILW, NYC, NKP, PRR, P&LE, SLSF, UP, WAB

H-12-44

Southern Pacific No. 1577 is a late H-12-44, with a shorter body and frame, vertical nose, no cab overhang, and thicker sideframe. *Fairbanks-Morse*

The H-12-44 used the same six-cylinder OP engine as the H-10, but boosted horsepower to 1,200. Early H-12-44s had the same body as the H-10-44. The body styling was simplified in September 1952, with the rear cab overhang and nose slant eliminated. Another change came in 1956, as the frame and body were shortened by three feet and the sideframe became deeper. The H-12-44 was F-M's most-popular diesel locomotive, with more than 330 built.

Major buyers: AT&SF, B&O, CN, C&NW, CG, IU, K&IT, MILW, MW, NYC, NKP, PRR, SLSF, Soo, SP, US Army, US Steel, WAB

H-12-44TS

The steam-generator-equipped H-12-44TS was designed for transfer work at Chicago's Dearborn Station.

Fairbanks-Morse

Fairbanks-Morse built three H-12-44TS (Transfer, Steam-generator) locomotives in 1956 for Santa Fe for switching passenger cars at Dearborn Station in Chicago. Mechanically it is the same as an H-12-44 switcher, with a six-cylinder OP engine providing 1,200 hp, but the TS has a short hood that houses a steam generator and it rides on a longer frame than the H-12-44. The nose makes the H-12-44TS look like a road switcher, but it rides on AAR type A switcher trucks and is designed for slow-speed operation.

H-12-44TS: AT&SF 541-543

Erie-Built

Santa Fe No. 90 is a late-production Erie-Built, as each windshield is curved at the top. *Fairbanks-Morse*

F-M's big Erie-Builts (named for being assembled at GE's Erie, Pa., plant), as with passenger diesels from other builders, rode on six-wheel trucks with center idler axles (either General Steel Castings or fabricated). Each Erie was powered by a single 10-cylinder OP diesel engine. Designed by Raymond Loewy, Eries have a distinctive nose shape ("boat-nosed," as many say) compared to PAs, with large rectangular radiator intake grilles at the rear of each side. Early Erie A units had rectangular windshields with square corners; later units had curved windshields (as on the Santa Fe locomotive above). All owners except Chicago & North Western also had matching B units.

Erie A: AT&SF 90, 90B; C&NW 6001A, B-6002A, B; KCS 60A, C-62A, C; MILW 5A, C-9A, C, 21A, B-22A, B; NYC 4400-4405, 5000-5005; PRR 9456A-9491A; UP 700-707

Erie B: AT&SF 90A; KCS 60B-62B; MILW 5B-9B, 21C; NYC 5100-5101; PRR 9456B-9478B (even); UP 700B, 702B-704B, 706B

CFA-16-4, CFA-20-4

Milwaukee Road CFA-16-4 No. 27A shows the C-Liner's shorter nose and body compared to the Erie-Built.

J.M. Gruber collection

Consolidation Line cab units have a similar look to Erie-Builts, but C-Liners are six feet shorter and have stubbier noses. All C-Liner bodies are identical externally. The freight-service ("F") 1,600-hp CFA-16-4 and cabless CFB-16-4 booster were the most common versions, using an 8-cylinder OP engine compared to the 10-cylinder OP used in the 2,000-hp CFA-20-4 (and CFB-20-4). These locomotives ride on C-Liner trucks, which resemble the AAR type B road truck but have a distinctive curve on the drop equalizer.

    CFA-16-4: CN 9300-9344 (even); MILW 23A-28A, 23C-28C; NYC 6600-6607; PRR 9448A-9455A, 9492A-9499A
    CFB-16-4: CN 9301-9305 (odd); MILW 23B-28B; NYC 6900-6903; PRR 9448B-9454B, 9492B-9498B (odd)
    CFA-20-4: NYC 5006-5017
    CFB-20-B: NYC 5102-5104

CPA-16-4

The steam generator stack and vent are visible at the rear of the roof on Canadian Pacific CPA-16-4 No. 4054.

Robert J. Yanosey collection

The CPA (and CPB B unit) locomotives were identical to the CFA/CFB, but were equipped with steam generators (at the rear of the body) for passenger service (the middle "P" in the model designation stood for "passenger"). Canadian Pacific received the only CPA-16-4s, which were built by CLC.

    CPA-16-4: CP 4052-4057, 4064, 4065, 4104, 4105
    CPB-16-4: CP 4449-4454, 4471, 4472

CPA-16-5, CPA-20-5, CPA-24-5

New York Central CPA-24-5 was powered by a 12-cylinder OP engine. *R.M. Stacy*

These five-axle passenger-service C-Liners had two-axle lead trucks (both powered) and three-axle A1A (center idler axle) rear trucks. The larger rear truck was designed to better carry the weight of the steam generator and water tank. The CPAs were built with three different engines (8-, 10-, or 12-cylinder OPs) rated at 1,600, 2,000, and 2,400 hp; B units (CPB) were built of the 1,600-hp version.

    Rosters: CN (CPA-16: 6700-6705; CPB-16: 6800-6805), LIRR (CPA-20: 2001-2008; CPA-24: 2401-2404), NYC (CPA-24: 4500-4507); NYNH&H (CPA-24: 790-799)

H-12-46

Number 1625 is an H-12-46, built exclusively for Canadian National. The body is rather spartan, and it rides on A1A trucks. *Canadian National.*

The 1,200-hp H-12-46 was a Canadian-only locomotive, built by CLC for lightweight branchline service on Canadian National. It rode on three-axle trucks with center idler axles (note the equal axle spacing).

    H-12-46: CN 7600-7629

H-15-44

Central of New Jersey H-15-44 has the classic Loewy-styled body shared with early H-16-44s. *Jerry A. Pinkepank*

The 1,500-hp H-15-44 featured another body designed by Raymond Loewy. The H-15 had sloped hood ends, curved cab-side windows, and louver-covered radiator openings that protruded slightly from the side of the hood. The locomotives rode on AAR type B trucks (long-wheelbase version).

H-15-44: ACY 200; CG 101-105; CNJ 1500-1513; CRI&P 400, 401; D&RGW 150-152; KCS 40, 41; LIRR 1503; MON 45, 46; UP DS1325-DS1329

H-20-44

The H-20-44 was a road switcher, even though it has an end cab. *Fairbanks-Morse*

Even though the 2,000-hp H-20-44 was F-M's most powerful four-axle road switcher, it's often mistaken for a switcher because of its lack of a short hood (note the AAR road trucks). Also note the MU connections, class lights, and road-style headlights. It has a bulge around the radiator shutters similar to the H-15-44 and H-16-44. It was powered by a 10-cylinder OP engine, compared to the eight-cylinder versions of the H-15 and H-16.

H-20-44: AC&Y 500-505; NYC 7100-7118; PRR 8917-8942, 9300-9311; P&WV 50-71; UP 1360-1370

H-16-44

Milwaukee Road No. 2460 is a mid-production H-16-44, with visible radiator fans, elevated walkway with step down at the radiator, and C-Liner trucks. *Fairbanks-Morse*

Late H-16-44s had tall walkways and elevated radiators. *Fairbanks-Morse*

The H-16-44 represented a bump in horsepower to 1,600 from the H-15-44. At first the difference was strictly internal, as the first H-16-44s were visually identical to the H-15 (and also used the same eight-cylinder OP engine). See page 241 for a photo of an early Missouri-Kansas-Texas engine. In January 1954 the sloped hood ends became vertical and the rounded cab windows were eliminated. The headlight casting was simplified from the initial oval housing (see the H-15 photo). In June 1954 the walkways were elevated, with a step down at the radiator (see the Milwaukee Road engine above). The screen-covered radiator fans were placed at an angle, becoming visible from the side. After March 1955 the walkway step was eliminated, with high-level running boards along the entire side and an elevated radiator intake at walkway level (as on the Virginian version above). Most H-16s built after 1950 have the C-Liner truck, spotted by its curved-bottom drop equalizer. This replaced the AAR type B trucks used earlier. Most had handrails on stanchions along the outside of the running boards, but some had handrails mounted on the sides of the hood. The H-16-44 was by far F-M's most-popular road locomotive, with 299 built. Virginian and Canadian Pacific were the biggest owners, each with 40.

H-16-44: AC&Y, AT&SF, B&O, BdeC, CN, CP, ChP, DL&W, LIRR, MILW, MKT, NYC, NYNH&H, P&WV, SOU, UP, VGN

H-16-66

Early H-16-66s, such as Chicago & North Western No. 1510, had curved cab windows, angled hood ends, and a stepped, low-level walkway. *Stan Mailer*

Late H-16-66s were longer and had exposed radiator fans and elevated walkways. Windows were squared and the angled hood ends eliminated. *Fairbanks-Morse*

The six-axle, 1,600-hp H-16-66 is powered by an eight-cylinder OP engine and rides on Commonwealth cast trucks. The first H-16-66s initially had the same Loewy-designed features as early H-16-44s, with rounded cab windows, slanted hood ends, and oval headlight housings. The first H-16-66s had screened body openings, which were replaced by louvered openings in 1952. In August 1953 the H-16-66 received a design overhaul that gave it an appearance more resembling the H-24-66: The body was lengthened almost seven feet, cab windows were squared, the walkway was elevated, and the slanted ends were made vertical. The radiator fans were angled, becoming visible from the sides. Dynamic brake-equipped engines (15 C&NW units) had small screened openings just behind the cab. Four C&NW engines had steam generators. The H-16-66 would eventually become known as the Baby Train Master.

H-16-66: C&NW 1510-1514, 1605-1612, 1668-1683, 1691-1700, 1901-1906; CStPM&O 150, 168-172; MILW 2125-2130; TVA 24; Alcoa 721001

H-24-66

Canadian National No. 3000 is a late H-24-66, with radiator fans placed adjacent to each other, a dip in the handrail to match the walkway, and fewer louvers than earlier models. *Canadian National*

This Delaware, Lackawanna & Western Train Master shows the early style of radiator fans, with a narrow panel between the two fans. *Jack Emerick*

Fairbanks-Morse's most-powerful—and most-celebrated—road switcher, the H-24-66 Train Master, can be identified by its sheer size. It has elevated running boards, tri-mount trucks, and a pair of angled radiator fans visible on each side through screen at the end of the long hood. The fans were initially separated by a narrow panel (as on the Lackawanna locomotive shown above), but were placed together starting in 1955 (see the Canadian National version above). The Train Master was rated at 2,400 hp, two years before Alco matched it with the RSD-7 and five years before EMD's SD24 hit the market. The first few TMs built had straight handrails; they were later modified to have a slight "dip" in the middle to match the walkway height. In 1955 the louver location and spacing were changed, with fewer louver sets along the tops of the sides. Southern and Wabash engines (see page 136) had low end platforms. The Train Master used a 12-cylinder OP engine, and although it was noted for its pulling power and quick accelleration, its performance suffered and problems arose when called upon for constant full-throttle operation or when running at high temperatures, high altitudes, and in tunnels. These locomotives had their best success on the Southern Pacific in Bay-area commuter service, where they served through the mid-1970s.

H-24-66: CN 3000; CP 8900-8920; CNJ 2401-2413; DL&W 850-861; PRR 8699-8707; RDG 800-808, 860-867; SOU 6300-6304; SP 4802-4815; VGN 50-74; WAB 552-554, 552A-554A

CHAPTER TEN

Rebuilds, slugs, and hydraulics

Illinois Central Gulf No. 8701 is what the railroad calls a GP11, rebuilt in 1979 from an older Geep. The locomotive received a 645C engine (replacing the original 567), new or upgraded electrical components, a new cab and chopped nose, and a new air filtration system. Although it's technically a rebuild, the 8701 emerged from the shop for all practical purposes as a new locomotive.
Illinois Central Gulf

Diesel locomotives enjoy fairly long lifespans. At least 15 years without major rebuilding is a standard expectation, with many engines lasting well beyond that. As the first generation of diesel locomotives approached and passed the 15-year mark, railroads began looking at options for overhauling and rebuilding engines to extend their service lives.

Rebuilding a locomotive can give it several more productive years of duty. It can be done to many levels, from a simple overhaul to an engine replacement to a complete disassembly with upgrade or replacement of all major components, new wiring, and new body. The result can be what is essentially a new locomotive, with a combination of new and rebuilt parts.

There are tax and financial benefits to rebuilding, depending upon who actually owns the locomotive (whether the locomotive was acquired via a bank equipment trust, through financing from the builder, or through a long-term lease). Rebuilding can reset the locomotive's value, allowing the owner to write off its depreciation over time.

Early rebuilds

The first attempts at rebuilding were in the 1950s, when railroads looked to upgrade older locomotives to current standards or replace worn or unreliable prime movers with new diesel engines.

Although Alco did some of this, EMD was a leader in rebuilding, establishing parts centers and rebuilding facilities in several locations across the country. Most of the work done at these centers involved upgrading older EMD locomotives. This involved replacing the older 567B or 567BC engines with 567C engines and replacing the alternator and traction motors with then-current components.

These often appear in rosters with "M", "R," or "U" suffixes ("modified," "rebuilt," or "upgraded"), but sometimes they appear as new models. Depending upon the level of work done, the builder and railroad may consider them new locomotives (and they'll receive new builder's plates) that received some components from the older locomotives, which were considered "trade-ins."

From the mid-1950s into the 1960s, many early Alco and Baldwin locomotives were refitted with new EMD 567 engines, either by EMD itself or by railroad shops. These re-engined locomotives sometimes retained their basic original appearance (perhaps with relocated exhaust stacks, fans, and grilles). Other engine replacements required rebuilding or replacing roofs or entire hoods to clear new engines

Electro-Motive re-engined many non-EMD locomotives, including Rock Island Alco RS-2 No. 453 in 1957. The new engine required a taller (GP-style) long hood, but the locomotive kept its original Alco nose, cab, frame, and trucks. *EMD*

Santa Fe used its Cleburne, Texas shops for its F7 to CF7 rebuild program, stripping locomotives to their frames and rebuilding the bodies. *J. David Ingles*

and components. The result was often a hybrid appearance, such as an Alco RS hood unit that retained its cab and nose but with an EMD-style long hood.

Results of these re-engining projects were mixed. Combining engines, cooling systems, and electrical components of two builders sometimes created new or additional problems, and a new engine itself didn't always result in a substantially increased lifespan for a locomotive. Some railroads, such as the Frisco, Missouri-Kansas-Texas, and Rock Island, went in big for re-engined locomotives; many others had one or a few done.

Major rebuilding programs

The first large-scale in-house rebuild program was undertaken by the Illinois Central starting in 1967 at its Paducah, Ky., shops. The resulting locomotives (primarily early EMD Geeps, but also

switchers) were nicknamed "Paducah Rebuilds" or "Paducah Geeps."

Faced with an aging fleet of GP7 and GP9 road switchers, the IC began rebuilding them instead of trading them in for new power. For the IC, rebuilding was a way to save money on new locomotives (including tax benefits by having a rebuilt locomotive that could again be depreciated over time) and keep its own shop forces employed.

The IC's rebuilding was extensive. Locomotives were stripped down to the frame and all components were removed. Individual parts and assemblies were rebuilt and refurbished, including the engine itself (which received new pistons and liners), crankshaft, generator, and traction motors. Wiring was redone and upgraded, and the brake system upgraded. Trucks were disassembled, and individual parts repaired or upgraded as

The road-switcher-style CF7 bears little resemblance to the original streamlined F unit. Early CF7s like this one retained the curved cab roof. *Charles M. Mizell, Jr.*

Morrison-Knudsen rebuilt four ex-Southern Pacific GE U25Bs with Sulzer engines in 1978, giving them a TE-70-4S designation. *Charles K. Marsh, Jr.*

needed before reassembly. After the first few locomotives, the IC began chopping the high short hoods to create low noses; other railroads and shops varied on this. After 1978, rebuilds received modular electrical equipment matching then-current EMD Dash-2 standards.

The resulting locomotives were extremely successful, and the IC (later Illinois Central Gulf) soon found itself rebuilding locomotives for other railroads and leasing companies on a contract basis. The IC also bought used Geeps and rebuilt them both for its own use and for resale.

Naming conventions for rebuilt locomotives can be convoluted. As mentioned earlier, many rebuilds carry— either formally or informally—the

original model number followed by an M, R, or U suffix. Others came up with new numbers. As examples, the IC termed its Geep rebuilds GP8s (former GP7s), GP10s (former GP9s), or GP11s (Geeps rebuilt to Dash-2 standards). The former Southern Ry. SD24s rebuilt by Paducah without turbochargers (to 2,000-hp units) became SD20s. The Santa Fe took a different approach with its SD24s, rebuilding the 567D3 engines with 645-series power assemblies (boosting the horsepower to 2,625) and calling them SD26s.

Other railroads embarked on similar projects. Milwaukee Road rebuilt old Geeps beginning in 1969, swapping 567 engines for 645s. This gave the engines

2,000 hp, so the Milwaukee called them GP20s (and went so far as to add "GP20" model plates to their sides, creating confusion with EMD's stock GP20s). Milwaukee also rebuilt old SDs, keeping their original engines and calling them SD10s.

The Santa Fe launched one of the most famous rebuild programs in 1970 when it began rebuilding more than 200 aging F units, turning them from cab units to road switchers and calling them CF7s (Converted F7s). The locomotives were stripped of all components and given new fabricated frames, since cab units rely on their side-wall framing for strength. The engine, traction motors, trucks, and electrical system components were rebuilt, brakes were upgraded, and a new body and cab added to the frame. The first few had rounded cab roofs (like the F unit), but it was found to be cheaper to fabricate angled-roof cabs instead.

The Santa Fe began rebuilding most of its other older EMD locomotives in the early 1970s, starting with Geeps and moving to GP20s, SD40s, SD45s, and switchers. Southern Pacific did likewise, as did Burlington Northern and other railroads.

New or rebuilt?

The success of railroad rebuild programs inspired independent companies to do likewise. In the 1970s, Morrison-Knudsen of Boise, Idaho, began offering locomotive rebuilding services. Among the company's more famous projects were in 1973 when it rebuilt Burlington Northern E units (with new single 645 engines replacing the original dual 567s) for Chicago commuter service, and in 1974 rebuilding the four existing Alco PA locomotives for Delaware & Hudson.

The company also offered "new" locomotives which used frames, trucks, and sometimes other components from retired locomotives. The first experiment came in 1978, when it took four ex-Southern Pacific GE U25Bs and rebuilt them with Sulzer V-12 diesel engines, marketing them as TE-70-4S locomotives. The conversion wasn't successful, and although they operated several years, no additional orders were ordered or converted.

A more-risky venture came in 1994 when Morrison-Knudsen built the first MK5000C demonstrators. Designed as an all-new locomotive to compete with EMD and GE, the MK5000C was rated at 5,000 hp and used Caterpillar diesel engines and Dofasco trucks. No production orders were placed.

Since that time, M-K successor MotivePower Inc. (MPI) has continued rebuilding locomotives and began offering a line of passenger diesels that—although they use trucks, EMD or GE prime movers, have new bodies. They are essentially new locomotives and are marketed as such. MPI has sold more than 200 of these MPXpress locomotives, mainly to commuter agencies. The largest customers have been GO Transit (Toronto), Metra (Chicago), and MARC (Washington D.C./Virginia).

Other major independent rebuilders since the 1970s have included VMV (operating from the IC's former shops at Paducah) and NRE (National Railway Equipment). Builders EMD and GE have both offered rebuilt-as-new locomotives including EMD's BL20-2 (rebuilt from older Geeps; only three demonstrators were built) and GE's Super 7 rebuilds (upgrades of older U-boats to Dash-7 standards; most went to Mexico).

Today, many rebuilt locomotives serve Class 1 railroads as well as short lines and regionals. As with older rebuilds, their designations vary widely by railroad and builder. Some simply carry an "M" or "R." A "-3" (such as an SD40-3) often indicates a locomotive with upgraded controls and electrical system; original SD40s (and SD45s rebuilt but derated to 3,000 hp) rebuilt to Dash-2 standards can be SD40M-2s (this applies to GPs as well), as can Dash 2 locomotives that have been rebuilt.

Gensets

Genset locomotives hit the market in 2005 as a way to both lower emissions and save fuel. Instead of a single large engine, gensets have multiple (usually two to four) small engine/generator combinations. Only as many engines as needed will run at any given time.

They have been built by several companies, including MPI, National

Genset locomotives, such as this RailPower RP20BD, have multiple engine/generator units (this one has three). Only as many as needed will run at any given time. This one is built on an old EMD GP38 frame. *RailPower Technologies*

The second unit in this Chicago & North Western consist is an Alco RS-2 converted to a slug (note the blanked cab windows). *J. David Ingles*

Railway Engineering (NRE), and RailPower Technologies. Gensets have been purchased by most major railroads, including BNSF, CSX, and Union Pacific.

Although the manufacturers listed provide standard models (deviating in total horsepower and number of gensets used), the locomotives are built on frames of retired locomotives, and typically use trucks reconditioned from older locomotives. Gensets largely fell out of favor by the mid-2010s.

Slugs

A slug is an older locomotive that has had its engine and generator removed, but retains its traction motors. It is then connected electrically to—and draws power from—one or two adjoining locomotives in a consist.

The idea is that in low-speed situations with heavy loads, a locomotive produces more electricity than its own traction motors can use. This excess power is routed to traction motors on the slug locomotive.

A typical arrangement is to position the slug between two conventional locomotives, with each locomotive providing power to one truck on the slug. Most have controls so that as speed increases (and the demands for high tractive effort diminish), the slug is phased out and the locomotives operate conventionally.

Slugs are most often used in slow-speed operations such as switching (especially hump-yard service) and helper service.

Dozens of types of locomotives have been converted to slugs. The basic conversion involves removal of the engine, generator, and other internal gear. Weight is added to make up for the loss of heavy components. Some

Canadian Locomotive Co. built several small H44A1 (DT-2) diesel-hydraulic locomotives for Canadian Pacific in the late 1950s. *Jim Shaughnessy*

Southern Pacific 9013 is one of several Krauss-Maffei diesel-hydraulics purchased by the railroad in the early 1960s. *Glenn C. Lee, Jr.*

The Kraus-Maffei diesels used hydraulic-mechanical differentials instead of traction motors to drive axles. *Kraus-Maffei*

railroads have removed cabs and built new hoods, creating a new appearance; others simply plate over cab windows and leave the body intact.

Diesel-hydraulics

From the 1920s onward, electric transmission has been the standard method of getting power from the diesel engine to the wheels. A hydraulic/mechanical transmission has been attempted a few times in an effort to find a more economical or reliable system.

A moderately successful attempt was the H44A1 center-cab switcher built by Canadian Locomotive Co. (CLC) for Canadian Pacific from 1957 to 1960. They resemble a GE 44-tonner, and only 14 were built, classified DT-2 by the CP. The DT-2 was small (44 tons), powered by a pair of 250-hp Caterpillar diesel engines. The drive system was known as DTC, for "diesel torque converter," a type of hydraulic/mechanical drive. Although no additional similar locomotives were built, some of the original models lasted in service into the 1970s.

A much larger attempt came in 1961, when Southern Pacific took delivery of three six-axle (C-C) ML-4000 diesel-hydraulic locomotives built by Kraus-Maffei in Germany. Each was powered by two Maybach V-16 diesel engines and rated at 3,540 hp. Rio Grande also purchased three, which it sold to SP in 1964. At that time, SP ordered an additional 15 locomotives.

The locomotives used hydraulic-mechanical transmissions made by Voith to transfer motion from the engines to the trucks. Alco also built three diesel-hydraulics for SP, delivered in 1964. These six-axle model 643DH locomotives also used twin diesel engines and were rated at 4,300 hp. They used Alco engines and components but the same German Voith transmissions as the K-M locomotives.

Unsatisfactory performance on mountain grades, the specialized nature of parts and repairs, and the coming of more-powerful (3,000 hp and higher) conventional diesel-electric locomotives doomed the diesel-hydraulics to experimental status. All were retired by 1968.

R O S T E R S

The following pages include diesel locomotive rosters for more than 120 railroads, including historical railroads, current Class I lines, and several independent regionals, all listed alphabetically. Rosters include diesel-electric and diesel-hydraulic locomotives. Not included are electric locomotives, slugs, locomotives converted to non-powered control units, and self-propelled motorcars (such as doodlebugs and Rail Diesel Cars). Each entry also includes a summary of that railroad's history with diesels, including last runs of steam (if applicable) and the date the railroad ceased to exist if it was merged, purchased, or abandoned.

Rosters include locomotives grouped by model number and class. Each line generally includes all locomotives of a given model type, unless numbering or other characteristics make such groupings difficult. Space precludes locomotive-by-locomotive listings or details on dates locomotives were sold or retired.

Rosters for the current Class I railroads (Amtrak, BNSF, Canadian National, Canadian Pacific, CSX, Kansas City Southern, and Norfolk Southern) include current locomotives in service only; all others (including "historical" versions of most of the above railroads) provide all-time lists, including locomotives retired and sold.

How to read the rosters

The first column in the chart includes original (as-delivered) road numbers. Second and third columns (when needed) indicate subsequent renumbering of locomotives, or in some cases, previous numbers if a merger was involved. A hyphen in a series (i.e. 300-349) indicates numbering is inclusive (50 locomotives numbered from 300 to 349). Two periods (300..349) indicate that all numbers were not used. If numbers were used more than once, a number in parenthesis indicates where

those locomotives fell in the sequence.

The number of locomotives in the group or class follows, followed by the model number and locomotive builder. The model is generally the designation given by the locomotive builder (for current Class 1 rosters, it is the railroad's designation). For rebuilt locomotives, the designation may be that of the builder, the railroad, or company that did the rebuilding (for example, Illinois Central classified its rebuilt GP7s and GP9s as GP8s, GP10s, and GP11s). These are explained in footnotes when possible.

Be aware that the dates built are not necessarily the dates acquired by the railroad. If locomotives were acquired used, this is indicated in footnotes; if practical, the previous owner and dates acquired are also indicated. Previous owners are indicated by "ex-" and original owners by "nee." For current railroads, an "R" before the year indicates the year rebuilt.

The "notes" column includes miscellaneous information such as previous owners and acquisition dates, rebuilding dates and information, or special equipment. Steam-generator-equipped locomotives are generally indicated in the notes (no notes are included for passenger locomotives that are assumed to have generators, including

EMD E units, FPs, and SDPs, and Alco PAs and FPAs.

Locomotives on short-term leases may not be listed; they are most likely to be included if they were painted in the railroad's colors.

Sources

Sources of printed rosters are included where applicable. These include magazines (usually *Diesel Era* and *Extra 2200 South*) as well as various railroad- and builder-specific books and communications (press releases and correspondence) from railroads and manufacturers. Many online sources were also used, including railroad historical societies and the sites Diesel Shop (thedieselshop.us) and American Rails (american-rails.com). Many of these rosters provide far more thorough coverage than is possible here, with—in many cases—unit-by-unit summaries with dispositions. Other general books with rosters include *Diesel Locomotive Rosters* (Wayner Publications), *Diesel Locomotive Rosters: U.S., Canada, Mexico,* Vols. 1, 2, and 3 (Kalmbach Publishing), and various editions of *The Official Locomotive Rosters & News* by James W. Kerr (DPA-LTA Enterprises, Inc.). Various editions of EMD's *Locomotive Reference Data* books were also used.

Akron, Canton & Youngstown
1942-1964

The Akron, Canton & Youngstown's first diesels were from Alco: an S-2 switcher in 1942 and an RS-1 road switcher in 1945 (six other second-hand S-2s would arrive later). However, the AC&Y would turn to Fairbanks-Morse in 1949 to dieselize its 171-mile main line and become known for its fleet of H-16-44 and H-20-44 diesels. The Norfolk & Western purchased the AC&Y in 1964, and although the railroad existed until the N&W's 1982 merger with Southern (forming Norfolk Southern), the AC&Y used parent N&W's diesels after 1964.

Number 202 was one of eight Fairbanks-Morse H-16-44 diesels on the AC&Y. *Trains magazine collection*

Road numbers	Qty.	Model	Builder	Dates built	Notes
101, 103-108	7	S-2	Alco	1942-47	1
102	1	RS-1	Alco	1945	2
200	1	H-15-44	F-M	1949	
201-208	8	H-16-44	F-M	1951-57	
501-508	8	H-20-44	F-M	1948-53	3

Notes:
1—No. 101 was built as no. D-1; 103 is ex-Delray Connecting 64; 104-105 are ex-Nickel Plate 1, 6; 106-108 are ex-Norfolk & Western 2032, 2038, 2042, nee NKP 32, 38, 42.
2—Delivered as no. D-2.
3—Nos. 506-508 are ex-N&W, nee Pittsburgh & West Virginia 68, 69, 67.

Published roster:
Diesel Locomotive Rosters (Wayner Publications)

Alaska Railroad
1944-current

The Alaska Railroad was owned by the U.S. Government until 1985 (run by the Department of the Interior until 1967, then the Federal Railroad Administration), when it was sold to the State of Alaska. Most of the ARR's early diesels were former U.S. Army locomotives, including oddballs such as military RSD-1s (many of which were shrouded to make RF1A and B locomotives) and MRS-1s, which were originally ordered by the government and built by both Alco and EMD. The railroad's main motive power today is a fleet of SD70MACs, several of which are equipped with head-end power (HEP) for passenger service.

Number 1074 is an RF1A, unique to the ARR and rebuilt from an Alco RSD-1. *Trains Magazine Collection*

Original road numbers	Second numbers	Qty.	Model	Builder	Dates built	Notes
50, 51		2	25-ton	GE	1941, 1944	1
60, 61		2	20GM15	Whitcomb	1940	2
1000, 1001		2	RS-1	Alco	1944	
1002, 1010-1036, 1041-1043, 1085, 1087, 1089		31	RSD-1	Alco	1941-45	3
1050-1052, 1054, 1070, 1072, 1074, 1078		8	RF1A	Alco	1947-50	4
1053, 1055, 1057, 1065, 1067, 1069, 1075-1077		9	RF1B	Alco	1950-53	4
1100-1107		8	65-ton	Porter	1941-43	5
1201-1204		4	SW1	EMD	1942	6
1300		1	Baldwin	VO1000	1945	7
1500-1508 (even)		5	F7A	EMD	1952-53	
1501 (1), 1501 (2), 1503-1511 (odd)		7	F7B	EMD	1949-52	8
1510-1514 (even)		3	FP7	EMD	1953	
1516		1	F3A	EMD	1948	9
1515-1525 (odd)		6	F7B	EMD	1949-52	10
1518-1532 (even)		8	F7A	EMD	1949-52	10
1551-1553		3	MP15	EMD	1976-77	11
1554		1	MP15DC	EMD	1980	11
1601-1613		13	MRS-1	Alco	1953	12
1714-1718, 1809 (1)		5	MRS-1	EMD	1952	12
1821, 1825-1831, 1834, 1836-1839	1801-1810	13	GP7	EMD	1951	13
2000	2504	1	GP30	EMD	1963	14
2001, 2002		2	GP38-2	EMD	1977-78	15
2003-2008		6	GP38	EMD	1968-69	16
2401, 2402		2	E9A	EMD	1955-56	17
2500, 2502, 2503	2501, 3051	3	GP35	EMD	1964-65	18
2801-2809		9	GP49	EMD	1983, 1985	
3000-3005, 3007-3015	3006	15	GP40-2	EMD	1975-78	19
3016-3020		5	GP40	EMD	1967	20
4001-4016, 4317-4328		28	SD70MAC	EMD	1999-2007	21
7107, 7109, 7112, 7123		4	S-2	Alco	1943	22
7249, 7324, 7331, 7356		4	45-tonner	GE	1941-42	23

Notes:
1—No. 50 is nee Todd-California Shipbuilding; 51 is ex-U.S. Army 51, acquired 1946.
2—Ex-U.S. Army 7654, 7655, acquired mid-1940s.
3—Ex-U.S. Army, acquired 1947-51; many were rebuilt to RF1As and RF1Bs.
4—Shrouded locomotives rebuilt from RSD-1s from 1947-50 (railroad's model designation). Nos. 1050, 1051 originally 1050A, 1050B.
5—Ex-U.S. Army, acquired 1947.
6—Ex-U.S. Army 7003, 7004, 7001, 7002, acquired 1947.
7—Ex-U.S. Army V1801, acquired 1949.
8—First 1501 wrecked 1962; second 1501 is ex-Great Northern 444C, acquired 1969. Nos. 1509, 1511 are ex-GN 444B, 450C, acquired 1969.
9—Ex-GN 438D, acquired 1969.
10—Ex-GN and Denver & Rio Grande Western engines, acquired 1969-70; 1523, 1524 rebuilt to F9m.
11—Nos. 1551-1552 are ex-Lake Erie, Franklin & Clarion 25-26, acquired 1992; nos. 1553-1554 are ex-Kelley's Creek & Northwestern 1-2, acquired 1993.
12—Ex-U.S. Army, acquired 1975-77.
13—Ex-U.S. Army, acquired 1960; ten rebuilt to GP7u and renumbered in 1976-77.
14—Rebuilt to GP30u and renumbered in 1974.
15—Ex-Rarus Railway, nee Missouri Pacific, acquired 1986.
16—Ex-Conrail, rebuilt to GP38u, no. 2008 is former GP40, acquired 1986.
17—Ex-Amtrak, no. 2401 is nee Union Pacific 957; no. 2402 is nee Milwaukee Road 202A, acquired 1981.
18—No. 2500 was renumbered 2501 in 1965; no. 2503 (later 3021) rebuilt to GP35u and renumbered in 1992
19—No. 3000 was renumbered 3006 in 1975.
20—Ex-Contrail, nee New York Central; rebuilt to GP40u and acquired 1983.
21—Nos. 4317-4328 equipped with HEP (head-end power) for passenger service.
22—Ex-U.S. Army (same numbers), acquired 1955.
23—Ex-U.S. Army (same numbers), acquired 1974.

Published roster:
Diesel Locomotive Rosters (Wayner Publications)

Algoma Central
1951-1995

Canadian line Algoma Central dieselized with General Motors Diesel (EMD's Canadian subsidiary) GP7s and switchers starting in 1951, and remained loyal to GMD through its final locomotive purchases in the 1980s. Wisconsin Central purchased Algoma Central in 1995.

Road numbers	Qty.	Model	Builder	Dates built	Notes
140, 141	2	SW8	GMD	1951-52	
150-170	21	GP7	GMD	1951-52	
171, 172	2	GP9	GMD	1963	1
180-182	3	SD40	GMD	1971	
183-188	6	SD40-2	GMD	1973	
190, 191	2	GP40u	GMD	1966-67	2
200-205	6	GP38-2	GMD	1981	
1750-1755	6	FP9	GMD	1954-57	3
1756	1	FP7	GMD	1953	4

Notes:
1—No. 172 was last GP9 built.
2—Ex-Soo Line 2108, 2134; nee Milwaukee Road 192, 161.
3—Ex-VIA Rail 6502, 6506, 6511, 6514, 6525, 6531; nee Canadian Pacific (same numbers).
4—Ex-VIA 6553; nee CP 4103.

Amtrak
Current (as of 2017)

Amtrak has replaced all of its EMD F40PH locomotives, converting them to NPCUs—non-powered control units—for push-pull operations. Amtrak now relies mainly on GE P32, P42 and EMD P40 diesels for road service, along with a variety of early EMD switchers.

Amtrak relies on a fleet of P42DCs for its passenger trains. *Alex Mayes*

Initial	Number series	Model	Builder	Dates
AMTK	1-207	P42DC	GE	
AMTK	406	CCU	EMD	1998
AMTK	450-470	F59PHI	EMD	1998
AMTK	500-519	P32-8BWH	GE	1991
AMTK	520-527	GP38H-3	EMD	2004
AMTK	530-539	MP15DC	EMD	1975
AMTK	540-541	SW1500	EMD	1973
AMTK	569	SW1001	EMD	1973
AMTK	570-579	MP15D	MotivePower	2004
AMTK	590	MP14B	MotivePower	2010
AMTK	591	MP21B	MotivePower	2010
AMTK	592, 593	MP14B	MotivePower	2013
AMTK	599	2GS12B-R	NRE	2006
AMTK	600-670	ACS-64	Siemens	2014
AMTK	680-694	HHP-8	Bombardier	
AMTK	700-717	P32AC-DM	GE	1995
AMTK	720-724	GP38-3	EMD	
AMTK	737	SW1	EMD	1941
AMTK	790-799	SW10	EMD	
AMTK	800-843	P40DC	EMD	1993
AMTK	901-953	AEM-7	EMD	
AMTK	1000, 1100	80-Ton	GE	1961
AMTK	2000-2039	Acela Power Car	Bombardier	2002
AMTK	90200-90413	NPCU	EMD	

Ann Arbor
1941-1976

Ann Arbor dieselized with Alco, starting with a pair of S-1 switchers during World War II and adding additional switchers along with RS-1 and FA-2 diesels for road freights in 1950. The line remained all-Alco until the arrival of GP35s (which rode on AAR trucks from traded-in FAs) in 1964.

Ann Arbor declared bankruptcy in 1973. Conrail took over its operations in 1976; the railroad was later purchased by the state of Michigan and operated by a succession of railroads.

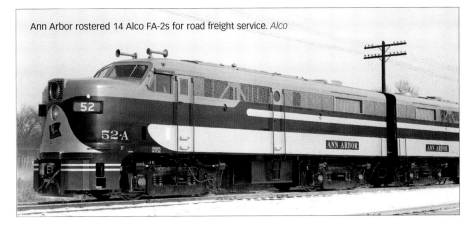

Ann Arbor rostered 14 Alco FA-2s for road freight service. *Alco*

Road numbers	Qty.	Model	Builder	Dates built	Notes
1	1	44-ton	Whitcomb	1941	
2, 3	2	S-1	Alco	1944	
4-7, 10	4	S-3	Alco	1950, 1952	1
20, 21	2	RS-1	Alco	1950	
50-56, 50A-56A	14	FA-2	Alco	1950	
385-394	10	GP35	EMD	1964	2

Notes:
1—No. 10 is ex-Manistique & Lake Superior 1, acquired 1968.
2—GP35s ride on AAR trucks from traded-in FAs.

Published roster:
Diesel Locomotive Rosters (Wayner Publications)

Arkansas & Missouri
1986-present

The Arkansas & Missouri was formed in 1986 from a former St. Louis-San Francisco line running from Van Buren, Ark., to Monett, Mo. The railroad became known for its all-Alco (and MLW) roster, acquiring locomotives second-hand from a variety of sources. In 2012 the railroad broke tradition by buying three EMD SD70ACe diesels, all former demonstrators.

Road numbers	Qty.	Model	Builder	Dates built	Notes
12, 14-18	6	T-6	Alco	1958-59	
20, 22	2	RS-1	Alco	1951, 1943	
30	1	RS-32	Alco	1961	
32, 34	2	C-424	Alco	1965	
40-56 (even), 57, 58-68 (even)	16	C-420	Alco	1964-67	
70 (1)	1	C-630M	MLW	1968	
70 (2), 72-76 (even)	4	M420	MLW	1974-81	
70 (3), 71, 72	3	SD70ACe	EMD	2012	

Atchison, Topeka & Santa Fe
1935-1995

The Santa Fe began dabbling in diesel power in 1935 with a pair of EMC six-axle passenger units (predecessors of E units), followed by switchers from various builders. The railroad dieselized mainly with EMD F units and Geeps, but purchased several Alcos and F-M locomotives as well. In later years, the railroad was a customer of high-horsepower road diesels from both GE and EMD.

The Santa Fe was a major rebuilder of older EMD locomotives, including switchers as well as road diesels. These are called out in the notes, and the Santa Fe designation generally calls for "u" or "m" suffix (sources vary) to the original model number. Be aware that these were sometimes not rebuilt in order or renumbered in the same sequence as their original numbers. The most extensive (and most famous) of these rebuilds was the CF7 program, where F units were remanufactured into road-switcher-style locomotives using a combination of new, used, and fabricated components. Space precludes a unit-by-unit listing of these locomotives.

The Santa Fe merged with Burlington Northern in 1995 to become Burlington Northern Santa Fe.

Santa Fe 303L, 303A, and 303B are an A-B-B set of passenger-service F7s. *Santa Fe*

Original road numbers	Second numbers	Third numbers	Qty.	Model	Builder	Dates built	Notes
1A, 1B	1, 10	1A, 2611	2	Boxcab	EMC	1935	1
2A, 3L-9L			8	E1A	EMC	1937-38	2
2B, 3A, 4A			3	E1B	EMC	1937-38	2
11L, 11A			2	E3A, E3B	EMC	1939	
12L-15L			4	E6A	EMC	1940-41	
12A, 13A, 15A			3	E6B	EMC	1940-41	
16L-36L, 16C-36C			42	F3A	EMD	1946-49	3
16A-36A, 16B-36B			42	F3B	EMD	1946-49	3
37L-47L, 37C-47C			22	F7A	EMD	1949-53	3
37A-48A, 37B-47C			23	F7B	EMD	1949-53	3
50L, 50A			2	DL-109, DL-109B	Alco	1941	
51L-62L, 51B-62B, 70L, 71L	63L-69L, 74L-78L		26	PA-1	Alco	1946-48	
51A-62A, 70A, 71A			14	PB-1	Alco	1946-48	
80L-87L			8	E8Am	EMD	1952-53	1, 2
80A-84A			5	E8Bm	EMD	1952-53	1, 2
90L, 90A, 90B			3	Erie A, B	F-M	1943	
100L-179L, 105C-179C	400..430		155	FTA	EMD	1940-45	4
100A-179A, 100B-179B, 100C-104C	400..430		165	FTB	EMD	1940-45	4
100-108 (2)	5940-5948	5990..5998	9	FP45	EMD	1967	5
100-162			63	GP60M	EMD	1990	
200-250			51	SD75M	EMD	1995	
200L, 200C, 201L, 201C			4	F3A	EMD	1949	
200A, 200B, 201A, 201B			4	F3B	EMD	1949	
202L-280L, 202C-280C			158	F7A	EMD	1949-53	
202A-280A, 202B-280B			158	F7B	EMD	1949-53	
281L-289L, 281C-289C			18	F9A	EMD	1956	
281A-289A, 281B-289B			18	F9B	EMD	1956	
300-314L, 325L-344L			35	F7A	EMD	1949-53	3
300A-314A, 300B-314B, 325A-344A, 325B-340B			56	F7B	EMD	1949-53	3
325-347			23	GP60B	EMD	1991	
350-359	7900-7909		10	U28CG	GE	1966	
400 (1)			1	44-ton	Whitcomb	1941	
400-405	8000-8005		6	U30CG	GE	1967	
450			1	44-ton	Davenport	1941	
460-468			9	44-tonner	GE	1942-44	
500-502 (1)			3	H-10-44	F-M	1945, 1948	
500-582 (2, 3)			83	B40-8W	GE	1990, 1992	
503-540, 544-564 (1, 2)	603..663		59	H-12-44	F-M	1950-57	
541-543 (1)			3	H-12-44TS	F-M	1956	
525-533 (1)	625-633		9	DS-4-4-7.5	Baldwin	1949	
600-611 (1)			12	RSD-7	Alco	1954-55	
600-611 (2), 612-699			100	C44-9W	GE	1994	
700-751	2900-2951	2244..2299	52	GP9	EMD	1956-57	6, 7
800-849 (1)	9800-9849		50	RSD-15	Alco	1959-60	8
800-926 (2)			127	C40-8W	GE	1992-93	
900-979 (1)	4500-4579	4600-4679	80	SD24	EMD	1959-60	9
927-951 (2)			25	C41-8W	GE	1993	
1100-1174	3100-3174	3000-3074	75	GP20	EMD	1960-61	10
1200-1284 (1)	3200..3284	2700..2785	86	GP30	EMD	1962-63	11
1300-1460	3301..3461	2801..2964	165	GP35	EMD	1964-65	12
1215-1217, 1220-1245 (2)			29	SSB1200	EMD	1974-79	13

Original road numbers	Second numbers	Third numbers	Qty.	Model	Builder	Dates built	Notes
1500-1537			38	S-4	Alco	1951-53	
1600-1615			16	U25B	GE	1962-63	
1700-1719	5000-5019		20	SD40	EMD	1966	14
1800-1889	5500-5589	5300-5370, 5408, 5426-5437	90	SD45	EMD	1966	5
1900-1939	5900-5939	5950-5989	40	F45	EMD	1968	5
2100-2109			10	RSD-4	Alco	1951	
2110 (1)	2099		1	RS-2	Alco	1950	15
2110-2162	9110-9162		53	RSD-5	Alco	1951-53	
2151-2153, 2301 (1)	2150, 650-653	1153, 1453	4	SC	EMC	1936-37	19
2200 (1)			1	VO660	Baldwin	1936	16
2201-2259	2450	1160	59	VO1000	Baldwin	1939-45	17
2200 (2), 2260-2299			41	DS-4-4-10	Baldwin	1948-49	
2300-2302			3	HH660	Alco	1934, 1937	18
2303, 2304			2	S-1	Alco	1944	
2310-2321			12	HH1000	Alco	1939	
2322-2391			70	S-2	Alco	1942-49	
2350-2352 (1)	2400-2402		3	NW	EMC	1937	20
2353-2367	2403-2417		15	NW2	EMD	1939-43	21
2370-2380			11	GP38-2	EMD	1977-78	22
2385-2388, 2394-2395	2396-2399		6	RS-1	Alco	1947-50	23
2418L, 2419L	1418L, 1419L		2	TR4A	EMD	1950-51	
2418A, 2419A	1418A, 1419A		2	TR4B	EMD	1950-51	
2420-2438 (1)			19	SW9	EMD	1953	
2439-2441 (1)	1441		3	SW1200	EMD	1959	
2417-2649			233	CF7	EMD	1970-78	24
2600-2605			7	DT-6-6-20	Baldwin	1948-49	
2650-2893	1310-1329, 2000-2027, 2050-2243		244	GP7	EMD	1950-53	6, 25
2788A-2792A	2244, 2258, 2270, 2288		5	GP7B	EMD	1953	6
2800-2819	3000-3019		20	H-16-44	F-M	1951-52	
3461	2964		1	GP40	EMD	1969	26
3500-3560	2300..2360		61	GP38	EMD	1970	27
3600-3705			106	GP39-2	EMD	1974-80	
3800-3809			10	GP40X	EMD	1978	
3810-3854			45	GP50	EMD	1981, 1985	
4000-4019 (1)	1556-1575		20	SD39	EMD	1969	28
4000-4039 (2)			40	GP60	EMD	1988-89	
5020-5192, 5200-5213			197	SD40-2	EMD	1977-81	
5250-5267			18	SDP40Fu	EMD	1973-74	29
5501, 5502 (1), 5502 (2), 5510-5517			11	SD45B, SD45-2B	EMD		30
5590-5624			35	SD45	EMD	1969-70	5
5625-5714			90	SD45-2	EMD	1972-73	
6300-6348			49	U23B	GE	1970-71	
6350-6418			69	B23-7	GE	1978-84	
7400-7402			3	B39-8	GE	1984	
7410-7449			40	B40-8	GE	1988-89	
7484-7499			16	B36-7	GE	1980	
7500-7519			20	U23C	GE	1969	
8010-8166			157	C30-7	GE	1977-82	
8500-8524			25	U33C	GE	1969	
8700-8799			100	U36C	GE	1972-75	

Notes:
1—Rebuilt to E8Am 83A, 84A by EMD, 1952.
2—Rebuilt to E8m by EMD, 1952-53.
3—Passenger service, steam-generator equipped (B units; A units carried water tanks).
4—Santa Fe numbered its FTs (and later Fs) with letter suffixes L, A, B, C: L (A units, for "lead") and C were A units, "A" was a B unit, and "C" could be an A or B depending upon whether it was an A-B-B-A or A-B-A consist. Many FTs were renumbered as consists were mixed and operated in A-B-B-A, A-B-B-B, or A-B-A configurations. Nos. 158-168LABC were equipped for passenger service.
5—SD45s rebuilt to SD45u in 1980-85; F45s rebuilt to F45u and FP45s to FP45u in 1980-83.
6—GP7s and GP9s were rebuilt to GP7u and GP9u and renumbered beginning in 1972.
7—Nos. 726-731 equipped with steam generators.
8—Nos. 9828, 9826, 9846 rebuilt to CRSD20 for hump service, renumbered 3900-3902, then 1300-1302.
9—Rebuilt by Santa Fe starting in 1973 with new horsepower rating of 2650, renamed SD26s.
10—GP20s remanufactured to GP20u in 1977-81.
11—No. 2785 is ex-TP&W 700, acquired 1984. GP30s remanufactured to GP30u in 1980-84.
12—Nos. 2961-2964 are ex-TP&W, acquired 1984. GP35s remanufactured to GP35u in 1979-84.
13—Rebuilt from older NW2 (1215-1217), SW9 (1220-1238), SW1200 (1239-1241), and TR4 (1242-1245) switchers by Santa Fe.
14—SD40s rebuilt to SD40u in 1980-81.
15—Former 1,600-hp Alco demonstrator 1600; steam-generator equipped.
16—Former Baldwin demonstrator 62000, acquired 1937.
17—No. 2220 was rebuilt with EMD engine and hood and renumbered 2450, then 1160.
18—No. 2300 is former Alco demonstrator no. 1, acquired 1935.
19—Rebuilt to SW900u by EMD, 1957.
20—Rebuilt to SW1200u by EMD, 1959, and renumbered 2439-2441.
21—Three NW2s were rebuilt to SSB1200s, nos. 1215-1217, in 1974-78.
22—Ex-Toledo, Peoria & Western 2001-2011, acquired with merger in 1984.
23—Nos. 2385-2388 equipped with steam generators; renumbered 2396-2399.
24—Rebuilt from older F3, F7, and F9 diesels by Santa Fe shops. Completed units were numbered in descending order.
25—Nos. 2650-2654, 2848, 2879-2893 are steam-generator equipped.
26—Ex-TP&W 1000, acquired 1984.
27—Rebuilt in 1984-85, reclassified GP38u.
28—SD39s rebuilt in 1985 to SD39u, renumbered.
29—Ex-Amtrak SDP40Fs; rebuilt in 1985 to SDP40Fu.
30—Rebuilt without cabs from various older SD45s and SD45-2s.

Published rosters:
Santa Fe Motive Power, by Joe McMillan (McMillan Publications, 1985), The Santa Fe Diesel, Vols. 1, 2, by Dr. Cinthia Priest (Paired Rail, 1997, 1998), CF7 Locomotives, by Cary Poole (Railroad Press, 1997)

Atlanta & St. Andrews Bay
1941-1994

The Atlanta & St. Andrews Bay, long known as "The Bay Line," dieselized with Alco S-2 switchers and RS-1 road switchers in the 1940s. It then added a variety of EMD power in the 1950s and later. The railroad was acquired by holding company Rail Management Corporation in 1994. RMC created a new company, the Bay Line, to operate the railroad, making its nickname official. Genesee & Wyoming acquired the Bay Line in 2005.

Original road numbers	Second numbers	Qty.	Model	Builder	Dates built	Notes
500-502 (1)	511 (1)	3	GP7	EMD	1952-53	1
500-507 (2), 511 (2)		8	GP38	EMD	1969	2
503-505 (1)		3	SD9	EMD	1956, 1958	
506 (1)		1	SD40	EMD	1966	
507 (1)		1	GP39	EMD	1970	
508-510		3	GP38-2	EMD	1973, 1975	
512		1	GP9	EMD	1956	3
901-913		13	RS-1	Alco	1941-50	
1001, 1002		2	S-2	Alco	1942	
1501		1	F3A	EMD	1947	
6416, 6418, 6419		3	GP40-2	EMD	1973	4

Notes:
1—No. 500 is ex-Reading 616; 502 was rebuilt in 1977 and renumbered 511.
2—Nos. 500, 501 are ex-Gulf, Mobile & Ohio 713, 707; 502-507, 511 are ex-Conrail (nee Penn Central) 7760, 7781, 7790, 7792, 7811, 7819, 7749.
3—Ex-Chesapeake & Ohio 6085.
4—Ex-Grand Trunk Western 6416, 6418, 6419 (nee Detroit, Toledo & Ironton 416, 418, 419).

Published roster:
Diesel Era, November-December 2007

Atlantic Coast Line
1939-1967

The Atlantic Coast Line began dieselizing passenger trains with EMC E units in 1939, followed by several sets of FT freight locomotives during World War II, and completed the job with later F units and GP7s through 1951. Second-generation power began arriving in the early 1960s from EMD as well as GE and Alco. The ACL merged with Seaboard Air Line to form Seaboard Coast Line on July 1, 1967.

The ACL's GE U30B diesels ride on EMD GP trucks from traded-in locomotives. *GE*

Original road numbers	Second numbers	Qty.	Model	Builder	Dates built	Notes
44-46		3	S-2	Alco	1943-44	1
50-59		10	SW8	EMD	1952	
70-71		2	Switcher	Whitcomb	1944	2
100-274		175	GP7	EMD	1950-51	3
300A-323A		24	FTA	EMD	1943-44	
300B-323B		24	FTB	EMD	1943-44	
324A-335A		12	F2A	EMD	1946	
324B-335B		12	F2B	EMD	1946	
336A-347A		12	F3A	EMD	1948	
336B-347B		12	F3B	EMD	1948	
348A-429A		82	F7A	EMD	1950-51	
392B-403B		12	F7B	EMD	1951	
500		1	E3A	EMC	1939	
501-523		23	E6A	EMD	1939-42	
524-543		20	E7A	EMD	1945-48	
544-548		5	E8A	EMD	1950	
600 (1)	25	1	HH1000	Alco	1940	
606-609, 616, 617-623 (odd)	10-18	9	VO1000	Baldwin	1942	
602, 604, 610, 612, 614, 618-642 (even)	26-43	18	S-2	Alco	1942, 1944	
601, 611, 613, 603, 615, 605	600-605 (2)	6	NW2	EMD	1940, 1942	
643-651		9	SW7	EMD	1950	
652-716		65	SW9	EMD	1951-52	
717, 718		2	SW7	EMD	1950	4

Original road numbers	Second numbers	Qty.	Model	Builder	Dates built	Notes
719, 720		2	SW9	EMD	1952	5
750-754		5	E6B	EMD	1940-42	
755-764		10	E7B	EMD	1945	
850-874		25	FP7	EMD	1951	
875-893	430-448	19	FP7	EMD	1951-52	
900-908		9	GP30	EMD	1963	
909-914		6	GP35	EMD	1963	
915-929		15	GP40	EMD	1966	
975-978		4	U30B	GE	1967	
1000-1023		24	SD35	EMD	1964-65	
1024-1033		10	SD45	EMD	1966	
1099		1	SDP35	EMD	1965	
1100-1104		5	GP7	EMD	1950-51	6
1503, 1504		2	GP9	EMD	1957	7
2000-2010		11	C-628	Alco	1963-64	
2011-2013		3	C-630	Alco	1965	
3000-3020		21	U25C	GE	1963-64	8
3021-3024		4	U28C	GE	1966	

Notes:
1—Ex-Richmond, Fredericksburg & Potomac 54, 56, 57.
2—Ex-Franklin & Carolina 100, 110.
3—Numbers 254-274 are ex-Charleston & Western Carolina, acquired with merger in 1959.
4—Ex-CW&C 800, 801, acquired 1959.
5—Ex-CW&C 802, 803, acquired 1959.
6—Ex-Columbia, Newberry & Laurens 100-104.
7—Leased to Winston-Salem Southbound.
8—Nos. 3011-3013 have 2800-hp engines and were classified U25Cm by ACL.

Published roster:
Extra 2200 South, July 1968

Baltimore & Ohio
Includes Baltimore & Ohio Chicago Terminal
1925-1973

The Baltimore & Ohio was an early internal-combustion user, buying the third boxcab oil-electric built by Alco-GE-Intersoll-Rand and acquiring Electro-Motive passenger diesels in the mid-1930s. In spite of this, the B&O was one of the last major railroads to completely dieselize, running steam as late as 1958. Early road diesels were primarily EMD F units and Geeps plus some Alco FA cab units, followed by later-model EMD GPs and SDs in the 1960s.

The B&O was closely tied to the Chesapeake & Ohio—in the early 1960s the C&O owned 90 percent of B&O stock. Many diesels were bought and sold between the two railroads, and by the mid-1960s many diesels were renumbered to avoid duplicate numbering between the railroads. The B&O had also undertaken a general renumbering of most locomotives in 1957, so many engines wore three numbers over the years.

This roster covers all locomotives owned by June 1973, when the B&O, C&O, and Western Maryland became subsidiaries of the newly formed Chessie System. See the Chessie System's separate entry for diesels owned at that time and later.

Original road numbers	Second numbers	Third numbers	Qty.	Model	Builder	Dates built	Notes
1 (1)	195	8000	1	Boxcab	A-GE-IR	1925	1
1-11, 1A-11A (odd)	101-111, 101A-111A (odd)	4400-4411	12	FTA	EMD	1942-43	2
1X-11X, 1AX-11AX (odd)	101X -111X,101AX-111AX (odd)	5400-5411	12	FTB	EMD	1942-43	2
19, 20	8801, 8802	8301, 8302	2	44-tonner	GE	1950	
25	8900		1	18-ton	Plymouth	1926	
26-32, 26A-32A (even)	1446-1453		8	E8A	EMD	1953	
34-40 (even)	1454-1457		4	E9A	EMD	1955	
50			1	AA	EMC	1935	
51, 52 (1), 53-56	1433..1437		6	EA	EMC	1937-38	3
51X-56X	2414-2419		6	EB	EMC	1937-38	3

GP30 No. 6900 was built in 1962. *EMD*

Original road numbers	Second numbers	Third numbers	Qty.	Model	Builder	Dates built	Notes
52 (2), 57-63	1408..1413		8	E6A	EMC	1940-41	
57X-63X	2407-2413		7	E6B	EMC	1940-41	
64-80, 64A-80A (even)	1415-1432		18	E7A	EMD	1945	
82X-88X, 82AX-86AX (even)	2400-2406	5520-5526	7	F3B	EMD	1947	
90-96, 90A-96A (even)	1438-1445	1463	8	E8A	EMD	1950	
113-171, 113A-171A (odd)	4420-4479		60	F3A	EMD	1948-49	
153X-171X (odd)	5420-5429		10	F7B	EMD	1950	
180-192, 180A-192A (even)	4480-4493		14	F7A	EMD	1949	
180X-192X, 180AX-192AX (even)	5430-5443		14	F7B	EMD	1949	
190 (1)	198	8820	1	80-ton	GE	1943	
194	8800		1	65-ton	GE	1943	
196, 197	9720, 9721		2	H-12-44	F-M	1953	
199	8422		1	SW	EMC	1936	4
200-215	8400-8415		16	SW1	EMD	1940	
216-221 (B&OCT)	8416-8421		6	SW1	EMD	1942	
222-227	8010-8015	9050-9055	6	S-1	Alco	1944	
231-297, 239A-297A (odd)	4494..4557		64	F7A	EMD	1950-51	
231X-237X, 249X-297X (odd)	5444-5472		31	F7B	EMD	1950-51	
300-309	9700-9709		10	H-10-44	F-M	1948	
310-319	9710-9719		10	H-12-44	F-M	1951	
320-329	9376-9385		10	LS-1200	Lima	1951	
330-339	9366-9375		10	LS-1000	Lima	1950	
340-353	9386-9399		14	LS-1200	Lima	1951	
361-365, 361A-365A, (odd), 367-374	4558-4571		14	F7A	EMD	1950-51	
361X-365X (odd), 363AX, 365AX, 367X-374X, 367AX-374AX	5473-5493		21	F7B	EMD	1950-51	
375	8200		1	VO660	Baldwin	1941	
376-399	9250-9273		24	DS-4-4-10	Baldwin	1950	
400-408	9500-9508		9	NW2	EMD	1940, 1943	

Original road numbers	Second numbers	Third numbers	Qty.	Model	Builder	Dates built	Notes
409-411 (B&OCT)	9509-9511		3	NW2	EMD	1943	
413-437	9200-9224		25	VO1000	Baldwin	1943-45	
438-462	9225-9249		25	DS-44-10	Baldwin	1948	
463-467	9274-9278		5	S-12	Baldwin	1953	
468-474, 534-545	9000-9018		19	S-4	Alco	1955	
475-533	9019-9077		59	S-2	Alco	1943-48	
550-589	9512-9551		40	NW2	EMD	1948-49	
590-597 (B&OCT)	9600-9607		8	SW9	EMD	1952	
598-603	9608-9613		6	SW9	EMD	1953	
625-653	9400-9428		29	SW900	EMD	1955	
675-696	6425-6446		22	GP9	EMD	1955	
720-731	6413-6424		12	GP7	EMD	1953	
740-746	3400-3406	6693-6699	7	GP7	EMD	1953	
747-752	3407-3412	6600-6605	6	GP9	EMD	1955	
760-764	7400-7404 (1)	1826-1830	5	SD7	EMD	1952-53	
765-774	7405-7414 (1)	1831-1840	10	SD9	EMD	1954-55	
801-837, 801A-837A (odd)	4000-4037 (1)	4128..4137 (1)	38	FA-2	Alco	1950-53	
801X-837X, 817AX, 837AX (odd)	5000-5020	4106..4110	21	FB-2	Alco	1950-53	
847, 849	4200, 4201		2	DR-4-4-15A	Baldwin	1948	5
847X, 849X	5200, 5201		2	DR-4-4-15B	Baldwin	1948	5
851-871, 851A-865A (odd)	4202-4220		19	RF-16	Baldwin	1950-53	
851X-861X, 865X-871X, 867AX-871AX (odd)	5202-5214		13	RF-16B	Baldwin	1952-53	
890-905	6200-6215	2234-2249	16	AS-16	Baldwin	1952-55	
906, 907	6700, 6701		2	H-16-44	F-M	1953	
910-922	6400-6412		13	GP7	EMD	1953	
925-927	6702-6704	9737-9739	3	H-16-44	F-M	1955	
929-993, 929A-973A, 977A-993A (odd)	4572-4636		65	F7A	EMD	1952-53	
929X-961X, 977X-993X (odd)	5494-5519		26	F7B	EMD	1952-53	
1400-1406	4637-4643		7	F3A	EMD	1947	6
1440 (2), 1460-1462, 1464-1467			8	E8A	EMD	1951	7
2007-2016			10	RSD-12	Alco	1956	8
2250			1	AS-616	Baldwin	1951	9
2400-2406	5520-5526		7	F3B	EMD	1947	6
3413-3425	6606-6618		13	GP9	EMD	1956	
3500-3519, 3540-3559, 3581			40	GP35	EMD	1964	
3684-3779			96	GP40	EMD	1966-71	
3800-3849			50	GP38	EMD	1967	
4000-4064 (2)			65	GP40	EMD	1971	
4100-4164 (2), 4185-4246			127	GP40-2	EMD	1972	
4412, 4413			2	FTA	EMD	1945	10
4644-4654			11	F7A	EMD	1950-51	11
4800-4819			20	GP38	EMD	1970	
5412, 5413			2	FTB	EMD	1945	10
5527-5537, 5540			11	F7B	EMD	1950-51	11
6447-6598			152	GP9	EMD	1956-58	12
6599			1	GP18M	EMD	1962	13
6650-6683			34	GP9	EMD	1956	14
6705-6709	9740..9743		5	H-16-44	F-M	1957	
6900-6976			77	GP30	EMD	1962-63	

Original road numbers	Second numbers	Third numbers	Qty.	Model	Builder	Dates built	Notes
7094, 7095			2	FP7	EMD	1952	14
7400-7419 (2), 7437-7440			24	SD35	EMD	1964-65	
7482-7494, 7497-7500			17	SD40	EMD	1967, 1969	
9078-9114			37	S-4	Alco	1956-57	
9115-9144			30	S-2	Alco		15
9145-9149			5	S-2	Alco	1942-44	16
9185, 9186			2	RS-1	Alco	1953	17
9614-9621			8	SW1200	EMD	1957	
9622, 9624			2	TR4A	EMD	1950	8
9623, 9625			2	TR4B	EMD	1950	8
9722-9726			5	H-12-44	F-M	1957	

Notes:
1—Alco-GE-Ingersoll-Rand 60-ton, oil-electric boxcab was the third built; renumbered in 1942 and 1957.
2—FTs originally had single numbers for four-unit (A-B-B-A) sets; letter suffixes were added in 1947.
3—EAs 51, 53-56 were rebuilt to E8Ams in 1953-54; EBs were rebuilt to E8Bm. EBs were numbered with their A units; X suffix was added in 1947.
4—Ex-Baltimore & Ohio Chicago Terminal 2, renumbered 199 in 1942, re-engined in 1955.
5—Ex-Elgin, Joliet & Eastern 700A-B, 701A-B, former Baldwin demonstrators, acquired 1955.
6—Steam-generator equipped.
7—Ex-C&O, transferred 1967-68.
8—Ex-C&O, transferred 1969.
9—Ex-C&O, transferred 1967.
10—Ex-New York, Ontario & Western, acquired 1957.
11—Nos. 4644-4654, 5527-5537 are ex-Bessemer & Lake Erie 701A-711A, 701B-711B, acquired 1962; no. 5540 is ex-C&O 7519.
12—No. 6571 is a GP9m, rebuilt from wrecked F7A 245 in 1957.
13—Rebuilt from F3 4428.
14—Ex-C&O, transferred 1968.
15—Ex-C&O, transferred 1963-64.
16—Ex-Lehigh Valley 150, 153, 155, 161, 162, acquired 1965.
17—Ex-C&O, transferred 1966.

Published rosters:
Extra 2200 South, March-April 1972; Chessie System Locomotives, by Jerry Doyle (TLC Publishing, 1999)

Bangor & Aroostook
1947-1995

The Bangor & Aroostook didn't purchase its first diesels (EMD F3s) until 1947, but dieselization then came quickly, with the last steam operations in 1949. The railroad kept its older diesels in good shape for a long time, supplanting them with GP38s in the late 1960s. BAR was purchased by rail holding company Iron Road Railways in 1995.

Original road numbers	Second numbers	Qty.	Model	Builder	Dates built	Notes
10 (2)		1	65-tonner	GE	1950	1
20 (2)		1	S-3	Alco	1954	2
20 (3), 21-23 (2), 24		5	GP7	EMD	1952	3
30-34 (1)		5	Y	GE	1936	4
30-34 (2), 35-39		10	SW9	EMD	1951	5
76-80		5	GP9	EMD	1954	
81-88	361, 358, 357, 365, 350, 352, 359, 360	8	GP38	EMD	1966-67	6
90-98	354, 362, 355, 353, 366, 363, 356, 364, 351	9	GP38	EMD	1966-70	6, 7
500A-507A	40-47	8	F3A	EMD	1947-48	
550-557	50-57	8	BL2	EMD	1949	
560-575	60-75	16	GP7	EMD	1950, 1952	
600B-603B		4	F3B	EMD	1947-48	8
700, 701	10 (1), 11	2	E7A	EMD	1949	
800-803	20-23	4	NW2	EMD	1949	

Notes:
All—General renumbering done in 1953.
1—Ex-Fraser Papers 6, acquired 1972.
2—Ex-Fraser 7, acquired 1972.
3—Ex-Santa Fe, acquired 1991.
4—Ex-New Haven 0901-0905, acquired 1952.
5—Nos. 30-36 are ex-Pittsburgh & Lake Erie, acquired 1972; 37-39 are ex-Pittsburgh, Chartiers & Youghiogheny 3-5, acquired 1975.
6—GP38s rebuilt and upgraded; BAR renumbered them and reclassified them GP38-3 after rebuilding.
7—Nos. 90-94 ex-Conrail, nee Pennsylvania-Reading Seashore Lines, acquired 1983; 95-98 ex-Missouri Pacific.
8—Sold to Pennsylvania RR in 1952 before renumbering.

Belt Railway of Chicago
1930-present

The Belt Railway of Chicago has operated a variety of locomotives over the years, including early boxcabs and switchers from EMD, Alco, and Baldwin, Alco Centuries, and newer EMD (and rebuilt EMD) locomotives. The railroad is currently owned by BNSF, Canadian National, Canadian Pacific, CSX, Norfolk Southern, and Union Pacific.

Belt Railway 500A and B are a TR2 cow/calf set, essentialy an NW2 plus a cabless B unit. *EMD*

Road Numbers	Qty.	Model	Builder	Dates built	Notes
140	1	2GS14B	NRE		1
150	1	MP15AC	EMD	—	5
210, 211	2	3G21B	NRE		1
230-237	8	GP23-ECO	EMD	2013-14	2
300, 302, 306	3	SD40-2	EMD	1980	3
300, 302, 303	3	HH600	Alco	1934-35	
301	1	Boxcab	GE-IR	1930	
304-306	3	S-1	Alco	1941-42	
400, 403, 404, 406-411	9	S-2	Alco	1941-50	
401, 402	2	VO1000	Baldwin	1942, 1944	
405	1	DS-4-4-10	Baldwin	1947	
420	1	S-6	Alco	1957	
450-458	9	RS-2	Alco	1949	
470-477	8	GP7	EMD	1951-52	
480-481	2	GP9	EMD	1956	
490-495	6	GP38-2	EMD	1972	
500, 501	2	TR-2A	EMD	1949	4
502-506	5	TR-4A	EMD	1950	4
510-511	2	TR-2B	EMD	1949	4
512-516	5	TR-4B	EMD	1950	4
520-523	4	SW9	EMD	1951	
524-526	3	SW1200	EMD	1963	
530-532	3	SW1500	EMD	1967-68	
533-536	4	MP15DC	EMD	1975, 1980	5
538-539	2	SW1500	EMD	1968, 1970	6
560, 561	2	SD40-3	EMD	1971	7
562-566	5	SD38-3	EMD	1971	7
570-574	5	SD38-2	EMD	1966-70	7
580-587	8	GP38-2	EMD	1978-79	8
600-605	6	C-424	Alco	1965-66	

Notes:
1—Genset locomotives.
2—Rebuilt from GP40s of various heritage.
3—Ex-Burlington Northern 8122, 8121, 8136.
4—Nos. 500-506, 510-516 are cow/calf switchers, originally numbered 500-506A, B.
5—No. 534 rebuilt to MP15AC and renumbered 150.
6—No. 538 is ex-Norfolk Southern 2321, nee Southern 2321; 539 is ex-Conrail 9225, nee Penn Central 9225.
7—Rebuilt from SD40s of various heritage.
8—Ex-NS, nee CR.

Published rosters:
Diesel Locomotive Rosters (Wayner Publications); Diesel Era January/February 1996

Bessemer & Lake Erie
1935-2004

The Bessemer & Lake Erie acquired several switchers and Baldwin road switchers in the late 1940s, then fully dieselized with a fleet of F7s (and a few SDs) from 1951-53. This roster covers the period until Canadian National acquired control of B&LE's holding company in 2004.

Electro-Motive F7s were B&LE's main road power beginning in the early 1950s. *B&LE*

Road numbers	Qty.	Model	Builder	Dates built	Notes
150-153, 160, 161	6	SW1500	EMD	1972-73	1
210	1	SD38-2	EMD	1975	2
281	1	65-tonner	Westinghouse	1936	
282	1	DS-4-4-10	Baldwin	1949	
285	1	SW8	EMD	1951	3
286	1	NW2	EMD	1947	4
291-292	2	S-4	Alco	1952	
401-407	7	DRS-6-6-15	Baldwin	1949-50	
408-409	2	AS-616	Baldwin	1952	
451-455	5	SD7	EMD	1953	
658	1	SD38-2	EMD	1974	5
701A-728A	28	F7A	EMD	1950-53	
701B-726B	26	F7B	EMD	1950-53	
801-803	3	SD7	EMD	1952	
821-847	27	SD9	EMD	1956-58	6
851-859	9	SD18	EMD	1960, 1962	7
861-863	3	SD38	EMD	1967	
864-869	6	SD38AC	EMD	1971	
870-879	10	SD38-2	EMD	1973	
881-886	6	RSD-15	Alco	1959	8
890-892	3	SD38-2	EMD	1975-76	
900-910	11	SD40T-3	EMD	1972-75	9

Notes:
1—Nos. 150-153 are ex-Conrail (nee Penn Central), acquired 1997; 160, 161 are ex-Union Railroad 6, 8, acquired 2000.
2—Ex-Duluth, Missabe & Iron Range 209, acquired 1980.
3—Ex-Donora Southern 802, acquired 1963.
4—Ex-Northampton & Bath 1002 (nee Lake Terminal 1002), acquired 1973.
5—Ex-Elgin, Joliet & Eastern 658, acquired 1986.
6—Ex-DM&IR, acquired 1964-80.
7—Nos. 858, 859 are ex-DM&IR 182, 181, acquired 2004.
8—Ex-DM&IR 50-55, acquired 1964.
9—Former St. Louis Southwestern and Southern Pacific SD45T-2s, rebuilt and acquired in 1999.

Published roster:
Diesel Era May/June 2012

Birmingham Southern
1937-2012

The Birmingham Southern was a shortline operating in the Birmingham, Ala., area. The railroad operated a variety of switchers into the 1970s, then acquired several second-hand road locomotives, including SD9s and GP38-2s. The line was purchased by Watco Companies in 2012, which renamed it the Birmingham Terminal Railway.

Original road numbers	Second numbers	Qty.	Model	Builder	Dates built	Notes
10-17	210, 212, 213	8	SW1000	EMD	1967-71	
18, 19	218, 219	2	SW1001	EMD	1973	
21-24		4	NW2	EMD	1948	1
71-75	91-95	5	NC1	EMC	1937	2
81-88		8	HH900	Alco	1937-38	
89		1	HH1000	Alco	1940	
100, 101		2	S-1	Alco	1941	
150, 151		2	RS-2	Alco	1949-50	
152-154		3	RS-3	Alco	1951-55	3
160		1	RSD-5	Alco	1953	
200, 201		2	SW1200	EMD	1957	
220-225		6	SW1001	EMD	1974	
260, 261		2	MP15	EMD	1976	
351-355		5	SW1500	EMD	1971	4
360		1	SW1504	EMD	1973	5
370		1	MP15	EMD	1976	6
371, 372		2	MP15DC	EMD	1976	6
373		1	SW1500	EMD		7
505		1	MP15DC	EMD	1976	7
519, 523, 525		3	S-2	Alco	1945	
574, 575, 588		3	SW9m	EMD	1953	8
601-603		3	SW1001	EMD	1976	9
629, 634, 639, 640, 649, 650, 652, 657, 658, 660, 661, 815		12	SD9	EMD	1957-59	10
700-704		5	GP38-2	EMD	1972	11
711, 714		2	GP35M	EMD	1964-65	12
743	243	1	RS-1	Alco	1943	13
820		1	SD18	EMD	1960	10

Notes:
1—Ex-Lake Terminal 1009, 1010, 1012, 1013, acquired 1962.
2—Rebuilt to SW900s and renumbered in 1958-60.
3—Nos. 153, 154 are ex-Federal Barge Lines 60, 61.
4—Ex-Conrail 9516, 9556, Southern Pacific 2469, Minnesota Transfer 306, St. Marys 503.
5—Ex-National of Mexico 8808.
6—Nos. 370-372 are ex-U.S. Steel 170, 967, 955.
7—Ex-St. Marys.
8—Rebuilt SW9s.
9—Ex-Union Railroad 601-603.
10—Ex-Duluth, Missabe & Iron Range; 820 is rebuilt (railroad classed SD-M).
11—Ex-Elgin, Joliet & Eastern.
12—Rebuilt ex-Southern Pacific GP35s.
13—Ex-Rock Island 743.

Published roster:
Diesel Locomotive Rosters (Wayner Publications)

BNSF
Current (as of 2017)

Most of BNSF's early power, including EMD SD40-2s and GP38-2, have been rebuilt or sold. Today, the railroad depends mainly on EMD SD70MAC and GE ES44 diesels for priority trains.

A BNSF SD70MAC leads a coal train in 2008.
Steve Schmollinger

Initial	Number series	Model	Builder	Dates
BNSF	50-60	TEBC6	VMV	1992
BNSF	61-70	Slug	ATSF	Various
BNSF	100-158	GP60M	EMD	1990
BNSF	145-159	GP60-3	EMD	1990
BNSF	160-200	GP60	EMD	1990-1991
BNSF	227-299	SD75M	EMD	1995-1997
BNSF	300-302	SD40-2B	EMD	1973-1980
BNSF	325-346	GP60B	EMD	1991
BNSF	500-559	B40-8W	GE	1990-1992
BNSF	561-597	B40-8	GE	1988-1989
BNSF	599-619	AC44C4M	GE	2014
BNSF	620-799	C44-9W	GE	1994-1997
BNSF	867-951	C40-8W	GE	1993
BNSF	960-1123	C44-9W	GE	1996-1997
BNSF	1205	HH20B	RP	2008
BNSF	1210	GG20B	RP	2005
BNSF	1211	RP14D	RP	2005
BNSF	1220-1292	3GS21B	NRE	2007-2010
BNSF	1293, 1294	3GS21B-DE	NRE	2010
BNSF	1300-1310	3GS21C	NRE	2010-2012
BNSF	1311-1316	3GS21C-DE	NRE	2014
BNSF	1320-1323	PR30C	Progress Rail	2009
BNSF	1350-1352	SD32ECO	EMD	R2013
BNSF	1400-1476	SD60M	EMD	1990-1991
BNSF	1500-1539	GP28-2	EMD	R1992
BNSF	1540-1549	GP28-2P	EMD	R1993

Initial	Number series	Model	Builder	Dates
BNSF	1550-1553	SD9-3	EMD	R1996
BNSF	1554-1558	SD38-3P	EMD	R1992
BNSF	1559-1562	SD38-2P	EMD	1966-1979
BNSF	1563, 1564	SD38-2	EMD	1979
BNSF	1565-1585	SD40-2R	EMD	R 2007-2013
BNSF	1590-1999	SD39-2/SD40-2	EMD	1973-1981
BNSF	2000-2039	GP38-2N	EMD	R 2006-2007
BNSF	2040-2107	GP38-2	EMD	1968-1974
BNSF	2112-2247	GP38/GP38-2R	EMD	1970-1971
BNSF	2249	GP38-2B	EMD	1976
BNSF	2256-2382	GP38-2/GP38-2R	EMD	1973-1978
BNSF	2390-2392	GP38-3R	EMD	R 2009
BNSF	2529-2699	GP35/GP39-3R	EMD	1964-1965
BNSF	2700-2739	GP39-2	EMD	1981
BNSF	2740-2768	GP39-2R	EMD	R 1989-1991
BNSF	2769-2799	GP39-2	EMD	1975
BNSF	2800-2834	GP39-2R	EMD	R 1989-1990
BNSF	2835-2869	GP39-2	EMD	1975-1979
BNSF	2870-2940	GP39-2R	EMD	R 1988-1991
BNSF	2941-2959	GP39-2	EMD	1979
BNSF	2961-2984	GP39-2R	EMD	R 1990
BNSF	3000-3029	GP40-2	EMD	1968
BNSF	3030-3038	GP25X	EMD	1978
BNSF	3039	GP25XE	EMD	1978
BNSF	3101-3105	GP50	EMD	1980-1985
BNSF	3110-3157	GP50+	EMD	1985
BNSF	3158-3161	GP50Q+	EMD	1985
BNSF	3162	GP50-3	EMD	1985
BNSF	3163-3199	GP50	EMD	1981-1985
BNSF	3764-3999	ET44C4	GE	2015
BNSF	4000-4199	C44-9W	GE	2002-2003
BNSF	4225-4299	ET44C4	GE	2016
BNSF	4300-5532	C44-9W	GE	1997-2004
BNSF	5600-5717	AC4400CW	GE	1999-2004
BNSF	5718-5747	AC4400EV	GE	2003
BNSF	5748-5837	ES44AC	GE	2005
BNSF	5838-5840	AC4400CW	GE	2004
BNSF	5844-6438	ES44AC	GE	2005-2009
BNSF	6500-7199	ES44C4	GE	2013
BNSF	7200-7920	ES44DC	GE	2005-2010
BNSF	7921-7999	ES44C4 (T4C)	GE	2014-2015
BNSF	8000-8291	ES44C4	GE	2013-2014
BNSF	8318-8399	ES44C4 (T4C)	GE	2014-2015
BNSF	8400-8499	SD70ACe	EMD	2014
BNSF	8500-8519	SD70ACe-P4	EMD	2014
BNSF	8520-8599	SD70ACe	EMD	2014
BNSF	8749-8799	SD70ACe	EMD	2013
BNSF	8800-8989	SD70MAC	EMD	1999-2000
BNSF	8990-9399	SD70ACe	EMD	2006-2014
BNSF	9400-9999	SD70MAC	EMD	1993-1999

Boston & Maine
1930-1983

The Boston & Maine began dieselizing early, with switchers in the 1930s and EMD's pioneering FTs during World War II. EMD Geeps and Alco RS units completed dieselization, with the railroad's last steam operations coming in 1956. This roster covers the period until Boston & Maine was purchased by Guilford in 1983.

Original road numbers	Second numbers	Qty.	Model	Builder	Dates built	Notes
1, 2		2	P12-42	F-M	1957	1
100		1	16-ton	Plymouth	1930	
101		1	ML-8	Plymouth	1938	
110-119		10	44-tonner	GE	1940-48	
200-212		12	GP38-2	EMD	1973	
300-317		18	GP40-2	EMD	1977	
800-807		8	SW8	EMD	1953	
860-865	1280-1283	6	S-5	Alco	1954	2
1100		1	Center-cab	GE	1935	
1101, 1102	1161, 1160	2	HH660	Alco	1938, 1934	
1103-1108		6	SC	EMC	1936, 1938	
1109-1132		24	SW1	EMD	1939-53	
1162		1	HH660	Alco	1939	
1163-1172		10	S-1	Alco	1944-49	
1173-1188		16	S-3	Alco	1950, 1952	
1200-1213		14	NW2	EMD	1941-49	
1220-1231		12	SW9	EMD	1952-53	
1260-1265		6	S-2	Alco	1944-45	
1266-1274		9	S-4	Alco	1950	3
1500-1504, 1530-1534		10	RS-2	Alco	1948-49	
1505-1519, 1535-1545		26	RS-3	Alco	1952-55	
1550-1553		4	BL2	EMD	1948	
1555-1577		23	GP7	EMD	1950-53	
1700-1749		50	GP9	EMD	1957	
1750-1755		6	GP18	EMD	1961	
3800-3820		21	E7A	EMD	1946-49	
3821		1	E8A	EMD	1950	
4200A-4223A		24	FTA	EMD	1943-44	
4200B-4223B		24	FTB	EMD	1943-44	
4224A, 4226A, 4225A (1)		3	F2A	EMD	1946	4
4224B-4226B		3	F2B	EMD	1946	
4227A, 4228A		2	F3A	EMD	1948	
4227B, 4228B		2	F3B	EMD	1948	
4250-4264	4225A (2)	15	F2A	EMD	1946	5
4265A-4268A		4	F7A	EMD	1949	
4265B-4268B		4	F7B	EMD	1950	
6000		1	AA	EMC	1935	6

Notes:
1—Cab units for ACF Talgo Train.
2—Nos. 860, 861, 865, 862 rebuilt to S-5m and renumbered in 1963.
3—No. 1274 rebuilt from no. 1174.
4—No. 4225A (1) wrecked in early 1950s.
5—No. 4263 renumbered to 4225A (2).
6—No. 6000 is shovel-nosed stainless-steel streamlined passenger unit Cheshire.

Published roster:
Extra 2200 South, December 1970

Burlington Northern
1970-1996

Burlington Northern was formed in 1970 with the merger of the Chicago, Burlington & Quincy, Great Northern, Northern Pacific, and Spokane, Portland & Seattle. The railroad continued to grow, merging the St. Louis-San Francisco (Frisco) in 1981 and absorbing subsidiaries Colorado & Southern in 1981 and Fort Worth & Denver in 1983. The result was a varied mix of locomotives from its predecessor roads, including early GEs, Alcos, and a sizeable fleet of F units. Former owners are listed in the notes column of the roster.

The railroad settled on six-axle diesels for mainline manifest freights and coal trains, including a large fleet of SD40-2s, with U30Cs and C30-7s on coal trains and GP38-2s and older Geeps on secondary trains.

The size of the BN roster precludes going into detail on most individual locomotives or locomotive orders, but for an excellent unit-by-unit summary, see Robert Del Grosso's *Burlington Northern Railroad Locomotives 1970-1996*. The BN merged with the Santa Fe in 1995, creating the Burlington Northern & Santa Fe, which later officially became BNSF.

Two new BN SD40-2s undergo final testing near the GMD plant at London, Ontario, in 1979. *Ron Bawhuis*

Original road numbers	Second numbers	Qty.	Model	Builder	Notes
1-5		5	44-tonner	GE	ex-CB&Q, NP
1, 5 (2), 14, 19		4	NW2	EMD	ex-GN
7		1	VO660	Baldwin	ex-NP
11		1	S-1	Alco	ex-SP&S
20-65		46	SW1500	EMD	ex-SLSF
70, 76-97, 102-104		26	SW1	EMD	ex-GN, CB&Q, FW&D
75-79, 107-145		44	SW7	EMD	ex-NP, C&S, CB&Q, GN
98-99, 101		3	SW8	EMD	ex-GN
100		1	SW900	EMD	ex-NP
106		1	SW1200m	EMD	1
146-161, 167-169		19	SW9	EMD	ex-GN, NP, CB&Q, SP&S
162-166, 170-259		95	SW1200	EMD	ex-GN, NP, CB&Q, C&S, FW&D
260-269		10	SW9	EMD	ex-SLSF
300-324		25	SW1500	EMD	2
375-394, 427-449, 574-585		53	SW1000	EMD	3
400-403, 405-406, 410-425, 450-573, 586-595		56	NW2	EMD	ex-C&S, FW&D, SLSF, GN, CB&Q, SP&S

Original road numbers	Second numbers	Qty.	Model	Builder	Notes
401..425		18	VO1000	Baldwin	ex-NP
406		1	DRS-4-4-15	Baldwin	ex-NP
407		1	DRS-6-6-15	Baldwin	ex-NP
601-604		4	GP9B	EMD	4
676..762 (even)		7	F3A	EMD	ex-GN, NP, SP&S
701-711, 763 (odd)		6	F3B	EMD	ex-GN, NP
600..796 (even)		68	F7A	EMD	ex-GN, NP, SP&S
621..761 (odd)		42	F7B	EMD	ex-GN, NP
800, 804-846 (even)		22	F9A	EMD	ex-NP
801-809, 813-853 (odd)		26	F9B	EMD	ex-NP, GN
798, 799		2	FTA, FTB	EMD	ex-NP
900-924, 934-940		32	S-2	Alco	ex-NP, SP&S
950		1	S-6	Alco	ex-NP
951-953		3	RS-1	Alco	ex-NP
986-995		10	NW5	EMD	ex-GN
1000-1004		5	MP15	EMD	ex-SLSF
1100, 1101		2	SL44	GE	5
1350-1365		16	GP9m	EMD	6
1375-1399		25	GP15-1	EMD	ex-SLSF
1400-1422, 1426, 1436, 1438		26	GP10	EMD	7
1500-1643, 1670-1673		148	GP7	EMD	
1500-1539, 1590-1599 (2)		50	GP28M	EMD	8
1700..1980		279	GP9	EMD	ex-NP, GN, CB&Q, SP&S
1990-1998		9	GP18	EMD	ex-NP
2000-2071		72	GP20	EMD	9; ex-GN, CB&Q
2072-2077, 2155-2189		41	GP38	EMD	10
2078-2109, 2150-2154, 2255-2369		152	GP38-2	EMD	11
2110-2138		29	GP38AC	EMD	ex-SLSF
2200-2254		55	GP30	EMD	ex-GN, CB&Q
2500-2545, 2550-2582		79	GP35	EMD	ex-GN, CB&Q, SLSF
2600, 2601		2	GP38-2B	EMD	12
2700-2739		40	GP39-2	EMD	
2750..2834, 2870..2984		160	GP39M, E, V	EMD	13
3000-3039		40	GP40	EMD	ex-CB&Q
3040-3064		25	GP40-2	EMD	ex-SLSF
3075-3084		10	GP40G	EMD	14
3100-3162		63	GP50	EMD	
3500-3523, 3550-3555		30	GP40M, E	EMD	15
4000-4002 (1)		3	RS-2	Alco	ex-SP&S
4000-4002 (2), 4003-4004 (1)		5	MP15	EMD	ex-SLSF
4000-4002 (3), 4003-4004 (2), 4005-4119		120	B30-7A (cabless)	GE	
4010-4011 (1)		2	C-415	Alco	ex-SP&S
4050-4078, 4081-4087 (1)		36	RS-3	Alco	ex-SP&S, GN, NP
4100..4126 (even)		12	FA-1	Alco	16
4180-4197		18	RS-11	Alco	ex-NP
4240-4246		7	C-424	Alco	ex-SP&S
4250-4265		16	C-425	Alco	ex-SP&S
4360-4369		10	C-636	Alco	ex-SP&S
5000-5141		142	C30-7	GE	
5200-5208		9	U23C	GE	ex-CB&Q

Original road numbers	Second numbers	Qty.	Model	Builder	Notes
5210-5233		24	U25B	GE	ex-SLSF
5300-5394, 5396-5399	5800-5805, 5900-5911	99	U30C	GE	17, 18
5400-5429		30	U25B	GE	ex-GN, CB&Q
5450-5465		16	U28B	GE	ex-CB&Q, GN
5470-5484		15	U30B	GE	ex-CB&Q
5485-5492		8	B30-7	GE	ex-SLSF
5497-5499		3	B32-8	GE	
5500-5599		10	C30-7	GE	
5600-5641		42	U25C	GE	ex-NP, CB&Q
5650-5677		28	U28C	GE	ex-CB&Q, NP
5700-5765		66	U33C	GE	19
5770-5799		30	U30B	GE	ex-SLSF
5806-5839, 5912-5944		67	U30C	GE	18
6000-6059, 6070-6089		80	SD7	EMD	ex-GN, CB&Q
6100-6206, 6215-6237		230	SD9	EMD	ex-GN, CB&Q
6240-6247 (1), 6249-6255		15	SD24	EMD	ex-CB&Q
6240-6247 (2)		8	SD7r	EMD	20
6260-6263		4	SD38-2	EMD	
6264-6270		7	SD38P	EMD	21
6289-6299		11	TEBC6	VMV	22
6300-6324, 6335-6347 (2)		38	SD40	EMD	23
6325-6334, 6335-6373 (1), 6348-6373 (2), 6374-6385	6912-6916, 6800-6823, 6900-6909	85	SD40-2	EMD	24
6330		1	SD40C	EMD	
6400-6567, 6570-6576		175	SD45	EMD	25
6600-6645		46	F45	EMD	26
6650-6696		47	SD45	EMD	ex-SLSF
6700-6799, 6824-6847, 6850, 6917-6928, 6950	6851	138	SD40-2	EMD	27
7000-7291		292	SD40-2	EMD	28
7300-7309		10	SD40	EMD	29
7500-7502, 7600		4	SD40-2B	EMD	30
7800-7940, 8000-8181		323	SD40-2	EMD	31
8300-8302		3	SD60	EMD	32
9200-9298, 1991		100	SD60M	EMD	
9400-9499, 9504-9775		372	SD70MAC	EMD	
9500-9503		4	SD60MAC	EMD	
9700..9766 (even, 1)	706, 710, 712	10	F3A	EMD	ex-GN, NP
9703..9777 (odd, 1)	703 (2)	11	F3B	EMD	ex-GN, NP
9712..9790 (even, 1)	704..724 (even, 2)	16	F7A	EMD	ex-GN, SP&S, NP
9792, 9794	726	2	FP7	EMD	ex-NP
9701..9771 (odd, 1)	705, 679	20	F7B	EMD	ex-GN, NP
9800-9830 (even)	766-796 (even)	16	F9A	EMD	ex-NP
9801-9821 (odd)	767-787 (odd)	11	F9B	EMD	ex-NP
9850-9855	6394-6399	6	SDP40	EMD	ex-GN
9856-9863	6592-6599	8	SDP45	EMD	ex-GN
9900-9931 (1)		32	E7A	EMD	ex-SP&S, GN, CB&Q
9932-9977	9900-9925 (2)	46	E8A	EMD	ex-CB&Q, 33
9980-9995		16	E9A	EMD	ex-CB&Q, 33
RN-1, BN-2		2	F9A, F9B	EMD	34
BN-3, BN-4		2	E9AM	EMD	34

Notes:
1—Rebuilt from Great Northern EMC NC 5101 in 1955.
2—Nos. 300-309 are ex-GN.
3—Nos. 574-585 are ex-Chicago, Burlington & Quincy.
4—Rebuilt without cabs from wrecked GP9s in 1982.
5—GE demonstrator switchers.
6—GP9s rebuilt using components from FT trade-ins, with lower (1,350-hp) rating. BN classed them as GP5s.
7—Rebuilt from several 1500-series GP7s in 1974-75.
8—Rebuilt in 1992-93 from older GP9s using 645 engines and new angled cabs.
9—Ten GP20s were rebuilt in 1989-90 with Caterpillar engines and renumbered 2000-2009 (2).
10—Nos. 2155-2189 are ex-Conrail; BN termed them GP38X.
11—Nos. 2150-2154 are ex-FW&D; 2255-2369 are ex-SLSF.
12—No. 2600 is ex-2136, rebuilt from a GP38 in 1989; no. 2601 is ex-2315, rebuilt from a GP38-2 in 1981.
13—Nos. 2750..2834 are GP30s and 2870..2984 are GP35s (BN predecessor and other heritage) rebuilt to GP39-2 standards. An M suffix indicates rebuilding by Morrison-Knudsen, E by EMD, and V by VMV Enterprises.
14—Ex-Baltimore & Ohio; rebuilt and leased from GATX.
15—Former 3000-series GP40s (ex-Chicago, Burlington & Quincy) rebuilt by Morrison-Knudsen (M) and EMD (E).
16—Ex-SP&S; 4146 is an FA-2.
17—Nos. 5396-5399 are ex-Colorado & Southern; no. 5336 was rebuilt to cabless (classified U30CB) 800B in 1981, then renumbered 4500.
18—Nos. 5300-5305, 5353-5364 renumbered 5800-5805, 5900-5911.
19—Nos. 5700-5714 are ex-GN; 5715-5724 are ex-NP.
20—Ex-Duluth, Missabe & Iron Range (6240, 6241) and Baltimore & Ohio; rebuilt in 1989 and classified SD9 by BN.
21—Ex-Southern, Western Maryland, and Louisville & Nashville SD35s, rebuilt in 1992-93 to SD38-2 standards.
22—Rebuilt from SD9s by VMV.
23—Nos. 6335-6347 are ex-Colorado & Southern.
24—Nos. 6335-6373 renumbered in 1974.
25—Nos. 6400-6471 are ex-NP, GN, CB&Q
26—Nos. 6600-6613 are ex-GN; 6614-6635 ordered by GN but delivered in BN colors.
27—No. 6794 wrecked in 1993, rebuilt and renumbered 6851; nos. 6840-6847 are ex-SLSF; 6850, 6950 are ex-C&S.
28—Nos. 7149, 7890 rebuilt to use either diesel fuel or liquified natural gas in 1991, reclassified DF40-2 by BN.
29—Ex-Missouri Pacific; classed SD40G by BN (the G for their lease from GATX).
30—SD40-2s 7221, 6337, 6352 and SD40 6302 rebuilt after wrecks (1981-84) into cabless B units (7600 is SD40B).
31—Nos. 7800-7831 are ex-C&S 930-961.
32—Demonstrators on short-term lease, painted in BN colors.
33—Nos. 9900-9925 (2) were rebuilt from E8s and E9s in 1973-78 and designated E9AM; used in Chicago commuter service.
34—BN-1 and -2 were rebuilt from ex-NP F9s to GP38-2 standards in 1990 for executive train operations. BN-3 and -4 were intended for the same purpose, but never used as such.

Published roster:
Burlington Northern Railroad Locomotives 1970-1996, by Robert C. Del Grosso (Great Northern Pacific Publications, 1999)

Canadian National (classic)
1929-1995

Canadian National dieselized relatively late, with its last scheduled steam run in 1960. Along with GP9s, the CN rostered a large fleet of RS-18s and unique-to-Canada lightweight GMD-1s, along with road-switcher versions of the SW1200, the SW1200RS. Second-generation power included Montreal Locomotive Works (Alco's Canadian licensee) road switchers along with wide-nose and cowl versions of the GP40-2 and SD40-2.

This roster covers new locomotive orders through 1995. It does not cover subsidiaries Central Vermont, Duluth, Winnipeg & Pacific, and Grand Trunk Western, each of which have their own entries, or Newfoundland Railway's narrow gauge lines. It also does not cover CN acquisitions of Illinois Central (1998) and Wisconsin Central (2001). See the current CN roster on the following spread.

Wide-nose MLW M-420 No. 2501 was delivered to CN in 1973. *MLW*

Original road numbers	Second numbers	Qty.	Model	Builder	Dates built	Notes
3-5		3	44-tonner	GE	1956	
74		1	80-tonner	GE	1947	1
500		1	center cab	Whitcomb	1929	2
991, 992		2	G12	GMD	1955, 1957	3
1000-1077		78	GMD-1	GMD	1958-60	
1227-1268, 1271-1397		169	SW1200RS	GMD	1956-60	
1544-1554, 1711-1729	1700-1710	30	RSC-13	MLW	1955-57	
1575-1597	1204-1221, 1504-1508	23	SW1200RS	GMD	1955-56	
1630-1659		30	H-12-44	CLC	1955-56	
1724-1750	4400-4426	27	GP9	GMD	1955	
1730-1734 (2)		5	RSC-13	MLW	1957	
1750-1787		38	RSC-18	MLW		4
1800-1803		4	RSC-24	MLW	1959	
1818-1840	3018-3040	23	RS-3	MLW	1954	
1841-1858	2200-2217	18	H-16-44	CLC	1955	
1863-1885	3058-3065, 3800-3814	23	RS-10	MLW	1955	
1900-1917		18	GMD-1	GMD	1958-59	
2000-2024 (1)	4451-4475	25	GP9	GMD	1955-56	
2000-2043 (2)		44	C-630M	MLW	1967-68	
2100-2119		20	HR-616	Bombardier	1982	
2300-2339		40	M-636	MLW	1970-71	
2400-2454		55	Dash 8-40CM	GE	1990-92	
2500-2522		23	Dash 9-44CWL	GE	1994	
2500-2579	3500-3579	80	M-420W	MLW	1973-77	
2580-2589	3580-3589	10	HR-412	Bombardier	1981	
3000	2900	1	H-24-66	F-M	1955	
3066-3093	3815-3822..	28	RS-10S	MLW	1957	
3100-3129		30	RS-18	MLW	1959	
3150-3155		6	RS-18M	MLW		5
3200-3240		41	C-424	MLW	1964-67	
3615-3745, 3830-3893		195	RS-18	MLW	1956-59	
4000, 4001	9300, 9301	2	GP35	GMD	1964	
4002-4017	9302-9317	16	GP40	GMD	1966-67	
4100-4133, 4147-4156, 4228-4353		170	GP9	GMD	1957-59	
4476-4538, 4560-4609, 4588-4601-4611 (2)	4200..4227	127	GP9	GMD	1956-58	6
4824		1	GP7m	GMD	1958	
5000-5240	6000-6028	241	SD40	GMD, EMD	1967-71	7
5241-5363		123	SD40-2W	GMD	1975-80	
5364-5387		24	SD40-2	EMD	1973-80	8
5400-5459		60	SD50F	GMD	1985, 1987	
5500-5559 (1)		50	GP38-2	GMD	1972-73	
5504-5563 (2)		60	SD60F	GMD	1989	
5560-5610	4760-4810	51	GP38-2W	GMD	1973-74	
5600-5625 (2)		26	SD70I	GMD	1995	
5700-5703		4	SD38-2	GMD	1975	9
6500-6542		43	FP9	GMD	1955-58	
6600-6637		38	F9B	GMD	1955-58	10
6700-6705		6	CPA-16-5	CLC	1955	
6706-6711	6750-6755	6	FPA 2	MLW	1955	
6760-6793		34	FPA-4	MLW	1958-59	
6800-6805		6	CPB-16-5	CLC	1955	

Original road numbers	Second numbers	Qty.	Model	Builder	Dates built	Notes
6806-6811	6850-6855	6	FPB-2	MLW	1955	
6860-6871		12	FPB-4	MLW	1958-59	
7000-7009	7700-7709	10	SW9	GMD	1952	
7020-7035	7731..7734	16	SW1200	GMD	1956-59	
7100-7107, 7300-7317		26	SW1200RM	GMD		11
7233-7261	7933-7942, 7600-7608	29	SW900	GMD	1957-58	
7555-7578	1700-1723	24	GP7	GMD	1953	
7600-7617	1600-1617	18	H-10-46	CLC	1951-52	12
7618-7629	1618-1629	12	H-12-46	CLC	1952-53	
7670-7674	850-854	5	G8	GMD	1954	
7700	77	1	400-hp B-B	CLC	1929	
7750		1	boxcab B-B	CNR	1932	
7751, 7752	7550, 7551	2	44-tonner	GE	1947	
7802-7819 (2)	1526-1543	18	70-tonner	GE	1950	
7803-7810 (1)		8	75-DE-12c	Whitcomb	1948	
7830-7847	3000-3017	18	RS-3	MLW	1953	
7936-7945, 7956-7973		28	NW2	EMD	1946-48	
7946-7955, 7975-7994	8112-8141	30	S-2	Alco, MLW	1949	
7995-8014, 8016-8025, 8028-8033, 8036-8079, 8163-8195	8142..8161	113	S-4	MLW	1949-57	
8206-8234		29	S-7	MLW	1957	
8235-8245		11	S-12	MLW	1958	
8450-8498		49	S-3	MLW	1951-54	
8500-8533	7150-7183	34	SW8	GMD	1951	
8500-8522 (2), 8600-8625	8700-8711	49	S-13	MLW	1959	13
8535-8559	7200-7224	25	SW900	GMD	1953-54	
8700-8744 (even)	9300-9344 (even)	23	CFA-16-4	CLC	1952-53	
8701-8705 (odd)	9301-9305 (odd)	3	CFB-16-4	CLC	1952	
9000, 9002, 9003, 9005		4	F3A	EMD	1948	
9001, 9004		2	F3B	EMD	1948	
9028-9142 (even)	9150-9179	58	F7A	GMD	1951-52	14
9029-9063 (odd)	9190-9199	18	F7B	GMD	1951-52	14
9400-9407 (1)		8	FA-1	MLW	1950	
9408-9456 (even)		25	FA-2	MLW	1951-53	
9409-9437 (odd)		15	FB-2	MLW	1951-52	
9400-9667		268	GP40-2L(W)	GMD	1974-76	
9668-9677		10	GP40-2	GMD	1973-75	15
9900-9903	5500-5503	4	SD50AF	GMD	1986	16

Notes:
1—Ex-National Harbours Board 1.
2— Thousand Islands Railway; center-cab locomotive rebuilt to twin-engine gas-electric from straight electric by the Oshawa Railway and Whitcomb.
3—Ex-London & Port Stanley L4, L5, acquired 1966.
4—Older RS-18s retrucked from B-B to A1A-A1A in 1975-76.
5—Rebuilt with auxiliary engines for lightweight Hawker-Siddeley-built Tempo trains in 1967-68.
6—Nos. 4602-4611 are ex-Northern Alberta Railways 201..211, acquired 1981.
7—29 units rebuilt and renumbered in 1992-95.
8—Rebuilt ex-Union Pacific (nee Missouri Pacific) units.
9—Ex-NAR, acquired 1981.
10—Steam-generator equipped.
11—Rebuilt from SW1200RS, 1987.
12—Upgraded to 1,200-hp and reclassed H-12-64 shortly after delivery.
13—12 units rebuilt to S-13u and renumbered in 1984-85.
14—30 A units and 10 Bs rebuilt to F7Au and F7Bu and renumbered in 1972-74.
15—Ex-GO Transit 700..710, acquired 1991.
16—Preproduction SD60Fs.
General: More than 200 GP9s were rebuilt to GP9rm starting in 1981. These were numbered 4000-4036 and 4100-4143 for road service and 7000-7083 and 7200-7280 for yard service. The CN also rebuilt many older GMD-1s with B-B trucks (from retired GP9s) and other upgrades. These were renumbered 1600-1614 and 1400..1444.

Published rosters:
Extra 2200 South, September-October 1974; Canadian National Railways Diesel Locomotives, Vol. 1 (by Kevin J. Holland and Ken Goslett) and Vol. 2 (by Glenn Courtney, Goslett, and Holland; both Canadian National Railways Historical Association, 2012 and 2014)

Canadian National
Current (as of 2017)

This roster is current as of early 2017, and includes units still lettered for merged railroads including British Columbia; Duluth, Missabe & Iron Range; Elgin, Joliet & Eastern; Illinois Central; Grand Trunk Western; and Wisconsin Central.

General Electric began delivering Tier-4 compliant ET44AC locomotives to CN in 2015. *Cody Grivno*

Initial	Number series	Model	Builder	Dates
CN	102, 103	E9A	EMD	1949-1956
CN	104-106	F40PHR	EMD	1977-1978
CN	200-263	YBU	GMD	R1980-1990
CN	268	YBU-M	CN	1964
CN	273-281	YBU	GMD	R1993
CN	500-526	HBU	GMD	R1978-1980
CN	1400-1444	GMD-1	GMD	R1988-1989
CN	1650, 1652, 1653	SD38-2	GMD	1975
CN	2000-2041	C40-8	GE	1989-1990
CN	2098,2099	C40-8W	GE	1992
CN	2100-2134	C40-8	GE	1991
CN	2135-2199	C40-8W	GE	1992
CN	2200-2205	C44-9W	GE	2004
CN	2220-2344	ES44DC	GE	2006-2010
CN	2400-2454	C40-8M	GE	1990-1992
CN	2500-2696	C44-9W	GE	1994-2004
CN	2727	C44-9W	GE	2005
CN	2800-2975	ES44AC	GE	2012-2013
CN	3000-3120	ET44AC	GE	2015-2016
CN	4018, 4028	GP9-RM	GMD	R1982-1984
CN	4100-4141	GP9-RM	GMD	R1984-1991

Initial	Number series	Model	Builder	Dates
CN	4700-4810	GP38-2	GMD	1972-1974
CN	5242-5386	SD40-2	GMD	1973-1980
CN	5400-5489	SD60	GMD	1986
CN	5500-5563	SD60F	GMD	1985-1989
CN	5600-5625	SD70I	GMD	1995
CN	5626-5800	SD75I	GMD	1996-1999
CN	6000-6028	SD40-3Q	GMD	R1992-1993
CN	7000-7083	GP9-RM	GMD	R1985-1993
CN	7200-7280	GP9-RM	GMD	R1985-1994
CN	7311	SW1200RB	GMD	R1987
CN	7500-7532	GP38-2	GMD	1973
CN	8000-8024	SD70M-2	EMD	2005-2006
CN	8100-8103	SD70ACe	EMD	2013
CN	8800-8964	SD70M-2	EMD	2007-2011
CN	9402-9486	GP40-2L	GMD	1974
CN	9513-9626	GP40-2L	GMD	1974-1975
CN	9639-9777	GP40-2	GMD	1974-1976
BCOL	4601-4626	C40-8M	GE	1990-1993
BCOL	4641-4654	C44-9W	GE	1995
BLE	862-868	SD38AC	EMD	1967-1971
BLE	878	SD38-2	EMD	1973
BLE	900-910	SD40-3	EMD	R1999-2000
DMIR	211, 212, 215	SD38-2	EMD	1975-1976
DMIR	400, 402-409	SD40-3	EMD	R1996
EJE	656-669	SD38-3	EMD	1973-1975
EJE	670-675	SD38-2	EMD	1973-1975
EJE	703	GP38-2	EMD	1972
GTW	4610-4633	GP9-RB	EMD	R1989-1993
GTW	4900-4934	GP38-2	EMD	1972
GTW	5812-5861	GP38-2	EMD	1977-1980
GTW	5930-5937	SD40-2	EMD	1975
GTW	5938-5955	SD40-3	GMD	R 1999
GTW	6221-6228	GP38-2	EMD	1978
GTW	6401	GP40	EMD	1968
GTW	6420, 6425	GP40-2	EMD	1973-1979
IC	1000-1039	SD70	EMD	1996-1999
IC	1200-1204	SW7RM	EMD/IC	R2006-2007
IC	1492-1506	SW14	EMD	R1978-1982
IC	2455-2466	C40-8W	GE	1994
IC	2697-2726	C44-9W	GE	2004
IC	3101-3140	GP40-2R	EMD	R1987-1991
IC	6100, 6200-6204	SD40-3	EMD	R1997-1998
IC	6250-6264	SD40-3	EMD	R1998-2000
IC	9560-9639	GP38-2	EMD	1972
WC	1552-1569	SW1500	EMD	R2001-2002
WC	1558-1565	SW1500	EMD	1968-1971
WC	1570, 1571	SW1500	EMD	R2001-2002
WC	2001-2006	GP38-2	GMD	1981
WC	3018	GP40	EMD	1970
WC	3026, 3027	GP40-2R	EMD	R1994

Canadian Pacific (classic)
1937-1998

The Canadian Pacific began buying diesel switchers in the 1930s and '40s, with road units following in the late 1940s into the 1950s. The railroad gradually dieselized through the 1950s, doing it district-by-district and then by train run until most steam was gone by 1959.

The railroad acquired an interesting mix of early diesels, including some unique-to-Canada models such as the RS-10 and RS-18. The railroad remained a long-time customer of Alco licensee Montreal Locomotive Works, buying M-630 and M-636 diesels into 1970. The railroad largely standardized on the EMD SD40-2 from 1972 onward, including variations such as the cowl-body SD40-2F.

This roster covers new locomotive orders through 1998 and includes the railroad's merger of Toronto, Hamilton & Buffalo (1987) and takeover of American subsidiary Soo Line. Soo had long been a CP subsidiary—CP acquired full ownership of Soo stock by 1990, and shortly thereafter began assimilating Soo locomotives into the CP roster (only Soo locomotives still active in 1990 are included). The current CP roster has its own entry on the following pages.

CP SD40-2Fs feature a cowl body with "Draper Taper" cutaway behind the cab.
GMD

Original road numbers	Second numbers	Qty.	Model	Builder	Dates built	Notes
10-23		14	DT-2	CLC	1957-60	
51-54		4	NW2	EMD	1948	1
55-58		4	SW9	GMD	1950-51	1
534		1	SD10	EMD	1953	2
749, 751, 752		3	SD40	EMD	1970	2
760, 762, 776-779, 783-786		10	SD40-2	EMD	1972-74	2
1000-1002		3	SW1200	EMD	1954	2
1405-1415		11	FP9	GMD	1954	
1682-1687		6	GP7u	GMD	1950-53	1
1688-1690		3	GP9u	GMD	1954	1
1800-1802		3	E8A	EMD	1949	
1900-1907		8	F9B	GMD	1954	
3000-3005		6	GP38AC	GMD	1970	
3006-3020		15	GP38	GMD	1971	
3021-3135		115	GP38-2	GMD	1983-86	
4000-4027		28	FA-1	Alco, MLW	1949-50	
4028-4041, 4058-4063, 4066-4075, 4099-4103	1400-1404, 1416-1434	34	FP7	GMD	1950-51	3
4042-4051, 4084-4093		20	FA 2	MLW	1951, 1953	
4052-4057, 4064, 4065, 4104, 4105		10	CPA-16-4	CLC	1951-54	4
4076-4081		6	CFA-16-4	CLC	1953	
4082, 4083, 4094-4098		7	FPA-2	MLW	1953	
4200-4250		51	C-424	MLW	1963-66	5
4400-4409 (2), 4421..4440, 4507, 4513		16	GP38-2	EMD	1977-80	2
4400-4423		24	FB-1	Alco, MLW	1949-50	
4424-4448, 4459-4462	1908-1919	29	F7B	GMD	1951-53	3
4449-4454, 4471, 4472		8	CPB-16-4	CLC	1952, 1954	
4455-4458		4	CFB-16-4	CLC	1953	
4463, 4464		2	FPB-2	MLW	1953	
4465-4470		6	FB-2	MLW	1953	
4500-4507		8	C-630	MLW	1968	

Original road numbers	Second numbers	Qty.	Model	Builder	Dates built	Notes
4508-4516, 4550-4557, 4570-4581	4558-4569	29	M-630	MLW	1969-70	
4598, 4599		2	GP39-2	EMD	1978	2
4600, 4602, 4609, 4611		4	GP40	EMD	1966-67	2
4700-4743		44	M-636	MLW	1969-70	
4744		1	M-640	MLW	1971	
5014-5023		10	GP35	GMD	1965	
5500-5564		65	SD40	GMD	1966-67	
5565-5879, 5900-6069	5388..5398	485	SD40-2	GMD, EMD	1972-85	6
6000-6057		58	SD60	EMD, GMD	1987, 1989	2
6058-6062		5	SD60M	GMD	1989	2
6400, 6403-6405, 6411		5	SD40	EMD	1970	2, 7
6406-6410		5	SD40A	EMD	1970	2
6500-6600		101	S-3	MLW	1951-57	8
6501-6613		13	S-10	MLW	1958	
6614-6623 (1)		10	S-11	MLW	1959	
6603..6622 (2)		11	SD40-2	EMD	1979-84	2
6700-6709		10	SW8	GMD	1950-51	
6710-6720		11	SW900	GMD	1955	
7000		1	600-hp	NSC	1937	9
7010-7064, 7076-7098		78	S-2	Alco, MLW	1943-49	
7065-7075		11	DS-4-4-10	Baldwin-CLC	1948	
7099-7118		20	S-4	MLW	1949-53	
7400-7405	1200-1205	6	SW9	GMD	1963	10
8000-8012		13	DRS-4-4-10	Baldwin-CLC	1948	
8013-8046		34	RS-23	MLW	1959-60	
8100-8171	1206-1214, 1237-1251, 1268-1276	72	SW1200RS	GMD	1958-60	10
8200, 8201	5000, 5001	2	GP30	GMD	1963	
8202-8213	5002-5013	12	GP35	GMD	1964	
8263, 8264, 8270, 8275		4	GP9	EMD	1954-57	2
8400-8408		9	RS-2	Alco, MLW	1949-50	
8409-8425	1500-1511	17	GP7	GMD	1952-53	10
8426-8461		36	RS-3	MLW	1954	
8462-8482, 8557-8568		33	RS-10	MLW	1955-56	
8483-8546, 8611-8708, 8801-8823, 8825-8839	1512..1697, 8200..8249	200	GP9	GMD	1955-59	10
8547-8556, 8601-8610, 8709-8728		40	H-16-44	CLC-FM	1955-57	
8569-8600, 8824		32	RS-10S	MLW	1956	11
8729-8800	1800..1868	72	RS-18	MLW	1957-58	10
8900-8920		21	H-24-66	CLC-FM	1955-56	
8921		1	RSD-17	MLW	1957	12
9000-9024		25	SD40-2F	GMD	1988	
9100-9160		61	SD90MAC	GMD	1998	
9300-9303		4	SD90MAC-H	GMD	1998	
9500-9683		184	AC4400CW	GE	1995-98	

Notes:
1—Ex-Toronto, Hamilton & Buffalo, acquired with CP absorption of TH&B in 1987; GP7s and GP9s rebuilt in 1987-88.
2—Ex-Soo Line, acquired with purchase of Soo in 1990.
3—Several FP7s and F7Bs were renumbered to 1400-series (passenger) numbers in 1954-55; these were changed back to their original numbers in the early 1960s.
4—Nos. 4164, 4165 are former CLC demonstrators 7005, 7006, acquired 1951.
5—No. 4200 was originally numbered 8300.
6—Nos. 5779-5789 and 5860-5864 were owned by Ontario Hydro but lettered CP; 11 were sold to CN in mid-1990s and repurchased by CP in 2000 and renumbered 5388..5398.
7—No. 6411 was rebuilt to Dash-3 standards and classed ESD40 by Soo.
8—Nos. 6560, 6561 are ex-Dominion Atlantic (same numbers).
9—End-cab, high-hood, B-B switcher built by National Steel Car with Harland Wolff 600-hp engine.
10—Many locomotives in these classes rebuilt to SW9u (1982-83), SW1200RSu (1981-84), GP7u (1980-84), GP9u (1980-90), RS-18u (1980-89) and renumbered.
11—No. 8824 rebuilt from wrecked FA-1 4016 in 1957.
12—Former MLW demonstrator; built as RSD-15m; only RSD-17 built.

Published rosters:
Extra 2200 South, January 1969; Canadian Pacific Diesel Locomotives, by Murray W. Dean and David B. Hanna (Railfare Enterprises, 1981); CP Rail: 1993 Review, by Gary Zuters (Hyrail Productions, 1994)

Candian Pacific
Current (as of 2017)

This roster includes all active locomotives on Canadian Pacific as of early 2017, including those still lettered for merged railroads and subsidiaries including Dakota, Minnesota & Eastern; Iowa, Chicago & Eastern; and Soo Line.

ES44AC No. 9353 was built in 2012.
Kent Johnson

Initials	Number series	Model	Builder	Dates
CP	1126-1128	GP35 Slug	GMD	1964-1965
CP	1401	FP9A	GMD	1958
CP	1900	F9B	GMD	1955
CP	2200-2329	GP20ECO	EMD	2012-2014
CP	3000-3020	GP38AC	GMD	1970-1971
CP	3021-3135	GP38-2	GMD	1983-1986
CP	4106-4107	FP9u	GMD	1957
CP	4650-4657	GP40-2	EMD	1977
CP	5000-5049	SD30ECO	EMD	2013/2015
CP	5708-6080	SD40-2	GMD	1972-1984
CP	6221-6257	SD60	EMD	1989
CP	6258-6262	SD60M	EMD	1989
CP	6601-6623	SD40-2	EMD	1979-1984
CP	6711	SW900	GMD	1955
CP	8500-8655	AC4400CW	GE	1998-2001
CP	8700-8960	ES44AC	GE	2005-2011
CP	9100-9160	SD90MAC	GMD	1998-2000
CP	9350-9379	ES44AC	GE	2012
CP	9500-9840	AC4400CW	GE	1995-2004
DME	3800 3801	GP38	EMD	1969
DME	4001-4006	GP40Q	EMD	1966-1970
DME	6056	SD40-3	EMD	1967-1980
ICE	6101	SD40-3	EMD	1966-1971
ICE	6212, 6215	SD40-2	EMD	1967-1976
SOO	2010	GP40	EMD	1966
SOO	2066	GP40	EMD	1969
SOO	6024-6053	SD60	EMD	1989
SOO	6061	SD60M	EMD	1989

Central of Georgia
1939-1971

The Central of Georgia began dieselizing with switchers just before World War II. EMD passenger cabs (E7s) arrived just after the war, with GP7s and RS-3s shortly after that to take over freight trains. The CofG was completely dieselized in 1953.

The Central of Georgia became a subsidiary of the Southern in 1963. This roster covers the CofG until 1971, when the CofG was restructured and merged the Georgia & Florida, the Savannah & Atlanta, and the Wrightsville & Southern. Although the CofG continued to exist (and still does on paper), the merged group was essentially absorbed into the Southern, with railroads losing their individual identities. For several years after this, locomotives were assigned to the CofG but wore Southern (and later Norfolk Southern) paint schemes with small "CofG" sublettering.

Number 201 was Central of Georgia's only SD7, built in 1953. *EMD*

Original road numbers	Second numbers	Qty.	Model	Builder	Dates built	Notes
1-3, 7		3	SW1	EMD	1939, 1941	
4, 6	329	2	S-1	Alco	1941	
5		1	VO660	Baldwin	1940	
20, 25		2	NW2	EMD	1941-42	
21, 23, 24, 28-35	330-335	11	S-2	Alco	1940-48	
22, 26, 27		3	VO1000	Baldwin	1940-44	
36, 37		2	DS-4-4-10	Baldwin	1949	
101-105		5	H-15-44	F-M	1949	
106, 107, 120-132		15	GP7	EMD	1950-51	1
108-119, 133-159		39	RS-3	Alco	1950-53	
160-170	6258-6268	11	GP9	EMD	1956	
171-178		8	GP18	EMD	1961	
201	197	1	SD7	EMD	1953	
202-207		6	SD9	EMD	1955	
210-214		5	GP35	EMD	1963	
215-224		10	SD35	EMD	1965	
301-310		10	SW9	EMD	1952-53	
311-314		4	S-12	Baldwin	1953	
315-318		4	H-12-44	F-M	1953	
801-810		10	E7A	EMD	1946, 1948	
811, 812		2	E8A	EMD	1950	
901-909		9	F3A	EMD	1947-48	
2025, 2026		2	RS-3	Alco	1952	2
2340-2347		8	SW1500	EMD	1970	
3184, 3185		2	SD40	EMD	1971	

Notes:
1—Nos. 123-132 steam-generator equipped.
2—Ex-Southern 2025, 2026.

Published roster:
Diesel Locomotive Rosters (Wayner Publications)

Central of New Jersey
1939-1976

The Central of New Jersey owned several switchers by 1940, then began buying road diesels after World War II. Most freight operations were dieselized by 1948, and passenger trains were all diesel by 1954. The CNJ had an eclectic mix of early Baldwin, EMD, and Alco power, returning to EMD for new engines in the 1960s. The CNJ became part of Conrail in 1976.

The GP40P had a steam generator in a hood extension at the rear (behind the flared radiator housing). *EMD*

Original road numbers	No.	Model	Builder	Dates built	Notes
A, B, C, D, E (1-5)	5	F3B	EMD	1947	1
K, L, M, R, S (11-15)	5	DR-4-4-15B	Baldwin	1947-48	1
10-29	20	F7A	EMD	1950-52	2
50-59	10	F3A	EMD	1947	
70-79	10	DR-4-4-15A	Baldwin	1947-48	
1000	1	Boxcab 60-ton	GE	1925	
1001	1	35-ton	GE	1941	3
1005-1008	4	SW	EMC	1939	
1009-1012	4	SW1	EMD	1939, 1942	
1020-1023	4	HH660	Alco	1938	
1024-1025	2	S-1	Alco	1941	
1040-1043	4	VO660	Baldwin	1942	
1053-1059	7	S-12	Baldwin	1951	
1060-1061	2	NW2	EMD	1942	
1062-1066	5	VO1000	Baldwin	1944	
1067-1071	5	S-2	Alco	1944	
1072-1074	3	DS-4-4-10	Baldwin	1950	
1080-1083	4	SW7	EMD	1950	
1084-1094	11	SW9	EMD	1951-52	
1200-1205	6	RS-1	Alco	1950-51	
1206-1209	4	RS-12	Baldwin	1953	
1500-1513	14	H-15-44	F-M	1948-49	
1514-1517	4	H-16-44	F-M	1950	
1520-1532	13	GP7	EMD	1952	
1540-1555	16	RS-3	Alco	1950, 1953	
1601-1614	14	RSD-4	Alco	1951-52	
1615	1	RSD-5	Alco	1953	
1700-1709	10	RS-3	Alco	1953	
2000-2006	6	DR-6-4-20	Baldwin	1946-48	4
2401-2413	13	H-24-66	F-M	1954, 1956	
2501-2512	12	SD35	EMD	1965	
3061-3069	9	SD40	EMD	1967	5
3671-3683	13	GP40P	EMD	1968	
6600-6605	6	GP9	EMD	1955	5
9225..9944	10	DS-4-4-10	Baldwin	1950	5

Notes:
1—Locomotives carried letters only (not numbers).
2—Leased; former Baltimore & Ohio and Norfolk & Western (nee Wabash) engines.
3—Ex-U.S. Army 2332.
4—Double-ended cab units.
5—Leased; former B&O engines.

Published roster:
Extra 2200 South, May 1968

Central Vermont
1942-1995

The Central Vermont was a subsidiary of Canadian National, and its locomotives were often transferred among other subsidiaries (Duluth, Winnipeg & Pacific and Grand Trunk Western). Locomotives of other subsidiaries and parent CN often appeared on the CV. The CV dieselized late—it was the last New England line to dieselize, with the last steam locomotives operating in 1957. Most Alcos were short-lived on the system; the railroad's GP9s were the usual mainline power until GP38ACs arrived in the late 1980s. The CV was purchased by RailTex in 1995, which renamed the line the New England Central.

Central Vermont's GP9s were the typical road power from the late 1950s into the 1980s.
Central Vermont

Original numbers	Second numbers	Qty.	Model	Builder	Dates built	Notes
1500, 1502		2	SW1200	EMD	1955	1
1859, 1860	3900, 3901	2	RS-3	Alco	1954	2
3600-3614		15	RS-11	Alco	1956	3
3602, 3614 (2)		2	GP18	EMD	1961, 1960	4
4547-4557, 4923-4929		18	GP9	EMD	1957	
5800-5810		11	GP38AC	EMD	1971	5
7917-7919	8093-8095	3	S-2	Alco	1942	6
8015, 8027, 8080, 8081	8162	4	S-4	Alco	1951-55	7

Notes:
1—Ex-Grand Trunk Western 1500, 1502, acquired 1963.
2—Renumbered in 1957.
3—Ex-Duluth, Winnipeg & Pacific, acquired 1967.
4—Ex-Rock Island 1345, 1334, acquired 1981.
5—Ex-GTW, acquired late 1980s.
6—No. 7917 is ex-GTW 7917.
7—No. 8015 was renumbered 8162.

Published rosters:
Diesel Locomotive Rosters (Wayner Publications); Extra 2200 South, September-October 1974

Chesapeake & Ohio
Including Pere Marquette
1947-1973

The Chesapeake & Ohio dieselized late, getting its first diesels through merger with Pere Marquette in 1947 but continuing to buy new steam locomotives as late as 1949. The railroad then dieselized rather quickly, mainly with EMD GP7s and GP9s and a handful of F units and Alco six-axle diesels, pushing out steam by 1956.

The C&O was closely tied to the Baltimore & Ohio—in the early 1960s the C&O owned 90 percent of B&O stock. Many C&O diesels were transferred to the B&O, and by the mid-1960s many diesels of both railroads were renumbered to group similar classes and avoid duplicate numbering.

This roster covers all locomotives owned by June 1973, when the B&O, C&O, and Western Maryland became subsidiaries of the newly formed Chessie System. See the Chessie System entry for diesels owned at that time and later.

Chesapeake & Ohio's six EMD BL2s were ordered by Pere Marquette but delivered to C&O after the merger. *EMD*

Original road numbers	Second numbers	Qty.	Model	Builder	Dates built	Notes
1	8303	1	44-tonner	GE	1946	1
2, 3	5297, 5298	2	NW2	EMD	1948	1
10, 11	1800 (1), 8401	2	SW1	EMD	1939, 1942	2
20-22	1810-1812	3	70-tonner	GE	1947	2
51-64	5275..5289	14	NW2	EMD	1942-46	2
80-85	1839	6	BL2	EMD	1948	3
95-98, 101-108	4510..4523	12	E7A	EMD	1946-48	2, 4
1800-1818	7300-7318	19	SD18	EMD	1963	5
1840-1847		8	BL2	EMD	1948-49	3
1850-1856	9558-9564	7	NW2	EMD	1948	4
2100-2103		4	C-630	Alco	1967	
2300-2329		30	U23B	GE	1969	
2500-2537	8100-8137	38	U25B	GE	1963-64	
3000-3047	3583, 3584	48	GP30	EMD	1962-63	6
3300-3312		13	U30C	GE	1967-68	
3520-3539, 3560-3575, 3582		37	GP35	EMD	1964	7
3780-3794, 4065-4099		50	GP40	EMD	1971	
3850-3899, 4820-4829		60	GP38	EMD	1967, 1970	
3900-3919		20	GP39	EMD	1969	
4000-4030		31	E8A	EMD	1952-53	
4165-4184		20	GP40-2	EMD	1972	
5000-5057		58	S-2	Alco	1949-50	
5060-5079, 5200-5213		34	NW2	EMD	1949	
5080-5093		14	SW9	EMD	1952-53	
5100-5113		14	S-4	Alco	1953	
5114, 5115		2	RS-1	Alco	1953	
5214-5239		26	SW7	EMD	1950	
5240-5265		26	SW9	EMD	1951	8
5500, 5501		2	RS-2	Alco	1949	
5528, 5529, 5533-5569	2202..2233	39	AS-616	Baldwin	1950-53	
5530-5532	2200, 2201	3	DRS-6-6-15	Baldwin	1949	
5570-5595	2000..2006	26	RSD-5	Alco	1952	

Original road numbers	Second numbers	Qty.	Model	Builder	Dates built	Notes
5600, 5601		2	RS-3	Alco	1955	
5700-5797, 5800-5900		199	GP7	EMD	1950-53	
5901-6263		363	GP9	EMD	1954-57	
6500A, 6501A	9552, 9555	2	TR3A	EMD	1949	
6500B, 6500C, 6501B, 6501C	9553, 9554, 9556, 9557	4	TR3B	EMD	1949	
6700-6709	2007-2016	10	RSD-12	Alco	1956	
6800-6811		12	RSD-7	Alco	1956	
7000-7093		94	F7A	EMD	1950, 1952	
7400-7431, 7425 (2), 7428 (2)		14	SD35	EMD	1964-65	9
7450-7469, 7475-7481, 7501-7536 (2)		63	SD40	EMD	1966-71	
7500-7546 (1)		47	F7B	EMD	1950, 1952	
8000-8015	7094, 7095	16	FP7	EMD	1952	
8200-8224		25	U30B	GE	1972	
8500-8506		7	F7B	EMD	1952	

Notes:
1—Ex-Manistee & Northeastern (same numbers), acquired in 1955 merger.
2—Ex-Pere Marquette (same numbers), acquired in 1947 merger.
3—Ordered by PM but delivered to C&O; nos. 80-85 steam-generator equipped; no. 83 wrecked 1960, rebuilt, and renumbered 1839.
4—Nos. 95-98, 1850-1856 were ordered by PM but delivered to C&O.
5—SD18s ride on Alco trucks from traded-in RSD-5s.
6—Nos. 3045, 3047 wrecked in 1965 and rebuilt by EMD into GP35s; later renumbered 3583, 3584.
7—Nos. 3537, 3563, 3574 wrecked in 1965 and rebuilt by EMD; listed as new for record-keeping.
8—Nos. 5240-5244 were built by GMD in Canada.
9—Nos. 7425 and 7428 wrecked in 1965 and replaced with new SD35s of same numbers.

Published rosters:
Extra 2200 South, March-April 1972; Chessie System Locomotives, by Jerry Doyle (TLC Publishing, 1999)

Chessie System
1973-1987

The Chessie System was formed in 1973 as a consolidation of the Chesapeake & Ohio, Baltimore & Ohio, and Western Maryland. The C&O controlled the B&O, and the two together owned 90 percent of WM stock. It wasn't a true merger: The railroads adopted a common paint scheme and numbering system for diesels but remained autonomous, with the owning railroad's initials on the cab.

Chessie System merged with Seaboard Coast Line (Family Lines) in 1980, forming CSX Industries. Although the intent was for the involved railroads to maintain their own identities, it wasn't to be. In 1983 B&O absorbed WM and in 1987 C&O merged B&O. On the other side, SCL merged Louisville & Nashville in 1982 to form Seaboard System; Seaboard System became CSX Transportation in 1986, and in 1987 C&O was merged into CSX, which adopted a new identity and paint scheme.

Chessie System SD50 No. 8556 was delivered in 1984.
Chessie System

Original road numbers	Second numbers	Railroad	Qty.	Model	Builder	Dates built	Notes
GM50	4164	B&O	1	GP40-2	EMD	1972	1
20-23	5632-5635	WM	4	GP7	EMD	1950	
25-45	6400-6420	WM	21	GP9	EMD	1954-57	
51-66, 231-242	7149-7176	WM	28	F7A	EMD	1947-52	
81, 82	7181, 7182	WM	2	BL2	EMD	1948	2
151, 152		WM	2	S-6	Alco	1956	
180-184		WM	5	RS-2	Alco	1947-50	
185-198		WM	14	RS-3	Alco	1953-54	
401-414	7135-7148	WM	14	F7B	EMD	1950-54	
1500-1524		C&O	25	GP15T	EMD	1981	
1826-1830		B&O	5	SD7	EMD	1952-53	
1831-1840		B&O	10	SD9	EMD	1954-55	
1977	4163	B&O	1	GP40-2	EMD	1972	1
2300-2329		C&O	30	U23B	GE	1969	
3000-3044, 3046		C&O	46	GP30	EMD	1963	3
3300-3312		C&O	13	U30C	GE	1967-68	
3500-3519, 3540-3559, 3581		B&O	41	GP35	EMD	1964-65	
3520-3539, 3560-3575, 3582-3584		C&O	39	GP35	EMD	1964-65	
3576-3580		WM	5	GP35	EMD	1963	
3684-3779, 4000-4064		B&O	161	GP40	EMD	1966-71	
3780-3794, 4065-4099		C&O	50	GP40	EMD	1971	
3795-3799		WM	5	GP40	EMD	1971	
3800-3849		B&O	50	GP38	EMD	1967	
3850-3899		C&O	50	GP38	EMD	1967	
3900-3919		C&O	20	GP39	EMD	1969	
4100-4162, 4185-4256, 4287-4311, 4322-4351, 4422-4447		B&O	206	GP40-2	EMD	1972-81	1
4165-4184, 4262-4286, 4372-4421		C&O	95	GP40-2	EMD	1972-80	
4257-4261, 4312-4321, 4352-4371		WM	35	GP40-2	EMD	1977-79	
4800-4819		B&O	20	GP38	EMD	1970	
4820-4829		C&O	10	GP38	EMD	1970	
5061..5089		B&O	12	NW2	EMD	1949	
5066..5093, 5200..5213		C&O	29	NW2	EMD	1949-52	
5215		B&O	1	SW7	EMD	1950	
5216..5239		C&O	29	SW7	EMD	1950	
5240..5265		C&O	23	SW9	EMD	1951	
5256, 5281		B&O	2	SW9	EMD	1945-51	
5600-5631		B&O	32	GP7	EMD	1953	
5700..5899		C&O	155	GP7	EMD	1950-53	
5900..5983, 6425..6683		B&O	252	GP9	EMD	1954-58	
5901..6263		C&O	278	GP9	EMD	1954-57	
6599		B&O	1	GP18m	EMD	1962	
6900..6976		B&O	70	GP30	EMD	1962-63	3
7300-7318		C&O	19	SD18	EMD	1963	4
7400-7419, 7437-7440		B&O	24	SD35	EMD	1964-65	
7420-7431		C&O	12	SD35	EMD	1964-65	
7432-7436		WM	5	SD35	EMD	1964	
7445-7449, 7470-7474, 7495, 7496	7545-7549, 7570-7574, 7595, 7596	WM	12	SD40	EMD	1967-69	
7500, 7591-7594, 7597-7599		B&O	8	SD40	EMD	1967-69	
7501-7536, 7550-7569, 7575-7581		C&O	63	SD40	EMD	1966-70	

Original road numbers	Second numbers	Railroad	Qty.	Model	Builder	Dates built	Notes
7600-7619		B&O	20	SD40-2	EMD	1977	
7700-7704		B&O	5	SD20-2	EMD	1964-65	4
8100-8137		C&O	38	U25B	GE	1963-64	
8200-8234		C&O	35	U30B	GE	1972-74	5
8235-8298		C&O	64	B30-7	GE	1978-79	
8401		C&O	1	SW1	EMD	1942	
8403..8421		B&O	10	SW1	EMD	1940-42	
8553-8575, 8624-8643		C&O	43	SD50	EMD	1984-85	
8576-8595		B&O	20	SD50	EMD	1984	
9001..9178		B&O	55	S-2	Alco	1942-57	
9400-9428		B&O	29	SW900	EMD	1955	
9500..9551, 9559..9564		B&O	52	NW2	EMD	1940-49	
9552..9557		B&O	5	TR3	EMD	1949	
9558, 9560-9562		C&O	4	NW2	EMD	1948	
9600-9613		B&O	14	SW9	EMD	1952-54	
9614-9621		B&O	8	SW1200	EMD	1957	
9622-9625		B&O	4	TR4	EMD	1945-48	

Notes:
1—Nos. GM50 (numbered for GM's 50th anniversary and painted gold) and 1977 (numbered for the year of B&O's 150th anniversary) were originally assigned nos. 4164 and 4163, but wore their commemorative numbers until 1984.
2—Renumbered 7171, 7172 in 1981.
3—Chessie rebuilt 67 GP30s into GP30Ms in 1981-83, keeping their same numbers.
4—Rebuilt in 1979-80 by Chessie from older SD35s; SD20-2 is Chessie designation. First 7700 was destroyed in 1980 and first 7702 was renumbered 7700.
5—Nos. 8223, 8224 are former GE demonstrators 301, 302, acquired 1972.

Published rosters:
Extra 2200 South, March-April 1972; Chessie System Locomotives, by Jerry Doyle (TLC Publishing, 1999)

Chicago & Eastern Illinois
1930-1976

Chicago & Eastern Illinois was a coal-hauling railroad and, other than some early switchers, stuck with steam through World War II. Three E7s and a bunch of F3s made quick work of dieselizing the line from 1946 onward, with the last steam operating in 1950. The Missouri Pacific assumed control of the C&EI in 1967, and the railroad was formally merged into the Missouri Pacific in October 1976.

Chicago & Eastern Illinois 1203 is a Phase IIb F3, with low radiator fans and screened side panels between portholes. *EMD*

Original road numbers	Second numbers (1967)	Qty.	Model	Builder	Dates built	Notes
95-99	6000, 6001	5	SW1	EMD	1942	
100, 101		2	SW	EMC	1938	
102		1	HH600	Alco	1938	
103-106		4	S-1	Alco	1938	
110		1	VO660	Baldwin	1942	
115-118		4	RS-1	Alco	1945	
120-125	1029-1034	6	NW2	EMD	1949	
126-133	1202-1205 (2), 1206-1209	8	SW7	EMD	1950	
200-202		3	BL2	EMD	1948, 1947	1
203-232	68-93	30	GP7	EMD	1950-51	2
221 (2), 229 (2)	86	2	GP9m	EMD	1958, 1959	2
233-238	340-345	6	GP9	EMD	1956-57	
239-241	590-592	3	GP30	EMD	1963	
242-272	650-680	31	GP35	EMD	1964-65	
1100-1102 (1)	27, 28	3	E7A	EMD	1946	3
1102 (2)	43	1	E8Am	EMD	1958	3
1200, 1201, 1202-1205 (1)		6	F3A	EMD	1948	4
1300, 1301		2	F3B	EMD	1948	4
1400-1409	750, 751	10	F3A	EMD	1948	5
1500-1504	750B-753B	5	F3B	EMD	1948	6
1570-1574		5	GP15-1	EMD	1976	7
1600-1609	933-942	10	FP7	EMD	1949	
3150-3163		14	SD40-2	EMD	1974	7

Notes:
1—Nos. 200-202 delivered as 1600-1602 (1) but renumbered in early 1949. No. 202 is former EMD demonstrator BL1 499, rebuilt to BL2 before delivery in 1948.
2—GP7s 221, 229 wrecked in 1958, 1959 and rebuilt to GP9ms of same numbers. Second 229 wrecked in 1963; not renumbered.
3—E7A 1102 wrecked 1958, rebuilt as E9Am 1102 (2).
4—Steam-generator equipped.
5—Nos. 1405, 1407 renumbered 750, 751 in 1967 and 824, 827 in 1968.
6—No. 1500 not renumbered. Others renumbered 933B-936B in 1968.
7—Purchased after Missouri Pacific control, delivered in MP colors but with C&EI buzzsaw herald.

Published roster:
Extra 2200 South, April-May-June 1983

Chicago & Illinois Midland
1955-1996

The Chicago & Illinois Midland was among the last all-steam Class I railroads, not acquiring its first diesel until a pair of SW1200s arrived in April 1955. By the end of that year, however, additional switchers and five SD9s arrived, and the last steam operated in December of that year. The coal-hauling railroad was purchased by Genesee & Wyoming in 1996 and renamed the Illinois & Midland.

Road numbers	Qty.	Model	Builder	Dates built	Notes
18-23	6	SW1200	EMD	1955	
30, 31	2	RS1325	EMD	1960	
40-43	4	SW1500	EMD	1970-72	1
50-54	5	SD9	EMD	1955	
60, 61	2	SD18	EMD	1961, 1962	
70-75	6	SD38-2	EMD	1974	
80-84	5	SD20	EMD	1959-60	2

Notes:
1—Ex-Southern Pacific 2559, 2556, 2653, 2595.
2—Former Southern SD24s, rebuilt by Illinois Central's Paducah shops in 1980.

Published rosters:
Diesel Locomotive Rosters (Wayner Publications); Extra 2200 South, September-October 1969

Chicago & North Western
Including Chicago, St. Paul, Minneapolis & Omaha
1938-1995

The Chicago & North Western dieselized with a wide variety of first-generation locomotives, but continued to rebuild older steam locomotives through 1949. Dieselization was complete in 1956. In the 1960s the C&NW began acquiring new second- and third-generation EMDs and GEs along with a fleet of rebuilt locomotives of its own as well as many acquired second-hand.

Into the 1950s, the C&NW had owned a majority of the Chicago, St. Paul, Minneapolis & Omaha (the Omaha Road). The Omaha Road largely operated as a separate company until 1957, including its own locomotives (albeit in a shared paint scheme but with CMO sublettering), but in 1957 the C&NW leased the CStPM&O, ending its independence. The North Western officially merged the Omaha Road in 1972. The North Western merged several other railroads, acquiring their locomotive fleets, including the Litchfield & Madison (1958), Minneapolis & St. Louis (1960), and Chicago Great Western (1968). The C&NW itself lost its identity when it was purchased by (and became part of) Union Pacific in 1995.

The C&NW's diesel fleet features complicated numbering, with many numbers used multiple times as locomotives left the roster and were replaced by others (including locomotives bought new or acquired used or through mergers). This wasn't helped as many early diesels were numbered in sequence as they were acquired, leading to multiple number groups of the same model type separated by other types.

The C&NW bought 22 GP30s in 1963.
EMD

Original road numbers	Second numbers	Third numbers	Qty.	Model	Builder	Dates built	Notes
10			1	44-ton	Whitcomb	1943	1
11 (1)			1	44-tonner	GE	1942	2
11 (2), 12-15	1216-1220		5	S-1	Alco	1948	3
16-31, 42 (2)	1016..1032		17	NW2	EMD	1948-49	3
32-41	1073-1075		10	DS-4-4-10	Baldwin	1948-49	3
50-54, 55-57 (2)			8	RS-2	Alco	1949	3
55 (1)	1207 (2)		1	SW1	EMC	1940	1
56, 57 (1), 69	1224 (2)		3	S-1	Alco	1944, 1948	1
58, 59 (1), 68	146, 147		3	VO660	Baldwin	1945	1
58A, 58B (2)			2	TR2	EMD	1948	3
59A-63A (2), 64A, 65A	1011..1015		7	TR2A	EMD	1949	3
59B-63B (2), 64B, 65B			7	TR2B	EMD	1949	3
60 (1)			1	SC	EMC	1938	2
61 (1)			1	SW	EMC	1938	2
66A, 66B	1014, 1103		2	TR2	EMD	1949	3
70			1	NW2	EMC	1940	1
71			1	DS-4-4-6	Baldwin	1949	1
86-89			4	VO1000	Baldwin	1942-45	4

Original road numbers	Second numbers	Third numbers	Qty.	Model	Builder	Dates built	Notes
90-93			4	S-2	Alco	1940, 1944	1
91 (2)			1	NW1	EMC	1938	2
92 (2)			1	HH1000	Alco	1939	2
94-98	1058..1067		5	H-10-44	F-M	1943, 1947	1
99, 100 (1)			2	DS-4-4-10	Baldwin	1949	1
100 (2), 101 (2)	201		2	NW2	EMC	1939-40	2
101 (1)	91 (3)		1	S-4	Alco	1953	1
102	92 (3)		1	S-2	Alco	1941	2
103			1	VO1000	Baldwin	1945	2
104A, 106A-115A, 101C, 107C-115C			21	F3A	EMD	1947-50	3
101B-112B, 101D-103D			15	F3B	EMD	1947-49	3
105D-116D, 113B-116B, 116E, F, G			19	F7B	EMD	1949-51	3
116A, 116C			2	FP7	EMD	1950	3
120			1	GP9m	EMD	1951	3
121			1	GP7	EMD	1951	3
126-129			4	SW8	EMD	1951	1
143			1	SC	EMC	1936	3, 5
146, 147			2	VO660	Alco	1945	1
150			1	H-16-66	F-M	1951	1
151-161			11	GP7	EMD	1951-52	1
162-167			6	RS-3	Alco	1952-53	1
168-172			5	H-16-66	F-M	1953	1
203..233			22	RS-1	Alco	1944-51	2
300, 301 (2)			2	SD7	EMD	1952	2
301 (1), 302, 303	905 (1)	406 (3)	3	RS-3	Alco	1952-56	6
310-321	1210-1221 (2)		12	SW1200	EMD	1960, 1962	
401-405, 408-410 (1)	42, 44		8	44-ton	Whitcomb	1941-45	
400-405 (2)			6	F3A	EMD	1948	2
406-410 (2), 411-413			8	F7A	EMD	1949-50	2
401-404 (3)			4	C-425	Alco	1966	
501-506			6	E8B/Am	EMD	1949-53	7
507-522			16	E8A	EMD	1949-53	8
600-608			9	GP9m	EMD	1956-57	2
700-713			14	GP9	EMD	1958	2
801			1	SW8	EMD	1952	
802-823			22	GP30	EMD	1963	9
824-866			43	GP35	EMD	1964-65	
867-896			30	SD40	EMD	1966-67	
901 (1)			1	NW1	EMC	1939	
900, 901 (2), 902, 903 (1)			4	RS-27	Alco	1962	
904 (1)			1	RS-36	Alco	1962	
901 (3), 902-905 (2), 906-920			20	SD45	EMD	1967	
921-929			9	SD40	EMD	1966	3
930-936			7	U30C	GE	1968	
937-977			41	SD45	EMD	1969	
1000-1002 (1)			2	Boxcab	Ingersoll	1926-27	
1000-1008 (2)			9	NW2	EMD	1941-47	10
1003-1015, 1025-1035, 1083-1092			33	S-2	Alco	1942-50	
1010 (2), 1014, 1015 (2)	1090, 1085		3	S-2	Alco	1947	3
1018-1022			5	DS-4-4-10	Baldwin	1949	
1024, 1037-1047			12	VO1000	Baldwin	1944-45	
1036, 1048-1065, 1070, 1082			21	H-10-44	F-M	1944-50	

Original road numbers	Second numbers	Third numbers	Qty.	Model	Builder	Dates built	Notes
1066-1069			4	RS-1	Alco	1953	
1071, 1072, 1110-1116			9	H-12-44	F-M	1950-53	
1073-1076, 1106-1109, 1117-1121, 1126-1128			16	S-12	Baldwin	1951-54	
1077-1079, 1093-1099			10	S-4	Alco	1951-55	
1080, 1081			2	RS-1	Alco	1944	
1101-1105, 1122-1125	1201-1209 (2)		9	SW9	EMD	1952-53	
1200			1	Boxcab	Ingersoll	1930	
1201			1	SW	EMC	1938	11
1202-1204, 1206, 1213, 1223-1236, 1247-1258			31	S-1	Alco	1941-48	
1205			1	80-ton	Whitcomb	1942	
1207-1212, 1214, 1215			8	SW1	EMD	1940, 1942	
1209 (2)			1	SC	EMC	1936	3
1224 (2)			1	S-1	Alco	1944	1
1237-1246			10	VO660	Baldwin	1945	
1259-1261			3	DS-4-4-6	Baldwin	1949	
1262-1267			6	S-3	Alco	1951	
1268-1279			12	SW1	EMD	1953	
1280, 1281			2	SW600	EMD	1954	
1301			1	SW1500	EMD	1968	12
1302-1316			15	MP15	EMD	1975	
1500-1502, 1504			4	DRS-6-4-15	Baldwin	1948	
1503			1	RS-2	Alco	1948	
1505-1509			5	DRS-6-6-15	Baldwin	1948-49	
1510-1514, 1605-1612			13	H-16-66	F-M	1951-52	
1515-1517, 1619, 1620			5	RSD-4	Alco	1951-52	
1518-1550, 1556-1559, 1625-1659, 1562-1599, 1601-1603			113	GP7	EMD	1952-53	
1551-1555, 1613-1618, 1621-1624			15	RS-3	Alco	1952-53	
1560, 1561, 1604			3	AS-616	Baldwin	1952	
1660-1664			5	SD7	EMD	1953	
1665-1667, 1684-1690			10	RSD-5	Alco	1953-54	
1668-1683, 1691-1700, 1901-1906			32	H-16-66	F-M	1953-56	
1701-1710, 1721-1724	6601-6614		14	SD9	EMD	1954-55	
1711-1720, 1725-1773			59	GP9	EMD	1954-59	
1774-1779			6	GP18	EMD	1960	
2000A, 2001A			2	TR2A	EMD	1949	
2000B, 2001B			2	TR2B	EMD	1949	
4051A-4054A			4	FTA	EMD	1945	13
4051B-4054B			4	FTB	EMD	1945	13
4055A-4066A, 4051C-4066C			28	F3A	EMD	1947	
4055B-4063B, 4065B, 4066B			11	F3B	EMD	1947	
4067A, C-4102A, C			72	F7A	EMD	1949-50	
4067B-4084B, 4091B-4094B			22	F7B	EMD	1949	
4101A, 4101C			2	F3A	EMD	1948-49	3
4102A, 4103A (2), 4102C			3	F7A	EMD	1949	3
4103A, 4104A (1)			2	FA-2	Alco	1950	
4103B, 4104B			2	FB-2	Alco	1950	
4100-4104 (2), 4105-4209			110	GP7	EMD	1950-53	14
4240-4249			10	RS-32	Alco	1962	
4250, 4251			2	RS-11	Alco	1957, 1960	
4252, 4253			2	HE15	EMD	1980	15

Original road numbers	Second numbers	Third numbers	Qty.	Model	Builder	Dates built	Notes
4301..4333, 4379-4399, 4496..4562			91	GP9m	EMD	1956-59	16
4310-4316, 4327-4332, 4334-4338, 4466-4495			48	GP7m	EMD	1951-54	16
4400-4424			25	GP15-1	EMD	1976	
4514-4528			15	GP9	GMD	1954-60	17
4600-4634			35	GP38-2	EMD	1979	
4701-4711			11	GP38r	EMD	1967	18
5000A			1	DR-6-2-10	Baldwin	1948	
5001A, B-5002A, B			4	E3A	EMC	1939	
5003A			1	E2A	EMC	1937	19
5004A			1	E6A	EMD	1941	19
5004B			1	E7A	EMD	1946	19
5005A, B-5006A, B			4	E6A	EMD	1941	
5007A			1	DL-109	Alco	1941	
5008A-5020A, 5007B-5019B			26	E7A	EMD	1944-49	
5021A-5031A, 5021B-5030B			21	E8A	EMD	1950-53	
5031B			1	E8Am	EMD	1952	20
5032A			1	E9Am	EMD	1959	21
5032B, 5033A			2	E8A	EMD	1952	21
5050-5099			50	GP50	EMD	1980	
5500-5537			38	GP40	EMD	1966-67	22
6001A, B-6002A, B			4	Erie A	F-M	1947	1
6500A, C-6505A, C			12	F7A	EMD	1949-50	1
6472..6491, 6500-6589			97	SD45	EMD	1966-70	23
6600			1	SDCAT	EMD	1968	24
6615-6621			7	SD7r	EMD	1954-55	25
6622-6647			26	SD18	EMD	1960	26
6650-6659			10	SD38-2	EMD	1975	
6701-6730			30	C-628	Alco	1965-66	27
6801-6935			135	SD40-2	EMD	1973-76	
7000-7035			36	SD50	EMD	1985	
8001-8055			55	SD60	EMD	1986	
8501-8577			77	Dash 8-40C	GE	1989-91	
8601-8730			130	Dash 9-44CW	GE	1994	
8801-8835			35	AC4400CW	GE	1994	

Notes:
1—Ex-Chicago, St. Paul, Minneapolis & Omaha, acquired with lease of Omaha Road in 1957.
2—Ex-Minneapolis & St. Louis, acquired with merger in 1960.
3—Ex-Chicago Great Western, acquired with merger in 1968.
4—No. 86 is ex-Litchfield & Madison 100, acquired with merger in 1958; 87-89 are ex-CStPM&O.
5—Rebuilt to SW900 in 1957.
6—Ex-L&M 301-303, acquired with merger in 1958; no. 310 renumbered 905, then 406.
7—B units rebuilt with cabs by C&NW (nicknamed "Crandall Cab" engines), owned by Regional Transportation Authority (RTA), Chicago.
8—Owned by RTA.
9—Nos. 802-809 are ex-CGW.
10—No. 1000 is ex-CGW 59A; others are ex-Grand Trunk Western, Kansas City Southern, Pittsburgh & Lake Erie, and Southern Pacific.
11—Former EMC demonstrator 655.
12—Ex-Minnesota Transfer.
13—Nos. 4051A-4054A rebuilt to FP9m and 4051B-4054B rebuilt to F9Bm in 1955.
14—Ex-Rock Island 4425-4478, 4500-4555, acquired 1980.
15—Geeps rebuilt with Cummins diesel engines.
16—Rebuilt from older C&NW and other railroads' GP7s and GP9s starting in 1972.
17—Ex-Quebec, North Shore & Labrador.
18—Ex-CSX, acquired early 1990s.
19—Originally owned jointly with Union Pacific and Southern Pacific for City of Los Angeles and City of San Francisco service. No. 5003A is former LA-1 (then 921A, 984J); 5004A is former SF-4 (904A, 985J); and 5004B is former LA-7 (927, 988J); all acquired in 1948.
20—Ex-Kansas City Southern 23, acquired 1970.
21—Nos. 5032A, 5032B, 5033A are ex-KCS 25, 27, 29, acquired 1970.
22—Ex-Conrail.
23—Ex-CR and Burlington Northern.
24—SD45 rebuilt with Caterpillar engine in early 1990s.
25—Rebuilt from older SD7s.
26—Ex Southern SD24s, rebuilt to 1800 hp, classified by C&NW as SD18.
27—Ex-Norfolk & Western 1100-1129, acquired 1973.
Many Baldwin switchers and road switchers were rebuilt by EMD with EMD engines.

Published roster:
Extra 2200 South, April-May 1970

Chicago, Burlington & Quincy
1929-1970

The Burlington Route was a diesel pioneer with its *Zephyr* passenger trains in the 1930s, and the railroad began dieselizing mainline freight trains with EMD FTs in 1943. The CB&Q continuing dieselizing with a large fleet of Fs and Geeps, with most steam locomotives pushed out by 1956. Other than a few wartime Baldwin and Alco switchers, the Q was a loyal EMD customer until a group of U25Bs arrived in 1964; it then purchased modern diesels from both EMD and GE until the 1970 Burlington Northern merger.

This roster includes the Burlington's Colorado & Southern and Fort Worth & Denver subsidiaries, with ownership noted next to the numbers. The CB&Q merged with the Great Northern, Northern Pacific, and Spokane, Portland & Seattle to form Burlington Northern in 1970.

Burlington Route acquired its first EMD FT diesels in 1943. *CB&Q*

Original road numbers	Second numbers	Third Numbers	Qty.	Model	Builder	Dates built	Notes
100 (1)	9100	8900	1	30-ton	Mack	1929	
101 (1)	9101	8901	1	12-ton	Whitcomb	1934	
111 (1)	9111	8902	1	44-ton	Porter	1930	
112 (1)	9120		1	60-ton	Porter	1932	
100-115 (3)			16	U25B	GE	1964-67	
100A, 100D (2)	150C, 151C		2	FTA	EMD	1943	
100B, 100C (2)	150B, 151B		2	FTB	EMD	1943	
101A (2), 101D (2)	152C, 201D	154C	2	FTA	EMD	1944	
101B (2), 101C (2)	152B, 201C	154B	2	FTB	EMD	1944	
102A, 102D	153C, 202D	155A	2	FTA	EMD	1944	
102B, 102C	153B, 202C	155B	2	FTB	EMD	1944	
103A, 103D	156A, 157A		2	FTA	EMD	1944	
103B, 103C	156B, 157B		2	FTB	EMD	1944	
104A, 104D	158A, 159A		2	FTA	EMD	1944	
104B, 104C	158B, 159B		2	FTB	EMD	1944	
105A-115A, 105D-115D			22	FTA	EMD	1944	
105B-115B, 105C-115C			22	FTB	EMD	1944	
116A-138A, 116D-138D	703A, 703D (C&S), 163C-166C		46	F3A	EMD	1947	1
116B-138B, 116C-138C	703B, 703C, (C&S), 163B-166B		46	F3B	EMD	1947	1
140-149			10	U28B	GE	1966	2
150-154 (2)			5	U30B	GE	1968	
150-153 (C&S)			4	NW2	EMD	1947-48	

Original road numbers	Second numbers	Third Numbers	Qty.	Model	Builder	Dates built	Notes
154 (C&S)			1	SW7	EMD	1950	
155 (C&S)			1	SW1	EMC	1940	
156-160 (C&S)			5	SW1200	EMD	1959	
150A-154A, 155C-159C			10	F2A	EMD	1946	
163A-169A, 167C-169C			10	F7A	EMD	1950	
167B-169B			3	F7B	EMD	1950	
170-189			20	GP40	EMD	1966-67	
200-267			68	GP7	EMD	1951-53	
270-289			20	GP9	EMD	1954	
300-324, 400-411			37	SD7	EMD	1952-53	
325-374, 430-459			80	SD9	EMD	1954-57	
460-468			9	U23C	GE	1969	
500-515			16	SD24	EMD	1959	
516-530			15	SD45	EMD	1969	
550-561			12	U25C	GE	1965	
562-577			16	U28C	GE	1966	
700A-702A, 700D-702D (C&S)			6	F7A	EMD	1950	3
700B-702B, 700C-702B (C&S)			6	F7B	EMD	1950	
703A, 703D (C&S)			2	F3A	EMD	1950	
703B, 703C (C&S)			2	F3B	EMD	1950	
750A-752A, 750D-752D (FWD)			6	F7A	EMD	1950	3
750B-752B, 750C-752C (FWD)			6	F7B	EMD	1950	
900-935			36	GP20	EMD	1961	
940-977			38	GP30	EMD	1962-63	
978-999			22	GP35	EMD	1964	
9103-9107	8903		4	44-tonner	GE	1940-41	
9121-9123			3	65-ton	Midwest	1933-34	
9130-9135			6	SW	EMC	1937	
9136-9153			18	SW1	EMC	1939-41	
9200-9201			2	NW1	EMC	1937	
9203-9248			46	NW2	EMD	1940-49	
9249-9268			20	SW7	EMD	1950	
9269, 9270			2	SW9	EMD	1951	
9271-9292			22	SW1200	EMD	1955, 1965	
9300-9308			9	S-2	Alco	1943, 1944	
9310-9321			12	SW1000	EMD	1966	
9350-9379			30	VO1000	Baldwin	1943-44	
9900-9903			4	AA	EMC	1934-35	4
9904, 9905, 9906A, 9907A, 9908			5	AA	EMC	1936-39	5
9906B, 9907B			2	AB	EMC	1936	5
9909	9953 (C&S)		1	E5A	EMC	1940	
9910A	9951A (C&S)		1	E5A	EMC	1940	
9911A	9982A (FWD)	9952A (C&S)	1	E5A	EMC	1940	
9912A, 9915A, 9914B, 9915B			4	E5A	EMD	1940-41	
9913, 9914A	9954, 9955 (C&S)		2	E5A	EMD	1940-41	
9910B	9951B (C&S)		1	E5B	EMC	1940	
9911B	9982B (FWD)	9952B (C&S)	1	E5B	EMC	1940	
9912B			1	E5B	EMC	1940	
9916A-9937A, 9916B-9936B, 9949B			44	E7A	EMD	1945-49	
9938A-9949A, 9937B-9948B			24	E8A	EMD	1949-50	
9950A			1	E5A	EMC	1940	
9950B			1	E5B	EMC	1940	

Original road numbers	Second numbers	Third Numbers	Qty.	Model	Builder	Dates built	Notes
9960A-9962A, 9960C-9962C			6	F3A	EMD	1947	
9960B-9962B			3	F3B	EMD	1947	
9964-9977			14	E8A	EMD	1952-53	
9981A, 9981B (C&S)			2	E8A	EMD	1952	
9985A-9989A, 9985B-9989B			10	E9A	EMD	1955-56	
9990-9995			6	E9A	EMD	1956	

Notes:
1—Nos. 163B-166B are former 137B, 137C, 138B, 138C; nos. 163C-166C are former 137A, 137D, 138A, 138D; nos. 703A-D are former 119A-D.
2—Locomotives rebuilt to 3,000 hp and classified U28Bm.
3—Numbers 700A and 750A wrecked in 1958 and rebuilt to F9Am.
4—Power units for articulated Zephyr trains; locomotives integral to trains.
5—Power units for Zephyr trains; locomotives separate from trains.

Published roster:
Extra 2200 South, May 1971

Chicago Great Western
1936-1968

The Chicago Great Western bought a few diesel switchers in 1936, but began heavily investing in diesels right after World War II. Electro-Motive F units took over most mainline freights, with steam making its last run in 1950. The railroad became known for running long, heavy freight trains behind matched sets of six or more F units, a practice it continued even after acquiring new GP30s and SD40s in the mid-1960s. The CGW was merged into the Chicago & North Western on July 1, 1968.

Chicago Great Western F3A No. 107A leads a string of seven F units at Oelwein, Iowa, in 1952. *Trains magazine collection*

Road Numbers	Qty.	Model	Builder	Dates built	Notes
5-7	3	SC	EMC	1936	
8-10	3	S-2	Alco	1947	
11-15	5	S-1	Alco	1948	
16-31, 42	17	NW2	EMD	1948-49	
32-41	10	DS-4-4-10	Baldwin	1948	
50-57	8	RS-2	Alco	1949	
58A-66A	9	TR2A	EMD	1948-49	
58B-66B	9	TR2B	EMD	1948-49	
101A-115A, 101C-115C	30	F3A	EMD	1947-49	
101B-112B, 101D-104D	15	F3B	EMD	1947-49	
113B-116B, 105D-116D, 116E, 116F, 116G	19	F7B	EMD	1949-51	
116A, 116C	2	FP7	EMD	1951	
120, 121	2	GP7	EMD	1951	1
150-152	3	F3A	EMD	1948, 49	2
153-156	4	F7A	EMD	1949	2
201-208	8	GP30	EMD	1963	
401-409	10	SD40	EMD	1966	

Notes:
1—No. 120 was rebuilt into a GP9m.
2—Steam-generator equipped.

Published roster:
Chicago Great Western: Iowa in the Merger Decade, by Phillip R. Hastings (Carstens Publications)

Chicago, Indianapolis & Louisville
(Monon)
1942-1971

Monon Alco RS-2 No. 23 was built in 1947. *P.F. Johnson*

The Monon began aggressively dieselizing in 1946 with EMD F units for mainline freight and passenger service with EMD BL2s and Alco RS-2s for locals. The last steam locomotive operated in 1949. New power came with Alco Century 628s in 1964, but the diesels proved too big for the Monon and they were quickly swapped for four-axle C-420s. The Monon was merged into Louisville & Nashville in 1971.

Original road numbers	Second numbers	Qty.	Model	Builder	Dates built	Notes
1, 5, 6		2	SW1	EMD	1949	1
11-17		7	NW2	EMD	1942, 1947	2
18		1	H-10-44	F-M	1946	
21-29	51-59	9	RS-2	Alco	1947	3
30-38		9	BL2	EMD	1948-49	
36, 37 (1)	45, 46	2	H-15-44	F-M	1947	4
51A, 51B, 61A-65A, 61B-65B	101-112	12	F3A	EMD	1946-47	5
61C-65C	301-305	5	F3B	EMD	1945-47	5, 6,
81A-85A, 81B-85B	201-210	10	F3A	EMD	1946-47	6, 7
400-408		10	C-628	Alco	1964	
501-518		18	C-420	Alco	1966-67	8
601-608		8	U23B	GE	1970	

Notes:
1—No. 1 delivered as DS50.
2—Nos. 11-13 delivered as DS1-DS3.
3—Upgraded to 1,600 hp in 1965 and 1966 and renumbered.
4—Rebuilt with EMD engines in 1960.
5—First 62B, 64A, 62C were wrecked and scrapped in 1947 and replaced by same-numbered new F3s. Second 62B, 64A, 62C were renumbered.
6—Nos. 85A, B, 65C were EMD demonstrators 754A1, 754A2, 754B1.
7—Steam-generator equipped.
8—Nos. 501, 502 steam-generator equipped with high noses.

Published roster:
Diesel Locomotive Rosters (Wayner Publications)

Chicago, Milwaukee, St. Paul & Pacific
1939-1986

The Milwaukee Road dieselized largely with EMD F units and Geeps, but acquired a variety of early power, including Erie-Built passenger units, a pair of DL-109s, and several Fairbanks-Morse and Baldwin switchers and road switchers. The Milwaukee renumbered locomotives often, and often re-used numbers. Also, as groups of locomotives were renumbered, they often weren't renumbered in sequence. See *The Milwaukee Road Diesel Locomotives* for an in-depth, unit-by-unit summary.

Most of the Milwaukee's remaining early diesels were retired when the railroad ended operations on its Pacific extension in 1980 and abandoned many branch lines. The Soo Line merged the Milwaukee Road on Jan. 1, 1986.

Milwaukee Road No. 3031 is an early SD40-2, built in 1972.

Louis A. Marre

Original road numbers	Second numbers	Third numbers	Qty.	Model	Builder	Dates built	Notes
1-5			5	FP45	EMD	1968	
5A-9A, 5C-9C, 21A, 22A, 21B, 22B	10A-14A, 11B-14B		14	Erie A	F-M	1946-47	1
5B-9B, 21C	10B		6	Erie B	F-M	1946-48	1
14A, 14B (1)			2	DL-109	Alco	1941	
15A, 15B			2	E6A	EMD	1941	
16A-20A, 16B-20B			10	E7A	EMD	1946	
21-30			10	SD40-2	EMD	1973	
23A-28A, 23C-28C			12	CFA-16-4	F-M	1951	
23B-28B			6	CFB-16-4	F-M	1951	
35A-47A, 35D-47D			26	FTA	EMD	1941-45	
35B-47B, 35C-47C			26	FTB	EMD	1941-45	
36A-38A, 36C-38C (2)			6	E9A	EMD	1961	
40-54			15	F40C	EMD	1974	2
48A-50A, 48C-50C, 68A-79A, 68C-79C			30	F7A	EMD	1950	
48B-50B, 68B-79B			15	F7B	EMD	1950	
80A-83A, 80D-83D	81C (3), 84A-86A (2)		8	F3A	EMD	1949	
80B-83B, 80C-84C	84B-86B (2)		8	F3B	EMD	1949	
84A-89A, 84D, 85D, 87C, 89C	106C-108C, 112A, 112C		10	F7A	EMD	1949	
84B, 84C, 85B, 85C, 87B, 89B (1)	106B-108B, 112B		6	F7B	EMD	1949	
81C-86C (2)	125A-128A, 125C, 127C (1)		6	F9A	EMD	1954	
81D-86D	125B-128B, 126C, 128C		6	F9B	EMD	1955	
90A-105A, 90C-105C (1)	60A..64A, 60C..64C		32	FP7	EMD	1950	
90B-121B	60B-64B, 84B, 84C, 85B, 85C		32	F7B	EMD	1949-51	3
106A-111A, 109C-111C, 113A-121A, 113C-121C			27	F7A	EMD	1950-51	
130-140 (1)	5506-5511, 6000-6003	5600-5603	11	U28B	GE	1966	
153-199 (1)	2000-2046 (2)	16 (1)	47	GP40	EMD	1966-67	
171-209 (2)	16-20 (2)		39	SD40-2	EMD	1973-74	
200A-205A, 200C-205C	30A-35A, 30C-35C		12	E9A	EMD	1956	
200B-205B	30B-35B (2)		6	E9B	EMD	1956	
280-331			52	GP9	EMD	1959	
340-355 (1)	1000-1015		16	GP30	EMD	1963	4

Original road numbers	Second numbers	Third numbers	Qty.	Model	Builder	Dates built	Notes
350-365 (2)			16	GP38-2	EMD	1973-74	
360-371 (1)	1500-1511		12	GP35	EMD	1965	
380-391	5000-5010 (1)	5050-5060	12	U25B	GE	1965	
380 (2), 393-398	6004, 5500-5505	5604	7	U28B	GE	1966	
434-497			64	MP15AC	EMD	1975-76	
532, 534, 543-561 (2)			21	SD10	EMD		5
581-590			10	SDL39	EMD	1969, 1972	
946-999 (3, 2)	212..277		54	GP20	EMD		6
961-963 (1)	870-872 (1)		3	RS-1	Alco	1950	
970, 971	926, 927		2	RS-12	Baldwin	1951-52	7
975-996	454..493, 576..597		22	RSC-2	Alco	1946-47	8
1600-1603	980-983		4	HH660	Alco	1939-40	
1610-1634	950..977	860..881	25	SW1	EMD	1939-41	
1643-1645	620-622		3	SW9	EMD	1951	
1637-1642	614-619		6	SW1200	EMD	1954	
1646	623		1	SW7	EMD	1950	
1647-1654	665-672		8	NW2	EMD	1940-47	
1649 (1)	1635		1	VO660	Baldwin	1940	
1657-1669, 1672-1674, 1678, 1679	822-839		18	S-2	Alco	1940-47	
1670, 1671	820, 821		2	HH1000	Alco	1939-40	
1676-1679	873, 874		4	RS-1	Alco	1941, 1943	
1680-1691	928-939	908	12	VO1000	Baldwin	1940-45	
1692-1697	940-945 (1)	931..941 (2)	6	DS-4-4-10	Baldwin	1948	
1690, 1700, 1701	991, 992, 1699	990 (2)	3	44-tonner	GE	1940-41	
1699, 1702-1707	993-996		7	44-ton	Whit.	1940-41	
1708, 1709	997		2	44-ton	Dav.	1942	
1802-1825	760-783		24	H-10-44	F-M	1944-50	
1826-1847	715-729, 750-756	746-749	22	H-12-44	F-M	1950-51	
1850-1862	840-852	807 (2)	13	S-2	Alco	1949-50	
1863-1896	800-819, 853-866		34	S-4	Alco	1950-53	
1901-1904	946-949 (1)	937-940 (2)	4	DS-4-4-10	Baldwin	1949	
1905-1925	900-914, 920-925	939	21	S-12	Baldwin	1950-54	
2000A, 2000B	696A, 696B		2	TR2A, TR2B	EMD	1949	
2001A-2006A	690A-695A		6	TR4A	EMD	1950-51	
2001B-2006B	690B-695B		6	TR4B	EMD	1950-51	
2020-2061 (1)	600-613, 625-652		42	SW1200	EMD	1954	
2047-2071 (2)	17, 19 (1)		25	GP40	EMD	1968-69	
2100A, 2101A, 2104-2107	2100, 2101, 564-567	560..569	6	AS-616	Baldwin	1951, 1953	
2100B, 2101B	2102, 2103	562, 563	2	AS-616B	Baldwin	1951	9
2125-2130	550-555 (1)	527-529, 547-549	6	H-16-66	F-M	1953	
2150-2155	570-575		6	RSD-5	Alco	1953	
2200-2223	500-523	534..561	24	SD7	EMD	1952-53	
2224-2237	530-543	500..557	14	SD9	EMD	1954	
2300-2325	700-710 (1), 730-744		26	H-12-44	F-M	1952-55	
2368-2443	200..277	800-809, 946..999	76	GP9	EMD	1954-58	
2450-2469, 2500-2516	400-436 (1)		37	H-16-44	F-M	1954, 1956	
2475-2495	450-470 (1)		21	RS-3	Alco	1953-55	
3000-3040	130-170 (2)		41	SD40-2	EMD	1972	
4000 4009	6-15		10	SD45	EMD	1968	
4800-4804	5000-5004 (2)		5	U23B	GE	1973	
5651-5658			8	U30C	GE	1974	

Original road numbers	Second numbers	Third numbers	Qty.	Model	Builder	Dates built	Notes
5800, 5801	E90, E91	1800, 1801	2	90-ton	Whit.	1929-30	
6005-6009	5605-5609		5	U30B	GE	1968	
8000-8003	5700-5703		4	U33C	GE	1968	
8500-8503	5800-5803 (2)		4	U36C	GE	1972	

Notes:
1—Nos. 5C, 6C, 8C, 21A, 22A, 7C, 9C, 21B, 22B, 21C renumbered (in 1947, except 13A, 13B, 14A in 1959).
2—F40Cs were owned by Northwest Suburban Mass Transit District (Chicago) but carried Milwaukee Road emblems and were maintained by MILW.
3—Nos. 90B-105B are steam-generator equipped.
4—These ride on AAR trucks from older RS-3s.
5—In 1974-1975, Milwaukee rebuilt 21 older SD7s and SD9s and chopped their noses, calling them SD10s.
6—From 1969-1973, Milwaukee rebuilt 54 older Geeps with new 2,000-hp 645 engines and chopped noses, calling them GP20s.
7—Steam-generator equipped.
8—Many RSC-2s were converted to RS-2s by swapping four-wheel trucks (some multiple times with multiple numbers). Four were rebuilt by Alco in 1965 with low noses and new engines, initially numbered 576-579.
9—Built as cabless, but had cabs/controls added by the mid-1950s.

Published rosters:
Extra 2200 South, July-August-September 1971; The Milwaukee Road Diesel Power, by Frederick Hyde and Dale Sanders (The Milwaukee Road Historical Association, 2009)

Chicago, Rock Island & Pacific
1930-1980

The Rock Island began buying diesel switchers before World War II, then received several sets of EMD FT cab units in 1944-45. In spite of this, the Rock continued buying steam locomotives, receiving new 4-8-4s in 1944 and 1946. The arrival of more F units, along with Geeps and Alco RS and FA diesels, put an end to steam operations in 1953. Second-generation diesels arrived beginning in the early 1960s from both EMD and GE, but the Rock was struggling financially by that time. The railroad ceased operations on March 31, 1980, but many of its diesels went on to operate on other railroads.

Rock Island took delivery of a dozen EMD GP7s in 1950.
Rock Island

Original road numbers	Second numbers	Third numbers	Qty.	Model	Builder	Dates built	Notes
1-3			3	LWT12	EMD	1955-56	1
38-49			12	F2A	EMD	1946	
70-99			30	FTA	EMD	1944-45	
70B-73B, 88B-99B			16	FTB	EMD	1944-45	
101 (1)	730		1	HH900	Alco	1939	

Original road numbers	Second numbers	Third numbers	Qty.	Model	Builder	Dates built	Notes
100-127			28	F7A	EMD	1949, 1951	
100B-109B, 120B-123B	10-23		14	F7B	EMD	1949	
145-160	128-143		16	FA-1	Alco	1948	
145B-152B	128B-135B	28-35	8	FB-1	Alco	1948	
190-199, 285-299			25	U33B	GE	1968-69	
200-238			39	U25B	GE	1963-65	
240-281			42	U28B	GE	1966	
300-333			34	GP35	EMD	1965	
340-396 (2)			57	GP40	EMD	1966-69	
345-350 (1)			5	30-ton	Davenport	1940-41	
351, 361-366 (1), 372-377 (1)			13	44-ton	Davenport	1939-42	
367-371 (1)			5	44-ton	Whitcomb	1940	
400, 401			2	H-15-44	F-M	1948	
402-411			10	FP7	EMD	1949	
415-424			10	C-415	Alco	1966	
425-429			5	BL2	EMD	1949	
430-441			12	GP7	EMD	1950	
450-454			5	RS-2	Alco	1948	
455-475, 485-499			36	RS-3	Alco	1950-51	
500-528			29	SW	EMD	1937-38	
529-546			18	SW1	EMD	1942, 1949	
550-563	915		14	SW900	EMD	1957	2
598, 599			2	S-1	Alco	1941	3
601-606			6	TA	EMD	1937	
613-620			8	E8B	EMD	1950, 1953	4
621-624			4	PA-1	Alco	1940-41	
625, 626			2	E3A	EMC	1939	
627-631			5	E6A	EMD	1940-41	
632-642			11	E7A	EMD	1946, 1948	
632B-634B, 637B-642B	602-604, 607-612		9	E7B	EMD	1946-48	
643-661			19	E8A	EMD	1949-53	5
662-665			4	E9A	EMD	1955	6
675-677			3	F7A	EMD	1949	
675B-677B	615, 617 (1)	25, 27	3	F7B	EMD	1949	
700-707			8	NW1	EMD	1938	
716-729, 731, 732			16	S-2	Alco	1942-48	7
735-749			15	RS-1	Alco	1941-44	
750, 751			2	AB	EMD	1940	
758, 759			2	S-12	Baldwin	1953	8
760-764			5	VO1000	Baldwin	1943-44	
765-774			10	NW2	EMD	1948-49	
775-779			5	SW9	EMD	1953	
795-797			3	NW2	EMD	1948	9
798, 799			2	112-ton	Davenport	1950	
800, 801			2	800-hp	Lima	1950	
802-806			5	S-8	Baldwin	1952	
811-840			30	SW8	EMD	1950-53	10
900-914	780		16	SW900	EMD	1959	
920-936			17	SW1200	EMD	1965	
940-949			10	SW1500	EMD	1966	
1000-1016			17	500-hp	Whitcomb	1950	11

Original road numbers	Second numbers	Third numbers	Qty.	Model	Builder	Dates built	Notes
1200-1237			38	GP7	EMD	1951	
1238, 1239			2	GP18m	EMD	1963	
1250-1311			62	GP7	EMD	1952-53	
1312-1332			21	GP9	EMD	1957, 1959	
1333-1353			21	GP18	EMD	1960-61	
3000-3006			7	GP40	EMD	1968-69	
4100-4111			12	F9B	EMD	1959	12
4150-4168			19	F9A	EMD	1959	13
4300-4355, 4368-4379			68	GP38-2	EMD	1976-78	
4700-4719			20	GP40	EMD	1970	
4790-4799			10	SD40-2	EMD	1973	
4800-4804			5	SW1	EMD	1939-46	14
4900-4909			10	NW2	EMD	1947, 1949	15
10000			1	Boxcab	Ingersoll	1930	

Notes:
1—Power units for experimental Jet Rocket and Aerotrain lightweight trains.
2—No. 560 was rebuilt and renumbered 915 in 1968.
3—Ex-Pullman RR 20, 21, acquired 1949.
4—Ex-Union Pacific 930B, 931B, 936B-939B, 946B, 947B, acquired 1969.
5—Nos. 657-661 are ex-UP 925, 930, 935, 937, 951, acquired 1969.
6—Ex-UP 900, 901, 903, 905.
7—Nos. 731, 732 are ex-Toledo Terminal 101, 102, acquired 1959.
8—Former Baldwin demonstrators 1200, 1201.
9—Ex-New York, Ontario & Western 111-113, acquired 1959.
10—Nos. 839, 840 are ex-Wichita Falls & Southern 801, 802.
11—Ex-Canadian National 7803-7817, 7819, 7820.
12—Rebuilt F3Bs, ex-UP 509B, 517B, 520B, 522B-524B, 531B, 532B, 536B, 539B, 540B, 542B, acquired 1972.
13 Rebuilt F3As, ex-UP 503, 507, 513, 515, 517-519, 521, 522, 524, 528, 529, 531, 533-535, 537, 538, 539, acquired 1972.
14—Ex-Illinois Central 600, 602, 604, 609, acquired 1970.
15—Ex-Pittsburgh & Lake Erie 8712, 8708, 8710, 8713, 8740-8742, 8747-8749.

Published rosters:
Diesel Locomotive Rosters (Wayner Publications); Rock Island Diesel Locomotives 1930-1980, by Louis A. Marre

Clinchfield
1948-1982

The coal-hauling Clinchfield got a late start on dieselizing, a process that started when EMD F3s arrived in 1948. The railroad then finished the job quickly with additional F units and Geeps, and steam made its last run in 1954. The railroad remained loyal to EMD other than a small order of GE U36Cs in 1971 (which it traded for SD45s six years later). The Clinchfield became part of the Family Lines system in the early 1970s, and its last diesels (GP38-2s, SD40-2s, and rebuilt GP7s) were delivered in the Family Lines paint scheme with Clinchfield sublettering. The railroad became part of Seaboard System on January 1, 1983.

Clinchfield's seven U36Cs were the first delivered. The CRR traded them to L&N for SD45s in 1977.
J. David Ingles

Road numbers	Qty.	Model	Builder	Dates built	Notes
200	1	FP7	EMD	1952	
250	1	F7B	EMD	1950	1
350-355	6	SW7	EMD	1950	
356-360	5	NW2	EMD	1949, 1947	2
361	1	NW3	EMD	1942	3
800-805	6	F3A	EMD	1948-49	4
806-823	18	F7A	EMD	1949-52	5
850-852	3	F3B	EMD	1948-49	4
853-863	11	F7B	EMD	1949-52	

Road numbers	Qty.	Model	Builder	Dates built	Notes
864-868	5	F9B	EMD	1955	
869	1	F7B	EMD	1950	6
900-916	17	GP7	EMD	1950, 1952	7
917, 918	2	GP9	EMD	1956	
919	1	GP7u	EMD	1950	8
2000-2009	10	GP38	EMD	1967	
3000-3024	25	SD40	EMD	1966-71	
3600-3606	7	U36C	GE	1971	
3607-3624	18	SD45-2	EMD	1972, 1974	
3625-3631	7	SD45	EMD	1971	9
6000-6006, 6045	8	GP38-2	EMD	1978-79	
8127-8132	6	SD40-2	EMD	1980-81	

Notes:
1—Ex-Louisville & Nashville 723.
2—No. 356 is ex-Jacksonville Terminal 36; Nos. 357-360 are ex-Apalachicola Northern 701-704; all acquired 1970.
3—Ex-Great Northern 180.
4—Rebuilt to F7 specifications in 1952; 805 wrecked 1955 and rebuilt to F9.
5—Nos. 821-823 are ex-L&N 1814, 1822, 914, acquired 1965.
6—Ex-L&N 1918, nee Nashville, Chattanooga & St. Louis 918, acquired 1965.
7—14 GP7s were rebuilt in 1979-80 and renumbered 4600-4613 (in Family Lines colors). The Clinchfield and FL called them GP16s.
8—Ex-L&N 1753, nee NC&StL 753, acquired 1965.
9—Ex-Seaboard Coast Line 2038-2044, acquired in trade for U36Cs 3600-3606 in 1977.

Published roster:
Extra 2200 South, July-August-September 1986

Conrail
1976-1998

Conrail was formed in 1976 with the consolidation of several bankrupt Northeastern railroads: Penn Central, Central of New Jersey, Erie Lackawanna, Lehigh & Hudson River, Lehigh Valley, Reading, and Pennsylvania-Reading Seashore Lines. This resulted in an eclectic mix of motive power, including switchers and F units dating back to the 1940s. About 80 percent of the original roster came from PC.

Over the next 20 years, the roster became more streamlined, with older power retired and new diesels joining the roster. This roster includes all diesels owned by Conrail that were assigned new numbers upon its formation (although space precludes listing the predecessor roads of specific locomotives) and new power acquired by CR during its existance. Be aware that not all predecessor locomotives were renumbered; some older engines were retired or sold before renumbering, or were stored at merger and never operated. In 1998, Conrail was acquired jointly by CSX and Norfolk Southern, which divided CR's locomotives.

Original road numbers	Second numbers	Qty.	Model	Builder	Dates built	Notes
500..568		67	C30-7	GE	1977-79	1
1600-1699		100	GP15-1	EMD	1979	
1900-2023		124	B23-7	GE	1978-79	
2021-2044 (1)		24	RS-32	Alco		
2030-2040 (2)		11	B30-7R	GE	1989-90	2
2048-2059		12	C-430	Alco	1966	
2060-2077		18	C-420	Alco	1963-66	
2100-2112		13	GP20	EMD		
2168-2249		82	GP30	EMD		
2250-2399		150	GP30	EMD		
2400-2414		15	RS-27	Alco		
2416-2446, 2450-2459	5060..5088	41	C-425	Alco	1964-65	
2474-2499		26	C-424	Alco	1963-67	
2500..2685		179	U25B	GE		
2557-2580 (2)		24	SD70	EMD	1998	
2700..2789		89	U23B	GE		
2800-2816		17	B23-7	GE	1977	

Original road numbers	Second numbers	Qty.	Model	Builder	Dates built	Notes
2822, 2823		2	U28B	GE		
2830-2889		60	U30B	GE		
2890-2970		81	U33B	GE		
3000..3274		272	GP40	EMD		
3275-3403		129	GP40-2	EMD	1973-80	
3400-3419		20	GP39-2	EMD	1974	
3620-3692		73	GP35	EMD		
3800-3839		40	GP9B	EMD		
3850-3873, 4156		25	F7B	EMD		
4000..4064		58	E8A	EMD		
4100-4112 (1)		13	GP40P	EMD		
4100-4129		30	SD80MAC	EMD	1995-96	3
4130-4144		15	SD70MAC	EMD	1998	
4151-4182		32	U34CH	GE	1970-73	
4211..4244		3	E7A	EMD		
4332..4373		22	FP7	EMD		
5000-5059 (1)		60	FL9	EMD	1956-60	
5000-5059 (2)		60	B36-7	GE	1983	
5060-5089		30	Dash 8-40B	GE	1988	
5200-5217		18	RS-2	Alco		
5229-5298, 5306..5593 (1)		158	RS-3	Alco		
5400..5462		49	GP8	EMD		4
5500-5543, 5545-5574 (2)		74	SD60M	EMD	1992	
5544, 5575-5653		80	SD60I	EMD	1994-95	
5600..5999		338	GP7	EMD		
6000-6051 (1)		52	SD35	EMD		
6000-6021		22	C39-8	GE	1986	
6025-6049		25	Dash 8-40C	GE	1989	
6050-6265 (2)		216	Dash 8-40CW	GE	1990-1994	
6066-6239 (1)		174	SD45	EMD		
6240-6357 (1)		118	SD40	EMD		
6358-6524		167	SD40-2	1977-79		
6500-6519		20	U25C	GE		
6520-6534		15	U28C	GE		
6535-6539, 6579-6583		10	U30C	GE		
6540-6578 (1)		39	U33C	GE		
6550-6599 (2)		50	C30-7A	GE	1984	
6587-6599 (1)		13	U36C	GE		
6600-6609		10	C30-7	GE	1977	
6610-6619		10	C32-8	GE	1984	
6620-6644		25	C36-7	GE	1985	
6654-6666		13	SD45-2	EMD		
6667-6699		33	SDP45	EMD		
6700-6834 (2)		135	SD50	EMD	1983-86	
6700-6718 (1)		19	U23C	GE		
6721-6752 (1)		32	C-628	Alco	1963-67	
6753-6779 (1)		27	C-630	Alco	1965-67	
6780-6794 (1)		15	C-636	Alco	1967-68	
6800..6805 (1)		4	RSD-5	Alco		
6812-6816 (1)		5	RSD-15	Alco		
6840-6867		28	SD60	EMD	1985, 1989	5

Conrail operated 167 EMD SD40-2s, including No. 6451.
Conrail

Original road numbers	Second numbers	Qty.	Model	Builder	Dates built	Notes
6855-6879		25	RSD-12	Alco		
6900-6924		25	SD9	EMD		
6925-6959		35	SD38	EMD		
6960-6999		40	SD40r	EMD		6
6998, 6999 (1)		2	SD7	EMD		
7000..7483, 7500..7559		461	GP9	EMD		
7496-7499		4	GP18	EMD		
7513..7597		76	GP10	EMD		4
7587-7612, 7617-7654		64	RS-11	Alco		
7656..7939		274	GP38	EMD		7
7940-8281		342	GP38-2	EMD	1972-79	
8267-8296 (1)		10	S-10	Baldwin		
8300-8303		4	RS-10	Baldwin		
8308..8352		27	S-12	Baldwin		
8353		1	S-8	Baldwin		
8397-8399		3	AS-16	Baldwin		
8400..8599		151	SW1	EMD		
8600-8627, 8664-8700, 9006		66	SW8	EMD		
8628..8663, 8701..8721		33	SW900	EMD		
8836..8910, 9035..9098, 9150		128	SW7	EMD		
8911..9026, 9042..9141		144	SW9	EMD		
9200-9296		97	NW2	EMD		

Original road numbers	Second numbers	Qty.	Model	Builder	Dates built	Notes
9301-9314		14	VO1000m	Baldwin		8
9315-9382		68	SW1200	EMD		
9400-9424		25	SW1001	EMD		
9500-9620		121	SW1500	EMD		
9621-9630		10	MP15	EMD		
9633..9701, 9729..9777, 9817..9833		30	S-4	Alco		
9705, 9731, 9732, 9780..9828, 9839..9855		27	S-2	Alco		
9844-9849		6	T-6	Alco		
9908..9938		9	RS-1	Alco		
9950..9998		40	RS-3m	Alco		9
9999		1	44-tonner	GE		

Notes:
1—Ex-Santa Fe, acquired 1993-94.
2—Ex-Monongahela 2300-2310, acquired 1993.
3—Nos. 4128, 4129 are former EMD demonstrators 8000, 8001.
4—GP8s were rebuilt from older GP7s (1,500 hp) and GP10s rebuilt from GP9s (1,800 hp) from 1976-79.
5—Nos. 6840-6842 are former EMD demonstrators, acquired in 1985.
6—Rebuilt from older SD40s in 1993.
7—Nos. 7656-7659 are GP38ACs.
8—Baldwin VO1000s rebuilt with EMD engines for Reading in 1959; railroad's model designation.
9—RS-3s rebuilt with EMD engines in 1970s.

Published rosters:
Conrail Motive Power Review 1986-1991, by Paul K. Withers (Withers Publishing, 1992), Conrail Motive Power Review, Vol. 1, by Gordon Lloyd Jr. and Louis A. Marre (Interurban Press, 1992), Conrail Power 1: 1976 (Rails Northeast, 1976)

CSX
Current (as of 2017)

This roster lists all locomotives active on CSX as of early 2017.

An AC4400CW and Dash 8-40CW lead a CSX train in 2007. *Alex Mayes*

Initial	Number series	Model	Builder	Dates
CSXT	1-602	CW44AC/H	GE	1994-2001
CSXT	603-699	CW46AC/H	GE	1998-2000
CSXT	700-999	ES44AH	GE	2007-2011
CSXT	1006-1018	MT6	Alco	1955-1958
CSXT	1021-1068	SWMT	—	1956-1957
CSXT	1100-1119	SW1500	EMD	1970-1971
CSXT	1122-1128	SW1001	EMD	1973
CSXT	1130-1139	MP15AC	EMD	1978
CSXT	1140-1149	MP15	EMD	1975
CSXT	1150-1194	MP15AC	EMD	1977-1978

Initial	Number series	Model	Builder	Dates
CSXT	1200-1241	MP15T	EMD	1984-1985
CSXT	1300-1315	3GS21B	NRE	2007-2010
CSXT	1316-1319	2GS14B	NRE	2010
CSXT	1320	RP20BD	RailPower	2012
CSXT	1321-1325	3GS21B	NRE	2010-2012
CSXT	1500-1524	GP15T	EMD	1982
CSXT	1534-1563	GP15-1	EMD	1979
CSXT	1600	3GS21C	NRE	2011
CSXT	1601-1603	RP20CD	RailPower	2011
CSXT	2000-2056	GP40-3	EMD	1973
CSXT	2200-2387	RDSLUG	EMD	1964-1971
CSXT	2411-2442	SD40-2	EMD	1974
CSXT	2443-2445	SD38-2S	EMD	1974
CSXT	2450-2454	SD38-2	EMD	1975
CSXT	2474-2499	SD50-2	EMD	1983-1984
CSXT	2500-2814	GP38-2	EMD	1972-1979
CSXT	3000-3174	ES44AH	GE	2012-2013
CSXT	3175-3249	ES44AH (T4C)	GE	2015
CSXT	3250-3374	ET44AH	GE	2015
CSXT	4000-4090	SD40-3	EMD	1979-1981
CSXT	4225-4299	SD40-3	EMD	R2015-2016
CSXT	4300-4319	GP39-2	EMD	1974
CSXT	4320-4390	SD40-3	EMD	R2015-2016
CSXT	4401-4452	GP40-2 /GP38-2S	EMD	1973-1980
CSXT	4500-4589	SD70MAC	EMD	1997-1998
CSXT	4675-4699	SD70M	EMD	1992-1995
CSXT	4701-4830	SD70MAC	EMD	2004
CSXT	4831-4850	SD70ACe	EMD	2004
CSXT	5000-5016	CW46AH	GE	2000
CSXT	5101-5122	CW44AH	GE	2002
CSXT	5200-5501	ES40DC	GE	2005-2007
CSXT	5930-5979	B20-8/B40-8	GE	1988
CSXT	6001-6499	GP40-2, GP38-2S	EMD	1972
CSXT	6500-6554	GP40-3	EMD	R2014-2015
CSXT	6897-6899	GP60	EMD	1985
CSXT	6900-6987	GP40-2	EMD	1971-1980
CSXT	7300-7396	C40-8W	GE	1990-1994
CSXT	7649-7929	C40-8W	GE	1991-1994
CSXT	8000-8488	SD40-2	EMD	1971-1981
CSXT	8219, 8249	SD38-2S	EMD	1977
CSXT	8500-8667	SD50, SD50-2, SD50-3	EMD	1983-1985
CSXT	8700-8721	SD60	EMD	1984-1989
CSXT	8722-8755	SD60I	EMD	1994-1995
CSXT	8756-8786	SD60M	EMD	1992-1993
CSXT	8787-8789	SD60	EMD	1984-1985
CSXT	8800-8888	SD40-2	EMD	1977-1979
CSXT	9000-9052	C40-9W	GE	1993-1994
CSXT	9151, 9156, 9157	RCPHG4	GE	R2003
CSXT	9241	RCPGH4	GE	R2003
CSXT	9969	GP40-3W	EMD	1967
CSXT	9992-9999	F40PH-2	EMD	1978-1980

Delaware & Hudson
1944-1991

The Delaware & Hudson was known for being a long-time loyal Alco customer. The railroad dieselized with S-2 switchers and RS-2 and RS-3 road switchers in the 1940s and early 1950s and didn't acquire an EMD locomotive until buying three SD45 demonstrators in 1966. The railroad was also noted for its former Santa Fe PAs that operated from the late 1960s through the mid-1970s, and for the pair of freight-service Baldwin Sharks it acquired in the early 1970s.

Guilford purchased D&H in 1984; the D&H subsequently declared bankruptcy in 1988 and in 1991 Guilford sold the railroad to Canadian Pacific, which eventually absorbed it.

The D&H bought 18 Alco Century 628 diesels in 1965. *Trains magazine collection*

Original road numbers	Second numbers	Qty.	Model	Builder	Dates built	Notes
16-19		4	PA-1	Alco	1947-48	1
301-316	2301..2316	16	U23B	GE	1968	
405, 414	422	2	C-420	Alco	1964	2
451-456, 461-463	70, 74, 75	9	C-424	Alco	1963	3
501-508		8	RS-3m	Alco		4
601-618		18	C-628	Alco	1965	
701-712		12	U30C	GE	1967	
751-762		12	U33C	GE	1968, 1970	5
801-803		3	SD45	EMD	1966	6
1205, 1216		2	RF-16	Baldwin	1951, 1952	7
3001-3032, 3004 (2)		33	S-2	Alco	1944-49	
3033-3050		18	S-4	Alco	1950	
4000-4025		26	RS-2	Alco	1946-49	
4026-4129		104	RS-3	Alco	1950-53	
5001-5011		11	RS-11	Alco	1960-61	
5012-5023		12	RS-36	Alco	1963	
7314-7325	7303, 7304, 7307, 7309, 7312, 225, 226, 231	12	GP38-2	EMD	1972	8
7400-7419, 7600-7620	371..388	20	GP39-2	EMD	1974, 1976	9

Notes:
1—Ex-Santa Fe 59L, 60L, 62L, 66L, acquired 1967; rebuilt by Morrison-Knudsen and often termed PA-4s.
2—Ex-Lehigh Valley 405, 414; no. 405 renumbered 422.
3—Ex-Conrail, nee Erie Lackawanna and Reading.
4—Rebuilt by Morrison-Knudsen from older RS-3s; M-K model designation TE56-4A.
5—Ex-EL.
6—Former EMD demonstrators 4352-4354.
7—Ex-Monongahela 1205, 1216; nee New York Central 3805, 3816, acquired 1974.
8—Ex-LV 314-325.
9—Nos. 7400-7419 are ex-Reading 3401-3420; several ex-Reading engines were then renumbered.

Published roster:
Diesel Locomotive Rosters (Wayner Publications)

Delaware, Lackawanna & Western
1933-1960

The Lackawanna bought several groups of switchers from Alco and Electro-Motive beginning in 1933, and dieselized its freight and passenger trains mainly with EMD F and E units starting in 1945. It kept things interesting by acquiring F-M Train Masters and H-16-44s as well. The railroad's last steam locomotive ran in 1953. The DL&W merged with the Erie to form Erie-Lackawanna on October 17, 1960.

Numbers 661 and 662 are Phase IIb F3s, delivered in 1948.
EMD

Road Numbers	Qty.	Model	Builder	Dates built	Notes
51-53	3	44-tonner	GE	1948	
401-411	11	HH660	Alco	1933-40	
425, 426	2	SC	EMC	1935	1
427-437	11	SW1	EMC	1940	
450-455	6	102-ton (center cab)	GE	1933-34	
461-465	5	NW2	EMD	1945	
475-491	17	S-2	Alco	1945, 1949	
501-511	11	SW8	EMD	1951-53	
551-560	10	SW9	EMD	1951-53	
561-568	8	SW1200	EMD	1957	
601A-604A, 601C-604C	8	FTA	EMD	1945	
601B-604C	4	FTB (FTSB)	EMD	1945	
605A, 606A, 605C, 606C, 621A, 621C, 655A-662A	14	F3A	EMD	1946-48	
605B, 606B, 621B, 655B-662B	11	F3B	EMD	1946-48	
611A, 611C, 631A-636A, 631C	9	F7A	EMD	1949	
611B, 632B-636B	6	F7B	EMD	1949	
651A-654A	4	FTA	EMD	1945	
651B-654B	4	FTB	EMD	1945	
801A-805A, 801C-805C	10	F3A	EMD	1946-47	2
801B-805B	5	F3B	EMD	1946-47	2
810-820	11	E8A	EMD	1951	3
850-861	12	H-24-66	F-M	1953, 1956	2
901-918	18	RS-3	Alco	1950-52	
930-935	6	H-16-44	F-M	1952	
951-970	20	GP7	EMD	1951-53	2

Notes:
1—The first EMC switchers, built at GE's Erie, Pa., plant in February-March 1935. They were built before true SC production began at LaGrange in May 1936.
2—Nos. 850-859, 966-970, and 800-series F3s are steam-generator equipped.
3—E8s 810 and 811 are former EMD demonstrators 810 and 811.

Published roster:
Extra 2200 South January-March 1983

Denver & Rio Grande Western
1941-1988

The Denver & Rio Grande Western began dieselizing with switchers and EMD FTs during World War II, but wasn't fully dieselized until 1956. The Rio Grande purchased Southern Pacific in 1988, but the new railroad retained the Southern Pacific name. The D&RGW initially retained much of its identity, and received its last diesel order (GP60s that were originally part of an SP order) in 1990.

Number 5305 is one of 10 SD9s purchased by Rio Grande in 1957. *EMD*

Original road numbers	Second numbers	Qty.	Model	Builder	Dates built	Notes
38-43		6	44-tonner	GE	1941-42	
50		1	30-ton	Davenport	1937	1
66-74		9	VO660	Baldwin	1941	
100		1	NW2	EMC	1941	
101-119		19	S-2	Alco	1943-44	
120-123		4	H-10-44	F-M	1948	
130-139		10	SW1200	EMD	1964-65	
140-149		10	SW1000	EMD	1966, 1968	
150-152		3	H-15-44	F-M	1948	
540A-551A, 540D-551D	5401..5514	24	FTA	EMD	1942-44	2
540B-551B, 540C-551C	5402..5513	24	FTB	EMD	1942-44	2
552A-554A, 552D-554D	5521..5544	6	F3A	EMD	1946	2
552B-554B, 552C-554C	5522..5543	6	F3B	EMD	1946	2
555A-564A, 555D-564A, 5651..5764	5551..5644	44	F7A	EMD	1949-52	2
555B-564B, 555C-564C, 5652..5753	5552..5643	42	F7B	EMD	1949-52	2
5762, 5763, 5772, 5773		4	F9B	EMD	1955	
5771, 5774		2	F9A	EMD	1955	
3001-3028		28	GP30	EMD	1962-63	
3029-3050		22	GP35	EMD	1964-65	
3051-3093		43	GP40	EMD	1966-71	
3094-3130		37	GP40-2	EMD	1972-83	
3131-3153		23	GP40	EMD	1968	3
3154-3156		3	GP60	EMD	1990	

Original road numbers	Second numbers	Qty.	Model	Builder	Dates built	Notes
4001-4003		3	ML-4000	Kraus-Maffei	1961	4
5100-5113		14	GP7	EMD	1950-52	5
5200-5204		5	RS-3	Alco	1951	
5300-5304		5	SD7	EMD	1953	
5305-5314		10	SD9	EMD	1957	
5315-5340		26	SD45	EMD	1967-68	
5341-5413		73	SD40T-2	EMD	1974-80	
5501-5517		17	SD50	EMD	1984	
5901..5954		24	GP9	EMD	1955-56	6
6001, 6003, 6011, 6013		4	PA-1	Alco	1947	
6002, 6012		2	PB-1	Alco	1947	

Notes:
1—Ex-Sumpter Valley 101, acquired 1963 (3-foot gauge).
2—When F units (564 and below) were renumbered in 1950, a fourth digit replaced the original letter suffix: 1 for A, 2 for B, 3 for C, and 4 for D (thus 540A became 5401, 544C became 5443, etc.). F units delivered after that were numbered in the same pattern.
3—Ex-Conrail (nee Penn Central) 3113..3169, acquired 1984.
4—Diesel-hydraulic locomotives; sold to Southern Pacific in 1964.
5—No. 5100 was originally first 5104; renumbered in 1951.
6—GP9s were numbered in a similar pattern as F units: 5901, 5902, 5903, 5904, 5911, 5912, etc., to 5954.

Published rosters:
Diesel Locomotive Rosters (Wayner Publications), Extra 2200 South, October-November 1970

Detroit & Toledo Shore Line
1950-1981

The Detroit & Toledo Shore Line dieselized with a fleet of 10 EMD GP7s and six EMD switchers from 1950-1953, and they remained the railroad's standard power until the line was merged by Grand Trunk Western in 1981.

Road numbers	Qty.	Model	Builder	Dates built	Notes
41-50	10	GP7	EMD	1951-53	
116-118	3	SW7	EMD	1950	
119-121	3	SW9	EMD	1951-52	

Published roster:
Diesel Locomotive Rosters (Wayner Publications)

Detroit, Toledo & Ironton
1941-1980

The Detroit, Toledo & Ironton began buying diesel switchers in 1941 and road units—EMD GP7s—in 1951, gradually adding more Geeps until dieselization was complete in 1955. The railroad owned EMD diesels exclusively until it was sold to the Grand Trunk Western in 1980.

As with most DT&I diesels, GP35 No. 353 lacks dynamic brakes. *EMD*

Original road numbers	Second numbers	Qty.	Model	Builder	Dates built	Notes
200-206		7	GP38	EMD	1966, 1969	1
210-214		5	GP38AC	EMD	1970	
215-217 (1)	209, 208, 207	3	GP38AC	EMD	1970	
215-217 (2)		3	GP38AC	EMD	1971	
218-220		3	GP38	EMD	1971	

Original road numbers	Second numbers	Qty.	Model	Builder	Dates built	Notes
221-228		8	GP38-2	EMD	1975	
250-252		3	SD38	EMD	1969	
253, 254		2	SD38AC	EMD	1971	
350-357		8	GP35	EMD	1964	
400-405		6	GP40	EMD	1968	
406-424		19	GP40-2	EMD	1973, 1979	
900, 901		2	SW1	EMD	1941	
910-916		7	NW2	EMD	1948	
920-924		5	SW7	EMD	1950	
950-973		24	GP7	EMD	1951-53	
980-992		13	GP9	EMD	1955, 1957	

Notes:
1—Nos. 201-204 ordered by Maine Central but delivered to DT&I; only dynamic-brake equipped diesels on the railroad.

Published roster:
Diesel Locomotive Rosters (Wayner Publications)

Duluth, Missabe & Iron Range
1949-2011

The Duluth, Missabe & Iron Range stuck with steam locomotives in freight service through the 1950s, acquiring used engines from other railroads. The railroad began putting its fleet of EMD SD9s together in 1956, and the last steam locomotives operated in 1960. The DM&IR was owned by U.S. Steel until 1988, and leased locomotives to and from other U.S. Steel railroads. The railroad's holding company sold the DM&IR to Canadian National in 2004, and the CN officially merged DM&IR in 2011.

EMD SD9s became the backbone of DM&IR's fleet in the late 1950s.
DM&IR

Original road numbers	Second numbers	Qty.	Model	Builder	Dates built	Notes
11 (2)		1	NW2	EMD	1949	1
11-25		15	SW9	EMD	1953	
50-55		6	RSD-15	Alco	1949	
101-174	300..322	74	SD9	EMD	1956-59	2
175-193	300..322	19	SD18	EMD	1960	2
201-208		8	SD38AC	EMD	1971	
209-213, 215	9002	6	SD38-2	EMD	1975-76	3
214, 216-217, 221-223, 225		7	SD38	EMD	1967, 1970	4
900-909		10	C-630	Alco	1966	5
400-419		20	SD40-3	EMD	See note	6

Notes:
1—Ex-Elgin, Joliet & Eastern 455 (nee Chesapeake & Ohio 5060), acquired 1998.
2—Several SD9s and SD18s were rebuilt and renumbered beginning in 1979; DM&IR classified these as SD-Ms. Locomotives were renumbered in order of rebuilding without regard to original model designation.
3—No. 211 renumbered 9002 in 1998 with special ISO 9002 lettering. No. 215 is ex-Bessemer & Lake Erie 892, acquired 1980.
4—Ex-EJ&E and Bessemer & Lake Erie engines, acquired 1992-93.
5—Ex-Union Pacific 2900-2909, acquired in 1973.
6—SD40-3s were rebuilt in 1996-97 from older SD40-2s (originally built 1972-74) from various sources.

Published roster:
Railroads Illustrated, September 1992

Duluth, Winnipeg & Pacific
1956-1995

The Duluth, Winnipeg & Pacific was a long-time subsidiary of Canadian National, and was popular among railfans for its fleet of Alco RS-11 diesels. The CN largely absorbed the DW&P in the early 1990s, with the DW&P's own scheme and locomotives disappearing, even though the railroad technically still existed until it was merged into another CN subsidiary, Wisconsin Central, in 2011.

The DW&P dieselized with Alco RS-11s in 1956. *Pierre Patenaude*

Road numbers	Qty.	Model	Builder	Dates built	Notes
3600-3614	15	RS-11	Alco	1956	
4429	1	GP9	EMD	1954	1
5726, 5727, 5850-5853	6	GP38-2	EMD	1973-78	2
5902-5911	10	SD40	EMD	1969	1
7902	1	NW2	EMD	1941	1

Notes:
1—Ex-Grand Trunk Western.
2—Ex-GTW; nee Rock Island.

Elgin, Joliet & Eastern
1936-2013

The Elgin, Joliet & Eastern was the outward-lying belt line around Chicago, and the heavy, slow trains it carried led to a roster of mostly switchers and lugging road diesels. It was known among railfans for its substantial fleet of big twin-engine Baldwin transfer locomotives. The EJ&E was owned by U.S. Steel until 1998, and its roster reflects many locomotives acquired from other U.S. Steel railroads (Duluth, Missabe & Iron Range and Bessemer & Lake Erie). Canadian National purchased most of the railroad in 2009 and officially merged it in 2013.

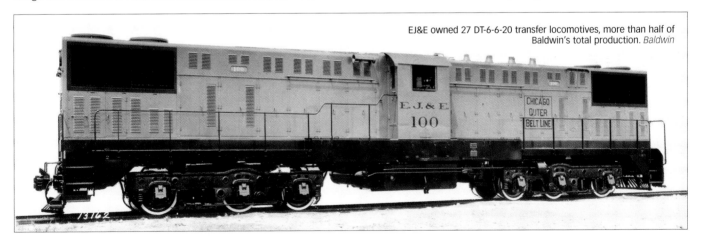

EJ&E owned 27 DT-6-6-20 transfer locomotives, more than half of Baldwin's total production. *Baldwin*

Original road numbers	Second numbers	Qty.	Model	Builder	Dates built	Notes
100-126	701..726, 903..925	27	DT-6-6-20	Baldwin	1946-50	1
200-208		9	SW	EMC	1936-37	
209-212		4	HH660	Alco	1937, 1940	
213-217		5	S-1	Alco	1940-41	
220-246, 249		28	SW1	EMD	1940-41, 1949	
270-272		3	VO660	Baldwin	1940-41	
300-307		8	SW1200	EMD	1960	
308, 309		2	TR5A, TR5B	EMD	1951	2
310-324		25	SW1200	EMD	1964-66	3

Original road numbers	Second numbers	Qty.	Model	Builder	Dates built	Notes
400-401		2	NW1	EMC	1937	
402 (1)	450 (1)	1	HH900	Alco	1937	
402 (2)		1	NC	EMC	1937	
403-407, 409-443		40	NW2	EMC	1940-49	
408 (1)		1	NW2	EMC	1937	4
408 (2)		1	NW2	EMD	1942	5
444-445		2	SW1001	EMD	1971	6
446-449		4	NW2	EMD	1942, 1947	7
451-462 (1)		12	S-2	Alco	1944	
450-452 (2)		3	NW2	EMD	1939	8
453 (2)		1	SW900	EMD	1956	8
454 (2)		1	SW9	EMD	1952	9
455 (2)		1	NW2	EMD	1949	10
456 (2)		1	SW9	EMD	1952	11
457 (2)		1	SW8	EMD	1952	12
458 (2)		1	NW2	EMD	1949	13
459 (2)		1	SW1000	EMD	1971	14
460-462		3	S-2	Alco	1944, 1949	
460 (2)		1	SW1500	EMD	1968	15
475-484		10	VO1000	Baldwin	1940-44	
500-501		2	DRS-6-6-15	Baldwin	1949	16
600-614		15	SD9	EMD	1957-59	17
615-616		2	SD18	EMD	1960	18
650-655		6	SD38	EMD	1970	
656-675		20	SD38-2	EMD	1973-75	19
700-701 (1)	700A, 701A	2	DR-4-4-15	Baldwin	1949	20
700B-701B		2	DR-4-4-15B	Baldwin	1949	20
700 (2), 701 (3), 702 (2), 703, 704 (2)		5	GP38-2	EMD	1972	
800-808, 809 (1)		10	RS-2	Alco	1948-49	
809 (2), 811, 813		3	SD18	EMD	1960	21
814, 815, 818		3	SD9	EMD	1959	21
820		1	SD18	EMD	1960	22
851-852		2	SD18	EMD	1962	23
891		1	SD38-2	EMD	1975	24

Notes:
1—All but 100 and 118 re-engined and renumbered from 1957-1962. Locomotives re-engined with Baldwin engines given new "7" first digits; those re-engined with EMD engines given new "9" first digits.
2—Ex-Union Pacific 1870, 1870B, acquired 1978.
3—Ex-Missouri Pacific, acquired 1986.
4—Ex-Youngstown & Northern, acquired 1946.
5—Ex-Whistler Corp. (nee U.S. Navy), acquired 1963.
6—Ex-U.S. Steel, acquired 1982
7—Ex-Monon and Union Pacific, acquired 1971-73.
8—Ex-Santa Fe, acquired 1974.
9—Ex-Lake Terminal (nee Chesapeake & Ohio), acquired 1975.
10—Ex-C&O, acquired 1975.
11—Ex-Bangor & Aroostook 38 (nee Pittsburgh, Chartiers & Youghiogheny 4), acquired 1976.
12—Ex-Norfolk & Western 2109 (nee Nickel Plate Road 109), acquired 1976.
13—Ex-Illinois Central Gulf 1011, acquired 1976.
14—Ex-New Orleans Public Belt, acquired 1989.
15—Ex-UP 1085 (nee St. Louis Southwestern 2483), acquired 2006.
16—Ex-Bessemer & Lake Erie 401, 402, acquired 1956.
17—Nos. 603-613 ex-Duluth, Missabe & Iron Range, acquired 1968-97.
18—Ex-DM&IR 175, 185, acquired 1997.
19—No. 669 ex-B&LE 891, acquired 1986; nos. 670-675 ex-B&LE, acquired 2001-02.
20—ex-Baldwin demonstrator 6001A, B, C, D, acquired 1950.
21—Ex-DM&IR 184, 180, 179, 162, 163, 172, acquired 1993, 1998.
22—Ex-DM&IR 176, acquired 1997.
23—Ex-B&LE 851, 852, acquired 1995.
24—Ex-B&LE 891, acquired 1986.

Published roster:
Diesel Era, January-February 1997

Erie
1926-1960

The Erie got involved with internal combustion early, buying several boxcab locomotives in the 1920s and several diesel switchers before World War II. It dieselized with a mix of Alco FA, PA, and RS engines, EMD F units and Geeps, and Baldwin road switchers, with the last steam run occurring in 1954. Erie merged with the Delaware, Lackawanna & Western to form Erie-Lackawanna on October 17, 1960.

Two of Erie's 14 EMD E8s lead a passenger train in the early 1950s. *Erie*

Original numbers	Second road numbers	Qty.	Model	Builder	Dates built	Notes
19, 20		2	300-hp bxcab	Alco/GE	1926, 1928	
21, 22		2	600-hp bxcab	Alco/GE	1927	
25		1	800-hp bxcab	GE	1931	
26		1	44-tonner	GE	1946	
300-305		6	HH-660	Alco	1939	
306-321		16	S-1	Alco	1950-57	
360		1	SW1	EMD	1948	
381-385		5	DS-4-4-6	Baldwin	1947, 1949	
386-389		4	DS-4-4-7.5	Baldwin	1949	
401-427		27	NW2	EMD	1939-49	
428-433		6	SW7	EMD	1950	
434-440		7	SW9	EMD	1951-52	
500-525		26	S-2	Alco	1946-49	
526-529		4	S-4	Alco	1951-52	
530-533		4	S-2	Alco	1947-48	1
600-616		17	DS-4-4-10	Baldwin	1947-49	
617-628		12	S-12	Baldwin	1951-52	
650-659		10	LS-1000	Lima	1949	
660-665		6	LS-1200	Lima	1950	
700A-705A, 700D-705D		12	FTA	EMD	1944	
700B-705B, 700C-705C		12	FTB	EMD	1944	
706A-708A, 706D-708D, 714A, 714D		8	F3A	EMD	1947-48	2
706B-708B, 706C-708C, 714B, 714C		8	F3B	EMD	1947-48	2
709A-712A, 709D-712D, 713C		9	F7A	EMD	1949, 1952	
709B-712B, 709C-712C		8	F7B	EMD	1949	
725A-735A, 725D-735D		22	FA-1	Alco	1947-49	

Original numbers	Second road numbers	Qty.	Model	Builder	Dates built	Notes
725B-735B, 725C-735C		22	FB-1	Alco	1947-47	
736A-739A, 736A-739D		8	FA-2	Alco	1951	
736B-739B, 736C-739C		8	FB-2	Alco	1951	
800A-806A, 800D-806D		14	F3A	EMD	1947	
800B-806B		7	F3B	EMD	1947	
807A, 807D	713A, 713D	2	F7A	EMD	1951	3
807B	713B	1	F7B	EMD	1951	3
820-833		14	E8A	EMD	1951	
850-861		12	PA-1	Alco	1949	
862-863		2	PA-2	Alco	1951	
900-913, 1000-1004	950-954	19	RS-2	Alco	1949	
914-933, 1005-1038		54	RS-3	Alco	1950-53	
1100-1105		6	DRS-4-4-15	Baldwin	1949	
1106-1120, 1140		16	AS-16	Baldwin	1951-52	
1150-1161		12	DRS-6-6-15	Baldwin	1950	
1200-1246, 1400-1404		52	GP7	EMD	1950-52	
1260-1265		6	GP9	EMD	1956	

Notes:
1—Ex-Delaware & Hudson 3012, 3014, 3016, 3017.
2—Nos. 714A-D are ex-New York, Ontario & Western 821, 821B, 822B, 822.
3—Built with steam generators; generators removed and locomotives renumbered in 1952.

Published rosters:
Erie Power, by Fred Westing (Alvin F. Staufer, 1983); Extra 2200 South, June 1968

Erie Lackawanna
1960-1976

Erie-Lackawanna was formed in October 1960 with the merger of the Erie and the Delaware, Lackawanna & Western (the hyphen was dropped in 1963). The merger resulted in a varied mix of power from all builders. Following the merger, EL continued to sample locomotives from multiple manufacturers, buying Century locomotives from Alco as well as four-and six-wheel U-Boats and Geeps from GE and EMD. Many early switchers and road switchers remained in service into the 1970s, but most cab units became trade-in material for the new locomotives purchased in the 1960s. This roster covers the railroad until it became part of Conrail in 1976.

Erie Lackawanna bought 34 EMD SD45s in 1967 and 1968.
Louis A. Marre collection

Erie-Lackawanna road numbers	Former Erie numbers	Former DL&W numbers	Qty.	Model	Builder	Dates built	Notes
19	19		1	65-ton	Alco-GE-IR	1928	
26, 51-53	26	51-53	4	44-tonner	GE	1946, 1948	
302-305	302-305		4	HH660	Alco	1939	
322-325		405, 406, 409, 410	4	HH600	Alco	1933, 1940	
306-321	306-321		16	S-1	Alco	1946-50	
349-360	360	427-437	12	SW1	EMD	1948, 1940	
361-371		501-511	11	SW8	EMD	1951-53	
381-385	381-385		5	DS-4-4-6	Baldwin	1946-49	
386-389	386-389		4	DS-4-4-7.5	Baldwin	1949	
401-427	401-427		27	NW2	EMD	1939-49	
428-433	428-433		6	SW7	EMD	1950	
434-440	434-440		7	SW9	EMD	1951-52	
441-445		461-465	5	NW2	EMD	1945	
446-455		551-560	10	SW9	EMD	1951-53	
456-463		561-568	8	SW1200	EMD	1957	
500-525	500-525		26	S-2	Alco	1946-49	
526-529	526-529		4	S-4	Alco	1951-52	
530-550	530-533	475-491	21	S-2	Alco	1945-49	
600-616	600-616		17	DS-4-4-10	Baldwin	1946-49	
617-628	617-628		12	S-12	Baldwin	1951-52	
650-659	650-659		10	LS-1000	Lima	1949	
660-665	660-665		6	LS-1200	Lima	1950	
801-803			3	SD45	EMD	1966	1
809-833	820-833	820, 810-819	25	E8A	EMD	1951	2
850-861	850-861		12	PA-1	Alco	1949	
862, 863	862, 863		2	PA-2	Alco	1951	
900-915, 950-954	900-915, 950-954		21	RS-2	Alco	1949-50	
916-933	916-933		18	RS-3	Alco	1951-53	
1005-1056	1005-1038	901-918	52	RS-3	Alco	1950-52	
1100-1105	1100-1105		6	DRS-4-4-15	Baldwin	1949	
1106-1120	1106-1120		15	AS-16	Baldwin	1951-52	
1140	1140		1	AS-16	Baldwin	1951	3
1150-1161	1150-1161		12	DRS-6-6-15	Baldwin	1950	
1200-1246	1200-1246		47	GP7	EMD	1950-52	
1260-1265	1260-1265		6	GP9	EMD	1956	
1270-1284		951-965	15	GP7	EMD	1951-52	
1400-1409	1400-1404	966-969, 670	10	GP7	EMD	1950-53	3
1850-1861		850-861	12	H-24-66	F-M	1953, 1956	
1930-1935		930-935	6	H-16-66	F-M	1952-53	
2401-2415			15	C-424	Alco	1963	
2451-2462			12	C-425	Alco	1964	
2501-2527			27	U25B	GE	1964-65	
2551-2586			36	GP35	EMD	1965	
3301-3315			15	U33C	GE	1968-69	
3601-3634			34	SD45	EMD	1967-68	
3635-3653			19	SDP45	EMD	1969	4
6011-6041 (by 10s), 6014-6044 (by 10s)		601A-604A, 601C-604A,	8	FTA	EMD	1945	
6012-6042 (by 10s)		601B-604B	4	FTB	EMD	1945	
6054, 6061, 6064, 6211, 6214		605C, 606A, C, 621A, C	5	F3A	EMD	1946, 1948	
6052, 6062, 6212		605B, 606B, 621B	3	F3B	EMD	1946, 1948	
6511-6541 (by 10s)		651A-654A	4	FTA	EMD	1945	
6512- 6542 (by 10s)		651B-654B	4	FTB	EMD	1945	
6551-6621 (by 10s)		655A-661A	8	F3A	EMD	1947-48	
6552-6612 (by 10s)		655B-661B	8	F3B	EMD	1947-48	

Erie-Lackawanna road numbers	Former Erie numbers	Former DL&W numbers	Qty.	Model	Builder	Dates built	Notes
7001-7051 (by 10s), 7004-7054 (by 10s)	700A-705A, 700D-705D		12	FTA	EMD	1944	
7002-7052 (by 10s), 7003-7053 (by 10s)	700B-705B, 705C-705C		12	FTB	EMD	1944	
7061-7101 (by 10s), 7064-7104 (by 10s)	706A-710A, 706D-710D		10	F3A	EMD	1947, 1949	
7062-7102 (by 10s), 7063-7103 (by 10s)	706B-710B, 706C-710C		10	F3B	EMD	1947, 1949	
7111-7131 (by 10s), 7114-7134 (by 10s)	711A-714A, 711D-714D		6	F7A	EMD	1950-51	
7112-7132 (by 10s), 7113-7133 (by 10s)	711B-714B. 711C-714C		6	F7B	EMD	1950-51	
7141, 7144	714A, 714D		2	F3A	EMD	1948	5
7142, 7143	714B, 714C		2	F3B	EMD	1948	5
7251-7351 (by 10s), 7254-7354 (by 10s)	725A-735A, 725D-735D		22	FA-1	Alco	1947-49	
7252-7352 (by 10s), 7253-7353 (by 10s)	725B-735B, 725C-735C		22	FB-1	Alco	1947-49	
7361-7391 (by 10s), 7364-7394 (by 10s)	736A-739A, 736D-739D		8	FA-2	Alco	1950-51	
7362-7392 (by 10s), 7363-7393 (by 10s)	736B-739B, 736C-739C		8	FB-2	Alco	1950-51	
8001-8061 (by 10s), 8004-8064 (by 10s)	800A-806A, 800D-806D		14	F3A	EMD	1947	
8002-8062 (by 10s)	800B-806B		7	F3B	EMD	1947	
8411-8451 (by 10s), 8414-8454 (by 10s)		801A-805A, 801C-805C	10	F3A	EMD	1946-47	
8412-8452 (by 10s)		801B-805B	5	F3B	EMD	1946-46	

Notes:
General: "Former" numbers are the most recent, if locomotives were renumbered by their original owners (see the DL&W and Erie listings for details).
Cab unit (EMD F units, Alco FAs) numbering was complex. Instead of renumbering locomotives in sequence, EL changed the third digit of four (i.e. 6551, 6561, 6571, etc.). This is indicated with "by 10s" in the chart. Thus, A unit numbers end in 1 or 4; B unit numbers end in 2 or 3.
1—Ex-Delaware & Hudson 801-803, nee EMD demonstrators 4354, 4352, 4353, acquired 1969.
2—Nos. 810, 811 are former EMD demonstrators 810, 811.
3—Steam-generator equipped.
4—Not equipped for passenger service; steam-generator compartment used for extra ballast (weight) and longer frame for larger fuel tank than standard SD45.
5—Nos. 714A, B, C, D are ex-New York, Ontario & Western 821, 821B, 822B, 822.

Published rosters:
Erie Power, by Fred Westing and Alvin Staufer; Extra 2200 South, June 1968

Escanaba & Lake Superior
1947-present

The Escanaba & Lake Superior was an early customer of Baldwin, dieselizing in the late 1940s with three switchers and subsequently adding other second-hand Baldwins. Since the 1960s the railroad has expanded its mileage and now operates with a mix of second-hand EMD locomotives.

Original road numbers	Second road numbers	Qty.	Model	Builder	Dates built	Notes
100		1	VO1000	Baldwin	1947	
101		1	DS-4-4-66	Baldwin	1947	
102		1	S-8	Baldwin	1952	
201, 202, 204		3	DS-4-4-10	Baldwin	1948, 1950	1
203		1	RS-12	Baldwin	1951	1
212, 213, 215	300	3	RS-12	Baldwin	1952-53	2
400 (1), 400 (2), 402	401	3	GP38	EMD	1969-70	3
500, 501		2	SD40-2	EMD	1973-74	4
600		1	FP7	EMD	1950	5
1200, 1201		2	SW8	EMD	1952	6
1205, 1216		2	RF-16	Baldwin	1951-52	7
1220-1224		5	SD9	EMD	1955-56	8
7908-7911		4	RS-12	Baldwin	1952	9

Notes:
1—Nos. 201-204 are ex-Calumet & Hecla 201-204; 204 is nee U.S. Corps of Engineers L-4.
2—Ex-Michigan Northern 212, 213, 215, nee Seaboard Air Line 1471, 1472, 1474; 215 renumbered 300.
3—400 (1) was renumbered 401; ex-Conrail, nee Penn Central.
4—Ex-Soo Line 6349, 6306, nee Milwaukee Road 182, 22.
5—Ex-Wisconsin & Southern, nee MILW 71A.
6—Ex-Reserve Mining 1200, 1201.
7—Ex-Monongahela 1205, 1216, nee New York Central.
8—Ex-RM 1220-1224.
9—Ex-Oregon, California & Western 7908-7911, nee SAL 1466, 1468-1470.

Published roster:
Diesel Locomotive Rosters (Wayner Publications)

Florida East Coast
1939-present

The Florida East Coast began dieselizing with Electro-Motive passenger E3s in 1939, but freight trains weren't fully dieselized until the mid-1950s with the arrival of GP7s and GP9s. The railroad settled on GP40s (and later Dash 2s) for its fast freight trains, then used SD40-2s. The FEC was an all-EMD railroad until 2014, when it received two dozen GE ES44C4s.

FEC acquired 14 GE ES44ACs in 2014, the first non-EMD locomotives on the railroad.
Tom Danneman

Original road numbers	Second road numbers	Qty.	Model	Builder	Dates built	Notes
100-107		8	SD70M-2	EMD	2006-08	
221-228		8	SW9	EMD	1952-53	
229-235		7	SW1200	EMD	1954	
401-410, 435, 436, 438, 442, 443	424, 2000	10	GP40	EMD	1971	1
411-423, 425-434, 437, 439-441		27	GP40-2	EMD	1972-86	2
444-453		10	GP40-3	EMD	1967-71	3
501-508 (1)		8	F3A	EMD	1949	
501-511 (2)		11	GP38-2	EMD	1977-78	
551-554		4	F3B	EMD	1949	
571-575		5	FP7	EMD	1951	
601-606		6	BL2	EMD	1948	
607-621		15	GP7	EMD	1952	
651-676		26	GP9	EMD	1954, 1957	
701-722		22	SD40-2	EMD	1977-80	4
800-823		24	ES44C4	GE	2014	
1001, 1002		2	E3A	EMD	1939	
1003-1005		3	E6A	EMD	1940, 1942	
1006-1022		17	E7A	EMD	1945, 1947	
1031-1035		5	E9A	EMD	1955	
1051		1	E6B	EMD	1942	
1052-1054		3	E7B	EMD	1945	

Notes:
1—No. 402 was wrecked in 1980, rebuilt to Dash-2 standards, and renumbered 424; nos. 435, 436, 438 are ex-Burlington Northern (nee Chicago, Burlington & Quincy); 442, 443 are ex-Conrail (nee Penn Central); no. 406 was renumbered 2000.
2—Nos. 439-441 are ex-Soo Line GP40s rebuilt to Dash-2 standards.
3—Rebuilt GP40s, various heritage.
4—Ex-Union Pacific.

Georgia Railroad
Includes Atlanta & West Point and Western Railway of Alabama
1944-1983

The Georgia Railroad, through a convoluted ownership arrangement, was intimately affiliated with the Atlanta & West Point and Western Railway of Alabama. The A&WP and WofA together were known as the West Point Route, and all three fell under ownership of the Louisville & Nashville and Atlantic Coast Line. Diesel locomotives of the three shared a common numbering system, with no duplicity among them. Orders of common diesel types were often split among the railroads, and in a few cases locomotives were transferred from one railroad to another (these are listed in the notes). These railroads began buying diesels relatively late, starting with four WofA Baldwin switchers in 1944, but a large order of GP7s starting in 1950, followed by GP9s, had the lines dieselized by 1954.

The Georgia, A&WP, and WofA continued operating following mergers of their parent railroads into Seaboard Coast Line and became part of the Family Lines grouping in the late 1970s. Seaboard System purchased the Georgia and assumed control of the three railroads, and they were bought by and merged into the Seaboard System in 1983.

Georgia RR	A&WP	WofA	Qty.	Model	Builder	Dates built	Notes
		501	1	F3A	EMD	1948	1
	(1005) (2)	502, 503	2	FP7	EMD	1949	2
		520-526	7	GP7	EMD	1950-53	3, 4
		530, 531	2	GP9	EMD	1954	
(1005) (1)	551-554		4	FP7	EMD	1949, 1951	5
(1019, 1020)	571-576		6	GP7	EMD	1950-52	4, 6
		621-624	4	VO1000	Baldwin	1944	7
	676, 677	630	2	DS-44-1000	Baldwin	1948-49	
	678		1	S-12	Baldwin	1951	
751-754	726-732	701-707	18	GP40	EMD	1967 70	
755, 756	733	708	4	GP40-2	EMD	1972, 1974	
901-905			5	NW2	EMD	1948-49	
906, 907			2	SW9	EMD	1951	
921			1	DS-44-1000	Baldwin	1949	
1001			1	F3A	EMD	1948	1
1002-1004			3	FP7	EMD	1949-50	
1021-1036			16	GP7	EMD	1950-53	8
1040-1042			3	GP9	EMD	1954	
4975	4976, 4978	4977, 4979	5	GP16	EMD	1981-82	9
6009, 6010	6007, 6008		4	GP38-2	EMD	1979	
6051, 6052		6045, 6046	4	GP38-2	EMD	1979-80	10

Notes:
(Parentheses indicate second numbers after locomotives were transferred).
1—Steam-generator equipped.
2—No. 502 became AW&P 1005 (2).
3—No. 520 is ex-Seaboard Coast Line 914, nee Seaboard Air Line 1734, acquired 1977.
4—Nos. 525, 526, 573, 574 are steam-generator equipped.
5—No. 551 became GRR 1005 (1).
6—Nos. 571, 572 became GRR 1019, 1020; no. 576 is ex-SCL 912, nee SAL 1732, acquired 1977.
7—Delivered as nos. 1-4.
8—Nos. 1024-1026, 1029, 1031-1036 steam-generator equipped.
9—Rebuilt by SCL from GP9 1042, GP7s 576, 524, and SCL GP7s 777, 729 in 1981-82. Classified GP16 by railroad.
10—Nos. 6045, 6046, 6051, 6052 delivered as Clinchfield 6045 and SCL 6046, 6051, 6052.

Published roster:
Extra 2200 South, July-August-September 1986

Grand Trunk Western

1938-1991

The Grand Trunk Western was among the last major railroads to fully dieselize, running its final steam-powered mainline train in March 1960. The GTW's first road diesels were EMD F3s in 1948, followed by GP9s in the mid-1950s. Locomotive number series have several breaks, as numbers were coordinated with parent Canadian National and other CN subsidiaries (Central Vermont and Duluth, Winnipeg & Pacific). Locomotives were often swapped among subsidiaries or with parent CN. The GTW acquired the DT&I in 1980 and merged the Detroit & Toledo Shore line in 1981, acquiring those railroads' locomotives in the process.

The roster covers the period until 1991, when the CN began marketing itself and its U.S. subsidiaries as CN North America. With that, the GTW lost its own identity and its locomotives began wearing parent CN's paint schemes.

The GTW received its first GP9s in 1954.
GTW

Original road numbers	Second numbers	Qty.	Model	Builder	Dates built	Notes
73		1	Boxcab	Brill	1926	1
952, 973		2	GP7	EMD	1951, 1953	2
982, 986, 989		3	GP9	EMD	1955	3
1200-1203, 1509-1519	1500-1503	15	SW1200	EMD	1955-60	
1751-1767, 1777-1781	4427-4441, 4900-4906	12	GP9	EMD	1954	
1950, 1951		2	RS-1	Alco	1957	
3606-3608, 3610, 3613		5	RS-11	Alco	1956	4
4134-4139, 4539-4546, 4552-4557, 4907-4933		47	GP9	EMD	1954-59	5
4600-4615, 4617-4632, 4634, 4635		34	GP9r	EMD	1954-58	6
4700-4707, 4950-4952		11	GP18	EMD	1960	7
4994-4996		3	GP38	EMD	1966, 1971	8
5800-5811	4997-4999	12	GP38AC	EMD	1971	9
5812-5836, 5844-5861		43	GP38-2	EMD	1977-80	10
5900-5929		30	SD40	EMD	1969-70	
5930-5937		8	SD40-2	EMD	1975	11
6041-6050		10	GP7	EMD	1951-53	12
6116-6118		3	SW7	EMD	1950	13
6119-6121		2	SW9	EMD	1951-52	13
6200-6220		21	GP38	EMD	1966-71	14
6221-6228		8	GP38-2	EMD	1975	14
6250-6254		5	SD38	EMD	1969	14
6350-6357		8	GP35	EMD	1964	14
6400-6405		6	GP40	EMD	1968	14
6406-6425		20	GP40-2	EMD	1972-79	14
7010-7016		7	SW9	EMD	1952-53	
7017-7019		3	SW1200	EMD	1955	
7225-7232, 7262-7268		15	SW900	EMD	1956, 1958	15
7800-7801	78, 79	2	SC	EMC	1938	
7900-7914, 7966-7974		24	NW2	EMD	1941-48	
7920-7935	8096-8104, 8106-8111	16	S-2	Alco	1944-46	
8026, 8027, 8034, 8035, 8082-8090	1000-1003	13	S-4	Alco	1953-55	16

Original road numbers	Second numbers	Qty.	Model	Builder	Dates built	Notes
8091-8095, 8119-8121		8	S-2	Alco	1941-47	17
8162, 8196-8205		11	S-4	Alco	1951, 1956	18
9006-9027		22	F3A	EMD	1948	

Notes:
1—Ex-Long Island 402.
2—Ex-Detroit, Toledo & Ironton 952, 973.
3—Ex-DT&I 982, 986, 989.
4—Ex-Duluth, Winnipeg & Pacific.
5—Nos. 4134-4138 are ex-Central Vermont.
6—Rebuilt (including chopped noses) by GTW from various GTW and CV Geeps.
7—Nos. 4950-4952 are steam-generator equipped.
8—Ex-DT&I 200, 201, 203.
9—Nos. 5800, 5801, 5807 renumbered.
10—Nos. 5844-5849 are ex-Pittsburgh & Lake Erie 2051-2056; nos. 5850-5861 are ex-Rock Island 4368-4379.
11—Nos. 5930-5937 are ex-Union Pacific (nee Missouri Pacific).
12—Ex-Detroit & Toledo Shore Line 41-50.
13—Nos. 6116-6121 are ex-D&TSL 116-121.
14—Nos. 6200-6228, 6250-6254, 6350-6357, 6400-6425 are ex-DT&I 200-228, 250-254, 350-357, 400-425.
15—Nos. 7225, 7226 are ex-Grand Trunk.
16—No. 8027 is ex-CV; nos. 8082, 8084, 8199, and CN 8186 rebuilt with Caterpillar engines and renumbered.
17—Nos. 8119-8121 are ex-Canadian National 7953-7955.
18—No. 8162 is ex-CV; 8205 is ex-GT.

Published roster:
Extra 2200 South, September-October 1974

Great Northern
1926-1970

The Great Northern was an early diesel operator, acquiring several diesel switchers and its first FTs before World War II. More F units and Geeps had the railroad essentially dieselized by the early 1950s, although steam continued operating during the grain harvest rush through 1957. Second-generation power included EMD SD45s as well as several groups of four- and six-axle GEs.

The GN merged with the Chicago, Burlington & Quincy, Northern Pacific, and Spokane, Portland & Seattle to form Burlington Northern on March 2, 1970.

An order of six U33Cs leave GE's Erie plant on their way to the GN in 1969. *GE*

Original road numbers	Second numbers	Third numbers	Qty.	Model	Builder	Dates built	Notes
1-10			10	S-2	Alco	1950	
11-13			3	SW7	EMD	1950	
14-23			10	SW9	EMD	1950-51	
24-28			5	S-12	Baldwin	1953	
29-33			5	SW1200	EMD	1957	
80-83			4	SW1	EMD	1950	
98, 99			2	SW8	EMD	1951	
139-144			6	VO1000	Baldwin	1944	
145-162			18	NW2	EMD	1945, 1949	
163-170			8	SW7	EMD	1950	
182-185			4	RS-1	Alco	1944	
186-195			10	NW5	EMD	1946	
197-199, 220-224	225-227 (2)		8	RS-3	Alco	1950	
200-211 (1), 212-219			20	RS-2	Alco	1949-50	
200-209 (2)			10	SW1500	EMD	1967	
225-231 (1)	271A, 271B (1), 275A (2), 360A, 360C, 361A, 361C	359A, 359C	7	F3A	EMD	1946-47	
228-232 (2)			5	RS-3	Alco	1953	
252A, 256A-258A	418A (2)		4	FTA	EMD	1945	
252B, 254B-258B	418B (2), 418C (2)		6	FTB	EMD	1945	
259A-267A, 262B-265B	366A, 367A		13	F3A	EMD	1947-48	
259B-261B, 266B, 267B	366B-369B		5	F3B	EMD	1947-48	
268A-275A, 271B-275B (2), 280A, 281A	370A, 367C, 368C, 474A, 474D, 363A, 363C, 369C, 370C		15	F7A	EMD	1949-52	1
268B-270B, 280B, 281B	370B-372B, 373B, 374B		3	F7B	EMD	1950-52	
276A, 276B (1)			2	FA-1	Alco	1950	
277A, B-279A, B			6	FA-2	Alco	1950	2
300A, 300C (2)	249A, 418D (2)		2	FTA	EMD	1945	
301A-305A	401A, 403A, 405A, 247A, 248A		5	FTA	EMD	1945	
301C-305C	401D, 403D, 405D, 247B, 248B		5	FTA	EMD	1945	
301B-305B	401B, 403B, 405B, 403C, 405C		5	FTB	EMD	1945	
306A, 306C	458A, 458D		2	F3A	EMD	1948	
306B	458B		1	F3B	EMD	1948	
307A-309A, 307C-309C, 311A-317A, 311C-317C			20	F7A	EMD	1950, 1952	
307B-309B, 311B-317B			10	F7B	EMD	1950, 1952	
310A, 310C			2	FA-1	Alco	1950	
310B			1	FB-1	Alco	1950	
320-325			6	SDP40	EMD	1966	
326-333			8	SDP45	EMD	1967	
350A-358A, 350C-358C	275A, 275B (3)		18	F3A	EMD	1947	
350B-358B			9	F3B	EMD	1947	
375C, 376C	362A, 362C		2	F3A	EMD	1948	

Original road numbers	Second numbers	Third numbers	Qty.	Model	Builder	Dates built	Notes
379A, 379C, 380A, 380C	364A, 364C, 365A, 365C		4	F7A	EMD	1950	3
379B, 380B (1)	364B, 365B		2	F7B	EMD	1950	3
400-426			27	SD45	EMD	1966-68	
427-440			14	F45	EMD	1969	
400A-428A (even), 400D-428D (even)			30	FTA	EMD	1943-45	4
400B-428B (even), 400C-428C (even)			30	FTB	EMD	1943-45	4
430A-438A (even), 430D-438D (even)			10	F3A	EMD	1948	
430B-438B (even), 430C-438C (even)			10	F3B	EMD	1948	
440A, 442A, 440D, 442D			4	FA-1	Alco	1948-49	
440B, 442B, 440C, 442C			4	FB-1	Alco	1948-49	
444A-456A (even), 444D-456D (even)			14	F7A	EMD	1949-50	
444B-456B (even), 444C-458C (even)			15	F7B	EMD	1949-52	
460A-468A (even), 460D-468D (even)			10	F7A	EMD	1952-53	4
460B-468B (even), 460C-468C (even)			10	F7B	EMD	1952-53	4
470B-474B (even), 470C-474C (even)			6	F9B	EMD	1954	
500A-504A	500, 503, 504, 506, 508		5	E7A	EMD	1945	
500B-504B (1)	500C-504C	500B-504B (3)	5	E7A	EMD	1945	
500B-504B (2)	359B-363B		5	F3B	EMD	1950	
510A-512A	510-512		3	E7A	EMD	1947	
550-572			23	SD7	EMD	1952-53	
573-599			27	SD9	EMD	1954-58	
600-655			56	GP7	EMD	1950-53	
656-732			77	GP9	EMD	1954-58	
733, 734, 900-915			18	GP9m	EMD	1958-59	
2000-2035			36	GP20	EMD	1960	
2500-2523			24	U25B	GE	1964-65	
2524-2529			6	U28B	GE	1966	
2530-2544			15	U33C	GE	1968-69	
3000-3016			17	GP30	EMD	1963	
3017-3040			24	GP35	EMD	1965	
5100			1	Boxcab	Ingersoll	1926	
5101 (1)	5300		1	NW	EMC	1938	
5101, 5102 (2), 5103-5105	75-79		5	SW1	EMC	1939, 1941	
5102 (1)	5301		1	NW1	EMC	1938	
5200, 5201	50, 51		2	44-tonner	GE	1940	
5302-5331, 5334-5336	102-131, 134-136		33	NW2	EMD	1939-42	
5332, 5333, 5337, 5338	132, 133, 137, 138		4	VO1000	Baldwin	1941	
5400-5406	175-181		7	NW3	EMD	1939-42	
5600A, 5700A, 5701A, 5900A, 5900C	200A, 250A, 251A, 300A (1), 300C (1)		5	FTA	EMD	1940-41	
5600B, 5700B, 5701B, 5900B	200B, 250B, 251B, 300B		4	FTB	EMD	1940-41	

Notes:
1—Nos. 272A, 272B are former EMD demonstrators 801, 802.
2—Nos. 278A, 279A, 278B, 279B are former Alco demonstrators 1602A, 1602D, 1602B, 1602C.
3—Locomotives were ordered with original numbers listed, but never wore them in service.
4—Nos. 418A-D wrecked; nos. 418D, 418C rebuilt to F7A 460D and F7B 460C in 1952.

Published roster:
X2200 South, January-February 1971

— 220 —

Green Bay & Western
(includes Kewaunee, Green Bay & Western)
1938-1993

Number 310 is an Alco RS-27 built in 1960. *Alco*

The Green Bay & Western was a favorite among railfans for its all-Alco roster. The railroad dieselized fairly early with switchers and Alco FAs and RS-2s, with the last steam operating in 1950. The roster includes subsidiary Kewaunee, Green Bay & Western (noted with initials by the numbers). The GB&W was absorbed by Wisconsin Central in 1993.

Original road numbers	Second numbers	Qty.	Model	Builder	Dates built	Notes
101		1	HH660	Alco	1938	
102, 103 (KGB&W)		2	S-1	Alco	1941, 1949	
201 (KGB&W)		1	S-2	Alco	1948	
301-304		4	RS-2	Alco	1950	
305-308		4	RS-3	Alco	1951, 1955	
309 (KGB&W)		1	RS-11	Alco	1956	
310, 316-318		4	RS-27	Alco	1960	1
311-313, 314 (KGB&W), 319-322		8	C-424	Alco	1963-65	2
315		1	C-430	Alco	1968	
323		1	C-420	Alco	1966	3
501-502 (KGB&W), 503 (1)	506	3	FA-1	Alco	1947	4
503 (2, KGB&W), 507		2	FA-1	Alco	1949	4
1201		1	S-6	Alco	1955	5
2400, 2403-2407		6	RSD-15	Alco	1959-60	6

Notes:
1—Nos. 316-318 are ex-Chicago & North Western 903, 902, 901, acquired in 1966.
2—Nos. 319-322 are ex-Conrail (originally Pennsylvania, Erie Lackawanna, and Reading) 2474, 2486, 2489, 2493, acquired in 1980.
3—Ex-Conrail 2075 (nee Lehigh & Hudson River 27), acquired in 1979.
4—First no. 503 renumbered to 506 in 1949 upon delivery of KGB&W 503.
5—Ex-Southern Pacific 1201, acquired in 1979 (never repainted).
6—Ex-Lake Superior & Ishpeming 2400, 2403-2407 (nee Santa Fe), acquired in 1989.

Published roster:
Extra 2200 South September-October 1969

Gulf, Mobile & Ohio
Includes Alton
1935-1972

The first GM&O FA-1s had a lower headlight grille than later models, and the same curved drip rail behind the cab as on PAs. *Alco*

The Gulf, Mobile & Ohio was one of the first major railroads to completely dieselize, with the last steam locomotive dropping its fire in October 1949. The GM&O was an early Alco customer, operating a large fleet of FA cab units before turning to EMD for GP30s, GP40s, and other power in the 1960s. The roster includes the Alton, which the GM&O merged in 1947 (former Alton engines are indicated in the notes). The GM&O merged with Illinois Central to form Illinois Central Gulf on August 10, 1972.

Road Numbers	Qty.	Model	Builder	Dates built	Notes
B1-B33	33	FB-1	Alco	1946-50	
B34-B37	4	FB-2	Alco	1955	
B60-B64	8	F3B	EMD	1947	
B65-B74	10	F7B	EMD	1947, 1949	
B80-B82	3	F3B	EMD	1947	1
10-24	15	S-2	Alco	1944-45	2
50-59	10	RS-1	Alco	1945	2
100A	1	EA	EMC	1937	2, 3
100-103, 101A-103A	7	E7A	EMD	1945, 46	2
270-272	3	DL-109	Alco	1940, 1943	
280, 281	2	DR-6-4-20	Baldwin	1947	
290-292	3	PA-1	Alco	1946-47	4
500-530	31	GP30	EMD	1962-63	5
601-648	48	GP35	EMD	1964-65	5
661-664	4	S-1	Alco	1940	
700, 701-720 (1), 721-754	55	FA-1	Alco	1946-47	
701-720 (2)	20	GP38	EMD	1969	
721-733	13	GP38AC	EMD	1971	
740-754	15	GP38-2	EMD	1972	
800A-811A, 800B-810B	23	F3A	EMD	1946-47	
811B-812B, 812A-813A	4	F7A	EMD	1949	
880A-885A, 880B-882B	9	F3A	EMD	1946-47	1
901-921	21	SD40	EMD	1966	
950	1	SD40X	EMD	1964	6
1001-1012	12	S-2	Alco	1941-46	
1051-1055, 1102-1117, 1120-1127	29	RS-1	Alco	1944-1950	7
1200	1	Boxcab	GE	1935	2
1501-1514	14	RS-2	Alco	1948-49	
1515-1523	9	RS-3	Alco	1950-52	
1900	1	4-S	Ingalls	1946	

Notes:
1—Steam-generator equipped.
2—Nos. 10-24, 50-59, 100A, 101, 1200 are former Alton engines (same numbers), acquired in 1947 when the Alton merged into the GM&O.
3—Former B&O no. 52.
4—No. 292 is former Freedom Train locomotive, acquired 1949.
5—Locomotives ride on AAR trucks from Alco trade-ins.
6—Former EMD demonstrator 434.
7—Nos. 1051-1055 are ex-Illinois Terminal, acquired 1970.

Published rosters:
Diesel Era, July/August 1993; Extra 2200 South, February-March 1970

Illinois Central

1929-1972

The Illinois Central, although an early buyer of boxcab switchers and passenger E units, was late to dieselize. A major rebuilding program begun in the 1930s provided the railroad with a fleet of modern steam locomotives, and it wasn't until the early 1950s that road freight diesels arrived in large numbers. The IC was known for its large fleet of EMD GP7s and GP9s, and for embarking on the country's first substantial diesel rebuilding program in 1967. The IC rebuilt its Geeps (along with many from other railroads) at its Paducah, Ky., shops, providing them with the nickname "Paducah Geeps" or "Paducah Rebuilds."

The IC merged with Gulf, Mobile & Ohio in 1972 to form Illinois Central Gulf (see the ICG roster on the following pages).

Number 4018 is an early E8 with horizontal-slit side grille panels. *EMD*

Original road numbers	Second numbers	Third numbers	Qty.	Model	Builder	Dates built	Notes
701-703			3	RS-2	Alco	1948-49	1
800-802			3	SW8	EMD	1952-53	2
1100-1105			6	C-636	Alco	1968	
1237-1243			7	SW9	EMD	1953	3
2036-2040			5	E9A	EMD	1955	4
3000-3074			75	GP40	EMD	1966-70	
3075			1	GP40X	EMD	1965	5
4000-4004	4001A, B, 4002A, B		5	E6A	EMD	1940-41	
4000 (2), 4005-4017			14	E7A	EMD	1946-48	

Original road numbers	Second numbers	Third numbers	Qty.	Model	Builder	Dates built	Notes
4018-4033	2021..2025		16	E8A	EMD	1950-53	
4034-4043			10	E9A	EMD	1954-61	
4100-4103			4	E7B	EMD	1946, 1948	
4104, 4105	2100		2	E8B	EMD	1952	
4106-4109			4	E9B	EMD	1956-57	
5000-5005			6	U30B	GE	1967	
5050-5059			10	U33C	GE	1968	
6000-6005			6	SD40	EMD	1967	
6006-6023			18	SD40X	EMD	1969-70	
7000			1	SD45	EMD	1965	6
8267, 8268, 8270-8286			19	GP8, GP10	EMD	1951-59	7
8390			1	GP18	EMD	1963	8
8800, 8801, 8850, 8851, 8900-8911, 8950-8981	7850..8269		48	GP7	EMD	1950-53	9
9000-9257 (2)	8000..8268		258	GP9	EMD	1954-57	9
9000-9005 (1)			6	Boxcab	GE-IR	1929-30	
9006-9013 (1)			8	HH660	Alco	1935	
9014-9032 (1)	600..617		19	SW1	EMD	1939-51	
9150-9166 (1)	1003-1016		17	NW2	EMD	1939-45	
9200 (1)			1	GX-66-18	GE-IR	1936	
9201 (1)	9202 (2)		1	T	EMC	1936	
9202 (1)	9201 (2)		1	GX-66-20	GE-IR-Sulz	1935	
9203A-9205A	1026A, 1027A, 1075	1300, 1302	3	TR-A	EMC	1940	
9203B-9205B	1026B, 1027B, 1235	1300B, 1301B	3	TR-B	EMC	1940	10
9206A-9208A	1028A-1030A		3	TR2A	EMD	1945-49	
9206B-9208B	1028B-1030B		3	TR2B	EMD	1945-49	
9250A, 9251A	1350A, 1351A		2	TR1A	EMD	1941	
9250B, 9251B	1350B, 1351B		2	TR1B	EMD	1941	
9275	400 (1)	200 (1)	1	44-tonner	GE	1947	
9300-9319 (1)	1200-1219		20	SW7	EMD	1950	
9320-9334	1220-1234		15	SW9	EMD	1952-53	
9400-9428 (2)			29	GP18	EMD	1960, 1963	
9400-9429 (1)	400-429		30	SW7	EMD	1950	
9429-9441 (2)			13	GP28	EMD	1964	11
9430-9484 (1)	430-484		55	SW9	EMD	1951-52	
9500-9519			20	GP38AC	EMD	1970	

Notes:
1—Ex-Peabody Short Line 701-703, acquired 1961.
2—Nos. 800, 801 are ex-Tremont & Gulf 75, 77, acquired 1959; no. 802 is ex-Louisiana Midland 12, acquired 1967.
3—Ex-Mississippi Central 201..210, acquired with merger in 1967.
4—Ex-Florida East Coast 1031-1035, acquired 1969.
5—Former EMD demonstrator 433A, acquired 1970.
6—Former EMD demonstrator 4351, acquired 1971.
7—Paducah Rebuilds (see note 9) using Geeps of other railroads, including Detroit, Toledo & Ironton, Florida East Coast, Southern Pacific, and Quebec, North Shore & Labrador.
8—Ex-Grand Trunk Western, acquired 1972.
9—GP7s and GP9s were rebuilt to GP8s and GP10s (IC designations) at IC's Pacucah shops starting in 1967 (and continuing into the ICG merger). Following rebuilding, engines were generally renumbered by lowering the number by 1000, but there were exceptions. See the Extra 2200 South issues listed below for unit-by-unit renumbering and dispositions.
10—Nos. 9205A, B rebuilt to NW2 and SW9 in 1954; renumbered in 1957.
11—No. 9441 is ex-MC 211, acquired with merger in 1967.

Published rosters:
Extra 2200 South, July-August 1972 (full roster), Extra 2200 South, October-November-December 1991 (Pacucah rebuild Geeps), Extra 2200 South, January-February-March 1992 (Paducah rebuild switchers and SDs)

Illinois Central Gulf/Illinois Central

1972-1999

The Illinois Central Gulf was formed in 1972 with the merger of Illinois Central and Gulf, Mobile & Ohio. Over the years, ICG spun off and abandoned a good share of the GM&O, and in 1988 the railroad's parent company in turn spun off the railroad, dropping the "Gulf" and reverting the name back to Illinois Central. Former GM&O locomotives are indicated in the "GM&O numbers" column; be aware that many of these (especially older locomotives) were never renumbered to their assigned IC numbers, or were retired at or shortly after the merger.

The Paducah Rebuild program begun by IC in the 1960s continued into the 1980s, covering the railroad's own Geeps, SDs, and switchers along with many from other railroads. Space precludes unit-by-unit tracking of rebuilds; see the *Extra 2200* issues referenced below for details. The railroad continued relying on rebuilds and older power until new SD70s began arriving in 1995. The IC was purchased by Canadian National in 1998 and officially merged in 1999, with the IC losing its identity within the CN system.

Number 2000 is a former SD24 rebuilt and rated at 2,000 hp; ICG calls them "SD20s." *ICG*

Original road numbers	Second numbers	GM&O numbers	Qty.	Model	Builder	Dates built	Notes
13			1	SW1R	EMD	1946	1
100-104 (1)			5	SW7, SW9	EMD	1950-51	2, 3
100-102			3	E9Au	EMD	1949, 1953	4
400..429	300..329		30	SW7	EMD	1950	2
430..484	1244-1250		54	SW9	EMD	1951-52	2, 5
603..615			4	SW1	EMD	1940-46	
800-802			3	SW8	EMD	1952-53	6
1000..1016 (1)			16	NW2	EMD	1939-45	2
1000-1039			40	SD70	EMD	1995-99	
1026A, 1027A, 1029A			3	TR-A, TR2A	EMC	1940-49	2
1026B, 1027B, 1029B			3	TR-B, TR2B	EMC	1940-49	2
1100-1105			6	C-636	Alco	1968	
1200..1219			19	SW7	EMD	1950	2
1220..1234			14	SW9	EMD	1952-53	2
1237-1243			7	SW9	EMD	1953	2, 7
1251-1289, 1133		50-59, 1051-1055, 1102..1132	39	RS-1	Alco	1945-49	8
1300-1311, 1300B-1302B			15	SW13	EMD	1940-52	2
1400-1511			112	SW14	EMD	1941-52	2
1600-1613, 1615-1620		800A..885A, 800B..880B	20	F3A	EMD	1946-47	
1614, 1615		811B, 812A	2	F7A	EMD	1949	
2000-2041			42	SD20	EMD	1953-60	9
2036 2040			5	E9A	EMD	1955	10
2250-2279	2601, 2602	500..530	30	GP30	EMD	1962-63	11
2500-2544		601..647	45	GP35	EMD	1964-65	

Original road numbers	Second numbers	GM&O numbers	Qty.	Model	Builder	Dates built	Notes
3000-3074	3076, 3077, 3100-3139		75	GP40	EMD	1966-70	12
3075			1	GP40X	EMD	1965	13
4020, 4022, 4023, 4027, 4028			5	E8A	EMD	1950-52	
4029, 4104			2	E10A, E10B	EMD	1952	14
4034-4042			9	E9A	EMD	1954-61	
4105-4108			4	E8B, E9B	EMD	1952-57	
5000-5005			6	U30B	GE	1967	
5050-5059			10	U33C	GE	1968	
6000-6005			6	SD40	EMD	1967	
6006-6023	6024		18	SD40A	EMD	1969-70	15
6030-6033, 6040-6049, 6100-6143			58	SD40-2	EMD	1973-76	16
6050-6070	6034	901-921	21	SD40	EMD	1966	15
6071			1	SDX40	EMD	1964	
7000			1	SD45	EMD	1965	17
7700..7746, 7800			48	GP8	EMD		18
8269..8466			102	GP10	EMD	1951-59	18
8390			1	GP18	EMD	1963	19
8701-8753, 8301, 8418			55	GP11	EMD	1951-59	18
8800, 8801, 8850, 8851, 8900-8911, 8950-8981	7850..8269		48	GP7, GP8	EMD	1950-53	18
9000-9257 (2), 9300-9389	8000..8268		348	GP9, GP10	EMD	1954-57	18
9400-9428 (2)			29	GP18	EMD	1960, 1963	
9429-9441 (2)			13	GP28	EMD	1964	20
9450, 9451			2	SD28	EMD	1965	21
9500-9519			20	GP38AC	EMD	1970	
9520-9539		701-720	20	GP38	EMD	1969	
9540-9552		721-733	13	GP38AC	EMD	1971	
9560-9574		740-754	15	GP38-2	EMD	1972	
9600-9639			40	GP38-2	EMD	1974	

Notes:
General: Former Gulf, Mobile & Ohio engines have their GM&O numbers listed in the "GM&O numbers" column. Be aware that, especially for older locomotives, all locomotives in a series may not have actually received their assigned IC numbers.
1—Rebuilt from SW1 no. 612 in 1968.
2—Most SW7s, SW9s, NW2s, and TRs were rebuilt to 1,300-hp SW13s (from 1971-75) and 1,400-hp SW14s (from 1978-82). Four engines (200, 236, 325, 379) had earlier been rebuilt to SW7R (in 1967). Engines with a B suffix are cabless SW13Bs, rebuilt from former TR B units.
3—Ex-Chicago & Illinois Western 100-104; no. 104 is an SW9.
4—Ex-Burlington Northern, nee Chicago, Burlington & Quincy, rebuilt and acquired for business train service in 1995-96.
5—Seven converted with multiple-unit connections and renumbered.
6—No. 800, 801 are ex-Tremont & Gulf 75, 77, acquired 1959; no. 802 is ex-Louisiana Midland 12, acquired 1967.
7—Ex-Mississippi Central 201..210, acquired with merger in 1967.
8—Nos. 1130-1133 were rebuilt with EMD 567 engines in 1972, reclassified RS-1E.
9—Rebuilt from earler SDs (various heritage) from 1979-82.
10—Ex-Florida East Coast 1031-1035, acquired 1969.
11—GM&O nos. 502, 514 were rebuilt to Dash-2 standards in 1981, renumbered 2601, 2601, and classed GP26.
12—Nos. 3035, 3070 rebuilt in 1974 to GP40A, renumbered 3076, 3077; 40 other GP40s rebuilt in 1987-91 by VMV, reclassified GP40R.
13—Former EMD demonstrator 433A, acquired 1970.
14—E8A and E8B rebuilt to E10A, E10B, 1969.
15—No. 6012 rebuilt and renumbered 6024 in 1974; 6069 rebuilt in 1982 and renumbered 6034.
16—Nos. 6040-6049 are ex-Rock Island 4790-4799; 6100-6143 are ex-Burlington Northern 6708..6752.
17—Former EMD demonstrator 4351, acquired 1971.
18—GP7s and GP9s were rebuilt to GP8s and GP10s (IC designations) at IC's Pacucah shops starting in 1967 (and continuing into the ICG merger). Following rebuilding, engines were generally renumbered by lowering the number by 1000, but there were exceptions. Geeps from other railroads were often rebuilt and added to the IC roster; these generally were in the 7700s, 8300s, and 8400s, but were mixed in throughout. Not all roster slots were filled. Beginning in 1978, Geeps were rebuilt to Dash-2 standards and termed GP11s (renumbered in 8700s). See the Extra 2200 South issues listed below for unit-by-unit renumbering and dispositions.
19—Ex-Grand Trunk Western, acquired 1972.
20—No. 9441 is ex-MC 211, acquired with merger in 1967.
21—Ex-Columbus & Greenville 701, 702.

Published rosters:
Extra 2200 South, July-August 1972 (full roster), Extra 2200 South, October-November-December 1991 (Pacucah rebuild Geeps), Extra 2200 South, January-February-March 1992 (Paducah rebuild switchers and SDs), Extra 2200 South April-May-June 1992, non-rebuilt locomotives

Illinois Terminal
1948-1981

The Illinois Terminal was an electric interurban line serving western Illinois down to the St. Louis area. In the mid-1950s the railroad abandoned its electric operations, moving to all-diesel operation—the last steam ran in 1950, and dieselization had begun with Alco RS-1s and S-2s 1948. The railroad had been owned by a group of 11 railroads since the 1950s. In 1981 the IT was purchased by the Norfolk & Western and ceased operations as an independent railroad.

Original road numbers	Second numbers	Qty.	Model	Builder	Dates built	Notes
700-711	1001-1012	12	S-2	Alco	1948, 1950	
725	801	1	SW8	EMD	1950	1
751-756	1051-1056	6	RS-1	Alco	1948, 1950	2
775-786	1201-1212	12	SW1200	EMD	1955	
1157, 1159	1507, 1508	2	F7B	EMD	1949-50	3
1220		1	SW1200r	EMD	1950	4
1221		1	SW7	EMD	1950	4
1509-1515		7	SW1500	EMD	1970	
1600-1605	1501-1506	6	GP7	EMD	1953	
2001-2004		4	GP38-2	EMD	1977	
2008, 2009		2	GP20	EMD	1960	5
2301-2306		6	SD39	EMD	1969	

Notes:
Most renumbering took place in 1967-68.
1—Former EMD demonstrator 800.
2—No. 753 was originally numbered 750; renumbered shortly after delivery.
3—Ex-Richmond, Fredericksburg & Potomac 1157, 1159.
4—No. 1220 is ex-Union Pacific 809 (built as SW7 and rebuilt), 1221 is ex-Chesapeake & Ohio 5228; both leased (1979-82) and painted in IT colors.
5—Ex-Union Pacific 712, 710; leased (1980-82); painted in IT colors.

Published roster:
The Illinois Terminal Railroad, by Dale Jenkins (White River Productions, 2005)

Indiana Harbor Belt
1948-present

The Indiana Harbor Belt was a longtime subsidiary of the New York Central, which shared ownership of the IHB with the Chicago & North Western and Milwaukee Road. Many of its early diesels follow NYC specifications, including fitting into NYC number series. The IHB did not accompany the NYC into the Penn Central merger in 1968, instead continuing to operate as an independent railroad. The railroad continues in operation in 2017, and is owned jointly between Canadian Pacific and Conrail Shared Assets.

Number 8774 is an EMD NW2 built in 1949. *EMD*

Original numbers	Second numbers	Qty.	Model	Builder	Dates built	Notes
2256, 2272		2	SW1200	EMD	1954, 1965	2
2920-2925		6	SD20	EMD	1959-60	3
3801, 3802		2	GP38-2	EMD	1973, 1971	4
3861, 3862		2	SD38-2	EMD	1974, 1974	5
8904, 8905		2	H-10-44	F-M	1949	
4010-4019		10	GP40-2	EMD	1974-78	6
7110-7118		9	H-20-44	F-M	1948-49	
8715-8739, 8774-8802, 8811-8834		78	NW2	EMD	1948-49	7
8835-8850, 8856-8879		40	SW7	EMD	1949-50	7

Original numbers	Second numbers	Qty.	Model	Builder	Dates built	Notes
9002-9008		7	SW9	EMD	1953	
9200-9222	1500..1524	23	SW1500	EMD	1966-70	8

Notes:
1—Genset locomotives.
2—No. 2256 is ex-Milwaukee Road 648; 2272 is ex-Southern Pacific 2272, acquired 1995-96.
3—Rebuilt by Illinois Central from early SDs in 1980-82 (railroad model designation), acquired 1996-98.
4—No. 3801 is ex-Norfolk Southern 5068; 3802 is ex-Altos Hornos Steel 141.
5—No. 3861 is ex-Soo Line 6354, nee Milwaukee Road 188; 3862 is ex-Burlington Northern SD40-2 6330, rebuilt in 1986, acquired 2001.
6—Ex-Union Pacific, nee Southern Pacific, all rebuilt, acquired 2002-03.
7—Six SW7s and NW2s were converted to powered B units ("booster units") and numbered BU50-55 in 1987-89. Several others were converted to slug units.
8—No. 9222 is ex-EMD 109. Most rebuilt in 2003-05 and renumbered.

Published roster:
Diesel Locomotive Rosters (Wayner Publications)

Kansas City Southern (classic)
1939-1991

The Kansas City Southern began buying diesels with Electro-Motive passenger E units in 1939, and began dieselizing freight trains after World War II with EMD F units and Geeps. Other than a few oddballs (Fairbanks-Morse Erie Builts and a few Alco and Baldwin switchers), KCS was primarily an EMD customer. This roster includes locomotives of subsidiary Louisiana & Arkansas, which wore KCS schemes (although some had the word "Lines" added after "Kansas City Southern." For a unit-by-unit summary, including L&A/KCS ownership, see the book *Kansas City Southern in the Deramus Era* (listed below the roster).

This roster covers all locomotives owned and delivered through 1991. Since then, KCS has greatly expanded and is now a Class I railroad with its acquisition of Mexican lines, now KCS of Mexico. For a current roster, see the following spread.

E3 No. 2, delivered in 1939, was soon renumbered 22. *EMC*

Original road numbers	Second numbers	Third numbers	Qty.	Model	Builder	Dates built	Notes
6, 7, 11, 12, 20			5	E7A	EMD	1946, 1948	1
21-23			3	E3A	EMC	1939-40	2
24, 25			2	E6A	EMD	1942	
26-29			4	E8A	EMD	1952	
30A-33A, 50A-58A, 50D-58D	77-85	95, 4050, 4051	22	F3A	EMD	1947-49	3
30B-33B, 50B-58B, 50C-58C			22	F3B	EMD	1947-49	3
40, 41	45		2	H-15-44	F-M	1949	
60A-62A, 60C-62C	60-65		6	Erie A	F-M	1946-47	
60B-62B			3	Erie B	F-M	1946, 1948	
59A, 59D, 70A-76A, 70C, 71C, 72D-76D	59, 70-76, 86-93	4053-4064	16	F7A	EMD	1948-51	3
59B, 59C, 70B-79B, 72C-78C,			19	F7B	EMD	1949-51	3
100-119	4100..4119		20	GP30	EMD	1962-63	
150-162	4150-4162		13	GP7	EMD	1951, 1953	
163-165	4163-4165		3	GP9	EMD	1959	
600-636			37	SD40	EMD	1966-71	
637-692			56	SD40-2	EMD	1972-78	

Original road numbers	Second numbers	Third numbers	Qty.	Model	Builder	Dates built	Notes
700-703			4	SD40X	EMD	1979	
704-713			10	SD50	EMD	1981	
714-759			46	SD60	EMD	1989-91	
748-795			48	GP40	EMD	1967-70	4
796-799			4	GP40-2	EMD	1979-81	
1100-1102, 1125, 1126, 1200-1226	4125, 4126, 4200..4226		32	NW2	EMD	1939-49	
1110-1113			4	RS-1	Alco	1943	
1114			1	S-2	Alco	1940	5
1120			1	HH900	Alco	1937	6
1121-1123			3	HH1000	Alco	1940	7
1150			1	VO660	Baldwin	1946	
1160-1163			4	S-12	Baldwin	1951	
1300-1315	4300-4315		16	SW7	EMD	1950-51	
1500-1542	4320-4362		43	SW1500	EMD	1966-72	
4000-4021			22	GP38-2	EMD	1973-78	8
4227-4231			5	NW2	EMD	1939-48	9
4363-4366			4	MP15	EMD	1975	

Notes:
1—Ex-Maine Central 705-709, acquired 1962-63.
2—Originally Nos. 1, 2, 3; renumbered to 21, 22, 23 (and shown as such in EMD Data Book; No. 21 is former EMC demonstrator 822.
3—Most F3s rebuilt to F7 specifications and several F7s to F9 specs in 1953-57.
4—Nos. 748-776 are ex-Conrail, acquired 1983-84; nos. 777-795 are ex-Illinois Central Gulf, acquired 1982.
5—Ex-Kansas City Terminal 51, acquired 1967.
6—Ex-Youngstown & Northern 211, acquired 1956.
7—Ex-Manufacturers Railway 201-203.
8—Nos. 4012-4021 are ex-Boston & Maine 200..211, acquired 1989.
9—Ex-Milwaukee Road 668, 670, 671 and ex-Soo Line 300, 2108, acquired 1981.

Published roster:
Kansas City Southern in the Deramus Era, by Louis A. Marre and Gregory J. Sommers (Withers Publishing, 1999)

Kansas City Southern
Current (as of 2017)

This roster is current as of early 2017, and includes locomotives of Kansas City Southern of Mexico (KCSM).

A trio of GE ES44ACs lead a freight at East St. Louis, Ill., in 2012. *Mark Mautner*

Initial	Number series	Model	Builder	Dates
KCS	1, 2	F9A-3	EMD	R1995-1996
KCS	3	F9B-3	EMD	R1995
KCSM	400-403	GPTEB-C	EMD	2009
KCS	400-407	SLUG	EMD	1961-1973
KCS	610	SD40-3	EMD	1967-1978
KCS	639-695	SD40-2	EMD	1967-1978
KCS	708-713	SD50	EMD	1981
KCS	1400-1401	RP14BD	Railpower	2005
KCS	1500-1574	SW1500	EMD	1966-1972
KCS	1902-2039	GP38-2	EMD	1973-1977
KCS	2020, 2036, 2040	GP32ECO	EMD	R2015
KCSM	2050-2099	GP38-2	EMD	1975-1982
KCSM	2400-2404	GP22ECO-M	EMD	2009
KCSM	2500-2513	GP22ECO	EMD	2009
KCS	2600, 2601	SD22ECO	EMD	2009
KCSM	2650, 2651	SD22ECO	EMD	1980
KCS	2800-3014	GP40-2/GP40-3	EMD	1979-1994
KCS	2831, 2841, 2853	GP32ECO	EMD	R 2016
KCSM	3000-3066	SD40	EMD	1968-1971
KCS	3100-3167	SD40-2	EMD	R1995-1996
KCSM	3200-3240	SD40-2	EMD	1972-1978
KCSM	3350-3367	C30-S7	GE	R1992
KCSM	3410-3468	C30-S7N	GE	R1990-1991
KCSM	3487-3499	CMP30-S7N	GE	1994
KCS	3800-3843	SD60	EMD	1989-1991
KCS	3900-3973	SD70MAC	EMD	1999-2000
KCSM	3997-4059	SD70ACe	EMD	2003
KCS	4060-4099	SD70ACe	EMD	2007
KCSM	4100-4199	SD70ACe	EMD	2008-2014
KCSM	4200-4224	SD70ACe	EMD	2015
KCS	4302	SW1001	EMD	1974
KCS	4320-4355	SW1500	EMD	1966-1972
KCS	4365	MP15DC	EMD	1975
KCS	4500-4574	AC4400CW	GE	1998-2000
KCSM	4575-4624	AC4400CW	GE	1999
KCS	4650-4679	ES44AC	GE	2006-2007
KCSM	4680-4709	ES44AC	GE	2007
KCSM	4710-4759	ES44AC	GE	2007
KCS	4760-4764	ES44AC	GE	2011
KCSM	4765-4869	ES44AC	GE	2011-2014
KCSM	4870-4894	ES44AC	GE	2015
KCS	7002-7024	SD50	EMD	1985

Kansas, Oklahoma & Gulf
(includes Midland Valley and Oklahoma City-Ada-Atoka)
1949-1970

Three railroads—the Kansas, Oklahoma & Gulf, Midland Valley, and Oklahoma City-Ada-Atoka—were all controlled by the Muskogee Company and operated jointly. Locomotives were lettered in a common scheme with a nameplate listing all three roads, although specific ownership was either by KO&G or MV. The Texas & Pacific acquired control of all three lines in 1964, selling the OCAA to the Santa Fe and formally merging the other two (MV in 1967 and KO&G in 1970).

Original road numbers	Second road numbers	Qty.	Model	Builder	Dates Built	Notes
151-154	106-109	4	GP7	EMD	1953	1
700, 701	570, 571	2	GP28	EMD	1964	
751-754	844-847	4	F7A	EMD	1949	
755B, 756B	846B, 847B	2	F7B	EMD	1949	
801-809	97-105	9	GP7	EMD	1952-53	

Notes:
General: All owned by KO&G except 151-154, owned by MV.
1—Nos. 151-154 renumbered 151, 154, 152, 153; nos. 152, 153 rebuilt to GP9m in 1958.

Published roster:
Diesel Locomotive Rosters (Wayner Publications)

Lake Superior & Ishpeming
1949-present

A Michigan Upper Peninsula ore hauler, the Lake Superior & Ishpeming became a railfan favorite by dieselizing with all Alco power in the 1950s. Along with its original fleet of RS-1, RS-2, RS-3, and RSD-12 locomotives, the railroad added several second-hand RSD-12s and RSD-15s in the early 1970s. The railroad also acquired new and second-hand GE diesels in the 1960s and later. All Alcos and early GEs are out of service, but several U30Cs and C30-7s remain, along with newer leased GE locomotives.

Original road numbers	Second numbers	Qty.	Model	Builder	Dates built	Notes
1001-1003		3	RS-1	Alco	1951	
1501-1503		3	RS-2	Alco	1949	
1604-1611		8	RS-3	Alco	1950-55	1
1801-1804		4	RSD-12	Alco	1956-63	
1800, 1805-1807	1850-1853	4	RSD-12	Alco	1956	2
2300-2304		5	U23C	GE	1968-70	
2400-2405	2406, 2407	6	RSD-15	Alco	1959-60	3
2500, 2501		2	U25C	GE	1964	
3000-3016, 3050-3053		21	U30C	GE	1974	4
3071-3074		4	C30-7	GE	1978	5

Notes:
1—No. 1611 is ex-Rock Island 466, acquired 1966.
2—Ex-Baltimore & Ohio (nee Chesapeake & Ohio), acquired 1972.
3—Ex-Santa Fe, acquired 1975; nos. 2401, 2402 renumbered 2406, 2407.
4—Nos. 3000-3011, 3050-3053 are ex-Burlington Northern, acquired 1989-90. Nos. 3012-3016 are ex-Detroit Edison, acquired 1995 mainly for parts only.
5—Ex-Burlington Northern Santa Fe, nee BN, acquired 1999.

Published roster:
Diesel Era, January 1990

Lehigh & New England
1948-1961

Anthracite carrier Lehigh & New England didn't acquire a diesel until 1948, but was completely dieselized—with an all-Alco roster—by 1949. The railroad was abandoned in 1961, with its relatively young diesels going to other owners (many to Louisville & Nashville).

Road numbers	Qty.	Model	Builder	Dates built	Notes
611-616	6	S-2	Alco	1948-49	
651-663	13	RS-2	Alco	1949	
701-710	10	FA-1	Alco	1948-49	
751-753	3	FB-1	Alco	1948-49	

Published roster:
Diesel Locomotive Rosters (Wayner Publications)

Lehigh Valley
1924-1976

The Lehigh Valley dieselized with EMD FTs and F3s and Alco FAs (the last steam ran in 1951), and remained a prolific Alco customer through the 1960s. For a small railroad, the LV had a wide variety of locomotives, from Baldwin as well as EMD and Alco. The LV had struggled financially through the 1960s, declared bankruptcy in 1970, and became part of Conrail upon its creation on April 1, 1976.

Lehigh Valley opted for low noses on its four Alco RS-11s, delivered in 1960. *Alco*

Original road numbers	Second numbers	Qty.	Model	Builder	Dates built	Notes
102, 103		2	300-hp	Alco	1931	
104	99	1	Boxcab	GE-Alco-IR	1926	
105, 116 (2)		2	HH-600	Alco	1932, 1939	
106-109; 110, 111 (2)		6	SW	EMC	1937-38	
110, 111 (1)	50, 51	2	45-ton	Mack	1929	
112 (1)	52	1	60-ton	Mack	1930	
112-114, 115 (2), 118, 119		6	SW1	EMD	1939-50	
115, 116 (1)	75, 76	2	Model 60	EMC	1930	
117		1	S-1	Alco	1950	
120-124, 125 (2), 126-130		11	NW1	EMC	1937-38	
125 (1)	101	1	Boxcab	GE/Brill	1927	
135-139		5	VO1000	Baldwin	1944	
140-148	148 (2), 141 (2)	9	DS-4-4-10	Baldwin	1949-50	
150-165		16	S-2	Alco	1942-49	
166, 167		2	S-4	Alco	1951	
180-186		7	NW2	EMD	1949	
200		1	DRS-4-4-15	Baldwin	1948	
210-212 (1), 213, 214, 217, 218		7	RS-2	Alco	1949-50	2
210-212 (2)		3	RS-2	Alco	1952-55	1
215, 216, 219		2	RS-3	Alco	1950	3
220-224		5	SW7	EMD	1950	
230-243	236 (2), 242 (2)	14	S-12	Baldwin	1950	

Original road numbers	Second numbers	Qty.	Model	Builder	Dates built	Notes
250-276		27	SW8	EMD	1950-52	
280-292		13	SW9	EMD	1951	
300, 301		2	GP9	EMD	1959	
302-305		4	GP18	EMD	1960	
310-313		4	GP38AC	EMD	1971	
314-325		10	GP38-2	EMD	1972	
400-403		4	RS-11	Alco	1960	
404-415		12	C-420	Alco	1964	
500, 501 (1), 502, 503 (1)	502 (2), 504, 506 (1)	4	FTA	EMD	1945	
500B, 501B, 502B, 503B	501, 503 (2), 505, 507 (1)	4	FTB	EMD	1945	
501-507 (3, 2), 508-512 (2)		12	U23B	GE	1974	
510-528 (even)		10	F3A	EMD	1948	
511-529 (odd)		10	F3B	EMD	1948	
530-548 (even)		10	FA-1	Alco	1948	
531-549 (odd)		10	FB-1	Alco	1948	
560-574 (even)		8	F7A	EMD	1950-51	
561-571 (odd)		6	F7B	EMD	1950-51	
580-594 (even)		8	FA-2	Alco	1950-51	
581-587 (odd)		4	FB-2	Alco	1950-51	
601-614		14	PA-2	Alco	1948	
625-641		17	C-628	Alco	1964-67	4
7640-7644, 7648		6	RS-11	Alco	1957	5

Notes:
1—Ex-Penn Central 5461, 5569, 5401 (nee Pennsylvania RR), acquired 1970-71.
2—Nos. 217, 218 are ex-Chesapeake & Ohio 5500, 5501, acquired 1950.
3—No. 219 is ex-Tennessee Central 251, acquired 1972.
4—Nos. 633-641 are ex-Monon 400-408, acquired 1967.
5—Ex-Pennsylvania RR 8640-8644, 8648, acquired 1964.

Published rosters:
Diesel Era, September/October 1998; Extra 2200 South September-October 1969

Long Island Rail Road
1928-present

The Long Island was an early user of internal combustion, operating what is regarded by many as the first diesel road freight locomotive (actually an oil-electric, Alco/General Electric/Ingersoll-Rand no. 401) in 1925. The mainly passenger railroad has operated a number of distinctive locomotives, including Fairbanks-Morse passenger-service cab units (CPAs) and passenger-service Alco C-420s.

Long Island's RS-1s had distinctive numbers on their radiator grilles.
Frederick J. Weber

Original road numbers	Second numbers	Qty.	Model	Builder	Dates built	Notes
100-107		8	SW1001	EMD	1977	
150-172		23	MP15AC	EMD	1977	
200-229		30	C-420	Alco	1963-68	1
250-277		28	GP38-2	EMD	1976-77	
300-302		3	FL9AC	EMD	1957	2
397-399		3	25-ton	GE	1956, 1958	
400 (1)		1	44-tonner	GE	1950	
401, 402 (1)		2	Boxcab	Alco-GE-IR	1925, 1928	
403A, B		2	Boxcab	Baldwin/West.	1928	
403 (1)		1	VO660	Baldwin	1945	
404-408 (1)		5	S-1	Alco	1946	
409-412 (1)		4	DS-4-4-66	Baldwin	1948	
413-421 (1)		9	S-1	Alco	1949	
400-421 (2), 422		23	DE30AC	EMD	1998	
439-449		11	S-2	Alco	1948-49	3
450		1	DS-4-4-10	Baldwin	1948	
451-460		10	S-2	Alco	1949	
461-469		9	RS-1	Alco	1949-50	1
500-522		23	DM30AC	EMD	1999	
1501-1509		9	H-16-44	F-M	1949-51	4
1551-1560		10	RS-3	Alco	1955	1
1571, 1572	1519, 1520	2	RS-2	Alco	1949	1, 5
2001-2008		8	CPA-20-5	F-M	1950	1
2401-2404		4	CPA-24-5	F-M	1951	1

Notes:
1—Steam-generator equipped.
2—Ex-Conrail 5003, 5000, 5047, nee New Haven 2003, 2000, 2047, rebuilt and acquired in 1991.
3—Nos. 439-445 are ex-Delaware & Hudson, acquired 1963-64.
4—No. 1503 is ex-Fairbanks-Morse H-15-44 demonstrator 1500; rebuilt to 1,600 hp and acquired in 1951.
5—Ex-Delaware & Hudson 4019, 4020, acquired 1962.

Published rosters:
Diesel Locomotive Rosters (Wayner Publications); Extra 2200 South, September-October 1969

Louisville & Nashville
1939-1982

Although the Louisville & Nashville acquired several diesel switchers from 1939 through the 1940s, it was a coal-hauling railroad and chose to stick with steam for mainline power longer than many other railroads (the L&N purchased new steam locomotives as late as 1949). The railroad began buying large numbers of road diesels by the early 1950s, and was dieselized by 1956.

The L&N merged the Nashville, Chattanooga & St. Louis in 1957, acquiring that railroad's diesels, and in 1971 did the same with the Monon. Starting in the mid-1970s, the L&N was marketed with owner Seaboard Coast Line as the "Family Lines." The L&N roster is complex and convoluted—mergers, impending mergers, rebuilt locomotives, and large numbers of locomotives purchased second-hand have resulted in many renumberings, with some locomotives renumbered multiple times and some number slots used three and four times. These have been indicated where practical, but a unit-by-unit listing would take more space than this book allows. See Louisville & Nashville Diesel Locomotives (Castner et al.) for a detailed list.

In 1982, the SCL and L&N merged to form the Seaboard System Railroad. The L&N briefly kept its own identity, but the last of it vanished with the coming of CSX in 1986.

Original road numbers	Second numbers	Third numbers	Qty.	Model	Builder	Dates built	Notes
10			1	HH660	Alco	1939	
11-15			5	SW1	EMD	1939, 1941	
16-19			4	S-1	Alco	1941	
20-23			4	VO660	Baldwin	1941	
24-29, 34-75			48	S-1	Alco	1945-50	
51-59 (2)	260 (2)		9	RS-2	Alco	1947	1

Number 100 is an Alco RS-3. *Alco*

Original road numbers	Second numbers	Third numbers	Qty.	Model	Builder	Dates built	Notes
100-154, 174-179, 104 (2), 173 (2)	186, 188, 193		67	RS-3	Alco	1947-55	2
125, 126	98, 99		2	70-tonner	GE	1948-49	
200-211	385..395		12	FB-2	Alco	1952-56	
214-264, 248-250 (2), 259 (2)	134..199		55	RS-3	Alco	1951-56	3
260-266 (2), 265-271			14	RS-2	Alco	1949	4
300-321, 353-369			39	FA-2	Alco	1952, 1956	
327-329, 391 (2)			4	FB-1	Alco	1948-49	5
330, 331, 383, 384	392, 393		4	FB-2	Alco	1953-54	
332, 333 (1), 333 (2), 334-341			11	FA-1	Alco	1948	5
350-352			3	FPA-2	Alco	1952-53	
388-395 (2), 396-440	490, 2200..2239, 2274, 2300, 2306 (2)	2266, 2300, 2369, 2376, 2381	53	GP7	EMD	1950-53	6
441-459	501-507, 523-534	2336-2338, 2412, 2413	19	GP9	EMD	1954-56	
450A-457A, 450B-457B	750-757, 770-777 (1946)		16	E6A	EMD	1942	
458A-461A, 458B-461B	758-761, 778-781		8	E7A	EMD	1945	
600-634, 657 (2), 663-668, 670-672			44	FP7	EMD	1951-52	
703-716, 723 (2)			15	F7B	EMD	1951, 1953	7
717-720			4	F9B	EMD	1956	
754 (2), 782-784, 790-793, 798, 799			10	E7A	EMD	1946-49	8
785-788, 794-797			8	E8A	EMD	1950-51	8
800-858, 900-918	909..964, 807..857		59	F7A	EMD	1947-50	
919-926	551-558		8	F9A	EMD	1956	
910-914			5	RS-36	Alco	1962-63	9
950-959			10	RS-11	Alco	1960	10
1000-1070			71	GP30	EMD	1962-63	11
1100-1128			29	GP35	EMD	1964-65	12
1200-1221, 1279-1288	4505..4523		32	SD35	EMD	1965	13
1225-1258			34	SD40	EMD	1966-71	

Original road numbers	Second numbers	Third numbers	Qty.	Model	Builder	Dates built	Notes
1259-1278			20	SD40-2	EMD	1974	
1289-1297			9	SDP35	EMD	1965	14
1300-1335, 1351-1378			64	C-420	Alco	1964-67	15
1400-1414			15	C-628	Alco	1964-65	
1425-1435			11	C-630	Alco	1966	16
1470-1499, 1534-1582			79	U30C	GE	1969-72	
1500-1525 (2)			26	U25C	GE	1963-65	17
1525-1532	1533		8	U28C	GE	1966	
1600-1626			27	U25B	GE	1963-64	
1700-1703 (2)	1221-1224	4524, 4537-4539	4	SDP35	EMD	1965	
1700-1731, 1750-1754	456..495	2345..2368	37	GP7	EMD	1950-54	18
1800-1808			9	F3A	EMD	1948-49	18
1809-1831, 1912-1919	800..865 (2)		31	F7A	EMD	1949-51	18
1900-1911	702 (2)		12	F3B	EMD	1948-49	18, 19
2101-2104 (1)	30-33		4	S-1	Alco	1941, 1946	18
2105-2111 (1)	2305-2311		7	S-2	Alco	1942-46	18
2115	11 (2)		1	SW1	EMD	1941	18
2119-2123	2210 (2), 2211-2214		5	NW2	EMD	1941, 1949	18
2124-2133	2224-2233		10	SW7	EMD	1950	18
2134-2138	2234-2238		5	SW9	EMD	1951	18
2150, 2151, 2160-2162			5	VO1000	Baldwin	1943	18
2200, 2201 (1), 2220-2224 (1)	2300 (2), 2301, 2320-2324		7	S-2	Alco	1943, 1949	
2202-2210 (1)	2102-2110 (2)		9	VO1000	Baldwin	1943-44	
2202-2209 (2)			8	NW2	EMD	1942-49	20
2221-2223 (2)			3	SW7	EMD	1950	21
2224-2233 (2)			10	SW7	EMD	1950	18
2234-2238			5	SW9	EMD	1951	18
2225-2232, 2350-2369	2325-2332		28	S-4	Alco	1951-63	
2240-2244	2215-2219		5	NW2	EMD	1949	
2245-2266			22	SW7	EMD	1950	
2267-2296			30	SW9	EMD	1951, 1953	
2297-2300	2240 (2)		4	SW1200	EMD	1957	22
2370-2374 (1)			5	S-2	Alco	1949	
2500, 2501 (1)	948, 949 (1950s)		2	F3A	EMD	1948	
2550-2552	747-749		3	F3B	EMD	1948	
2500-2504 (2)			5	U28B	GE	1966	
2505-2509			5	U30B	GE	1967	
2700-2772, 2800-2824, 2803 (2)			99	U23B	GE	1970-1975	23
3000-3029			30	GP40	EMD	1966-67	
3100-3103			4	44-tonner	GE	1950	18
3554-3613			60	SD40-2	EMD	1974-77	
4000-4019			20	GP38	EMD	1970	
4020-4049			30	GP38AC	EMD	1971	
4050-4144			95	GP38-2	EMD	1972-73	
4225-4234			10	MP15AC	EMD	1978	
4500-4504			5	SD38-2	EMD	1975	
5000-5029			30	SW1500	EMD	1970-72	
5030-5039			10	MP15	EMD	1975	
5115-5129			15	B23-7	GE	1978	
5600-5602	2244, 2247, 2260		3	C-430	Alco	1965-67	24
6011-6044			34	GP38-2	EMD	1979	

Original road numbers	Second numbers	Third numbers	Qty.	Model	Builder	Dates built	Notes
6600-6616			17	GP40-2	EMD	1980	
7000-7015, 7032-7051, 7062-7069			44	C30-7	GE	1979-80	
7513-7523			11	C-628	Alco	1963-64	25
8000-8039, 8067-8086, 8095-8126, 8133-8162			122	SD40-2	EMD	1979-81	
8007-8009 (1)	1433-1435 (1979)		3	C-630	Alco	1965	26
8500-8524			25	SD50	EMD	1983	

Notes:
Most renumbering occurred in 1965.
1—Ex-Monon 51-59; assigned numbers 260-268 at merger but only 51 was renumbered, to 260.
2—No. 104 (2) is ex-Great Northern RS-2 201, rebuilt and acquired 1966; nos. 150-154 steam-generator equipped.
3—Nos. 256-264 are ex-Rutland 200-208, acquired 1963; nos. 248-250, 259 are ex-Tennessee Central, acquired 1968; nos. 240-243 steam-generator equipped.
4—Nos. 260-266 (2) are ex-Monon 51-57; nos. 265-271 are ex-Lehigh & New England, acquired 1963.
5—Nos. 332-341, 327-329 are ex-L&NE 701-710, 751-753, acquired 1963; 333 (2), 391 (2) are ex-St. Louis-San Francisco 5205, 5300, repowered by EMD in 1956 and acquired 1966.
6—Nos. 388 (2)-399 are ex-Missouri Pacific (nee Chicago & Eastern Indiana).
7—No. 723 (2) is ex-Clinchfield 853.
8—Second 754 is ex-MP 20, rebuilt; nos. 782-784, 785-788 are ex-SLSF, acquired 1965; nos. 798, 799 are ex-MP 27, 28, acquired 1969.
9—Ex-TC 301-305, acquired 1968.
10—Ex-Seaboard Coast Line 1202-1211, acquired 1976.
11—Nos. 1058-1060 are ex-MP (nee C&EI), nos. 1061-1070 are ex-Seaboard (nee ACL and SAL).
12—Nos. 1116-1128 are ex-MP (nee C&EI) 260-272.
13—Nos. 1279-1288 are ex-SCL 7025-7038.
14—Ex-ACL and SAL.
15—Nos. 1316, 1317 ex-TC 400, 401; nos. 1318-1335 ex-Monon 501-518; 1351-1378 ex-SCL 1212-1239; nos. 1318, 1319 steam-generator equipped.
16—Nos. 1433-1435 are ex-SCL 8007-8009 (nee ACL 2011-2013).
17—Nos. 1518-1525 are ex-Oro Dam Contractors 8012..8019.
18—Ex-Nashville, Chattanooga & St Louis.
19—No. 1907 rebuilt to F7B and renumbered in 1965; all steam-generator equipped.
20—Nos. 2202-2206 are ex-Monon; nos. 2207-2209 are ex-MP, acquired 1969.
21—Ex-MP 1202-1204, acquired 1969.
22—No. 2300 renumbered 2240 in 1965.
23—Nos. 2700-2707 are ex-Monon 601-608.
24—Ex-SCL, acquired 1976.
25—Ex-SCL 2200-2210, acquired 1977.
26—Ex-SCL 2211-2213, acquired 1977.

Published rosters:
Extra 2200 South, February 1968; Diesel Locomotive Rosters (Wayner Publications); Louisville & Nashville Diesel Locomotives, by Charles B. Castner et al. (TLC Publishing, 1998)

Maine Central
1939-1981

The Maine Central acquired a few diesel switchers before and during World War II and began buying road diesels from both EMD and Alco after the war, even though it purchased used steam locomotives as late as 1947. The railroad was fully dieselized in 1954. For second-generation locomotives, MEC went to both EMD (GP38s) and GE (U25Bs and U18Bs). This roster covers the Maine Central until it became part of Guilford in 1981.

Maine Central had seven EMD E7s, including No. 708. *EMD*

Road numbers	Qty.	Model	Builder	Dates built	Notes
11-17	7	44-tonner	GE	1941-47	
225-238	14	U25B	GE	1965	1
251-263	13	GP38	EMD	1966-67	
301-303, 311, 312	5	S-2	Alco	1949-50	
313-317	5	S-4	Alco	1951, 1954	
331-333	3	SW7	EMD	1950	
334, 335	2	SW9	EMD	1951, 1953	

Road numbers	Qty.	Model	Builder	Dates built	Notes
400-409	10	U18B	GE	1975	
450	1	GP9	GMD	1963	2
466, 469	2	RS-3	Alco	1950	3
551-555	5	RS-2	Alco	1949	
556, 557	2	RS-3	Alco	1953	4
561-569, 571-581	20	GP7	EMD	1950-52	5, 6
590-593	4	GP7	EMD	1950, 1953	7
671A, 672A	2	F7A	EMD	1947	4
671B, 672B	2	F7B	EMD	1947	4
681-686	6	F7A	EMD	1948	
705-711	7	E7A	EMD	1946, 1948	
801, 802	2	RS-11	Alco	1956	8
951, 952	2	HH660	Alco	1939	
953-960	8	S-1	Alco	1941-49	
961, 962	2	S-3	Alco	1953	

Notes:
1—Ex-Rock Island 225-238. Nos. 227, 233, 235-237 for parts only.
2—Ex-Algoma Central 171, acquired 1981.
3—Ex-Rock Island 466, 469; leased 1965.
4—Steam-generator equipped.
5—GP7s 571-573, 575-580 steam-generator equipped.
6—No. 581 is ex-Portland Terminal 1082, acquired 1957.
7—Ex-Louisville & Nashville 439, 433, 388 (nee Chicago & Eastern Illinois), 393 (nee C&EI).
8—No. 802 ex-PT 1082, acquired 1956.

Published rosters:
Diesel Era, September/October 2013; Extra 2200 South September-October 1969

Maryland & Pennsylvania
1946-1999

Shortline Maryland & Pennsylvania dieselized with EMD switchers in the late 1940s. Owner Emons Industries merged the Ma & Pa with Yorkrail in 1999 to form the York Railway (which was later purchased by Genesee & Wyoming).

Road numbers	Qty.	Model	Builder	Dates built	Notes
70	1	SW1	EMD	1946	
80, 81, 85	3	NW2	EMD	1946, 1941	1
82, 84	2	SW9	EMD	1951-52	2
83	1	SW900m	EMD	1937	3
1500, 1502, 1504	3	CF7	EMD/ATSF	1978	4
1506	1	GP7	EMD	1953	5

Notes:
1—No. 85 is ex-Reading 92, acquired 1976.
2—No. 84 is ex-Montour 85, nee Pittsburgh & Lake Erie 8952, acquired 1976.
3—Built as SW, rebuilt 1957; ex-Steelton & Highspire 23, nee Philadelphia, Bethlehem & New England 206, acquired 1967.
4—ex-Santa Fe 2417, 2426, 2425; rebuilt F7s (Santa Fe model designation).
5—ex-Reading 621, originally numbered 86, acquired 1976.

Published roster:
The Ma & Pa—A History of the Maryland & Pennsylvania Railroad, by George Hilton

McCloud River
1948-1992

The McCloud River was primarily a logging and wood products line operating in northern California. It became popular among railfans largely because of its fleet of Baldwin diesels acquired in the 1940s and 1950s. It was sold in 1992 and renamed the McCloud Railway.

Road numbers	Qty.	Model	Builder	Dates built	Notes
28, 29	2	DRS-6-6-15	Baldwin	1948, 1950	
30	1	S-12	Baldwin	1953	
31	1	S-8	Baldwin	1953	
32, 33	2	RS-12	Baldwin	1955	
34	1	AS-616	Baldwin	1952	1
35	1	DRS-6-6-15	Baldwin	1949	1
36-38	3	SD38	EMD	1969	
39	1	SD38-2	EMD	1974	

Notes:
1—Nos. 34, 35 are ex-Southern Pacific 5253, 5204.

Published roster:
Diesel Locomotive Rosters (Wayner Publications)

Minneapolis & St. Louis
1938-1960

The Minneapolis & St. Louis began buying diesel switchers in 1938, followed by road diesels in the form of EMD F units, Alco RS-1s, and EMD Geeps. The last run of steam was in 1951. The railroad originally used a unique (and cumbersome) numbering system loosely based on the month and year a locomotive was purchased; in 1956 (prior to the GP9s' arrival) these were renumbered into more-conventional number blocks. The M&StL was merged into the Chicago & North Western in 1960.

Minneapolis & St. Louis F7s 151A and 151C were built in 1950. *M&StL*

Final road numbers	Original road numbers	Qty.	Model	Builder	Dates built	Notes
D340		1	VO1000	Baldwin	1940	1
10-12	D742, D842, D149	3	44-tonner	GE	1942, 1948	
60	D438	1	SC	EMC	1938	
61	D838	1	SW	EMC	1938	
66	D939	1	HH660	Alco	1939	
90, 91	D538, D738	2	NW1	EMC	1938	
92	D539	1	HH1000	Alco	1939	
100, 101	D139, D740	2	NW2	EMC	1939, 1940	
102	D741	1	S-2	Alco	1941	
103	D145	1	VO1000	Baldwin	1944	
200-234	244, 744, 944, 1044, 1144, 645, 745, 845, 945, 146, 246, 346, 446, 546, 646, 746, 846, 946, 1046, 547, 948, 1048, 1148, 849, 949, 1049, 1149, 1249, 950, 1050, 1150, 1250, 751, 851, 951	35	RS-1	Alco	1944-51	
300, 301	852, 952	2	SD7	EMD	1952	
400-405	248A, 248C, 348A, 348C, 448A, 448C	6	F3A	EMD	1948	
406-413	150A, 150C, 250A, 250C, 350A, 350C, 151A, 151C	8	F7A	EMD	1949-50	
500, 501	147A, 147C	2	F2A	EMD	1946	
502-505	445A, 445C, 545A, 545C	4	FTA	EMD	1945	

Final road numbers	Original road numbers	Qty.	Model	Builder	Dates built	Notes
550	147B	1	F2B	EMD	1946	
551, 552	445B, 545B	2	FTB	EMD	1945	2
600-608, 700-713		23	GP9	EMD	1956-58	3

Notes:
1—Traded in for no. D145 (103) in 1944.
2—FT B units were FTSB version.
3—GP9s 600-608 re-used many components from traded-in FTs and F2s 500-505 and 550-552.

Published roster:
Minneapolis & St. Louis In Color, by Gene Green (Morning Sun, 1996)

Minneapolis, Northfield & Southern
1940-1982

The Minneapolis, Northfield & Southern dieselized with Baldwins, including six of the builder's distinctive large twin-engine, center-cab transfer locomotives. The railroad switched to EMD switchers and SD39 road diesels in the 1960s. The MN&S was merged into the Soo Line in 1982.

Initial road numbers	Second numbers	Qty.	Model	Builder	Dates built	Notes
1	61	1	VO660	Baldwin	1942	
10		1	H-12-44	F-M	1951	1
11		1	H-10-44	F-M	1946	1
12		1	VO1000	Baldwin	1944	2
15		1	DRS-6-6-15	Baldwin	1950	
20-24		5	DT-6-6-20	Baldwin	1948	
25		1	RT-624	Baldwin	1953	
30-35		6	SW1200	EMD	1962-65	
36, 37		2	SW1500	EMD	1966	
40, 41		2	SD39	EMD	1968	
600	60	1	VO660	Baldwin	1940	

Notes:
1—Nos. 10, 11 are ex-Minnesota Western 10, 51, acquired 1956.
2—Ex-Elgin, Joliet & Eastern 482, acquired 1954.

Published roster:
Diesel Locomotive Rosters (Wayner Publications)

Missouri-Kansas-Texas
1947-1988

The Katy was late to buy diesels, with the first switchers and EMD F units arriving in 1947. However, the locomotives' success let to quick dieselization, with the last steam locomotives running in 1952. Early diesels included samples from all major builders, including a significant number of Baldwins. By the 1960s the M-K-T settled on EMD, with GP38, GP40, and SD40 types dominating. The Katy was purchased by Missouri Pacific in 1988.

Original road numbers	Second numbers (renumbered 1960)	Qty.	Model	Builder	Dates built	Notes
1-6		6	SW1200	EMD	1957	
50-58		9	SW1500	EMD	1967-68, 1980	
101A, 101C	51A, 51C	2	E7A	EMD	1947	
106A, 107A, 106C, 107C	52A, 53A, 52B, 53C	4	E8A	EMD	1950-51	1
121A-124A, 121C-124C	78A-81A, 78C-81C	8	FP7	EMD	1952	
121B-124B	78B, 78D, 78E, 78F	4	F7B	EMD	1952	
151A, 151C, 152A, 152C	57A, 57C, 58A, 58C	4	PA-1	Alco	1949	
153A-157A, 153C-157C	59A-63A, 59C-63C	10	PA-2	Alco	1950-51	
170-230		61	GP40	EMD	1966-69	
201A-207A, 201C-207C	64A-70A, 64C-70C	14	F3A	EMD	1947, 1949	2

Number 1734 is an early production Fairbanks-Morse H-16-44.
Donald Sims

Original road numbers	Second numbers (renumbered 1960)	Qty.	Model	Builder	Dates built	Notes
201B-207B	64B, 64D-H, 65B	7	F3B	EMD	1949	
208A-211A, 208C-211C	71A-74A, 71C-74C	8	F7A	EMD	1949	
208B-211B	65D-G	4	F7B	EMD	1949	
226A-229A, 226C-229C	75A-77A, 77C, 65H, 70C	8	F7A	EMD	1949	
226B-229B	75B, 75D-F	4	F9B	EMD	1955	
231-248		18	GP40	EMD	1968	3
300-303		4	GP38	EMD	1969	
304-321		18	GP38-2	EMD	1973-76	
322-335, 337-343		21	GP38AC	EMD	1967, 1970	4
326A-334A, 326C-334C	82A-90A, 82C-90C	18	FA-1	Alco	1948-49	
350-352		3	U23B	GE	1973	
360-388		29	GP39-2	EMD	1977, 1984	5
400	94	1	25-ton	GE	1950	
600-636	637	37	SD40-2	EMD	1978-81	6
1000-1010	22-32	11	DS-4-4-10	Baldwin	1947-47	7
1026-1030	7-11	5	NW2	EMD	1947	
1201-1215	33-47	15	S-12	Baldwin	1951	
1226-1235	12-21	10	SW9	EMD	1952	
1501-1529	91-119	29	GP7	EMD	1950-52	
1551-1563	144 156	13	RS-3	Alco	1951	
1571-1586	126-141	16	AS-16	Baldwin	1951-53	8
1591	157	1	H-16-44	F-M	1950	

Original road numbers	Second numbers (renumbered 1960)	Qty.	Model	Builder	Dates built	Notes
1651-1654		4	70-tonner	GE	1950	
1655	92	1	12-ton	Whitcomb	1949	
1656	93	1	25-ton	Whitcomb	1949	
1701, 1702	142, 143	2	RS-3	Alco	1951	9
1731-1734	158-161	4	H-16-44	F-M	1951	
1761-1764	120-123	4	GP7	EMD	1952	
1787, 1788	124	2	AS-16	Baldwin	1950	8

Notes:
1—Nos. 53A, 54C rebuilt to E9 by EMD in 1957.
2—Nos. 64A, D, E rebuilt to F9 by EMD, 1955-57.
3—Ex-Conrail, acquired 1983.
4—Nos. 322-324 ex-Conrail (nee Penn Central) 7795, 7801, 7813, acquired 1985; 325-335, 337-343 ex-Illinois Central Gulf 9500-9509, 9511, 9513-9519, acquired 1986.
5—Nos. 380-388 ex-Kennecott Copper 779-783, 785, 787-789; built 1977 and rebuilt and acquired 1984.
6—No. 628 wrecked 1985, rebuilt and renumbered 637.
7—Re-engined by EMD, 1959-60.
8—AS-16s re-engined by EMD, 1958-60; no. 1788 off roster before renumbering/rebuilding.
9—Several RS-3s re-engined by EMD, 1959.

Published rosters:
Katy Power, by Joe Collias and Raymond B. George, Jr. (M M Books, 1986), Diesel Era, July-August 1991

Missouri Pacific
Includes Fort Worth Belt; International-Great Northern; Missouri-Illinois; and St. Louis, Brownsville & Mexico
1937-1986

The MoPac merged several railroads during the diesel era, notably the International-Great Northern and St. Louis, Brownsville & Mexico in 1956, the Texas & Pacific (which it had long controlled) and Chicago & Eastern Illinois (which it had controlled since 1967) in 1976, and the Fort Worth Belt and Missouri-Illinois in 1977. The MP also purchased the Alton & Southern (1968). Locomotives originally owned by these smaller subsidiaries are indicated with the road number or in the notes. Texas & Pacific and C&EI each have their own listings; T&P and C&EI locomotives are only included here if they were still active at the time those railroads were merged into MP.

The Missouri Pacific merger into the Union Pacific was approved in 1982, with MP initially becoming a subsidiary of UP. Missouri Pacific diesels at first retained MP's own paint scheme, then in 1984 they began receiving yellow and gray paint but with "Missouri Pacific" lettering. This continued, with a couple of additional locomotive orders by MP, until 1986, when all subsequent repainting was into UP colors and lettering.

Original road numbers	Second numbers	Third numbers	Qty.	Model	Builder	Dates built	Notes
1 (FWB)	6018 (FWB)		1	SW1	EMC	1939	
2 (FWB)	1020 (FWB)		1	NW2	EMD	1946	
42			1	E8A	EMD	1950	1
51 (MI)	1028 (MI)	1028	1	NW2	EMD	1949	
62-74 (MI)	961-973 (MI)	1065..1095	13	RS-3	Alco	1951-55	2
201-208			8	DR-4-4-15	Baldwin	1948	3
201B-204B			4	DR-4-4-15B	Baldwin	1948	
301-320			20	FA-1	Alco	1948	
301B-310B			10	FB-1	Alco	1948	
321-392	1370..1392		72	FA-2	Alco	1950-54	4
321B-325B, 331B-335B, 345B-356B, 370B-392B	1373..1391B		45	FB-2	Alco	1950-54	
400-499, 534-550 (2)	1900..1994, 1892..1896		117	GP18	EMD	1962-63	
500-504 (2)	1850-1854		5	GP18	EMD	1960	5
501-512 (1)			12	FTA	EMD	1943-45	
501B-512B			12	FTB	EMD	1943-45	
513-576 (1)	700..746, 765-774, 790-795		64	F3A	EMD	1947-48	6, 4
513B-518B, 525B-526B, 553B-556B, 561B-570B	790B..810B		22	F3B	EMD	1947-48	4
577-626 (1)	785, 786, 796-843 (1)	1808..1842	50	F7A	EMD	1949-51	6, 4
587B-596B, 619B, 620B	811B-822B		12	F7B	EMD	1949-51	6
551-564 (2)	1837..1849		14	GP9	EMD	1957	5

Missouri Pacific RS-3s have steam-style number boxes and class lights.
Missouri Pacific

Original road numbers	Second numbers	Third numbers	Qty.	Model	Builder	Dates built	Notes
572-577 (2)	852-857	2002-2007	6	GP38	EMD	1966	
600..665			25	GP40	EMD	1966-70	7
615-639	2514..2536	2608..2614	25	GP35	EMD	1964-65	
637, 640			2	GP7	EMD	1952	5
668-674	2250-2256 (1)	4500-4506 (2)	7	U23B	GE	1973	
700-789	3000-3089		90	SD40	EMD	1967-71	
790-814 (2, 3)	3090-3114		25	SD40-2	EMD	1973	
800, 801, 811-815	3500..3503		7	44-tonner	GE	1941-42	8
802-810	3504, 3505		9	44-ton	Misc.	1940-41	9
848B, 849B			2	F7B	EMD	1950	10
858-959	2009-2110		102	GP38-2	EMD	1972-73	
900, 901, 904, 907 (2)			4	GP40-2	EMD	1979-80	7
960-969, 974-988	1-10, 15-29	3300-3309, 3314-3328	25	U30C	GE	1968-69	11
1100-1166, 1175-1201, 1255-1299	1253, 1254		139	SW1200	EMD	1963-66	12
1202-1204, 1400			4	SW7	EMD	1950	
1222-1227, 1229-1231, 1410, 1412, 1419, 1422			13	SW9	EMD	1951	5
1254	1218	1421	1	SW9	EMD	1952	13
1356-1392			37	MP15DC	EMD	1982	

Original road numbers	Second numbers	Third numbers	Qty.	Model	Builder	Dates built	Notes
1415, 1417			2	SW7	EMD	1950	5
1518-1521			4	SW1500	EMD	1972	
1530-1554			25	MP15DC	EMD	1974-75	
1555-1714 (2)			160	GP15-1	EMD	1976-82	14
1715-1744 (2)			30	GP15AC	EMD	1982	
1627-1633, 1641-1644 (1)	627..643		11	GP7	EMD	1951-52	5
1634-1636 (1)			3	GP7	EMD	1951	15
1826, 1827			2	GP9	EMD	1956	15
1848 (1)			1	F7A	EMD	1950	10
2000, 2001			2	GP28	EMD	1964	5
2111-2334 (2)			224	GP38-2	EMD	1974-81	16
2257-2288 (1)	4507..4537 (2)		32	U23B	GE	1974-77	
2289-2338 (1)	4600-4649		50	B23-7	GE	1978-79	
2500-2513, 2537-2564	2601..2617		42	GP35	EMD	1964-65	5
3000 (1)	2400		1	30-ton	Plymouth	1931	17
3001 (1)			1	WLD 2	Plymouth	1932	
3004 (1)	2401		1	JDT-25	Plymouth	1961	
3115-3321			207	SD40-2	EMD	1973-80	18
3216-3235 (1)	6000-6019		20	SD40-2	EMD	1976	19
3310-3313, 3329-3334	2975-2978, 2994-2999		10	U30C	GE	1969-74	5
3500-3529			30	GP50	EMD	1980-81	
4100, 4101			2	NC2	EMC	1937	
4102, 4103			2	NW4	EMC	1938	20
4104-4111			8	BL2	EMD	1948	
4112-4115 (StLB&M)			4	DRS-4-4-15	Baldwin	1949	
4116-4194, 4197-4325	131..336	1600..1786	208	GP7	EMD	1950-54	21
4195, 4196, 4326-4331	941-946	935-940	8	AS-16	Baldwin	1951-54	22
4332-4371	346-385	1787..1825	40	GP9	EMD	1955	
4501-4526	974-999	1074..1089	26	RS-3	Alco	1955	2
4601-4612	488-499	944-955	12	RS-11	Alco	1959	2
4650-4684			35	B23-7	GE	1980-81	
4801-4829 (1)	505-533	1855..1881	29	GP18	EMD	1960-62	
4800-4854			55	B30-7A	GE	1981-82	
5000-5059			60	SD50	EMD	1984	
6005, 6006 (1)			2	SW	EMC	1938	23
6008			1	SW1	EMD	1947	23
6020-6073			54	SD40-2	EMD	1979-80	19
6602-6606			5	S-1	Alco	1940-47	24
7000, 7001			2	E3A	EMC	1939	
7002, 7003	11, 12		2	E6A	EMD	1941	
7002B, 7003B	11B, 12B		2	E6B	EMD	1941	
7004-7017	13-26		14	E7A	EMD	1945-48	25
7004B, 7010B-7012B, 7014B-7017B	13B-20B		8	E7B	EMD	1945-48	
7018-7021	38-41		4	E8A	EMD	1950	
7100			1	AA	EMC	1940	
8001-8008 (1)	44-51		8	PA-1	Alco	1949	25
8009-8036	52-79		28	PA-2	Alco	1950-52	
8000-8007 (2)	1401..1416		8	SW8	EMD	1952	5
9000-9059 (2)			60	C36-7	GE	1985	
9000-9003 (1)	1023, 6007, 6009 (1)		4	SC	EMC	1937	
9004-9006 (1), 9011, 9016-9021	6010..6017 (1)		10	SW1	EMD	1939-41	

Original road numbers	Second numbers	Third numbers	Qty.	Model	Builder	Dates built	Notes
9007, 9008	6600, 6601		2	S-1	Alco	1940	
9009, 9010, 9012, 9022	6612, 6613		4	VO660	Baldwin	1940-41	
9102	1035		1	HH1000	Alco	1939	
9103, 9117-9119, 9150-9155, 9160, 9161	1062-1065, 1084-1091		10	VO1000	Baldwin	1939-45	26
9104-9106	1021, 1022		3	NW2	EMC	1939-41	
9107-9116, 9128-9132, 9156-9159, 9168, 9169	1036-1056		17	S-2	Alco	1941-49	26
9120-9127, 9133-9141, 9148, 9149, 9162-9167	1066..1083, 1092-1097		25	DS-4-4-10	Baldwin	1948-50	26
9142-9146	1210-1214		5	SW7	EMD	1950	
9170-9191	1232-1253		22	SW9	EMD	1951	27
9200-9205 (IGN)	9016-9021 (1, IGN)	6014..6017 (1)	6	SW1	EMC	1939-41	
9200-9239	1260-1299	1365..1395	40	S-12	Baldwin	1951-53	27

Notes:
1—Ex-Boston & Maine 3821, acquired 1962.
2—Rebuilt with EMD engines.
3—Baldwin cabs with "baby-face" nose.
4—Nos. 361-373, 387-392, 561-570, 561B-570B, 603-606, 611-614, 617, 618 equipped with steam generators.
5—Ex-Texas & Pacific, acquired in merger.
6—Nos. 525-528, 525B, 526B, 553-560, 553B-556B, 595-606, 595B, 596B, 617, 618 are International-Great Northern; 529-552, 607-616 are St. Louis, Brownsville & Mexico.
7—Nos. 600-645 are ex-Rock Island, acquired 1984-85; 651..665 and 900..907 are ex-Western Pacific.
8—No. 812 is nee IGN, then StLB&M; nos. 813, 814 are StLB&M; 815 is ex-Beaumont, Sour Lake & Western.
9—Built by Porter (802), Davenport-Bessler (803, 808-810), and Whitcomb (804-807).
10—Ex-Rio Grande F7Bs 5683, 5693, F7A 5684, acquired 1967.
11—Subsequently renumbered 2965-2974, 2979-2993.
12—No 1260 is ex-Bauxite & Northern 11; 1261 and 1262 are ex-Rockdale, Sandow & Southern 8, 9; 1275-1299 are ex-T&P (same numbers), acquired in merger.
13—Ex-B&N 10, acquired 1964.
14—Nos. 1570-1574 are ex-Chicago & Eastern Illinois (same numbers).
15—Ex-C&EI.
16—Nos. 2238-2289 are ex-Rock Island 4300-4351, acquired 1980.
17—Ex-New Orleans & Lower Coast 3000.
18—Nos. 3115-3138 are ex-T&P; 3150-3163 are ex-C&EI (all same numbers).
19—Nos. 6000-6073 had dynamic brakes and Pacesetter control and were designated SD40-2c by MP, the "c" for "coal service."
20—Steam-generator equipped.
21—Nos. 4116-4120, 4159-4165, 4203-4207, 4249-4253, 4284-4286, 4298, 4323, 4324 are StLB&M; 4121-4123, 4153-4158, 4197-4202, 4254, 4255, 4287-4297, 4325 are IGN; nos. 4142-4165, 4241-4260, 4316-4325 are steam-generator equipped.
22—Nos. 4195, 4196 are IGN; 4326-4331 are StLB&M.
23—Nos. 6005, 6006, 6008 are ex-St. Joseph Belt 5, 10, 12.
24—Nos. 6602, 6603 are ex-Texas Pacific Missouri Pacific Terminal 3, 4; 6604-6606 are ex-NO&LC 9013-9015.
25—Nos. 7008, 7009 are StLB&M; nos. 7007, 7012, 7013, 7012B, 8011, 8012 are IGN.
26—Nos. 9150-9152, 9156-9158, 9168-9169 are IGN; 9148, 9149, 9153-9155, 9159-9167 are StLB&M.
27—Nos. 9187-9191, 9227-9229 are StLB&M; 9230-9232 are IGN; 9233-9239 are ex-Union Terminal.

Published rosters:
Extra 2200 South, April 1968; Missouri Pacific Diesel Power, by Kevin EuDaly (White River Productions, 1994)

Monongahela
1951-1993

The Monongahela, a small coal-hauling railroad on the Pennsylvania-West Virginia border, began dieselizing with Baldwin S-12 switchers in 1952, using them for both yard and mainline service. The last steam ran in 1954 with the arrival of the last of 27 S-12s. The railroad became well-known later mainly for buying eight Baldwin RF-16 sharks from the New York Central in 1967. It was also one of the only U.S. buyers for GE Super 7 rebuilt locomotives.

Conrail merged the Mongahela into its system in 1993.

Road numbers	Qty.	Model	Builder	Dates built	Notes
400-426	27	S-12	Baldwin	1952-54	
1205, 1207, 1209, 1210, 1211, 1213, 1216	7	RF-16	Baldwin	1951-52	1
3708	1	RF-16B	Baldwin	1952	1
1500-1510	11	GP7	EMD	1951-53	2
2000-2004	5	GP38	EMD	1969	3
2300-2310	11	Super 7-23B	GE	1972	4

Notes:
1—Ex-New York Central (same numbers), acquired 1967.
2—Ex-Pittsburgh & Lake Erie 1506..1533, acquired 1974.
3—Specially ballasted; they were the heaviest GP38s built.
4—Ex-Western Pacific U23Bs (2251..2265), rebuilt to Dash 7 standards by GE Montreal and acquired 1989-90.

Published roster:
Diesel Era, July/August 2008

Montana Rail Link
1987-present

Montana Rail Link began service in 1987 on former Burlington Northern lines in its namesake state. All of its diesels other than SD70ACes have been acquired used from BN and a variety of other sources; space precludes listing predecessor roads for individual locomotives. Non-standard model numbers reflect rebuilt locomotives, with model designations those of the railroad or company performing the rebuilding.

Montana Rail Link relied on used locomotives until buying its first SD70ACe diesels in 2005. *Tom Danneman*

Road numbers	Qty.	Model	Builder	Dates built	Notes
11	1	NW2m	EMD	1939	
12-18	7	SW1200	EMD	1956-57	1
51, 52	2	SW1500	EMD	1968, 1970	
102-135	34	GP9	EMD	1951-58	2
151	1	GP19-1	EMD	1957	
200..225	19	SD40	EMD	1966-71	
250-265	16	SD40-2R	EMD	1966-74	
290	1	SDP40R	EMD	1966	
301-313	13	SD45-2	EMD	1974	
314-331, 342..388	55	SD45R	EMD	1966-70	
332	1	SD45-2R	EMD	1970	
390-393	4	F45, F45M	EMD	1971	
401-406	6	GP35	EMD	1964-65	
600-612	13	SD9	EMD	1953-56	
651, 652	2	SD19-1	EMD	1956-57	
701-705	5	SD35	EMD	1965	
1701, 1718	2	SD45	EMD	1966	
1721, 1731, 1744	3	GP9	EMD	1956-57	
4300-4315, 4400-4408	25	SD70ACe	EMD	2005-14	

Notes:
1—No. 16 is an SW9.
2—No. 129 is a GP7, built 1950.

Nashville, Chattanooga & St. Louis
1941-1957

The Nashville, Chattanooga & St. Louis began dieselizing with switchers from several builders in the early 1940s. Mainline freight and passenger trains were dieselized with EMD GP7s and F units starting in 1948; the last steam operated in 1953. The NC&StL had been under Louisville & Nashville control since before the turn of the 20th century, and the L&N merged the NC&StL in 1957.

Dixie Line GP7 No. 754 is equipped with a steam generator (in the short hood). *EMD*

Original road numbers	Second numbers	Qty.	Model	Builder	Dates built	Notes
1-4		4	S-1	Alco	1941-46	
5-9, 10 (2), 11		7	S-2	Alco	1942-46	
10	40	1	VO660	Baldwin	1941	1
20	15	1	SW1	EMD	1941	2
19-23		5	NW2	EMD	1941, 1949	
24-29, 30-33 (2)		10	SW7	EMD	1950	
34-35 (2), 36-38		5	SW9	EMD	1951	
30-35 (1)	50-55	6	VO1000	Baldwin	1941-43	3
100-103		4	44-tonner	GE	1950	
700-731, 750-754		37	GP7	EMD	1950-52	4, 5
800-808		9	F3A	EMD	1948-49	
809-831		23	F7A	EMD	1949-51	
900-911		12	F3B	EMD	1948-49	4
912-919		8	F7B	EMD	1949-50	4

Notes:
1—Renumbered in 1945.
2—Renumbered in 1949.
3—Renumbered in 1950.
4—GP7s 750-754 and all F3B and F7B locomotives steam-generator equipped.
5—GP7s 700-705 rode on AAR trucks.

Published rosters:
L&N Historical Society Archive No. 88C1.2, Nashville, Chattanooga & St. Louis Ry. Equipment Data Series (L&N Railroad Historical Society, 1988); Nashville, Chattanooga & St. Louis: A History of the Dixie Line, by Dain L. Schult (TLC Publishing, 2002)

National of Mexico (N de M)
1944-1993

Ferrocarriles Nacionales de Mexico (FNM, known in the U.S. as National Railways of Mexico, or N de M) was Mexico's major state-owned railway system. N de M purchased both steam and diesel locomotives from U.S. builders, acquiring its first diesels in 1944 and its last new steam in 1946. Dieselization was slow; steam still operated into the mid-1960s. This roster covers all new locomotive deliveries through 1993; the railroad also acquired hundreds of used diesels from U.S. railroads. In 1995 the decision was made to privatize N de M, a process completed in 1998.

Number 5800 is a G12, an EMD export locomotive rated at 1,250-hp with a 12-cylinder 567 engine. *EMD*

Original road numbers	Second numbers	Qty.	Model	Builder	Dates built	Notes
5000-5004		5	S-1	Alco	1944	
5100-5102		3	70-tonner	GE	1948	
5300		1	S-6	Alco	1956	
5400-5416		17	GA8	EMD	1964, 1967	

Original road numbers	Second numbers	Qty.	Model	Builder	Dates built	Notes
5500-5522		23	S-2	Alco	1944, 1950	
5523-5530		8	S-4	Alco	1951	
5600-5663		64	RS-1	Alco	1950-60	
5700-5705		6	RSD-1	Alco	1946	
5800-5889		90	G12	EMD	1955-64	
5900-5904		5	RSD-35	MLW	1963	
6000-6002	6100	3	DR-6-4-20	Baldwin	1945-46	1
6200A-6213A		14	F2A	EMD	1946	
6200B-6213B		14	F2B	EMD	1946	
6300-6308, 6328A-6334A		16	FP7	EMD	1950-51	
6309-6318, 6319A-6327A, 6335-6338		23	F7A	EMD	1950-51	
6319B-6334B		16	F7B	EMD	1951	
6400-6413		14	DR-12-8-30	Baldwin	1948	2
6500, 6501, 6502A-6506A, 6523A-6533A		18	FPA-2	Alco, MLW	1950-54	
6502B-6506B, 6528B-6533B		11	FPB-2	Alco	1951, 1954	
6507A-6522A, 6519A (2), 6534A		18	FA-2	Alco	1951-54	
6507B-6527B, 6519B (2), 6534B		23	FB-2	Alco	1951-54	
6700-6706 (1)		7	RS-3	Alco	1952, 1956	
6700-6799, 9600-9656, 11001-11148		305	C30-7	GE	1979-83	
6800-6819	6820, 6821	20	AS-616	Baldwin	1954	3
6900, 6901		2	RSD-5	Alco	1955	
7000A-7009A		10	F9A	EMD	1954	
7000B-7009B		10	F9B	EMD	1954	
7010-7034		25	FP9	EMD	1956	
7100-7107, 7101-7102 (2)	7108	10	GP9	EMD	1956-59	4
7200-7293	7294	94	RS-11	Alco, MLW	1956-64	4
7300-7323		24	G16	EMD	1958-60	
7400-7472	7473	73	RSD-12	Alco	1958-62	4
7500-7536		37	GP18	EMD	1961-62	
8000-8009		10	UD18B	GE	1956	
8100-8144		45	C-424	Alco	1964-65	
8200-8254		55	GP35	EMD	1964-65	
8300-8331		32	C-628	Alco	1967-68	
8400-8409		10	GP40	EMD	1967	
8500-8521, 8536-8585		72	SD40	EMD, GMD	1968-72	
8522-8535		14	SDP40	EMD	1968-70	
8600-8619		20	M-630	MLW	1972	
8700-8798, 13001-13004		103	SD40-2	EMD	1972-86	
8800-8859		60	SW1504	EMD	1973	
8900-8937, 8958-8986, 9300-9316		84	U36C	GE	1973-75	
8938-8957		20	U36CG	GE	1974	
9000-9044		45	U18B	GE	1974	
9100-9129		30	U23B	GE	1975-77	
9130-9180, 10001-10052, 12000-12011, 1-01 to 1-08		122	B23-7	GE	1979-81	
9200-9299, 9400-9414, 9901-9909		104	GP38-2	EMD	1975-82	
9317-9341		25	C36-7	GE	1979-80	
14000-14098		99	C30-S7	GE	1989-93	5

1—Nos. 6000, 6001 are ex-Baldwin demonstrators 2000, 2001; no. 6002 was renumbered 6200.
2—Baldwin Centipedes.
3—N de M rebuilt two locomotives from AS-616 and other parts, numbering them 6820 and 6821 and classing them SLP-4 and SLP-1.
4—No. 7108 is an SLP-8, rebuilt from a wrecked GP9 and F units; 7294 is an SLP-2, rebuilt from a retired RS-11; 7473 is an SLP-5 rebuilt from a retired RSD-12 and FB-2.
5—GE "Super 7" rebuilds, rebuilt to Dash 7 standards from older GE locomotives of varied heritage.

Published roster:
Extra 2200 South, March-April 1974

New York Central
1928-1968

The New York Central was one of the country's largest railroads and it remained devoted to steam later than most. The railroad owned some early boxcabs and acquired a small fleet of diesel switchers during World War II. As the railroad began to dieselize, it did so with locomotives from all the builders, making it popular among railfans, and the railroad wasn't completely dieselized until 1957.

The New York Central System included several subsidiary railroads that were operated as part of the NYC. Some lacked their own identity; others carried road names or initials but wore NYC paint schemes. This roster includes the Boston & Albany, "Big Four" (Cleveland, Cincinnati, Chicago & St. Louis), and Michigan Central, along with the Peoria & Eastern, Cleveland Union Terminal, and Chicago River & Indiana. It does not include subsidiaries Pittsburgh & Lake Erie and Indiana Harbor Belt, neither of which become part of Penn Central and both of which have their own listings in this book.

Many early locomotives went through multiple renumberings (especially switchers); see the renumbering dates in parentheses for clarification. Most locomotives were renumbered in 1966 in anticipation of the Penn Central merger; these are listed in their own column. The NYC merged with longtime rival Pennsylvania Railroad in February 1968 to form Penn Central.

Fairbanks-Morse CFA-20-4 is one of 12 2,000-hp C-Liners purchased by NYC in 1950. *Fairbanks-Morse*

Original road numbers	Subsequent numbers (dates)	1966 (pre-PC) renumbering	Qty.	Model	Builder	Dates built	Notes
20			1	RP-210	Baldwin	1956	1
501, 502	750, 751 (1943)		2	VO660	Baldwin	1941-42	
506-513			8	70-ton	GE	1940-42	
567-573			7	SC	EMC	1936	
574-599, 600-621		8400..8447	48	SW1	EMD	1939-50	
590	811 (1948)	9300	1	S-1	Alco	1940	
600-654	650-704 (1949)	8448..8500	55	SW1	EMD	1939-42	
614-618	674-678 (1939), 800-804 (1948)		5	HH660	Alco	1939	
679-684	805-810 (1948)		6	HH660	Alco	1939	
685-692	900-907 (1948), 950-957 (1950)	9404-9409, 9382, 9410	8	S-1	Alco	1940-41	

Original road numbers	Subsequent numbers (dates)	1966 (pre-PC) renumbering	Qty.	Model	Builder	Dates built	Notes
693-744	812-863	9301..9338	52	S-1	Alco	1942-45	
752-761			10	VO660	Baldwin	1942, 1944	
780-789	8500-8509 (1944)	9600..9608	10	S-2	Alco	1943-44	
851, 869		9704, 9705	2	S-2	Alco	1949	2
864-873		9340..9347	10	S-1	Alco	1950	
874-916		9348..9371	43	S-3	Alco	1950-51	
1000-1043	1056, 1110, 1119 (1964)		44	FA-1	Alco	1947-49	
1044-1123	1000, 1031, 1033 (1964-65)		80	FA-2	Alco	1951-52	
1505	505 (1936)		1	250-hp	GE/Buda	1923	
1525-1562	525-562 (1936)		38	300-hp	Alco-GE-IR	1928-30	
1550	See note		1	Boxcab	Alco-GE-IR	1928	3
1600-1603			4	FTA	EMD	1944	
1604, 1605			2	F2A	EMD	1946	
1606-1635			30	F3A	EMD	1947-48	
1636-1875, 1877			241	F7A	EMD	1949-52	4
2050-2059			10	C-430	Alco	1967	
2300-2322	3300-3322 (1951)		23	FB-1	Alco	1947-49	
2400-2403			4	FTB	EMD	1944	
2404-2419			16	F3B	EMD	1947-48	
2420-2476		3423..3432	57	F7B	EMD	1949-52	4
2500-2569			70	U25B	GE	1964-65	
2822, 2823			2	U28B	GE	1966	
2830-2889			60	U30B	GE	1967	
3000-3104			105	GP40	EMD	1965, 1967	
3200-3203	3504-3507 (1955)		4	DR-6-4-15	Baldwin	1947-48	
3300, 3301	3602, 3603 (1955)		2	DR-6-4-15B	Baldwin	1947-48	
3323-3372	3320 (1965)		50	FB-2	Alco	1951-52	
3400-3403	3800-3803 (1951)		4	DR-4-4-15	Baldwin	1948	5
3500-3503	1874..1877 (1958-61)		4	F3A	EMD	1947	6
3600, 3601	2475, 2476 (1958-59)		2	F3B	EMD	1947	6
3700, 3701			2	DR-4-4-15B	Baldwin	1948	
3702-3709			8	RF-16B	Baldwin	1951-52	
3804-3821		1204-1221	18	RF-16	Baldwin	1951-52	
4000-4035			36	E7A	EMD	1945-49	7
4036-4095			60	E8A	EMD	1951-53	
4100-4113			14	E7B	EMD	1945-48	
4200-4203			4	PA-1	Alco	1948	5
4208-4212			5	PA-2	Alco	1950	8
4300-4303			4	PB-1	Alco	1948	
4304			1	PB-2	Alco	1950	8
4400-4405			6	Erie A	F-M	1949	
4500-4507			8	CPA-24-4	F-M	1955-56	
5000-5005			6	Erie A	F-M	1947-49	5
5006-5017			12	CFA-20-4	F-M	1950	5
5100, 5101			2	Erie B	F-M	1948-49	5
5102-5104			3	CFB-20-4	F-M	1950	5
5600-5675, 5686-5712, 5738-5827		5900..5930	193	GP7	EMD	1950-53	9
5800-5815	6200-6215 (1953)	8062, 8063	16	LRS-1200	Lima	1950	5
5820-5836	6220-6236 (1953)	8067-8083	17	RS-12	Baldwin	1951-52	

Original road numbers	Subsequent numbers (dates)	1966 (pre-PC) renumbering	Qty.	Model	Builder	Dates built	Notes
5900-6075		7300..7518	176	GP9	EMD	1954-57	
6100-6114		2100..2112	15	GP20	EMD	1961	
6115-6124		2188-2197	10	GP30	EMD	1962	
6125-6155		2369-2399	31	GP35	EMD	1963-65	
6600-6607			8	CFA-16-4	F-M	1952	
6900-6903			4	CFB-16-4	F-M	1952	
7000-7012		5100..5112	13	H-16-44	F-M	1951	
7100-7118			19	H-20-44	F-M	1948-49	10
7530-7533	563-566 (1936)		4	300-hp	Alco-GE-IR	1930	
8000-8008		7600-7608	9	RS-11	Alco	1957	
8020-8044		2020-2044	25	RS-32	Alco	1961-62	
8100-8113		9900-9913	14	RS-1	Alco	1948, 1950	
8200-8222		5207..5221	23	RS-2	Alco	1948-50	
8223-8357		5223..5352	135	RS-3	Alco	1950-53	11
8300, 8301	7300, 7301 (1951)	5991	2	DRS-4-4-15	Baldwin	1948	5
8400-8405			6	LS-1000	Lima	1949	
8406-8411			6	LS-1200	Lima	1951	12
8505, 8510-8589		9605, 9609..9662, 9707..9732	81	S-2	Alco	1944-50	2, 13
8590-8667		9663-9703, 9729..9766	78	S-4	Alco	1952-53	13
8600-8607	9300-9307 (1951)		8	DS-4-4-10	Baldwin	1944-45	
8700-8704, 8715, 8794-8802		8907	15	NW2	EMD	1946-49	14
8842-8855, 8872-8874, 8880-8903, 8911-8921			34	SW7	EMD	1950-51	15
8922-8930, 8941-8951, 8962-9001			60	SW9	EMD	1951-53	
9104-9110		8204..8210	7	H-10-44	F-M	1949-50	16
9111-9137		8301..8326	27	H-12-44	F-M	1950-52	
9200-9221			22	SW1500	EMD	1966-68	17
9308-9328		8092-8112	21	S-12	Baldwin	1951-52	
9500-9516		8683-8699	17	NW2	EMD	1948	18
9600-9627		8600-8627	28	SW8	EMD	1952-53	19
9628-9646		8628-8646	19	SW900	EMD	1954-55	
9800-9820			21	LS-800	Lima	1951	12

Notes:
1—Streamlined power unit for experimental lightweight Pullman X-Plorer train.
2—Nos. 851, 869, 8505 are ex-Delaware & Hudson 3024, 3031, 3032.
3—Renumbered 1510 in 1929, 510 in 1936 and 500 in 1941.
4—Nos. 1874, 1875, 1877, 2475, 2476 rebuilt from F3s in 1958-61.
5—Nos. 3803, 4302, 5001, 5006-5017, 5101-5104, 5810, 5811, 7300, 7301 were rebuilt with EMD engines in 1955-57.
6—Passenger units converted to freight in 1958-61.
7—Nos. 4003, 4020 rebuilt after wreck to E8A.
8—Nos. 4212, 4304 are ex-GE 8375A and B, used on GE's More Power to America train in 1950-51.
9—Nos. 5818-5827 are ex-Chesapeake & Ohio 5720-5729, acquired 1956. Several GP7s subsequently renumbered in 5700s in 1967-68.
10—Nos. 7110-7118 are ex-Indiana Harbor Belt, acquired 1949-50.
11—Nos. 8353-8357 are ex-Pittsburgh & Lake Erie, acquired 1966.
12—Chicago River & Indiana.
13—Nos. 8537-8549, 8633-8667 are ex-P&LE, acquired 1966.
14—Nos. 8715, 8794-8802 are ex-IHB (no. 8715 renumbered 8907), acquired 1966-67.
15—Nos. 8842-8850 (1967), 8872-8874 (1967) are ex-IHB; nos. 8898-8903 (1951) ex-CR&I.
16—Nos. 9104, 9105 are ex-IHB, acquired 1950.
17—Nos. 9216-9221 delivered to Penn Central.
18—Ex-New York, Ontario & Western, acquired 1957.
19—Nos. 9600, 9601 ex-CR&I, acquired 1951.

Published rosters:
Diesel Locomotives of the New York Central System, by W. D. Edson et al. (New York Central System Historical Society, 1978); Diesel Locomotive Rosters (Wayner Publications)

New York, Chicago & St. Louis
(Nickel Plate Road)
1942-1964

The Nickel Plate was late to dieselize, buying switchers during World War II but holding off on passenger power until the late 1940s (PA-1s) and freight locomotives until the 1950s. Steam lasted in mainline service until all districts were dieselized in 1958. Diesel switchers and freight units were a mix of models from various builders, with the railroad purchasing new Alcos (RS-36s) and EMDs (GP30s) shortly before the railroad's merger into the Norfolk & Western in 1964.

Number 706 is an EMD GP18, one of 10 delivered in 1960. *NKP*

Original numbers	Qty.	Model	Builder	Dates built	Notes
1-6, 25-45	27	S-2	Alco	1942-50	
7-22	16	NW2	EMD	1942-48	
46-61, 65-83	35	S-4	Alco	1951-53	
85	1	S-1	Alco	1950	
90	1	44-tonner	GE	1949	
95-98	4	NW2	EMD	1940-41	1
100-101	2	VO1000	Baldwin	1947	
105-106	2	SW1	EMD	1950	
107-114	8	SW8	EMD	1952	
125-133	9	H-10-44	F-M	1949	
134-155	22	H-12-44	F-M	1953-58	
180-190	11	PA-1	Alco	1947-48	
230-232	3	SW7	EMD	1950	
233-244	12	SW9	EMD	1951-52	
305-308	4	LS-1000	Lima	1949	
309-312	4	LS-1200	Lima	1950	
320-323	4	AS-16	Baldwin	1953-54	2
325-333	9	RSD-12	Alco	1957	
340-359	20	SD9	EMD	1957	
400-447	48	GP7	EMD	1951, 1953	
448-534	87	GP9	EMD	1955-59	3, 4
482, 496, 497, 503 (2)	4	GP9	EMD	1957	4

Original numbers	Qty.	Model	Builder	Dates built	Notes
535-557	23	RS-3	Alco	1954	
558-577	43	RS-11	Alco	1956-60	
578	1	C-420	Alco	1964	
700-709	10	GP18	EMD	1960	
800-814	15	GP9	EMD	1959	
850-864	15	RS-11	Alco	1959	
865-875	11	RS-36	Alco	1962	3
900-909	10	GP30	EMD	1962	
910	1	GP35	EMD	1964	

Notes:
1—Ex-Wheeling & Lake Erie.
2—Re-engined in 1959 by Alco (320, 321) and EMD (322, 323).
3—Nos. 477-485, 874, 875 steam-generator equipped.
4—First nos. 482, 496, 497, 503 wrecked 1956; replaced by new GP9s with same numbers in 1957.

Published roster:
Diesel Era November-December 1993

New York, New Haven & Hartford

1931-1968

The New Haven was known for its eclectic mix of diesels from all the major builders, with EMD playing only a minor role (20 switchers and 30 GP9s until the unique FL9s arrived). The railroad finished dieselizing in 1952, with Alco FAs and RS diesels on the main line. Notable are New Haven's large fleet (60) of Alco DL-109 prewar passenger cabs, which it used for both passenger and freight trains, and its 60 dual-power FL9s, its last EMD diesels (1957 and 1960). For second-generation power, the NH stuck to Alco (C-425s) and GE (U25Bs).

The New Haven spent much of its diesel era in financial troubles, entering reorganization in the early 1960s. The Interstate Commerce Commission ordered Penn Central (formed in February 1968 by merger of New York Central and the Pennsylvania Railroad) to purchase the New Haven, which it did on December 31, 1968.

New Haven's high-hood Alco RS-11s were delivered in 1956. *New Haven*

Original road numbers	Second numbers	Qty.	Model	Builder	Dates built	Notes
0400-0429		30	FA-1	Alco	1947	
0450-0464		15	FB-1	Alco	1947	
465-469		5	FB-2	Alco	1951	
0500-0516		17	RS-2	Alco	1948	
517-559, 560-561 (2)		45	RS-3	Alco	1950-52	
560-561 (1), 562-564	590-599	10	H-16-44	F-M	1950	
0600-0621		22	S-2	Alco	1944	
630-639		10	LS-1000	Lima	1950	
640-659		20	SW1200	EMD	1956	

Original road numbers	Second numbers	Qty.	Model	Builder	Dates built	Notes
0660-0671		12	RS-1	Alco	1948	
0700-0759		60	DL-109	Alco	1942-45	
0760-0786		27	PA-1	Alco	1948-49	
790-799		10	CPA-24-5	F-M	1951-52	1
0800-0818		19	44-tonner	GE	1940-47	
0900		1	HH660	Alco	1931	2
0901-0910		10	98-ton	GE-IR	1936-37	
0911-0930		20	HH600	Alco	1938, 1940	
0931-0995		65	S-1	Alco	1941-49	
1200-1229		30	GP9	EMD	1956	
1400-1414		15	RS-11	Alco	1956	
1600-1614		15	H-16-44	F-M	1956	
2000-2059		60	FL9	EMD	1957, 1960	
2500-2525		26	U25B	GE	1964-65	
2550-2559		10	C-425	Alco	1964	
3000, 3001		2	RP-210	Baldwin	1956	3
3100, 3101		2	P12-2	F-M	1957	4

Notes:
1—Nos. 790, 791 former Fairbanks-Morse demonstrators 4501, 4502.
2—Former Alco demonstrator 600 (first HH locomotive built).
3—Baldwin power units for Pullman-Standard Train X articulated passenger train.
4—Fairbanks-Morse power units for ACF Talgo passenger train.

Published roster:
Extra 2200 South, May 1968

New York, Ontario & Western
1941-1957

The New York, Ontario & Western began buy-ing diesels in 1941 with five GE 44-tonners. Road diesels arrived in 1945 with EMD FTs, with F3s following three years later. Financial troubles plagued the line, and the NYO&W was abandoned in 1957.

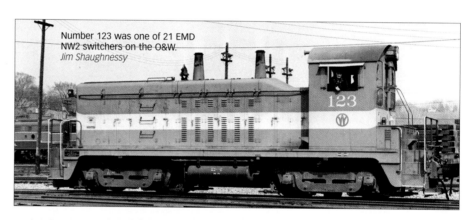

Number 123 was one of 21 EMD NW2 switchers on the O&W.
Jim Shaughnessy

Original road numbers	No.	Model	Builder	Dates built	Notes
101-105	5	44-tonner	GE	1941-42	
111-131	21	NW2	EMD	1948	
501-503	3	F3A	EMD	1948	
601, 801-808	9	FTA	EMD	1945	
601B, 801B-808B	9	FTB	EMD	1945	
821-822	2	F3A	EMD	1948	
821B-822B	2	F3B	EMD	1948	

Published roster:
Diesel Era, November/December 1992

Norfolk & Western
1947-1982

The Norfolk & Western was the last major American railroad to dieselize, as it continued buying and building new steam locomotives until 1953. The arrival of large numbers of EMD GP9s in the late 1950s enabled the railroad to finally retire its last steam locomotives in 1960. For second-generation power, the N&W bought a sizable fleet of EMD SD45s, SD40-2s, and GE C30-7s.

The N&W acquired several groups of locomotives through mergers. The N&W merged the Virginian in 1959, acquiring that railroad's diesels (notably its F-M Train Masters and H-16-44s), then in 1964 acquired the diesels of the Nickel Plate Road (merger) and Wabash (lease). These are indicated in the notes following the roster. The roster covers orders through June 1, 1982, when the N&W merged with the Southern Railway to form Norfolk Southern.

Norfolk & Western painted SD45 No. 1776 in a special scheme to celebrate the Bicentennial in 1976. Most N&W hood units had tall noses. *Jim Hediger*

Original road numbers	Second numbers	Qty.	Locomotive type	Builder	Dates built	Notes
10-13 (2), 14-49		40	T-6	Alco	1959	
10-13 (1)	710-713	4	GP9	EMD	1955	
50-71		22	H-20-44	F-M	1947-53	1
90-93		4	H-16-44	F-M	1956-57	1
110-149		40	H-16-44	F-M	1954-57	2
150-174		25	H-24-66	F-M	1954-57	2
200-239		40	GP35	EMD	1963-64	
300-307		8	RS-3	Alco	1955-56	
308-406		99	RS-11	Alco	1956-61	
407-412		6	RS-36	Alco	1962	
413-420		8	C-420	Alco	1964	
500-521, 620-699, 714-761, 768-914		297	GP9	EMD	1957-59	3
522-565		44	GP30	EMD	1962	
915-962		48	GP18	EMD	1959-61	
1000-1016		17	C-425	Alco	1964-65	
1100-1129		30	C-628	Alco	1965-66	
1130-1139		10	C-630	Alco	1966-67	4
1300-1328		29	GP35	EMD	1964-65	

Original road numbers	Second numbers	Qty.	Locomotive type	Builder	Dates built	Notes
1329-1388		60	GP40	EMD	1966-67	
1500-1579		80	SD35	EMD	1965	
1580-1624		45	SD40	EMD	1966, 1971	
1625-1652		28	SD40-2	EMD	1973	
1700-1833		134	SD45	EMD	1966, 1970	
1900-1929		30	U28B	GE	1966	
1930-1964		35	U30B	GE	1967	
2011-2022		12	NW2	EMD	1947-48	5
2025-2045		21	S-2	Alco	1947-50	5
2046-2061, 2065-2083		35	S-4	Alco	1951-53	5
2085		1	S-1	Alco	1950	5
2105, 2106		2	SW1	EMD	1950	5
2107-2114		8	SW8	EMD	1952	5
2125-2133, 2139-2145		16	H-10-44	F-M	1949, 1957	5
2134-2138, 2146-2155		15	H-12-44	F-M	1953, 1958	5
2230-2232		3	SW7	EMD	1950	5
2233-2244		12	SW9	EMD	1951-52	5
2320-2323	7902, 7903	4	AS-16	Baldwin	1953-54	5, 6
2325-2333	250-258	9	RSD-12	Alco	1957	5
2340-2359		20	SD9	EMD	1957	5
2400-2447		48	GP7	EMD	1951-53	5
2448-2534		87	GP9	EMD	1955-59	5
2535-2557		23	RS-3	Alco	1954	5
2558-2577		20	RS-11	Alco	1956-60	5
2578		1	C-420	Alco	1964	5
2700-2709		10	GP18	EMD	1960	5
2800-2814		15	GP9	EMD	1959	5
2850-2864		15	RS-11	Alco	1959	5
2865-2875		11	RS-36	Alco	1962	5
2900-2909		10	GP30	EMD	1962	5
2910-2918		19	GP35	EMD	1964	5
3109, 3110		2	SW1	EMD	1949	7
3120-3132		13	SW8	EMD	1950-53	7
3320, 3321		2	S-2	Alco	1949	7
3322-3324		3	S-4	Alco	1953	7
3346-3352		7	NW2	EMD	1941-49	7
3355-3362		8	SW7	EMD	1950	7
3363-3374		12	SW9	EMD	1952-53	7
3375-3379		5	SW1200	EMD	1954, 1957	7
3380-3383		4	H-10-44	F-M	1946, 1949	7
3384-3386		3	H-12-44	F-M	1953	7
3450-3483		34	GP7	EMD	1950-53	7
3484-3495		12	GP9	EMD	1954, 1956	7
3515-3529	8138-8151	15	U25B	GE	1962, 1965	7
3540-3547		8	GP35	EMD	1964	7
3592-3599		8	H-24-66	F-M	1954, 1956	7
3606, 3608		2	F7B	EMD	1949-50	7
3611..3726		103	F7A	EMD, GMD	1951-53	7
3800..3815		14	E8A	EMD	1949-53	7
3900-3906	421-425	7	C-424	Alco	1964	7
4100-4159		60	GP38AC	EMD	1971	

Original road numbers	Second numbers	Qty.	Locomotive type	Builder	Dates built	Notes
5000-5003		4	GP9r	EMD	1955-56	
6073-6207		135	SD40-2	EMD	1975-80	
6500-6505		6	SD50	EMD	1980	
8000-8002		3	U30C	GE	1974	
8003-8082		80	C30-7	GE	1978-79	
8465-8539		75	U30B	GE	1970-71	
8500-8542		43	C36-7	GE	1981, 1984	

Notes:
1 – Ex-Pittsburgh & West Virginia.
2—Former Virginian Ry., acquired with merger in 1959.
3—Nos. 500-505 were delivered as 762-767 but quickly renumbered.
4—Nos. 1135-1139 ride on trucks from traded-in H-24-66s.
5—Former Nickel Plate Road, acquired with merger in 1964.
6—Nos. 2320, 2321 re-engined and rebuilt by Alco and 2322, 2323 by EMD in 1957.
7—Former Wabash locomotives, acquired 1964 when Wabash was leased to N&W.

Published rosters:
Extra 2200 South, January 1968; Norfolk & Western First Generation Diesels, by Paul K. Withers and Robert G. Bowers (Withers Publishing, 1990); Norfolk & Western Second Generation Diesels, by Paul K. Withers and Robert G. Bowers (Withers Publishing, 1989)

Norfolk Southern
1946-1974

The original Norfolk Southern was a loyal Baldwin customer, dieselizing with several types of switchers and road switchers from 1946 through the mid-1950s. When Baldwin left the locomotive business, the railroad turned to EMD in the 1960s for GP18s and GP38s. The NS was purchased by the Southern Ry. in 1974; the Norfolk Southern name would be resurrected in 1982 when Southern merged with Norfolk & Western.

Road Numbers	Qty.	Model	Builder	Dates built	Notes
1-17	17	GP18	EMD	1963	
661-663	3	DS-4-4-66	Baldwin	1946-47	
701-703	3	70-tonner	GE	1948	
1001, 1002	2	DS-4-4-10	Baldwin	1946	
1501-1510	10	DRS-6-4-15	Baldwin	1947-48	
1601-1617	17	AS-416	Baldwin	1951-55	
2001-2007	7	GP38	EMD	1966-67	

Published roster:
Diesel Era, November/December 1998

Norfolk Southern
Current

This Norfolk Southern roster is current as of early 2017.

A GE Dash 9-40CW leads a Norfolk Southern freight.
Kermit Geary, Jr.

Initial	Number series	Model	Builder	Dates
NS	98-99	RCP4	EMD	R2009
NS	100-103	RP20BD	Railpower	2007-2011
NS	130-141	PR43C	Progress Rail	2008-2012
NS	525-566	B32-8	GE	1989
NS	600-601	GPTEB	EMD	R2011
NS	610-649	RP-M4C	EMD	R2013
NS	700-753	RP-E4C	EMD	R2009-2011
NS	799	CNG Tender	NS	2014
NS	850-869	RPU6	ALCO	1978-1979
NS	870-888	RPU6	EMD	R2007
NS	911	SD60E	EMD	2015
NS	912-913	RP-E4	EMD	1983
NS	914-941	RP-E4D	EMD	1984-1988
NS	944	RP-E4U	EMD	1976
NS	952-962	RP-E4U	EMD	1983-1990
NS	999	BP4	Brookville	2009
NS	1000-1174	SD70ACe	EMD	2011-2014
NS	1625-1652	SD40-2	EMD	1973-1974
NS	1700-1705	SD45-2	EMD	1972
NS	2100-2105	SW1001	EMD	1973
NS	2120-2121	RP14BD	Railpower	R2008
NS	2350-2432	MP15DC/MP15E	EMD	1977-1982
NS	2423	MP21E	EMD	R2011
NS	2501-2580	SD70	EMD	1993-1994
NS	2581-2648	SD70M	EMD	2000-2003
NS	2649-2778	SD70M-2	EMD	2005-2006
NS	2797-2799	SD70M	EMD	1994
NS	2800-2806	SD75M	EMD	1995
NS	2835	GP38AC	EMD	1971
NS	3000-3102	GP40-2	EMD	1973-1980
NS	3201-3584	SD40-2	EMD	1972-1979
NS	3830	RP20CD	Railpower	2008
NS	4000-4001	AC44C6M	GE	2015
NS	4148, 4150	GP38AC	EMD	1971
NS	4270-4271	F9A	EMD	1952
NS	4275-4276	F7B	EMD	1950
NS	4609-4641	GP59	EMD	1985-1989
NS	4650-4661	GP59E	EMD	R2013
NS	4700-4729	GP33ECO	EMD	R2014
NS	5001-5360	GP38-2	EMD	1972-1979
NS	5601-5673	GP38-3	EMD	R2005-2006
NS	5801-5837	GP38-3	EMD	R2005-2006
NS	5900-5901	GP22ECO	EMD	R2011
NS	6073-6206	SD40-2	EMD	1975-1980
NS	6300-6357	SD40E	EMD	R2008-2013
NS	6514-6716	SD60	EMD	1984-1991
NS	6717-6762	SD60I	EMD	1994-1995
NS	6763-6815	SD60M	EMD	1992-1993
NS	6900-7018	SD60E	EMD	R2010-2013
NS	7036-7083	GP50	EMD	1980-1981
NS	7100-7150	GP60	EMD	1991-1992

Initial	Number series	Model	Builder	Dates
NS	7200-7228	SD80MAC	EMD	1995-1996
NS	7229-7328	SD90MAC/SD70ACU	EMD	1995-2015
NS	7500-7719	ES44DC	GE	2004-2008
NS	8000-8165	ES44AC	GE	2008-2013
NS	8300-8313	C40-8	GE	1989
NS	8314-8467	C40-8W	GE	1990-1995
NS	8500 8513	C40-8.5	GE	2014
NS	8689-8763	C40-8	GE	1990-1992
NS	8764-8888	C44-9	GE	1995
NS	8889-9978	C44-9W	GE	1996-2004

Northern Pacific
1930-1970

The Northern Pacific dabbled in switchers from all the major builders, then settled mainly on EMD F units and Geeps for mainline freight power into the 1960s. When it came time to replace early units, NP went to six-axle power from both GE (U25Cs, U28Cs, U33Cs) and EMD (SD45s).

The NP was among major railroads that chose F units over E units for passenger service. The railroad's F unit numbering is complex. Freight Fs were numbered in the 5400, 6000, and 7000 series; passenger units were 6500s, 6600s, and 6700s. Confusion comes in as the railroad broke up its original A-B-B passenger sets, turning them into A-B-A sets by buying new A units and renumbering the original B units. The railroad then renumbered and reassigned many Fs from passenger to freight service (and sometimes back again), with some engines wearing four numbers. The roster that follows is a summary; for a complete unit-by-unit list, see *Northern Pacific Diesel Era* by Schrenk and Frey.

The roster covers the NP's diesels until the railroad merged with the Chicago, Burlington & Quincy, Great Northern, and Spokane, Portland & Seattle to form Burlington Northern on March 2, 1970.

Northern Pacific was the largest owner of GE U25Cs, with 30 locomotives. *Northern Pacific*

Original road numbers	Second numbers	Third numbers	Qty.	Model	Builder	Dates built	Notes
98, 99 (1)			2	44-tonner	GE	1943, 1946	
99 (2), 101-106			7	NW2	EMD	1940-48	1
100			1	NW	EMC	1938	
107, 108 (1), 113-118 (1), 150-152 (1)	700-710		11	S-2	Alco	1941-44	

Original road numbers	Second numbers	Third numbers	Qty.	Model	Builder	Dates built	Notes
107-114 (2)			8	SW7	EMD	1949	
109-112 (1), 119-124 (1), 153, 154 (1), 159-174 (1)	400-427		28	VO1000	Baldwin	1941-45	
115-118 (2)			4	SW9	EMD	1952-53	
125-127 (1)	600-602		3	HH660	Alco	1940	
128-130 (1)	650-652		3	VO660	Baldwin	1940, 1942	
131 (1)	603		1	S-1	Alco	1945	
119-131 (2), 132-149, 150-177 (2)			59	SW1200	EMD	1955-58	
155-158 (1)	800-803		4	RS-1	Alco	1945	
175, 176 (1)	500, 501		2	DRS-4-4-15	Baldwin	1948	2
177	525		1	DRS-6-6-15	Baldwin	1948	2
200-375			176	GP9	EMD	1954-58	
376-384			9	GP18	EMD	1960	
550-569			20	GP7	EMD	1950-53	3
711, 712			2	S-2	Alco	1949	
713-724			12	S-4	Alco	1951, 1953	
750			1	S-6	Alco	1955	
850-863			14	RS-3	Alco	1953, 1955	
900-917			18	RS-11	Alco	1958, 1960	
2500-2529			30	U25C	GE	1964-65	
2800-2811			12	U28C	GE	1966	
3300-3309			10	U33C	GE	1969	
3600-3629			30	SD45	EMD	1966-68	
6000A-6010A, 6000D-6010D (1)	5400A, D-5410A, D		22	FTA	EMD	1944-45	
6000B, C-6010B, C (1)	5400B, C-5410B, C		22	FTB	EMD	1944-45	
6011A-6017A, 6011D-6017D (1)	6000A, D-6006A, D (2)	6051A, 6052A	14	F3A	EMD	1947-48	4
6011B-6017B (1), 6011C-6017C (1)	6000B-6006B (2), 6000C-6006C (2)		14	F3B	EMD	1947	4
6007A-6017A (2), 6007D-6017D (2)			22	F7A	EMD	1950-51	
6007B-6017B (2), 6007C-6017C (2)			22	F7B	EMD	1950-51	
6018A-6020A, 6018D-6018D			6	F7A	EMD	1951	
6018B-6020B, 6018C-6018C, 6050B			7	F7B	EMD	1951	
6500A-6506A			7	F3A	EMD	1947	5
6500B-6506B, 6500C-6506C (1)	6016B, C, 6017B, C (1)	6005C, 6006B, C; then 6551B, 6552B	14	F3B	EMD	1947	4, 5
6500C-6502C (2)			3	F7A	EMD	1949	4, 5
6503C-6506C (2)			4	F3A	EMD	1948	4, 5
6507A-6513A, 6507C-6513C			14	F7A	EMD	1949-50	4, 5
6510B-6513B, 6550B			5	F7B	EMD	1949-52	4, 5
6600A, 6601A			2	FP7	EMD	1952	
6700A-6704A, 6700C (1), 6701C			7	F9A	EMD	1954-56	4, 5
6700B, 6701B			2	F9B	EMD	1956	5
7000A-7014A, 7000D-7014D			30	F9A	EMD	1954-56	4
7000B-7014B, 7000C-7014C			30	F9B	EMD	1954-56	4

Notes:
Most renumbering was done in 1950.
1—No. 99 (2) is ex-New York, Ontario & Western 115, acquired 1957.
2—Re-engined by EMD.
3—Nos. 550-563 originally steam-generator equipped.
4—Several F units were renumbered and/or converted from passenger to freight engines multiple times around 1950 and again around 1960 (some had four numbers). For a complete unit-by-unit summary, see Northern Pacific Diesel Era by Schrenk and Frey.
5—Steam-generator equipped.

Published rosters:
Extra 2200 South, March 1968; Northern Pacific Diesel Era, by Lorenz P. Schrenk and Robert L. Frey (Golden West Books, 1988)

Pan Am
2006-present

Pan Am Railways is the renamed version of Guilford Transportation, which started out in 1981 as a holding company for several New England railroads, including Maine Central, Portland Terminal, Springfield Terminal, and Boston & Maine. Delaware & Hudson was owned by Guilford from 1984-1991. Although the railroads still exist individually, Pan Am locomotives wear a common scheme with sublettering indicating specific railroad ownership. This roster indicates latest ownership; previous owners are not indicated.

Road numbers	Qty.	Model	Builder	Dates built	Notes
1, 2 (PAR)	2	FP9	GMD	1954	
007 (PAR)	1	SW1	EMD	1948	
12, 15, 25 (ST)	3	GP7r	EMD	1950, 1953	
45, 51, 52, 54, 62, 71, 72, 77 (ST)	8	GP9	EMD	1957	
200-216 (ST)	17	GP35	EMD	1963-65	
300-310 (MEC), 312-321 (MEC), 326-328 (BM), 330-342 (BM), 343-354 (MEC), 370-382 (MEC)	62	GP40	EMD	1965-69	
500-519 (MEC)	20	GP40-2LW	GMD	1974-76	
600-619 (MEC)	20	SD40-3, SD40-2, SD40M-2	EMD	1969-74	1
621, 643 (ST)	2	SD26	EMD	1959-60	2
681 (ST)	1	SD45	EMD	1970	
690 (BM)	1	SD39	EMD	1969	
3400-3404, 3468, 3470, 3471, 3474, 3476, 3482, 3489, 3491 (MEC)	13	SD40-2	EMD, GMD	1972-80	

Railroad Key: BM—Boston & Maine; MEC—Maine Central; PAR—Pan Am Railways; ST—Springfield Terminal

Notes:
1—This series includes a mix of original SD40-2s and older SD40s and SD45s that have been rebuilt.
2—Rebuilt ex-Santa Fe SD24s (Santa Fe designation).

Pennsylvania
1928-1968

Into the 1960s the Pennsylvania was the country's largest railroad, with the biggest diesel roster—more than 3,000 locomotives. The railroad was late to dieselize, building and acquiring steam locomotives until the late 1940s (and keeping some steam in service through 1957). However, once the Pennsylvania began buying diesels it did so quickly and in large numbers. The railroad was known for sampling locomotives from all builders, creating a diverse mix of early diesel power.

Instead of grouping locomotives by numbers by locomotive type and class, the Pennsy tended to number its locomotives in sequence as they were ordered—meaning locomotives of various types are intermixed. In 1966, the PRR and New York Central renumbered most locomotives for their pending merger. These numbers are listed in the chart, but be aware that renumbering was not always done in sequence, and there are many gaps in the new number groups. For a unit-by-unit summary, see *Pennsy Diesels* by Douglas and Weiglin.

The Pennsy merged with longtime rival NYC in February 1968 to form Penn Central.

Original road numbers	1966 (pre-PC) renumbering	Qty.	Model	Builder	Dates built	Notes
2000A-2027A		28	RF-16	Baldwin	1951-52	
2000B-2026B (even)		14	RF-16B	Baldwin	1951-52	
2200-2251	..2198, 2199	52	GP30	EMD	1963	
2252-2370	..5657-5660..2309-2310	119	GP35	EMD	1963-65	
2400-2414		15	RS-27	Alco	1962	
2415		1	C-424	Alco	1963	
2416-2446		31	C-425	Alco	1964-65	
2500-2548, 2649-2658	2600-2648..	59	U25B	GE	1962-65	
3905-3907		3	A6, A6b	PRR	1928-30	1
4041..4048		6	RS-3	Alco	1950	2
5550-5590	7950..7990	41	DS-4-4-10	Baldwin	1950	
5591-5594	8051-8053	4	DRS-4-4-10	Baldwin	1950	
5595-5618	7886..7911	24	DS-4-4-7.5	Baldwin	1950	
5619-5640	9919..9940	22	RS-1	Alco	1950	

The Pennsy owned 24 A-B sets of Baldwin DR-4-4-15 sharknose diesels. This one, from the last order, shared the body of the RF-16. *Don Wood*

Original road numbers	1966 (pre-PC) renumbering	Qty.	Model	Builder	Dates built	Notes
5641-5660	9785, 9802..9842	20	S-2	Alco	1950	
5661-5670	9461..9470	10	S-1	Alco	1950	
5671-5683		13	LT-2500	Lima	1950	
5700A-5716A, 5760A-5769A, 5788A-5810A, 5835A-5539A, 5884A-5899A, 5902A-5905A	4246..4319	75	E8A	EMD	1950-52	
5750A-5759A		10	PA-1	Alco	1947	
5750B-5758B (even)		5	PB-1	Alco	1947	
5770A-5787A		18	DR-6-4-20	Baldwin	1948	
5770B-5786B (even)		9	DR-6-4-20B	Baldwin	1948	
5811-5834		24	DR-12-8-30	Baldwin	1947-48	
5840A-5883A, 5900A, 5901A	4200..4245	46	E7A	EMD	1947-49	
5840B-5864B, 5900B	4114-4127	14	E7B	EMD	1945-48	
5907-5909, 5932-5937, 5941-5943		12	VO660	Baldwin	1942, 1945	
5910, 5944-5953, 5987-5999	8510, 8544-8553, 8587-8599	24	SW1	EMD	1942-48	
5911	8511	1	SW	EMC	1937	3
5912, 5921-5925	8677, 8651-8654, 8678	6	NW2	EMD	1941-47	4
5913-5920		8	VO1000	Baldwin	1943, 1945	
5926-5931	9820-9821, 9826-9829	6	S-2	Alco	1948	
5954-5956	9454-9456	3	S-1	Alco	1947	
5957-5966	7858..7866	10	DS-4-4-66	Baldwin	1948	
5967-5979	7938..7947, 8038, 8039	13	DS-4-4-10	Baldwin	1948	
5980-5986	8211-8217	7	H-10-44	F-M	1948	
6000-6039		40	SD35	EMD	1965	

Original road numbers	1966 (pre-PC) renumbering	Qty.	Model	Builder	Dates built	Notes
6040-6104		65	SD40	EMD	1966	
6105-6234		130	SD45	EMD	1966-68	
6300-6314		15	C-628	Alco	1965	
6315-6329		15	C-630	Alco	1966	
6500-6519		20	U25C	GE	1965	
6520-6534		15	U28C	GE	1966	
6535-6539		5	U30C	GE	1967	
7000-7269		270	GP9	EMD	1955-59	
7175B-7204B, 7230B-7239B	3800-3839	40	GP9B	EMD	1957, 1959	
7600-7624	6900-6924	25	SD9	EMD	1957-58	
7900-7934	9050-9058, 9009-9034	35	SW1200	EMD	1957-58	
8100-8104	8134-8136, 8165, 8167	5	S-12	Baldwin	1954	
8105-8110	8085..8091	6	RS-12	Baldwin	1954	
8111, 8112, 8114	6975-6977	3	AS-616	Baldwin	1951-1954	5
8113	8966	1	RT-624	Baldwin	1954	
8424-8429	9844-9849	6	T-6	Alco	1958	
8430-8434, 8487-8499	9768-9777, 9815, 9822, 9823, 9830-9834	18	S-4	Alco	1952-54	
8435-8445, 8452-8484, 8590-8605, 8817-8856	5400..5470, 5537..5584	67	RS-3	Alco	1951-53	
8446-8451	6800-6805	6	RSD-5	Alco	1952-53	
8485, 8486	9914, 9915	2	RS-1	Alco	1952	
8500-8512, 8545-8587	5845-5850, 5852-5882, 5884-5892, 5950-5959,	56	GP7	EMD	1952-53	
8513-8544	9113-9141, 9042-9044	32	SW9	EMD	1952-53	
8588, 8589	6950, 6951	2	SD7	EMD	1953	
8606-8610	6806-6810	5	RSD-7	Alco	1955-56	
8611-8616	6811-6816	6	RSD-15	Alco	1956	
8617-8654	7617-7654	38	RS-11	Alco	1956-57	
8655-8679	6855-6879	25	RSD-12	Alco	1957-58	
8699-8707	6700-6708	9	H-24-66	F-M	1956	
8708-8723	8327-8342	16	H-12-44	F-M	1952-54	
8724-8731		8	RT-624	Baldwin	1952	
8732-8775, 8777-8796, 8976-8993	8113..8199	82	S-12	Baldwin	1951-52	
8776, 8975	8084, 8086	2	RS-12	Baldwin	1951-52	
8797-8806	5840-5844, 5895-5899	10	GP7	EMD	1952	
8807-8816	5151..5158	10	H-16-44	F-M	1952	
8857, 8858	9917, 9918	2	RS-1	Alco	1951	
8859, 8860, 8869, 8870	9059, 9060, 9095, 9096	4	SW9	EMD	1951	
8862-8868, 8871, 8872	9061-9067, 9094..9098	9	SW7	FMD	1951	
8873-8885	9473-9485	13	S-3	Alco	1950-51	
8886-8901	9788-9801, 9803, 9817	16	S-4	Alco	1950-51	
8902-8916	5406-5409, 5414, 5557..5565	15	RS-3	Alco	1951	
8917-8942, 9300-9311	7700..7741	38	H-20-44	F-M	1951	
8952-8965		14	RT-624	Baldwin	1951	
8966-8974	6966..6974	9	AS-616	Baldwin	1951	
8994-8999	7896, 7898	6	S-8	Baldwin	1951	
9000-9049, 9110-9121, 9210-9236	7801..7882	62	DS-4-4-66	Baldwin	1948-49	
9050-9079, 9122-9136, 9177-9183, 9251-9275, 9429-9434	7914..8046	93	DS-4-4-10	Baldwin	1948-49	
9080-9099, 9184-9199, 9288-9299	8218.. 8261	48	H-10-44	F-M	1948-49	
9100-9103, 9237-9246	9437-9446, 9450-9453	14	S-1	Alco	1948-49	
9104, 9137-9154, 9200-9203, 9205-9209, 9396-9428	8501..8580	61	SW1	EMD	1949-50	

Original road numbers	1966 (pre-PC) renumbering	Qty.	Model	Builder	Dates built	Notes
9105-9109, 9204, 9278-9287	9778..9787, 9804-9809	16	S-2	Alco	1948-49	
9155-9176, 9247-9250	8647-8650, 8655-8676	26	NW2	EMD	1948	
9312-9357	9999	46	44-tonner	GE	1947-50	
9358-9395	9035..9049, 9068-9093	38	SW7	EMD	1950	
9448A-9455A, 9492A-9499A		16	CFA-16-4	F-M	1950	
9448B-9454B (even), 9492B-9298B (even)		8	CFB-16-4	F-M	1950	
9456A-9491A		36	Erie A	F-M	1947-48	
9456B-9478B (even)		12	Erie B	F-M	1947-48	
9500A-9561A, 9563A-9567A, 9677A-9689A	1402..1425	80	F3A	EMD	1947-48	
9500B-9528B, 9530B-9536B (even), 9540B-9546B, 9948B-9554B (even)	3501..3506	44	F3B	EMD	1947-49	6
9547B-9555B (even)	3508	5	F7B	EMD	1949	
9568A-9583A, 9700A-9707A		24	DR-4-4-15	Baldwin	1949-50	
9568B-9583B, 9700B-9707B		24	DR-4-4-15B	Baldwin	1949-50	
9594A-9599A, 9708A-9745A		44	RF-16	Baldwin	1951	
9594B-9496B (even), 9708B-9714B (even), 9728B-9744B (even)		16	RF-16B	Baldwin	1951	
9600A-9607A		8	FA-1	Alco	1948, 1950	
9600B-9607B		8	FB-1	Alco	1948, 1950	
9608A-9631A		24	FA-2	Alco	1951	
9608B-9630B (even)		12	FB-2	Alco	1951	
9632A, 9632B, 9633A		3	ABF-18		1959	7
9640A-9656A, 9661A-9676A, 9690A-9699A, 9764A-9831A, 9872A-9879A	1440..1538, 1905, 1906	119	F7A	EMD	1949-51	
9640B-9648B, 9650B-9654B (even), 9667B-9676B, 9764B-9818B (even), 9832B-9858B (even), 9872B-9878B (even)	3512..3563, 4150-4163,	64	F7B	EMD	1949-51	
9832A-9871A	4332-4371	40	FP7	EMD	1952	

Notes:
1—Home-built two-axle boxcab gas-electrics; nos. 3905, 3906 had Winton 400-hp gas engines; 3907 had a Brill-Westinghouse 535-hp engine and later a Hamilton 450-hp engine.
2—Ex-Delaware & Hudson, leased 1956, purchased 1958.
3—Originally no. 3908; renumbered 5911 in 1942; rebuilt and re-engined with an EMD 567 in 1956.
4—No. 5912 was originally no. 3909; renumbered in 1942.
5—No. 8114 is ex-Pittsburgh & West Virginia 40; leased in 1954, purchased in 1963.
6—Nos. 9530B-9536B (even) are ex-Bangor & Aroostook 600B-603B, acquired 1952.
7—Two Baldwin RF-16 A units and a DR-4-4-15 B unit rebuilt and re-engined by Alco in 1959.

Published rosters:
Pennsy Diesels, 1924-1968, by Kenneth L. Douglas and Peter C. Weiglin (Hundman Publications, 2002)

Pennsylvania-Reading Seashore Lines
1950-1976

The Pennsylvania-Reading Seashore Lines was co-owned by the Pennsylvania (two-thirds ownership) and Reading. The railroad was notable for dieselizing with Baldwin and maintaining an all-Baldwin roster until the arrival of EMD GP38s in 1967. Locomotives wore a simple dark green scheme, except for AS-16s 6011-6016, which were delivered in a lighter ("Ivy Green") color and nicknamed "Green Hornets." They were repainted dark green by the mid-1950s. The railroad was mainly a passenger line, with business dwindling through the 1960s. The PRSL became part of Conrail in 1976.

Road numbers	Qty.	Model	Builder	Dates built	Notes
2000-2009	10	GP38	EMD	1967, 1969	
6000-6005	6	DRS-4-4-1500	Baldwin	1950	1
6006	1	S-8	Baldwin	1951	
6007-6016, 6022-6027	16	AS-16	Baldwin	1953-56	1
6017-6021, 6028-6033	11	S-12	Baldwin	1953, 1956	

Notes:
1—Equipped with steam generators, except 6024, 6025.

Published rosters:
Diesel Locomotive Rosters (Wayner Publications); Extra 2200 South, September-October 1969

Pittsburgh & Lake Erie
1946-1992

The Pittsburgh & Lake Erie was a longtime New York Central subsidiary. When NYC successor Penn Central entered bankruptcy in 1970, the P&LE—which was then solvent—began operating independently, and eventually became its own entity. The railroad continued to operate through the 1980s, but the decline in the region's steel industry caused a sharp drop in business. The railroad ceased operations in 1992, with remaining routes acquired by a CSX subsidiary.

Through the 1960s, the railroad's locomotives followed the NYC's specifications, including fitting into NYC number series. Many P&LE diesels were later purchased by the NYC (see the NYC roster for details).

Original road numbers	Second numbers	Third numbers	Qty.	Model	Builder	Dates built	Notes
1534-1563			30	SW1500	EMD	1971-73	
1574-1598			25	MP15DC	EMD	1974-75	
2025-2041			17	GP38	EMD	1969	1
2051-2060			10	GP38-2	EMD	1977, 1976	2
2800-2821			22	U28B	GE	1966	
4204-4207			4	PA-1	Alco	1949	
4213, 4214			2	PA-2	Alco	1952	
5676-5685, 5713-5734	1503..1533		32	GP7	EMD	1951-53	3
5735-5737	5928-5930	1500-1502	3	GP7	EMD	1953	3
8537-8549			13	S-2	Alco	1948-49	
8633-8667			35	S-4	Alco	1953	
8705-8714, 8740-8749			20	NW2	EMD	1947, 1949	
8800, 8801, 8902, 8903	9100-9103		4	H-10-44	F-M	1946, 1948	4
8931-8940, 8952-8961			20	SW9	EMD	1951-52	
8353-8357	5353-5357		5	RS-3	Alco	1953	
9280-9289	1564-1573		10	SW1500	EMD	1971	3

Notes:
1—Ex-Conrail, nee Penn Central.
2—Nos. 2057-2060 are ex-Rock Island 4352-4355.
3—Renumbered in reverse order (9280 became 1573, etc.).
4—Nos. 8800, 8801 briefly renumbered 8900, 8901 in 1948; renumbered 9100, 9101 in 1949.

Published roster:
Diesel Locomotive Rosters (Wayner Publications)

Providence & Worcester
1973-2016

The Providence & Worcester dates to the 1800s, but had been leased by the New York, New Haven & Hartford since 1892. Shortly after the New Haven was merged into Penn Central in 1969, the P&W petitioned the Interstate Commerce Commission to be discharged from the lease and resume operations on its own. The ICC granted the request in late 1972; the lease was terminated and the P&W began operating independently in February 1973.

The P&W operated with many second-hand locomotives, mainly Alco in its early days and GE from the late 1970s onward, along with GP38-2s and MLW M-420Rs acquired new. The roster lists the most recent owner (for used diesels) and the date acquired by P&W (if known). The P&W was purchased by holding company Genessee & Wyoming in 2016.

P&W road numbers	Previous owner and numbers (date acquired)	Qty.	Model	Builder	Dates built	Notes
8	MV 8	1	50-tonner	GE	1950	
101	Warwick 101 (1984)	1	40-ton	GE	1924	
104	Warwick 104 (1984)	1	50-ton	Atlas	1940	
106	MV 9 (1984)	1	65-ton	GE	1943	
120	CCC 1201 (1997)	1	RS-3m	Alco	1951	1
150, 151	NHT (1992-93)	2	25-ton	GE	1945	
161-165	D&H (1973)	5	RS-3	Alco	1952	
668	Amtrak 456	1	E9B	EMD	1954	2
1201, 1202	CR 8845, 8851 (1991)	2	SW7	EMD	1950	3

P&W road numbers	Previous owner and numbers (date acquired)	Qty.	Model	Builder	Dates built	Notes
1501, 1601	MEC, SOU (1976-77)	2	RS-2	Alco	1949, 1951	
1602	SOU 2141 (1976)	1	RS-3	Alco	1951	
1701, 1702	CR 7189, 7205	2	GP9	EMD	1982	4
1801		1	U18B	GE	1976	
1802	CCC 53	1	GP9e	EMD	1954	5
2001-2005		5	M-420R	MLW	1974-75	
2006-2009		4	GP38-2	EMD	1980, 1982	
2010, 2011	CR 7808, 7794	2	GP38	EMD	1969	6
2201		1	B23-7	GE	1978	
2202-2211	CR, L&N (1993-95)	10	U23B	GE	1974-77	
2212-2214	L&N (1995)	3	B23-7	GE	1978	
2215, 2216	UP 531, 525 (1998)	2	B23-S7R	GE	1972	7
3001-3003	GRR (1999)	3	GP40	EMD	1966-71	8
3004-3008	BN (2001)	5	B30-7A	GE	1982	
3901-3909	LMX (2002-03)	9	B39-8E	GE	1987-88	
4001-4004	NYS&W (2004)	4	Dash 8-40B	GE	1988	
4005, 4006	BNSF 561, 562	3	Dash 8-40BW	GE	1992	9
4301, 4302	FEC 100, 102	2	SD70M-2	EMD	2006	

Road name key:
BNSF (Burlington Northern Santa Fe), CCC (Cape Cod Central), CR (Conrail), GRR (Georgetown Railroad), L&N (Louisville & Nashville/Seaboard System), LMX (LMX Leasing), MEC (Maine Central), MV (Moshassuck Valley), NHT (New Haven Terminal), NYS&W (New York, Susquehanna & Western), SOU (Southern), UP (Union Pacific)

Notes:
1—Nee New York Central 8246 (later 5246); rebuilt.
2—Nee Union Pacific 952B.
3—Nee NYC 8845, 8851.
4—Nee Pennsylvania 7189, 7205.
5—Nee Texas & New Orleans 283; rebuilt.
6—Nee Penn Central.
7—Nee Western Pacific; rebuilt to Dash 7 standards.
8—Nee Baltimore & Ohio 4021, Seaboard Air Line 617, Seaboard Coast Line 1571.
9—Nee Santa Fe.

Published roster:
Diesel Era, March/April 2005

Reading
1926-1976

The Reading acquired diesel switchers early, followed by EMD FTs in 1945, but it wasn't until the arrival of EMD GP7s, Alco RS-3s, and Baldwin AS-16s in the early 1950s that steam began to give way. Dieselization was finally complete in 1956. The railroad continued placing orders with all major builders through the 1960s. Reading became part of Conrail in 1976.

Reading No. 302 is an Alco FA-2/FB-2 set built in 1948. *Trains magazine collection*

Original road numbers	Second numbers	Qty.	Model	Builder	Dates built	Notes
10-15		6	SW	EMC	1937	
16-24		9	SW1	EMD	1939-41	
26-39		14	DS-4-4-10	Baldwin	1946-47	
40, 41		2	HH900	Alco	1937	
42-47		6	S-2	Alco	1946-47	
50-54		5	S-1	Alco	1940-41	
55-59		5	VO1000	Baldwin	1944	
60-70		11	VO660	Baldwin	1940-42	
71-89		19	VO1000	Baldwin	1943-44	
90-92		3	NW2	EMD	1940-41	
97		1	Center-cab	F-M/St. L	1939	1
98, 99		2	Boxcab	GE/I-R	1926, 1928	2
100-104		5	NW2	EMD	1947	
250A-259A		10	FTA	EMD	1945	
250B-259B		10	FTB	EMD	1945	
260A-265A		6	F3A	EMD	1946	
260B-265B		6	F3B	EMD	1948	
266A-283A		18	F7A	EMD	1950	
266B-271B		6	F7B	EMD	1950	
300A-305A		6	FA-2	Alco	1948	
300B-305B		6	FB-2	Alco	1948	
444-450, 460-475, 481-524		67	RS-3	Alco	1951-53	
530-554, 560-563, 576-589		43	AS-16	Baldwin	1951-53	
600-636, 660-666		44	GP7	EMD	1952-53	
700-729		30	DS-4-4-10	Baldwin	1948-49	
800-808, 860-867	201-203, 260-265	17	H-24-66	F-M	1953-56	3
900-907		8	FP7	EMD	1950, 1952	
1501-1515		15	SW900	EMD	1961, 1963	
1516-1521		6	SW900m	EMD	1970-71	4
2601-2625		25	SW1001	EMD	1973	
2701-2719		19	SW1200	EMD	1959, 1963	5
2750-2770		21	SW1500	EMD	1966, 1969	
2771-2780		10	MP15DC	EMD	1974	
3401-3420		20	GP39-2	EMD	1974	
3626-3656		31	GP35	EMD	1964	
3671-3675		5	GP40-2	EMD	1973	
5201-5210		10	C-424	Alco	1963	
5211-5212		2	C-430	Alco	1966	
5300-5311		12	C-630	Alco	1967	
5501-5520	3600-3619	20	GP30	EMD	1962	6
6300-6304		5	U30C	GE	1967	
6501-6506	3620-3625	6	GP35	EMD	1963	6
7600-7604		5	SD45	EMD	1967	

Notes:
1—*Originally no. 35, renumbered in 1940. Built by St. Louis Car Co., powered by Fairbanks-Morse.*
2—*Originally nos. 50, 51; oil-electric boxcab, 300 hp, built by Alco/GE/Ingersoll-Rand.*
3—*Nos. 801, 806, 808, 860, 862-865, 867 renumbered 201-203, 260-265 in 1967.*
4—*Rebuilt from SW nos. 10-15.*
5—*Nos. 2701-2714 rebuilt from VO1000s, 1959.*
6—*Renumbered in 1964.*

Published roster:
Diesel Locomotive Rosters (Wayner Publications)

Richmond, Fredericksburg & Potomac
1942-1991

Number 1001 is one of 15 EMD E8 passenger diesels on the roster. *EMD*

The Richmond, Fredericksburg & Potomac bought a large group of Alco S-2 switchers starting in 1942, then followed with EMD E and F units for passenger and freight service starting in 1948. The last steam was retired in 1954. Modern power included EMD SW1200 and SW1500 switchers and GP35 and GP40 road switchers in the 1960s. The RF&P was absorbed by CSX in 1991.

Original road numbers	Second numbers	No.	Model	Builder	Dates built	Notes
1 (1)		1	S-2	Alco	1944	
1-8		8	SW1500	EMD	1967	
50		1	SW1	EMC	1939	1
51-71		21	S-2	Alco	1942-48	2
81-85		5	SW1200	EMD	1965	
91		1	SW1500	EMD	1966	
101-104		4	GP7	EMD	1950, 1953	
111-118	131-138	8	GP35	EMD	1965	3
121-127		7	GP40	EMD	1966-67	
141-147		7	GP40-2	EMD	1972	
1001-1015		15	E8A	EMD	1949-53	
1051-1055		5	E8B	EMD	1949	
1101-1110		10	F7A	EMD	1949-50	
1111		1	F3A	EMD	1948	4
1151-1160		10	F7B	EMD	1949-50	
1201-1203		3	FP7	EMD	1950	

Notes:
1—Ex-Atlantic Coast Line 1901, acquired in 1944.
2—Nos. 62, 70, 71 rebuilt to slug units A, B, and C in 1967.
3—Renumbered in 1969.
4—Former Aberdeen & Rockfish 201, acquired in 1952.

Published rosters:
Diesel Era, September-October 1999; Extra 2200 South September-October 1969

Rutland
1951-1961

The Rutland dieselized rapidly with Alco RS-1s and RS-3s in 1951 and 1952, and they—along with a GE 70-tonner—remained the railroad's only diesels until 1961. In that year, a strike effectively ended service, and when management and workers couldn't work out a compromise, the railroad was abandoned (although portions were later operated by other railroads).

Road numbers	Qty.	Model	Builder	Dates built	Notes
200-208	9	RS-3	Alco	1951-52	1
400-405	6	RS-1	Alco	1951	
500	1	70-tonner	GE	1951	

Notes:
1—No. 200 is former Alco demonstrator 1601.

Published roster:
Diesel Locomotive Rosters (Wayner Publications)

St. Louis-San Francisco
1941-1980

The Frisco began dieselizing in 1941 with switchers from several builders. Its first road diesels were Alco RS-1s, followed by EMD Es, Fs, and GP7s. The railroad was dieselized in 1952. The railroad dabbled with Alco, but stayed primarily with EMD except for a few orders of GE U-Boats. The Frisco stuck with four-axle freight power except for SD45s and a handful of SD40-2s. The Frisco was merged into the Burlington Northern on November 21, 1980; its GP50s were actually delivered to BN after the merger.

The Frisco was GE's first customer for the U25B. *Louis A. Marre collection*

Road numbers	Qty.	Model	Builder	Dates built	Notes
1-2	2	44-ton	Davenport	1942	
3	1	44-ton	Whitcomb	1943	
4-8	5	44-tonner	GE	1943	1
10	1	SW1	EMD	1941	2
11	1	45-tonner	GE	1941	3
12	1	70-tonner	GE	1950	4
60-61	2	VO660	Baldwin	1942	
100-111 (1)	12	RS-1	Alco	1944-47	5
100-111 (2), 112-124	25	GP15-1	EMD	1977	
200-237	38	VO1000	Baldwin	1941-46	6
238-241	4	DS-4-4-10	Baldwin	1948	
250-265	16	NW2	EMD	1948-49	
270-281, 286	13	H-10-44	F-M	1948-49	
282-285	4	H-12-44	F-M	1951, 1948	7
290-295, 296-298 (1)	5	S-2	Alco	1948-49	8
296-298 (2), 299	4	SD38-2	EMD	1979	
300-304	5	SW7	EMD	1950-51	
305-314	10	SW9	EMD	1952	
315-360	46	SW1500	EMD	1968-73	
361-365	5	MP15DC	EMD	1975	
400-478	79	GP38-2	EMD	1973-76	
500-549, 555-632	128	GP7	EMD	1950-52	9
550-554	5	RS-2	Alco	1949	10
633-662	30	GP38AC	EMD	1971	
663-699	37	GP38-2	EMD	1972	
700-732	33	GP35	EMD	1964-65	
750-774	25	GP40-2	EMD	1979	
790-799	10	GP50	EMD	1980	
800-831	32	U25B	GE	1961-66	11, 12
832-862	31	U30B	GE	1968-75	
863-870	8	B30-7	GE	1977-78	
900-948	49	SD45	EMD	1967-71	
950-957	8	SD40-2	EMD	1972	
2000-2005	6	E7A	EMD	1947	
2006-2022	17	E8A	EMD	1950	
5000-5017	18	F3A	EMD	1948	
5018-5039	22	F7A	EMD	1949-50	

Road numbers	Qty.	Model	Builder	Dates built	Notes
5040-5051	12	FP7	EMD	1950-51	
5100-5117	18	F3B	EMD	1948	
5118-5139	22	F7B	EMD	1949-50	
5140-5152	13	F9B	EMD	1954, 1957	
5200-5231	32	FA-1	Alco	1948-49	13
5300-5315	16	FB-1	Alco	1948-49	13

Notes:
1—Nos. 6, 8 are ex-Kansas City, Memphis & Birmingham, acquired 1947.
2—Ex-Burlington Northern 77, nee Great Northern 5103, acquired 1979.
3—Ex-Alabama, Tennessee & Northern 11, acquired 1948.
4—Ex-Okmulgee Northern, acquired 1964.
5—Ex-AT&N 100-111, acquired 1948.
6—Nos. 200-206, 210, 215 re-engined by EMD.
7—No. 286 is ex-Denver, Rio Grande & Western 122.
8—Nos. 295-298 are ex-Northeast Oklahoma 703-706, acquired 1964.
9—Nos. 500-514, 557-572, 598-618 steam-generator equipped.
10—Re-engined by EMD.
11—Nos. 804-807 are former GE demonstrators 753-756; 812-815 are former GE demonstrators 51-54.
12—Nos. 812, 813 are former GE demonstrators 51, 54.
13—FA-1s 5200-5209, 5211-5213, 5215-5219 and FB-1s 5300-5311 repowered by EMD.

Published rosters:
Diesel Locomotive Rosters (Wayner Publications); Frisco Diesel Power, by Louis A. Marre and John Baskin Harper

St. Louis Southwestern (Cotton Belt)
1942-1996

The St. Louis Southwestern, better known as the Cotton Belt Route, was Southern Pacific's principal subsidiary. Its diesel locomotives were painted in the railroad's own scheme in the 1940s, but after 1949 they wore SP colors with "Cotton Belt" lettering. They were numbered in sequences to match SP locomotives.

The SSW acquired diesel switchers in the early 1940s, followed by EMD FTs for mainline freight service. The railroad was completely dieselized in 1953. Like parent SP, the Cotton Belt ran freights behind F units, then transitioned to high-horsepower EMD four- and six-axle diesels from the late 1960s onward. The SSW was a major owner of EMD GP60s and SD45s. Cotton Belt was included with parent SP's merger into Union Pacific in September 1996.

Cotton Belt ordered 20 of EMD's first turbocharged four-axle diesel, the GP20.
EMD

Original road numbers	Second numbers (1965 unless noted)	Qty.	Model	Builder	Dates built	Notes
260		1	DT-6-6-20	Baldwin	1948	
270-272	2888-2890	2	RSD-5	Alco	1953	
300, 301		2	PA-1	Alco	1949	
304		1	GP7	EMD	1950	1
306		1	FP7	EMD	1950	
308-311, 313, 314, 350-360	2800-2816	17	RS-3	Alco	1951-52	2
750-759	5000-5009	10	GP30	EMD	1963	
760-781	6500-6519, 6680, 6681	22	GP35	EMD	1964-65	
800-819	4030-4049	20	GP20	EMD	1960-62	
820-831	3641-3652	12	GP9	EMD	1957, 1959	
850-859	5150-5159	10	RSD-15	Alco	1960	
901, 903, 907-913 (odd), 917-923 (odd)		10	FTA	EMD	1944-45	
902-908 (even), 912-918 (even), 922, 924		10	FTB	EMD	1944-45	
925-975 (odd)		26	F7A	EMD	1950-52	
926-958 (even)		17	F7B	EMD	1950-52	
1000-1022	1850	23	VO1000	Baldwin	1942-45	
1023-1027	1851..1854	5	DS-4-4-10	Baldwin	1947	
1050-1053	1900-1903	4	NW2	EMD	1949	
1054-1057	2200-2203	4	SW7	EMD	1950	
1058-1061	2204-2207	4	SW9	EMD	1951	
1062-1073, 2289-2293	2250-2261	17	SW1200	EMD	1964-66	
2481-2492, 2511-2522		24	SW1500	EMD	1968, 1969	
3808-3813, 3871-3874		10	GP9e	EMD	1957, 1959	3
4200-4203		4	GP35R	EMD	1964-65	4
6869-6892		24	SD45T-2R	EMD	1972-75	5
7248-7273, 7628-7657		56	GP40-2	EMD	1978-84	
7274-7293		20	GP40M-2	EMD		6
7600-7607	7960-7967 (1980s)	8	GP40	EMD	1966	7
7770-7773		4	B36-7	GE	1980	
7774-7799		26	B30-7	GE	1980	
8040-8094		55	Dash 8-40B	GE	1988-89	
8964-8981, 9052-9068, 9152-9156		40	SD45	EMD	1968-71	
9157-9165, 9261-9301, 9371-9404		84	SD45T-2	EMD	1972-75	
9620-9714		95	GP60	EMD	1988-90	

Notes:
1—Steam-generator equipped.
2—Nos. 308-311, 313, 314 steam-generator equipped.
3—Rebuilt GP9s.
4—Rebuilt GP35s (turbochargers removed).
5—Rebuilt SD45T-2s.
6—GP40s rebuilt to Dash-2 standards in 1990-91.
7—Rebuilt to GP40R and renumbered 7960-7967.

Published rosters:
Extra 2200 South, February-March 1969; Cotton Belt Locomotives, by Joseph A. Strapac (Shade Tree Books, 1977)

Seaboard Air Line
1938-1967

The Seaboard Air Line started dieselizing passenger trains with E units in 1938, followed by diesel switchers from EMC, Alco, and Baldwin. A mix of EMD Fs and Geeps and a sizable number of Alco RS units completed dieselization in 1953. Second-generation diesels from EMD, Alco, and GE arrived in the early to mid-1960s. The SAL merged with Atlantic Coast Line on July 1, 1967 to form the Seaboard Coast Line.

Seaboard Air Line purchased 35 EMD GP30s in 1962 and 1963. *EMD*

Road Numbers	Qty.	Model	Builder	Dates built	Notes
100-109	10	RS-11	Alco	1960	
110-136	27	C-420	Alco	1965	
500-534	35	GP30	EMD	1962-63	
535-544	10	GP35	EMD	1965	
600-650	51	GP40	EMD	1966-67	
800-814	15	U30B	GE	1966-67	
400-409	10	GP18	EMD	1960	
1100-1119	20	SDP35	EMD	1964	
1200	1	SW1	EMD	1939	
1201	1	S-1	Alco	1941	
1202	1	VO660	Baldwin	1941	
1400-1402	3	VO1000	Baldwin	1941	
1403-1405, 1425-1434	13	S-2	Alco	1942, 1946	
1406-1412	7	NW2	EMD	1942	
1413-1416	4	VO1000	Baldwin	1944	
1417-1424, 1435-1461	35	DS-4-4-10	Baldwin	1946-51	
1462-1465, 1476-1481	10	S-12	Baldwin	1952-53	
1466-1475	10	RS-12	Baldwin	1952-53	
1482-1491	10	S-4	Alco	1953	
1492	1	VO1000	Baldwin	1942	1
1500-1531	32	RSC-2	Alco	1947, 1949	2
1532-1543	10	RSC-3	Alco	1950-51	
1600-1604	5	RS-2	Alco	1949	
1605-1684	80	RS-3	Alco	1950-52	
1685-1687	3	RS-2	Alco	1949	3
1688-1691	4	RS-3	Alco	1950-56	4
1700-1822	123	GP7	EMD	1950-52	
1900-1929, 1954-1978	55	GP9	EMD	1955-57	
2700-2702	3	DR-6-4-15	Baldwin	1947	
3000-3013	14	E4A	EMD	1938-39	
3014-3016	3	E6A	EMD	1940-41	
3017-3048	32	E7A	EMD	1945-49	
3049-3059	11	E8A	EMD	1950, 1952	
3060	1	E9A	EMD	1963	
3100-3104	5	E4B	EMD	1938-39	
3105-3107	3	E7B	EMD	1948	
4000-4021	22	FTA	EMD	1942, 1944	
4022-4032	11	F3A	EMD	1948	

Road Numbers	Qty.	Model	Builder	Dates built	Notes
4100-4121	22	FTB	EMD	1942, 1944	
4200-4202	3	FA-1	Alco	1948	
4300-4302	3	FB-1	Alco	1948	
4500-4513	14	DR-12-8-1500	Baldwin	1945, 1947	

Notes:
1—Ex-Macon, Dublin & Savannah 1000.
2—A total of 19 RSC-2s were converted to B-B trucks (making them RS-2s) in 1954-55.
3—Ex-MD&S 1700-1702.
4—Ex-MD&S 1705, 1703, 1704, 1706.

Published roster:
Extra 2200 South, July 1968

Seaboard Coast Line
1967-1982

The Seaboard Coast Line was formed in July 1967 by a merger of the Seaboard Air Line and Atlantic Coast Line. Locomotives acquired via the merger are listed in the second column with their previous road numbers. The SCL lasted until December 1982, when it merged with Louisville & Nashville to form the Seaboard System.

Seaboard Coast Line GE U30Bs ride on EMD GP trucks from a trade-ins. *SCL*

Road numbers	Former numbers (ACL or SAL)	Qty.	Model	Builder	Dates built	Notes
1-8		8	H15	EMD		1
10-19	ACL 50-59	10	SW8	EMD	1952	
20-25	ACL 600-605	6	NW2	EMD	1940, 1942	
26	SAL 1201	1	S-1	Alco	1941	
27	SAL 1202	1	VO660	Baldwin	1941	
28-30, 37-40, 84	SAL 1400-1402, 1413-1416, 1492	7	VO1000	Baldwin	1941-53	
31-36	SAL 1406..1412	6	NW2	EMD	1942	
41-50	SAL 1425-1434	10	S-2	Alco	1946, 1948	
51-73	SAL 1439-1461	23	DS-4-4-10	Baldwin	1950-51	
74-83	SAL 1482-1491	10	S-4	Alco	1953	
85-95 (1)		11	VO1000	Baldwin	1943-44	2
91-93 (2)		3	DS-4-4-10	Baldwin	1948	3
96-98, 107-124	ACL 26-46	21	S-2	Alco	1942-44	
99-106	ACL 10..18	8	VO1000	Baldwin	1942-44	
125-133, 199, 200	ACL 643-651, 717, 718	11	SW7	EMD	1950	
134-198, 201, 202	ACL 652-716, 719, 720	67	SW9	EMD	1951-52	

Road numbers	Former numbers (ACL or SAL)	Qty.	Model	Builder	Dates built	Notes
203-206, 217-222	SAL 1462-1465, 1476-1481	10	S-12	Baldwin	1952-53	
207-216	SAL 1466-1475	10	RS-12	Baldwin	1952, 53	4
225-230		6	S-4	Alco	1954	5
231		1	NW2	EMD	1949	6
232-234		3	SW900	EMD	1954	6
235		1	DS-4-4-10	Baldwin	1949	6
250-261, 300-392 (2)		105	U18B	GE	1973-74	
300-315 (1)	ACL 408-418	16	F7A	EMD	1951	
316 (1), 318-335 (1)	ACL 430-448	19	FP7	EMD	1951-52	
317 (1)	ACL 317	1	F9Am	EMD	1957	
336-347 (1)	ACL 336-347	12	F3A	EMD	1948	
336B-347B	ACL 336B-347B	12	F3B	EMD	1948	
348-392 (1), 393-413	ACL 348-413	66	F7A	EMD	1950-51	
392B-403B	ACL 392B-403B	12	F7B	EMD	1951	
500-555 (2)		56	GP38-2	EMD	1973	
501-523 (1)	ACL 501-523	23	E6A	EMD	1939-42	
525-531 (1)	ACL 524..531	7	E7A	EMD	1945	
524 (1), 532 (1), 574-581	ACL 500, 532, 544..550	10	E8A	EMD	1950-53	7
533-555 (1), 556-573	ACL 532..543, SAL 3017..3048	41	E7A	EMD	1945-49	8
582	ACL 551	1	E9Am	EMD	1957	
583-598	ACL 552-556, SAL 3049-3059	16	E8A	EMD	1950-52	
599	SAL 3060	1	E9A	EMD	1963	
600-620	ACL 1099, SAL 1100-1119	21	SDP35	EMD	1964-65	9
655B, 656B	ACL 751, 753	2	E6B	EMD	1940-41	
657B-669B	ACL 755-764, SAL 3105-3107	13	E7B	EMD	1945, 1948	
670B, 671B	ACL 765, 766	2	E8B	EMD	1949	
675-698	ACL 850..874	24	FP7	EMD	1951	
700-1002	ACL 100-279, SAL 1700-1822	303	GP7	EMD	1950-52	
1003-1055	SAL 1900..1979	53	GP9	EMD	1955-57	10
1056-1065	SAL 400-409	10	GP18	EMD	1960	
1100-1105	SAL 1502..1531	6	RSC-2	Alco	1947-49	
1106-1117	SAL1532-1543	12	RSC-3	Alco	1950-51	
1118	SAL 1604	1	RS-2	Alco	1949	
1119-1201	SAL 1605..1691	83	RS-3	Alco	1950-56	
1202-1211	SAL 100-109	10	RS-11	Alco	1960	
1212-1237	SAL 110-136	26	C-420	Alco	1965-66	
1238, 1239		2	C-420	Alco	1966	11
1250-1259		10	RS-3	Alco	1950-56	11
1275-1277		3	C-430	Alco	1967	12
1300-1343	ACL 900-908, SAL 500-534	44	GP30	EMD	1962-63	
1400-1415	ACL 909-914, SAL 535-544	16	GP35	EMD	1963, 1965	
1500-1565	ACL 915-929, SAL 600-650	66	GP40	EMD	1966-67	
1566-1635		68	GP40	EMD	1968-71	
1636-1656		21	GP40-2	EMD	1972	
1700-1718	ACL 975-978, SAL 800-814	19	U30B	GE	1966-67	13
1719-1747		29	U33B	GE	1967-69	13
1748-1855		108	U36B	GE	1970-72	
1900-1923	ACL 1000-1023	24	SD35	EMD	1964-65	
2000-2009	ACL 1024-1033	10	SD45	EMD	1966	
2010-2044		35	SD45	EMD	1968-71	
2045-2059		15	SD45-2	EMD	1974	

Road numbers	Former numbers (ACL or SAL)	Qty.	Model	Builder	Dates built	Notes
2100-2120	ACL 3000-3020	21	U25C	GE	1963-65	14
2121-2124	ACL 3021-3124	4	U28C	GE	1966	
2125-2131		7	U36C	GE	1971	15
2200-2210	ACL 2000-2010	11	C-628	Alco	1963-64	
2211-2213	ACL 2011-2013	3	C-630	Alco	1965	
4000-4019, 4200-4224		45	MP15AC	EMD	1977-78	
4614-4630, 4700-4750		66	GP16	EMD/SCL		16
5100-5114, 5140-5154, 5500-5516		47	B23-7	GE	1978, 1980	
5130-5139		10	BQ23-7	GE	1978-79	
6047-6050, 6053, 6054		6	GP38-2	EMD	1979-80	
6617-6621		5	GP40-2	EMD	1980	
7016-7031, 7052-7061		26	C30-7	GE	1979-80	
8040-8066, 8087-8130		71	SD40-2	EMD	1979-81	

Notes:
1—SD35s and SDP35s derated to 1500 hp for hump use.
2—Ex-Chicago, Burlington & Quincy 9350..9379.
3—No. 91 (2) is ex-Western of Alabama 630; 92, 93 (2) are ex-Kentucky & Indiana Terminal 53, 54.
4—Steam-generator equipped.
5—Ex-Piedmont & Northern 1000-1005.
6—Nos. 231-234 are ex-Jacksonville Terminal 33, 37-39; 235 is ex-Atlantic & West Point 677.
7—Nos. 524, 532 are ex-Fort Worth & Denver 9981A, 9981B.
8—Nos. 556-559 are ex-Durham & Southern 2000-2003.
9—Renumbered 1950-1970.
10—Nos. 1051, 1052 are ex-Winston-Salem Southbound 1503, 1504.
11—Nos. 1238, 1239, 1250-1259 are ex-P&N 2000, 2001, 1600-1609.
12—Former Alco demonstrators 430-1, 430-2, 430-3.
13—Equipped with EMD trucks from trade-ins.
14—Nos. 2111-2113 equipped with 2800-hp engines.
15—Ex-Clinchfield 3600-3606, acquired 1977.
16—Early Geeps rebuilt by SCL (railroad designation GP16).

Published roster:
Extra 2200 South, July 1968

Soo Line
Includes Wisconsin Central (1938-1961) and Duluth, South Shore & Atlantic
1938-1992

The Minneapolis, St. Paul & Sault Ste. Marie had long been known by its nickname, the Soo Line. The railroad adopted that name officially in 1961 when it merged the Wisconsin Central and Duluth, South Shore & Atlantic, both of which the Soo had long controlled. The WC followed the motive power leadings of the Soo, and its locomotives were painted in the Soo Line scheme but with small "WC" sublettering. The DSS&A favored Baldwin locomotives (other than a group of four Alco RS-1s), and its locomotives wore DSS&A's own paint scheme.

In 1982 the Soo acquired the Minneapolis, Northfield & Southern, and in 1986 merged the bankrupt Milwaukee Road, acquiring both railroads' active locomotives in the process. These are indicated in the notes. Canadian Pacific, which had long owned a slight majority of Soo Line stock, acquired full ownership of Soo in 1990 and fully absorbed the railroad in 1992.

Soo Line FP7 No. 500A is paired with F7B No. 500B. The FP7 is a former EMD demonstrator. *EMD*

Original road numbers	Second numbers	Qty.	Model	Builder	Dates built	Notes
100-107 (DSS&A)		8	RS-1	Alco	1945-51	
200A-204A, 200B-204B		10	F3A	EMD	1947-48	
205A-211A, 205B-211B		14	FA-1	Alco	1948-49	
212A-214A, 212B-214B		6	F7A	EMD	1951-52	
300-301		2	NW2	EMD	1939	
310		1	VO1000	Baldwin	1945	
311, 312		2	DS-4-4-10	Baldwin	1949	
313, 314		2	S-12	Baldwin	1952	
315-319		5	H-12-44	F-M	1952, 1954	
320		1	SW1	EMD	1939	
321-328		8	SW1200	EMD	1954-55	
330		1	44-tonner	GE	1941	
350-353		4	RS-1	Alco	1954	
360-367		8	DRS-4-4-15	Baldwin	1947-48	
368-369	370-371 (2)	2	RSC-2	Alco	1949	1
370-371 (1)		2	RSC-2	Alco	1949	1
372-374		3	RSC-3	Alco	1950	1
375-378, 381-383		7	GP7	EMD	1950-52	
379, 380		2	AS-16	Baldwin	1951	
384-387 (DSS&A 200-204)		4	DRS-6-6-15	Baldwin	1949-50	
388-395 (DSS&A 205-211)		8	AS-616	Baldwin	1951-52	2
396-399 (DSS&A 300-303)		4	DT-6-6-20	Baldwin	1949-50	
400-414		15	GP9	EMD	1954-57	
415, 416		2	RS-27	Alco	1962	
500A-503A, 504, 505		6	FP7	EMD	1949-52	3
500B-501B	500C, 501C	2	F7B	EMD	1949	4
502C-503C		2	F7B	EMD	1951	
532, 534, 543 (MILW)		3	SD10	EMD	1952-54	5, 6
550-558	4225-4233	9	GP9	EMD	1954-56	7
700-721		22	GP30	EMD	1963	8, 9
722-731		10	GP35	EMD	1964-65	
732-735	4600-4603	4	GP40	EMD	1967	7
736-756		21	SD40	EMD	1969-71	
757-789		33	SD40-2	EMD	1972-73	
800-809		10	U30C	GE	1968	
1200-1205 (MN&S 30-35)		6	SW1200	EMD	1962-65	10
1206..1220 (MILW 700-715)		7	SW1200	EMD	1954	5
1400, 1401 (MN&S 36, 37)		2	SW1500	EMD	1966	10
1500-1563 (MILW 434-497)		64	MP15AC	EMD	1975-76	5
2000-2071 (MILW)	4604-4660	72	GP40	EMD	1966-69	5
2100-2102, 2108 (WC)		4	NW2	EMC	1938, 1948	
2103-2107, 2109, 2110 (WC)		7	S-2	Alco	1942-49	
2111-2115, 2117-2119 (WC)		8	SW9	EMD	1952-53	
2116 (WC)		1	S-4	Alco	1952	
2120-2127 (WC)		8	SW1200	EMD	1955	
2200A, 2200B (WC)		2	F3A	EMD	1948	
2200C (WC)		1	F3B	EMD	1948	
2201A-2203A, 2201B-2203B (WC)		6	F7A	EMD	1949	
2201C-2204C (WC)		4	F7B	EMD	1949, 1952	
2220A-2223A, 2220B-2220B (WC)		8	FA-1	Alco	1949	
2224A-2230A, 2224B-2230B (WC)		14	F7A	EMD	1950-1953	

Original road numbers	Second numbers	Qty.	Model	Builder	Dates built	Notes
2360-2368 (WC)		9	RS-1	Alco	1950-52	
2380 (WC)		1	RSC-3	Alco	1951	
2381 (WC)		1	SD9	EMD	1954	
2400-2413 (WC)		14	GP9	EMD	1954-57	
2500A, 2501A (WC)		2	FP7	EMD	1949-50	3
2500B, 2501B (WC)	2500C, 2501C	2	F7B	EMD	1949	
2550-2556 (WC)		7	GP9	EMD	1954-56	
3013-3019		7	GP38	EMD		11
4100-4106		7	GP9r	EMD	1952	12
4200-4204		5	GP9m	EMD	1954-57	13
4300-4335 (MILW 212..277)		36	GP20	EMD		5, 14
4300-4302 (2)		3	GP30m	EMD	1961-63	15
4400-4452		53	GP38-2	EMD	1977-81	
4500-4515 (MILW 350-365)		16	GP38-2	EMD	1973-74	5
4598, 4599		2	GP39-2	EMD		16
5000, 5003, 5004 (MILW 4800, 4802, 4803)		3	U23B	GE	1973	5
5651-5658 (MILW)		8	U30C	GE	1974	5
5800, 5802, 5803 (MILW)		3	U36C	GE	1972	5
6000-6057		58	SD60	EMD	1987, 1989	
6058-6062		5	SD60M	EMD	1989	
6103-6120 (MILW 544-561)		18	SD10	EMD	1952-54	5, 4
6200-6208 (MILW 582-590)		9	SDL39	EMD	1969, 1972	5
6240, 6241 (MN&S 40, 41)		2	SD39	EMD	1968	10
6300-6388 (MILW)		89	SD40-2	EMD	1972-74	5
6400-6405		6	SD40	EMD	1970	17
6406-6410		5	SD40A	EMD	1970	18
6411		1	SD40	EMD	1966	19
6450		1	SD40B	EMD	1971	20
6491, 6492		2	SD45	EMD	1971	21
6600-6623		24	SD40-2	EMD	1979-84	

Notes:
All—Numbers in parentheses are numbers worn on former railroads.
1—Most RSC locomotives were eventually fitted with four-wheel trucks.
2—No. 395 is former Baldwin demonstrator 1600.
3—No. 500A is former EMD demonstrator 9051; 2500A is former EMD demonstrator 7001.
4—Former EMD demonstrators 9052, 9053.
5—Former Milwaukee Road engines, acquired in 1986 merger.
6—Early SDs rebuilt by Milwaukee Road in 1974-75, given SD10 designation by railroad.
7—Renumbered in 1986.
8—GP30s ride on AAR trucks from traded-in Alco FAs.
9—No. 727 was renumbered 1776 in 1976, painted in bicentennial scheme.
10—Former Minneapolis, Northfield & Southern engines, acquired in 1982 merger.
11—Acquired used in mid-1990s.
12—Ex-Conrail locomotives rebuilt with Caterpillar engines, sometimes called GP15Cs, acquired 1990-91.
13—Ex-Conrail, acquired 1991.
14—Early Geeps rebuilt by Milwaukee Road with 645 engines, given GP20 designation by railroad.
15—Ex-Union Pacific, rebuilt with Caterpillar engines, acquired 1990.
16—Ex-Kennecott Copper 793, 794, acquired late 1980s.
17—Ex-Kansas City Southern 621-626, acquired late 1980s.
18—Ex-Illinois Central 6019-6023, acquired late 1980s.
19—Ex-Baltimore & Ohio 7500, acquired late 1980s.
20—Ex-Burlington Northern 6302, cabless B unit rebuilt from SD40 7600, acquired late 1980s.
21—Ex-BN 6678, 6659, nee St. Louis-San Francisco 930, 910, acquired late 1980s.

Published roster:
Extra 2200 South, September-October 1972

Southern Ry.
1940-1982

The Southern began buying passenger diesels and switchers before World War II, then was an early owner of EMD's FT diesel, getting its first in 1941. The railroad continued buying F units through the F7 model, along with Geeps. The railroad remained a key EMD customer, buying SD35s, SD40-2s, and GP38-2s in large numbers, and also buying a fair number of second-generation GEs. Southern (along with eventual merger partner Norfolk & Western) became known for continuing to order high-nose hood units long after other railroads were opting for low noses.

The roster includes locomotives of subsidiaries AGS (Alabama Great Southern), CNO&TP (Cincinnati, New Orleans & Texas Pacific), G&F (Georgia & Florida), and NO&NE (New Orleans & Northeastern). To say Southern numbering was convoluted is an understatement.

Numbers for single models of locomotives are often divided among several number series depending upon the owning subsidiary. In addition, many locomotives were renumbered over the years, and again as subsidiaries were absorbed. Locomotives of Southern subsidiaries Central of Georgia (and its own subsidiaries) and the original Norfolk Southern, which have their own listings in this book, are included only if they were still active at their mergers (in 1971 and 1974, respectively). The Southern merged with N&W in 1982 to form Norfolk Southern.

Most Southern road switchers, like this new GE U23B, were delivered with high noses. *GE*

Original road numbers	Second numbers	Qty.	Model	Builder	Dates built	Notes
1-6 (2)		6	RS-1	Alco	1943-51	1
1-4		4	RS-2	Alco	1948	
5-10, 30-39		16	RS-3	Alco	1953-56	2
11		1	RS-11	Alco	1956	3
1, 15, 292, 300, 301, 701, 703		7	60-tonner	GE	1945-48	4
5, 2005		2	VO660	Baldwin	1940-41	
6, 329, 2000, 2001, 2006, 6000, 6001, 6500-6502		10	S-1	Alco	1940-44	
12		1	DS-4-4-660	Baldwin	1948	
21..29, 332-335, 2208-2232, 6057-6059		39	S-2	Alco	1940-44	
22, 26, 27, 2205		4	VO1000	Baldwin	1940-44	
36, 37, 2285-2289		7	DS-4-4-10	Baldwin	1948-49	
67-83		17	SW1500	EMD	1966-74	5
73, 1000-1007, 1087, 2002-2004, 2007-2011	1008-1014	17	SW1	EMD	1937-47	6
91		1	NW1	EMC	1937	6

Original road numbers	Second numbers	Qty.	Model	Builder	Dates built	Notes
100-107		8	DRS-6-4-15	Baldwin	1948	
108-110 (1)		3	AS-416	Baldwin	1950-52	
108-119, 133-159		39	RS-3	Alco	1950-53	7
171-196		26	GP18	EMD	1960, 1963	8
201	197	1	SD7	EMD	1953	7
202-207	198, 199	6	SD9	EMD	1955	7
210-214	240-244	5	GP35	EMD	1963	7
215-224	2990-2999	10	SD35	EMD	1966	7
301-310, 1133	1134-1143, 1733	11	SW9	EMD	1950-53	9
311-314, 2290-2299		14	S-12	Baldwin	1952-53	
400, 401		2	F2A	EMD	1946	
402, 403, 1950-1955, 6040, 6520, 6840		11	44-tonner	GE	1944-45	10
405		1	RS-1	Alco	1951	
701, 703		2	70-tonner	GE	1948	11
801-810		10	E7A	EMD	1946-48	
1015		1	SW8	EMD	1950	6
1016-1086		71	NW2	EMD	1940-48	12
1606-1617		12	AS-416	Baldwin	1952-55	13
2025-2062, 2131-2145		53	RS-3	Alco	1951-53	
2100		1	NW5	EMD	1947	
2101-2130		30	RS-2	Alco	1949	
2146-2155		10	H-16-44	F-M	1951	
2300-2347		48	SW1500	EMD	1968-70	
2348-2493		46	MP15DC	EMD	1977, 1979	
2400-2404	1088-1092	5	TR2A	EMD	1947	
2450-2454	1093-1097	5	TR2B	EMD	1947	
2502-2524	6300-6304, 6326-6343	23	SD24	EMD	1959	
2525-2644		120	GP30	EMD	1962-63	
2645-2715		71	GP35	EMD	1965	
2716-2822, 2879-2886	2732	115	GP38	EMD	1966-70	14
2800-2802 (1), 2900-2903		7	E6A	EMD	1941	
2823-2878		56	GP38AC	EMD	1971	
2904		1	DL-109	Alco	1942	
2905-2922		18	E7A	EMD	1946-49	
2923-2929	6900-6905, 6916	7	E8A	EMD	1951	
2950-2953		4	E6B	EMD	1941	
2954		1	DL-110	Alco	1941	
3000-3099		100	SD35	EMD	1965-66	
3100-3104 (1)	3800-3804	5	U30C	GE	1967	
3100-3169 (2)		70	SD45	EMD	1967, 1970	
3170-3200		31	SD40	EMD	1971	
3201-3328		128	SD40-2	EMD	1972-79	
3500-3521		22	B30-7A1	GE	1982	
3805-3814		10	U33C	GE	1970, 1972	
3815-3820		6	B36-7	GE	1980	
3900-3969		70	U23B	GE	1972-77	

Original road numbers	Second numbers	Qty.	Model	Builder	Dates built	Notes
3970-4023		54	B23-7	GE	1978-81	
4100-4127		28	FTA	EMD	1943-45	
4128-4206		79	F3A	EMD	1946-49	
4207-4269		63	F7A	EMD	1949-52	
4300-4319		20	FTB	EMD	1943-45	
4320-4384		65	F3B	EMD	1946-49	
4385-4429		45	F7B	EMD	1949-52	
4600-4605		6	GP39X	EMD	1980	
5000-5256		257	GP38-2	EMD	1972-79	
6060-6073, 6505-6509, 6852-6863, 8200-8203	1098-1132	35	SW7	EMD	1950	
6074, 6075		2	S-4	Alco	1951	
6100-6105, 6800-6803		10	FTA	EMD	1941-45	
6106-6113, 6702-6713, 6804-6806		23	F3A	EMD	1946-47	
6114-6120, 6714-6719		13	F7A	EMD	1950-52	
6130-6149	3496-3499	20	FP7	EMD	1950	
6150-6155, 6825-6828		10	FTB	EMD	1941-45	
6156-6159, 6750-6755, 6829		11	F3B	EMD	1946-47	
6160-6183, 6756-6758		27	F7B	EMD	1950-52	
6206, 6207		2	RS-2	Alco	1949	
6210-6239, 6875-6882		38	RS-3	Alco	1950-52	
6245-6268		21	GP9	EMD	1955-57	15
6300-6304		5	H-24-66	F-M	1955	
6305-6325, 6950-6953	..6344-6347	25	SD24	EMD	1959-60	
6400, 6401		2	DL-109	Alco	1941	
6425, 6426		2	DL-110	Alco	1941	
6545-6550		6	H-16-44	F-M	1950	
6700, 6701		2	F2A	EMD	1946	
6841		1	45-tonner	GE	1941	16
6900-6905 (1)		6	PA-2	Alco	1953	
6906-6915		10	E8A	EMD	1953	
7000-7002		3	GP40X	EMD	1978	
7003-7092		90	GP50	EMD	1980-81	
8210-8213, 8216-8300		89	GP7	EMD	1950-52	17

Notes:
Most system renumbering done in 1972.
1—Ex-Tennessee RR 1-6, acquired with merger in 1973.
2—Nos. 5, 6 are ex-Danville & Western 1, 2; 7, 8 are ex-Blue Ridge 1, 2; 10 is ex-Carolina & Northwestern 10; 30-39 are ex-Interstate 30-39, acquired with merger in 1961.
3—Ex-C&N 11.
4—Nos. 701, 703 are ex-Norfolk Southern, acquired with purchase of NS in 1974.
5—Ex-Kentucky & Indiana Terminal.
6—Nos. 73, 91 are ex-Georgia & Florida; 1000, 1001, 1003 are ex-Central of Georgia; 1002 is ex-Chattanooga Traction Co. 4; 1004-1006 are ex-G&F 70-72; 1007 is ex-Atlantic & East Carolina 404; 1015 is ex-Georgia Northern 1310; 1087 is an SW1m; 2002-2004 and 2007-2011 were renumbered 1008-1014.
7—Ex-CofG, acquired with merger in 1971.
8—Nos. 171-178 are ex-CofG; 179 is ex-Tennessee, Alabama & Georgia 50, acquired with purchase of TA&G in 1971; nos. 180-196 are ex-NS 1-17.
9—No. 1133 is ex-CTC 5; 1134-1143 are ex CofG 301-310; 1142 was renumbered 1733 in 1977.
10—Nos. 402, 403 are ex-A&EC 6, 7; 1954, 1955 are ex-CTC 2, 3.
11—Ex-NS 701, 702.
12—Nos. 1016, 1017 are ex-CofG.
13—Ex-NS.
14—No. 2879 is ex-TA&G 80; 2880-2886 are ex-NS 2001-2007; 2716 was renumbered 2732 (2).
15—Nos. 6250, 6251 are ex-Live Oak, Perry & Gulf; 6256, 6257 are ex-Georgia Southern & Florida; 6258-6268 are ex-CofG 160-170.
16—Ex-North Carolina Shipbuilding 3002.
17—Nos. 8210-8213 are ex-GS&F (same numbers); 8216-8229 are ex-CofG 106, 120-132; 8230 is ex-A&EC 406; 8231-8234 are ex-G&F 701-704; 8235-8237 are ex-TA&G 705-707.

Published rosters:
Extra 2200 South, November-December 1969 and July-August-September 1979; Southern Railway Diesel Locomotives and Trains, 1950-1982, Vol. 1, by Curt Tillotson, Jr. (TLC Publishing, 2003); Southern: A Motive Power Pictorial, 1968-82, by Paul K. Withers and Tom L. Sink (Withers, 1987)

Southern Pacific

1938-1996

Through the early diesel era, Southern Pacific was one of the largest railroads in the U.S., second only to Santa Fe in route miles. "Southern Pacific Lines" included SP's main subsidiary, Texas & New Orleans, which covered all lines east of El Paso, Texas. The SP merged the T&NO in 1961. Diesels of the T&NO wore standard SP paint schemes, but into the 1960s were numbered below 1000 and carried TNO sublettering. The SP undertook a major renumbering in 1965 to group together locomotives of each model among SP, T&NO, St. Louis Southwestern (SSW) and other subsidiaries.

The SP dieselized largely with EMD F units, but also had a diverse mix of early diesels from Alco, Baldwin, and Fairbanks-Morse. The railroad operated steam fairly late, with the last steam freight run in late 1956 and the final passenger movement in January 1957. The SP was a proponent of rebuilding older locomotives, and most early EMDs from GP9s through SD45s were rebuilt. The SP initially added an "E" suffix to the model number for bookkeeping purposes; later the more-common "R" was used.

The sheer size of the SP roster precludes providing specific details about individual locomotives. Some diesels wore four or more numbers during their lifespans, and this roster may not include all of them. This roster does not include locomotives of SP's key subsidiary, St. Louis Southwestern (Cotton Belt), which has its own listing on page 270. The Rio Grande purchased the SP in 1988, although the new parent company was named Southern Pacific. The roster covers the period until the SP was purchased by Union Pacific in 1996.

Southern Pacific Alco PA-1 No. 210 carries numbers for Train 13, the *Sunbeam*, in its train-indicator boards in 1954.
R.S. Plummer

Original road numbers	Second numbers	Third numbers	Qty.	Model	Builder	Dates built	Notes
1, 2			2	switcher	Plymouth	1932	
10			1	S-1	Alco	1941	
11			1	SW1	EMD	1941	
12-16	1104-1108		5	SW8	EMD	1953	
17			1	44-tonner	GE	1944	
30-71, 89-94	1721..1765		48	S-2	Alco	1943-50	
72-88	1914-1930		17	NW2	EMD	1949	1
95-104 (1)	1782-1791		10	S-4	Alco	1951	
100-378 (2)			279	AC4400CW	GE	1995	
105-107, 121, 122 (1)	2121-2125		5	S-12	Baldwin	1952	
108-112 (1)	2208-2212		5	SW9	EMD	1953	
113-118, 123-128 (1)	2213..2223		12	SW1200	EMD	1954, 1957	
130-139 (RG)			10	SW1200	EMD	1964-65	
140-149 (RG)			10	SW1000	EMD	1966, 1968	
155-176, 185, 186 (1)	2850..2887		24	RSD-5	Alco	1953	

Original road numbers	Second numbers	Third numbers	Qty.	Model	Builder	Dates built	Notes
177-184 (1)			8	AS-616	Baldwin	1952	
187-190 (1)			4	DRS-6-6-15	Baldwin	1949	
200A-205A, 200B-205B	200-211 (1)	6055-6066	12	PA-1	Alco	1949	
240-249, 280-283 (1), 400-458	3400-3420, 3424-3440, 3551-3570, 3653-3662, 5892-5895	3300..3435	73	GP9	EMD	1954	2
250-252 (1)	5160-5162	3100-3102	3	RSD-15	Alco	1959	
538-553	8286-8289, 8304		16	F7B	EMD	1951-53	
1000, 1004-1016			14	SW1	EMC	1939-41	
1001-1003			3	HH660	Alco	1939	
1017-1020			4	S-1	Alco	1941	
1021, 1022			2	VO660	Baldwin	1941	
1023-1032			10	S-3	Alco	1951	
1033-1090	1200-1257		58	S-6	Alco	1955-56	
1300-1309 (1), 1330-1370 (1, 2), 1386-1392, 1426-1441 (1)	1700-1720, 1766-1781		74	S-2	Alco	1941-50	
1310-1319 (1), 1403-1425 (1)	1904-1913, 1931-1953		33	NW2	EMD	1941-49	1
1320-1329 (1), 1371-1385	1858-1862		25	VO1000	Baldwin	1941-44	
1393-1402 (1)	1863-1869		10	DS-4-4-10	Baldwin	1948	
1442-1463, 1492-1513, 1539-1550	2100-2120, 2126-2157		56	S-12	Baldwin	1951-53	
1464-1485, 1514-1528, 1551-1567	1792-1845		54	S-4	Alco	1951-55	
1486-1491, 1529-1538, 1568-1596	2350-2394		45	H-12-44	F-M	1952-53	
1597-1623	2262-2288		27	SW1200	EMD	1964-65	
1900-1905			6	44-tonner	GE	1942-46	3
2690-2701			12	MP15	EMD	1974-75	
2702-2759			57	MP15AC	EMD	1975	
2971-2976			6	SD38-2	EMD	1973	
3001..3028 (RG)			24	GP30	EMD	1962-63	
3029-3050 (RG)			22	GP35	EMD	1964-65	
3051..3093, 3131-3153 (RG)			64	GP40	EMD	1966-71	
3094..3130 (RG)			36	GP40-2	EMD	1972-83	
3154-3156 (RG)			3	GP60	EMD	1990	
3197-3199			3	GP40P-2	EMD	1974	
3200-3209			10	SDP45	EMD	1967	
4600-4603	1100-1103		4	TR6A	EMD	1950-51	
4604-4623	1109-1128		20	SW8	EMD	1953-54	
4624-4633	1170-1179		10	SW900	EMD	1954	4
4700-4703	1150-1153		4	TR6B	EMD	1950-51	
4800-4815 (1)	3020-3035		16	H-24-66	F-M	1953-54	5
4800-4844 (2)			45	GP38-2	EMD	1980	
4816-4844 (1)	6900-6928	6950..6978	29	SD35	EMD	1964-65	6
4845..4873	7101..7128	3110-3136	27	C-628	Alco	1964-65	7
5100-5120 (1)			21	70-tonner	GE	1949-55	
5100-5114			15	B23-7	GE	1980	
5200-5202			3	DRS-6-4-15	Baldwin	1948	
5203-5226			24	DRS-6-6-15	Baldwin	1949-50	
5227	5500 (1)	4900	1	DRS-6-6-15B	Baldwin	1950	
5228-5278			51	AS-616	Baldwin	1950-52	
5279-5293, 5308-5335 (1)	2700-2742 (1)	1400-1442 (2)	43	SD7	EMD	1952-53	
5294-5307 (1), 5336-5339 (1), 5445-5448, 5494-5507 (2)	2871		37	RSD-5	Alco	1953-56	
5300-5325 (2)			26	SD39	EMD	1968, 1970	
5300-5304 (RG)			5	SD7	EMD	1953	

Original road numbers	Second numbers	Third numbers	Qty.	Model	Builder	Dates built	Notes
5305-5314 (RG)			10	SD9	EMD	1957	
5315-5340 (RG)			26	SD45	EMD	1967-68	
5339-5352, 5354-5444, 5449-5493	3800-3830, 3850-3966	4300..4451	148	SD9	EMD	1954-56	8
5341..5413			71	SD40T-2	EMD	1974-80	
5501-5505 (1)	4901-4905		5	AS-616B	Baldwin	1951	
5501-5517 (RG)			17	SD50	EMD	1984	
5600-5697, 5699-5713, 5715-5719, 5730-5844, 5872-5891	3002-3009, 3441-3640, 3663-3727	3300..3435	253	GP9	EMD	1954-59	2
5720-5729, 5845-5871	2900-2936		37	RS-11	Alco	1956, 1959	
5762, 5763 (RG)			2	F9B	EMD	1955	
5771			1	F9A	EMD	1955	
5903..5954			13	GP9	EMD	1955-56	
5918-5924			7	PB-2	Alco	1950-53	
6000A-6004A	6000-6004		5	E7A	EMD	1947	
6000B-6004B, 6011B, 6000C-6004C, 6011C	5900-5909, 5916, 5917		12	E7B	EMD	1946-47	
6005A-6010A, 6005C-6010C	6005-6016		12	PA-1	Alco	1948-49	
6005B-6010B	5910-5915		6	PB-1	Alco	1948-49	
6011A	6017		1	E2A	EMD	1937	
6018			1	E8A	EMD	1950	
6019-6045			27	PA-2	Alco	1950-53	
6046-6054			9	E9A	EMD	1954	
6100A-6139A, 6100D-6139D	6100-6179	300-319	80	F3A	EMD	1947-49	
6100B-6139B, 6100C-6139C	8000-8079		80	F3B	EMD	1947-49	
6140A-6169A, 6140D-6169D, 6240-6423, 6440-6445	6180-6239		250	F7A	EMD	1949-53	
6140B-6169B, 6140C-6169C, 8140-8285, 8290-8303 (1)	8080-8139		220	F7B	EMD	1949-53	
6446-6461			16	FP7	EMD	1953	
7000-7020	2950-2970		21	RSD-12	Alco	1961	
7025-7028			4	U28B	GE	1966	
7150-7159			10	U28C	GE	1966	
7200-7237	4050-4087	4100..4133	38	GP20	EMD	1962	9
7240-7247			8	GP40-2	EMD	1984	
7300-7309	4000-4009		10	RS-32	Alco	1962	
7400-7407	5010-5017		8	GP30	EMD	1963	
7408-7484, 7700-7782	6520-6679		160	GP35	EMD	1963-65	
7500-7567	6700-6767	6800, 6801	68	U25B	GE	1962-63	10
7600-7607	7960-7967		8	GP40	EMD	1966	11
7608-7627, 7658-7677, 7940-7959			60	GP40-2	EMD	1978-80	
7754-7769			16	B36-7	GE	1984	
7800-7810, 7812-7814	3140-3153		14	C-630	Alco	1966	
7801-7883 (2)			83	B30-7	GE	1978-79	
7900-7936			37	U30C	GE	1968-69	
8000-8039			40	B39-8	GE	1987	
8100-8200			101	Dash 9-44CW	GE	1994	
8300-8306 (2), 8350-8356			14	SD40T-2	EMD	1974	
8400-8402 (1)	9500-9502 (1)	9900-9902	3	DD35B	EMD	1964	
8400-8488 (2)	7300-7385		89	SD40	EMD	1966, 1968	11
8500-8502	9550-9552	9950-9952	3	U50	GE	1964	
8585-8796			212	U33C	GE	1969-75	
8800-9156, 8992 (2), 9136 (2)	7400..7566		359	SD45	EMD	1966-71	11

Original road numbers	Second numbers	Third numbers	Qty.	Model	Builder	Dates built	Notes
9000-9017 (1), 9021-23 (1)	9100-9120 (1)		21	ML4000	K-M	1961-64	11
9018-9020 (1)	9150-9152	9800-9802	3	C-643H	Alco	1964	12
9157-9404	6767..6856		248	SD45T-2	EMD	1972-75	
9500-9505 (2)			6	SD45X	EMD	1970-71	13
9600-9619, 9715-9794			100	GP60	EMD	1988-94	
9800-9824			25	SD70M	EMD	1994	

Notes:
Locomotives with (RG) following the number were acquired with the Rio Grande merger in 1988.
1—Most rebuilt to NW2E beginning in 1971.
2—Most rebuilt to GP9E beginning in 1970.
3—No. 1903 is ex-Visalia Electric 501, acquired 1950; 1904, 1905 are ex-Petaluma & Santa Rosa 1, 2, acquired 1958.
4—Rebuilt to SW900E beginning in 1974.
5—Nos. 4800, 4801 are former F-M demonstrators TM-3, TM-4, acquired 1953.
6—Most rebuilt to SD35E beginning in 1974.
7—Nos. 4870-4873 are former Alco demonstrators 628-1 to 628-4, acquired 1964.
8—Most rebuilt to SD9E beginning in 1970.
9—Nos. 7234-7237 are ex-EMD demonstrators 5625-5628, acquired 1962. Most converted to GP20E in mid-1970s.
10—Nos. 6708, 6724 rebuilt to U25BE and renumbered 6800, 6801 in 1975-76.
11—Most GP40s, SD40s, and SD45s rebuilt to GP40E, SD40E, SD45E, 1980-85.
12—Diesel-hydraulic locomotives built by Alco (9018-9020) and Kraus-Maffei; nos. 9021-9023 are ex-Rio Grande, acquired 1964.
13—Nos. 9503-9505 are former EMD demonstrators 4201-4203, acquired 1972.

Published rosters:
Extra 2200 South (all-time roster in seven parts, from October-November-December 1975 through April-May-June 1977); Southern Pacific Review: 1952-82, by Joseph A. Strapac (Shade Tree Books, 1983)

Spokane, Portland & Seattle
1940-1970

The Spokane, Portland & Seattle was known for its predominantly Alco diesel roster, including early FAs and RS units as well as second-generation Century diesels. Diesel switchers began arriving in 1940, and the last steam locomotives operated in 1956. The SP&S merged with the Chicago, Burlington & Quincy, Great Northern, and Northern Pacific to form Burlington Northern on March 2, 1970.

Number 61 is one of five Alco RS-2s owned by SP&S. Donald Sims

Road Numbers	Qty.	Model	Builder	Dates built	Notes
10, 11	2	S-1	Alco	1941	
20-28	9	S-2	Alco	1940-43	
30-34	5	VO1000	Baldwin	1940-45	
40-42	3	NW2	EMD	1948	
43-45	3	SW9	EMD	1951	
50-55	6	RS-1	Alco	1945	
60-64	5	RS-2	Alco	1947-50	1
65-84, 90-98	29	RS-3	Alco	1950-55	2
100-105	6	C-415	Alco	1968-69	
150-155	6	GP9	EMD	1956	
200-211	12	FB-1	Alco	1948-50	3
212, 213	2	FB-2	Alco	1950	
300-306	7	C-424	Alco	1964	
310-317, 320-327	16	C-425	Alco	1965-66	
330-335, 340-343, 350, 351	12	C-636	Alco	1968-69	
750	1	E7	EMD	1948	

Road Numbers	Qty.	Model	Builder	Dates built	Notes
800-802	3	F3A	EMD	1947-48	4
803-806	4	F7A	EMD	1953	4
850-867	18	FA-1	Alco	1948-50	5
868, 869	2	FA-2	Alco	1950	

Notes:
1—Nos. 63, 64 are ex-Great Northern 200, 201, acquired 1963.
2—Nos. 83, 84 are ex-GN 231, 232, acquired 1959.
3—Nos. 206-209 are ex-GN 440B, 440C, 442B, 442C, acquired 1950.
4—Steam-generator equipped.
5—Nos. 862-865 are ex-GN 440A, 440D, 442A, 442D, acquired 1950.

Published roster:
Extra 2200 South, April 1969

Tennessee, Alabama & Georgia
1951-1971

The Tennessee, Alabama & Georgia, known as the TAG Route, dieselized with EMD GP7s in the 1950s. Through the 1960s, the line was owned by the same family that owned a steel mill in Chattanooga; the railroad was sold to the Southern on Jan. 1, 1971.

GP18 No. 801 was quickly renumbered to 50 (stenciled on the lower cab). *EMD*

Original road numbers	Second numbers	Third numbers	Qty.	Model	Builder	Dates built	Notes
1	80	2879	1	GP38	EMD	1968	
50	179		1	GP18	EMD	1960	
707	8237		1	GP7	EMD	1951	
708, 709	705, 706	8235, 8236	2	GP7	EMD	1951	

Published roster:
Diesel Locomotive Rosters (Wayner Publications)

Tennessee Central
1939-1968

The Tennessee Central was noted for its entirely non-EMD roster, running Alcos and a trio of Baldwin road switchers. The TC was abandoned in 1968, with locomotives dispersed and portions of the railroad purchased and operated by several other railroads.

Road numbers	Qty.	Model	Builder	Dates built	Notes
50	1	HH660	Alco	1939	
51	1	S-1	Alco	1941	
75-77	3	DRS-4-4-10	Baldwin	1948	
248-250	3	RS-3	Alco	1951	1
251-254	4	RS-2	Alco	1950	
255-260	6	RS-3	Alco	1952, 1956	
301-305	5	RS-11	Alco	1962-63	
400, 401	2	C-420	Alco	1966	
801-805	5	FA-1	Alco	1949	
801B	1	FB-1	Alco	1949	

Notes:
1—Ex-Reading 502, 508, 518.

Published roster:
Diesel Locomotive Rosters (Wayner Publications)

Terminal Railroad Assn. of St. Louis
1940-present

The Terminal Railroad Association of St. Louis provides switching and transfer operations among railroads in the St. Louis area, and through the 1960s provided switching operations for all passenger trains at St. Louis Union Station. The railroad dieselized with a variety of switchers from all five builders, finally settling on EMD SW1200s and SW1500s by the late 1960s. The railroad still operates, and is co-owned by the five remaining Class I railroads. As of 2017, motive power is a variety of rebuilt EMD GP and SD diesels.

Road numbers	Qty.	Model	Builder	Dates built	Notes
501-508	8	SW1	EMD	1940, 1947	
521-524	4	S-1	Alco	1940-41	
531-534	4	VO660	Baldwin	1940, 1942	
551-567	17	NW2	EMD	1941-49	
569-590	22	S-1	Alco	1941-49	
591-601	11	VO1000	Baldwin	1941-44	
602, 603	2	DS-44-10	Baldwin	1949	
700-703	4	H-10-44	F-M	1947, 1949	
1200-1205	6	LS-1200	Lima	1950-51	
1206-1218	13	SW9	EMD	1952	
1219-1243	25	SW1200	EMD	1955, 1965	
1250-1253	4	S-12	Baldwin	1952	
1501-1511	11	SW1500	EMD	1967, 1969	
1600-1603	4	RS-3	Alco	1950	
1751	1	SD7r	EMD	1953	1
2000-2011	12	GP38-3	EMD	1967-71	2
3001	1	SD45T-2	EMD	1978	3
3002, 3004 (1), 3004 (2), 3005 (1), 3005 (2), 3006	6	SD40-2	EMD	1968-78	4
3003	1	SD38-2	EMD	1966	5

Notes:
1—Ex-Conrail 6999, nee Pennsylvania 8589; rebuilt.
2—Rebuilt from GP38s and GP40s of mixed heritage.
3—Ex-Southern Pacific 8515.
4—Acquired used; mixed heritage, some rebuilt; no. 3004 (1) was rebuilt to SD40-3 and renumbered 300.
5—Ex-Southern Pacific SD40 8458, rebuilt.

Published roster:
Extra 2200 South, September-October 1969

Texas & Pacific
1946-1976

The Texas & Pacific was long controlled by the Missouri Pacific, and although the T&P continued operating most trains with steam after World War II, MoPac diesels began appearing on T&P trains in 1947. Dieselization then followed quickly, mainly with EMD F units and Geeps, with the last steam running in 1952.

The T&P acquired control of the Muskogee Company railroads (Midland Valley, Kansas, Oklahoma & Gulf, and Oklahoma City-Ada-Atoka) in 1964. The T&P sold the OCAA to the Santa Fe, then merged the other two in 1967 and 1970. The MoPac merged the Texas & Pacific in 1976.

Original road numbers	Second numbers	Third numbers	Qty.	Model	Builder	Dates built	Notes
97-107	1637-1640, 1688-1694		11	GP7	EMD	1952-53	1, 2
108, 109	1695, 1696		2	GP9m	EMD	1958	2
570, 571	850, 851	2000, 2001	2	GP28	EMD	1964	3
600-614, 640-667	2500..2513, 2537-2547		43	GP35	EMD	1964-65	4
811-818 (1)	8000-8007		8	SW8	EMD	1952	
816-839	3115-3138		24	SD40-2	EMD	1973-74	
844-847			4	F7A	EMD	1949	5
846B, 847B			2	F7B	EMD	1949	5
970-973	11-14	3310-3313	4	U30C	GE	1969-70	

GP7 No. 1130 wears T&P's original orange and black scheme.
Trains magazine collection

Original road numbers	Second numbers	Third numbers	Qty.	Model	Builder	Dates built	Notes
1000-1019			20	NW2	EMD	1946-49	
1020-1023	1215-1218	1202..1204	4	SW7	EMD	1950	
1024-1036	1219-1231		13	SW9	EMD	1951	
1061, 1062, 1100	1063		3	RS-2	Alco	1948-49	6
1071			1	RS-3	Alco	1956	6
1110-1130	110-130		21	GP7	EMD	1950-52	
1131-1144	386-399		14	GP9	EMD	1957	
1145-1149	500-504		5	GP18	EMD	1960	
1275-1299			25	SW1200	EMD	1966	
1500-1582	850-932	1850..1932	83	F7A	EMD	1949-51	7
1500B-1534B			35	F7B	EMD	1949-52	7
2010-2017	30-37		8	E8A	EMD	1951	
3329-3334			6	U30C	GE	1974	

Notes:
1—Nos. 97-105 are ex-Kansas, Oklahoma & Gulf 801-809.
2—Nos. 106-109 are ex-Midland Valley 151, 154, 152, 153; 152, 153 rebuilt from GP7 to GP9m following 1958 wreck.
3—Ex-KO&G 700, 701.
4—Nos. 650-667 are ex-C&EI (same numbers).
5—Ex-KO&G 751-754, 755B, 756B.
6—Nos. 1061, 1062, 1071 are ex-Texas Pacific Missouri Pacific Terminal 956, 957, 959; no. 1100 was transferred to TPMPT, then re-acquired and renumbered 1063.
7—Nos. 1500, 1501, 1531B-1534B are steam-generator equipped.

Published rosters:
Extra 2200 South, April 1968; Missouri Pacific Diesel Power, by Kevin EuDaly (White River Productions, 1994)

Toledo, Peoria & Western
1946-1983

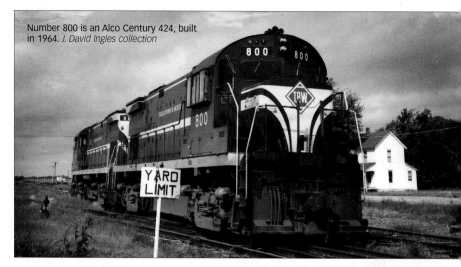

Number 800 is an Alco Century 424, built in 1964. *J. David Ingles collection*

The Toledo, Peoria & Western dieselized with a mix of Alco and EMD RS-2s and Geeps, along with a trio of Lima switchers. The railroad sampled both EMD and Alco diesels in the 1960s, then returned to EMD for GP38-2s in the late 1970s. The TP&W was co-owned by the Santa Fe and Pennsylvania from 1960 onward. Santa Fe acquired full ownership from a Conrail subsidiary in 1979 and merged the TP&W in 1983. This roster does not cover the new TP&W, which was formed in 1989.

Road numbers	Qty.	Model	Builder	Dates built	Notes
100	1	F3A	EMD	1945	1
101	1	F3B	EMD	1945	1
102, 103	2	GP7	EMD	1952	
200-206	7	RS-2	Alco	1948-49	
207	1	RS-3	Alco	1950	
300-302	3	LH-1000	Lima	1949-50	2
303-306	4	SW1500	EMD	1968, 1970	
400-402	3	RS-11	Alco	1958-59	
600	1	GP18	EMD	1961	
700	1	GP30	EMD	1963	
800, 801	2	C-424	Alco	1964	
900-902	3	GP35	EMD	1965	
1000	1	GP40	EMD	1969	3
2001-2011	11	GP38-2	EMD	1977-78	

Notes:
1—Former EMD demonstrators 291A-B, acquired 1946.
2—No. 302 is former Lima-Hamilton demonstrator 1004.
3—Former EMD demonstrator 21.

Published roster:
Diesel Era, November-December 2005

Union Pacific (classic)
1934-1994

The Union Pacific was an early buyer of diesels for passenger service—notably for its M-10000 fleet of streamliners beginning in 1934—along with diesel switchers (mainly from Electro-Motive and Alco). However, the railroad continued buying new steam locomotives into the 1940s and didn't begin dieselizing freight trains until 1947, and then did so largely with EMD F3s and GP9s. As those diesels were retired, the UP standardized on EMD's SD40 and SD40-2, acquiring a large fleet through the 1980s.

The UP's locomotive fleet grew substantially as the railroad itself grew in size with acquisitions over the years. This roster covers UP diesel orders through 1994 and includes locomotives acquired through its mergers of Western Pacific (1982), Missouri Pacific (merged in 1982, but not fully absorbed until several years later), and Missouri-Kansas-Texas (1988). It does not cover UP acquisitions of Chicago & North Western (1995) or Southern Pacific (1996), as that period saw both a huge influx of new locomotives as well as a mass renumbering of existing locomotives. See the following entry for a current UP roster.

Original road numbers	Second numbers	Third numbers	Qty.	Model	Builder	Dates built	Notes
LA-1, SF-1	921A, 901A	984J, 983J	2	E2A	EMC	1937	1
LA-2, -3, SF-2, -3	922B, 923B, 902B, 903B	984BJ, CJ, 983BJ, CJ	4	E2B	EMC	1937	1
LA-5, -6 (1)	5M1A, 5M1B	951A, 952B	2	E3A, E3B	EMC	1939	
7M1, 7M2, 8M1, 8M2, 9M1, 9M2, LA-4, SF-4	992-997, 985J, 987J		8	E6A	EMC	1940-41	1

The Union Pacific had a substantial fleet (220) of EMD GP9s, along with 125 cabless GP9Bs (second unit). *Union Pacific*

Original road numbers	Second numbers	Third numbers	Qty.	Model	Builder	Dates built	Notes
LA-5, -6, SF-5, -6	905B, 906B, 925B, 926B	985BJ, 985CJ, 987BJ, 987CJ	4	E6B	EMC	1941	1
31-53 (1)			23	U50	GE	1963-65	
50-79 (2, 3)			30	GP50	EMD	1980-81	2
60, 61 (2)			2	C-855	Alco	1964	
60B			1	C-855B	Alco	1964	
60-65			6	SD45 Sulzer	EMD		3
70-84 (2)			15	DD35	EMD	1965	
72B-98B			27	DD35B	EMD	1963-64	
100-184 (2)			85	B23-7	GE	1980-81	2
130-349			220	GP9	EMD	1954, 1957	
130B-204B, 300B-349B			125	GP9B	EMD	1954, 1957	
200-254 (2)			55	B30-7A	GE	1981-82	2
257-259 (2)			3	B23-7M	GE	1980-81	2
400-429, 445-448	3999	99	34	SD24	EMD	1958-60	
500-516 (2), 581-599			36	GP40	EMD	1966-69	4
530-571 (2)			42	U23B	GE	1974-77	2
500-540 (1)			41	F3Au	EMD		5
500B-542B			43	F3Bu	EMD		5
600-650 (2)			51	GP40	EMD	1966-71	6

Original road numbers	Second numbers	Third numbers	Qty.	Model	Builder	Dates built	Notes
651-691 (2, 3)			41	GP40	EMD	1966-71	7
667-684 (2)	9951-9966		18	GP40	EMD	1968	4
604-607 (1)			4	PA-1	Alco	1949	
604B-607B			4	PB-1	Alco	1949	
620, 621, 620B, 621B			4	UM20BA, B	GE	1954	8
625-640 (1)			16	U25B	GE	1961-62	9
675-678 (1)			4	RS-27	Alco	1959-60	10
700-707 (1)	650-657		8	Erie A	F-M	1945-48	11
700B, 702B-704B, 706B (1)	650B, 652B-654B, 656B		5	Erie B	F-M	1945-48	11
700-729 (2, 1)	100-129		30	GP7	EMD	1953	
700-729 (3, 2)	470-499		30	GP20	EMD	1960	
700-735 (4, 3)			36	GP30	EMD	1963	
700B-739B (2)			40	GP30B	EMD	1963	12
740-763			24	GP35	EMD	1963-64	13
775-784	450-459		10	SD7	EMD	1953	
782-799 (2)			18	GP35	EMD	1963-65	7
800-875			76	GP30	EMD	1961-62	13
900-914 (1), 943-962			35	E9A	EMD	1954-64	
900B-904B, 910B-913B, 950B-974B			34	E9B	EMD	1954-63	
907A, 927A, 930A, 931A, 959A, 960A, 988	986, 989, 990, 998, 999		7	E7A	EMD	1946	
908B, 909B, 928B, 929B, 961B-963B	986B, 986C, 988B, 990B, 994B, 996B, 998B		7	E7B	EMD	1946	
925-942			18	E8A	EMD	1950-53	
922B-949B			28	E8B	EMD	1950-53	
905-910 (2), 964A-968A	900-904	1451-1461	11	F3A	EMD	1947-48	14
905B-909B (odd), 905C-909C (odd), 969B-978B	900B-904B, 900C-904B	1451B-1458B, 1451C-1458C	16	F3B	EMD	1947-48	14
911, 912 (1)	1498, 1499		2	FP7	EMD	1952	
910B, 910C	1498A, C		2	F7B	EMD	1952	14
900-914 (2)	3002-3007, 1461-1469		15	GP40-2	EMD	1979-80	7
994A-997A	600-603		4	PA-1	Alco	1947	
998B, 999B	600B, 602B		2	PB-1	Alco	1947	
1000-1014 (2)	1300-1314		15	MP15DC	EMD		15
1000-1095 (1, 2)			96	NW2	EMD	1939-48	
1036-1054 (1), 1119-1153	1100-1118		54	S-2	Alco	1943-45	
1055-1060 (1)	1200-1205		6	VO1000	Baldwin	1943-44	
1180-1190	1280-1290		11	RSC-2	Alco	1947-48	16
1191-1195	1291-1295		5	RS-2	Alco	1947-49	
1206-1210			5	DS-4-4-10	Baldwin	1948	
1211-1222			12	RS-1	Alco	1949-53	17
1250 (1)			1	DRS-6-4-15	Baldwin	1946	18
1250 (2)			1	S-3	Alco	1950	19
1251			1	HH1000	Alco	1940	19
1260-1265			6	AS-616	Baldwin	1951-52	
1270			1	RS-1m	Alco	1943	20
1300-1304			5	H-10-44	F-M	1945, 1947	
1315-1327 (2)			13	SW1500	EMD	1967-80	2, 4, 7
1325-1329 (1)			5	H-15-44	F-M	1948	
1330-1392 (2)			63	MP15	EMD	1974-82	2
1340-1342 (1)			3	H-16-44	F-M	1950	
1360-1370 (1)			11	H-20-44	F-M	1947	21

Original road numbers	Second numbers	Third numbers	Qty.	Model	Builder	Dates built	Notes
1393-1428 (2)			36	MP15AC	EMD		22
1399	03999	903999	1	44-tonner	GE	1947	
1400-1409 (2)			10	SDP35	EMD	1965	
1400-1463 (1)	1500..1528	502..536	64	F3A	EMD	1947-48	23
1400B-1458B (even), 1400C-1458C (even)	1500B..1526B, 1500C..1526C	500B..540B	60	F3B	EMD	1947-48	23
1464-1483			20	F7A	EMD	1950-52	
1464B-1498B (even), 1464C-1498C (even)			36	F7B	EMD	1951-52	
1500A-1523A, 1542A, 1543A	1600-1625		26	FA-1	Alco	1947	
1524B-1541B	1600B-1616B, 1600C-1616C (even)		18	FB-1	Alco	1947	
1550-1563			14	F3A	EMD	1948-49	
1550B-1562B (even), 1550C-1562C (even)			14	F3B	EMD	1948-49	
1626-1643			18	FA-1	Alco	1948	
1618B-1642B (even), 1618C-1642C (even)			26	FB-1	Alco	1948	
1555-1714 (2)			160	GP15-1	EMD	1976-82	2
1715-1744			30	GP15AC	EMD	1982	
1800-1828	300-328		29	GP38-2	EMD	1974-81	2
1800-1824	1200..1274		25	SW7	EMD	1950	24
1825-1866	1200..1274		42	SW9	EMD	1953	24
1870-1877			8	TR5A	EMD	1951	
1870B-1877B			8	TR5B	EMD	1951	
1975-1981			7	GP38	EMD	1967-69	4
1982-1999			18	GP38AC	EMD	1967-70	4
2000-2059	500-559		60	GP38-2	EMD	1974-75	
2060..2348, 2380-2389	349-363, 560-563, 611..848		325	GP38-2	EMD	1973-81	2, 4
2350-2378	1200-1208		29	GP39-2	EMD	1977-84	4
2400-2539			140	C30-7	GE	1977-80	25
2800-2809			10	U28C	GE	1966-70	
2810-2959			150	U30C	GE	1972-74	
2900-2909 (1)			10	C-630	Alco	1966	
3000-3039, 3048-3122			115	SD40	EMD	1966-71	
3000, 3001 (2)			2	GP40	EMD	1968	4
3002-3007 (2)			6	GP40-2	EMD	1979-80	7
3040-3047			8	SD40X	EMD	1965	
3123-3239, 3275-3304, 3335-3399, 3410-3583, 3609-3808			586	SD40-2	EMD	1972-80	
3809-3844			36	SD40-2	EMD	1978-81	4
3900-3973, 4090-4321			307	SD40-2	EMD	1973-80	2
3600-3649 (1)	1-50 (2)		50	SD45	EMD	1968	
4000-4089			90	SD40	EMD	1967-71	2
5000-5039 (1)			40	U50C	GE	1969-71	
5000-5059 (2)			60	SD50	EMD	1984	2
6000-6084	2155-2239		85	SD60	EMD	1986	
6085-6365	2240-2520		281	SD60M	EMD	1988-1992	
6900-6946			47	DDA40X	EMD	1969-71	
8000-8099	3240..3608		100	SD40-2	EMD	1973-79	26
9000-9005 (1)	90-95		6	GP40X	EMD	1977-78	
9000-9059 (2)			60	C36-7	GE	1985	2
9100-9355			256	Dash 8-40C	GE	1987-89	
9356-9405			50	Dash 8-40CW	GE	1989-90	

Original road numbers	Second numbers	Third numbers	Qty.	Model	Builder	Dates built	Notes
9406-9559			154	Dash 8-41CW	GE	1990-93	
9700-9739			40	Dash 9-44CW	GE	1994	
9997-9999	6700-6702		3	AC4400CW	GE	1994	
M10000, M10001, M10002A-M10006A			7	A unit	EMC	1934-37	27
M10002B-M10006B			5	B unit	EMC	1936-37	27

Notes:
General: Many early diesel switchers originally had a "D.S." prefix to their numbers (NW2, S-2, RS-2, RSC-2, 44-tonner). This was eliminated in 1953. Early cab unit numbering was complex—see Extra 2200 South for unit-by-unit details.
1—LA and SF locomotives were assigned to the City of Los Angeles and City of San Francisco trains and were jointly owned with train co-operators Chicago & North Western and (for the SF set) Southern Pacific. The "J" suffix dropped after joint ownership ended in 1948; locomotives were divided among owners.
2—Former Missouri Pacific engines, acquired with 1982 merger.
3—Rebuilt from retired SD45s with new Sulzer engines by Morrison-Knudsen in 1980-82.
4—Former Missouri-Kansas-Texas engines, acquired with 1988 merger.
5—F3s rebuilt to F9s in 1958-59; the railroad considered them F9s (as opposed to rebuilt F3s).
6—Ex-Rock Island.
7—Ex-Western Pacific, acquired with 1982 merger.
8—Experimental A-B-B-A cab units.
9—Nos. 633-636 are former GE demonstrators 2501-2504.
10—Former Alco demonstrators 640-2, -3, -4, -5.
11—The first Erie-Builts were an A-B-A set numbered 50M1A, 50M3B, and 50M2A, which were renumbered 981A, 983B, 982A. The next were 984A, 985A, 986B, 987B; they were renumbered to 700-series in 1948.
12—Nos. 727B-739B are steam-generator equipped.
13—Nos. 762, 763, 875 are former EMD demonstrators 5652, 5654, 5629.
14—Steam-generator equipped.
15—Ex-Pittsburgh & Lake Erie.
16—No. 1190 is former Alco demonstrator 1190.
17—Ex-Spokane International 200-211, acquired with merger in 1958.
18—Former Baldwin demonstrator 1500.
19—Nos. 1250 (2), 1251 are ex-Mount Hood 50, 51, acquired 1968.
20—Ex-Bamberger; re-engined by EMD in 1951, acquired 1959.
21—Nos. 1365, 1366 are former F-M demonstrators (both numbered 2000).
22—Ex-MKT, Soo Line.
23—F3As 1400-1423 briefly wore "A" suffix; F3Bs to 1428B and C briefly wore 1442B-1471B.
24—Rebuilt to SW10 (railroad designation) and renumbered, beginning in 1980.
25—Nos. 2400-2414 initially numbered 2960-2974; renumbered shortly after delivery.
26—SD40-2s with high-speed gearing. Their renumbering falls into gaps in 3000 series.
27—EMC power units for Pullman-built streamlined trains. M10000 had a Winton distillate engine (later converted to butane); the rest were Winton diesels.

Published rosters:
Extra 2200 South, January-February-March 1979, April-May-June 1979, July-August-September 1979, October-November-December 1979, January-February-March 1980.

Union Pacific
Current

This roster is current as of early 2017.

Initial	Number series	Model	Builder	Dates
UP	96	SW10	EMD	1982
UP	238, 282	GP38-2	EMD	1972-1980
UP	500-847	GP38-2/GP38N	EMD	1972-1981
UP	949951	E9A (E38-2)	EMD	1955
UP	963B	E9B (E38B-2)	EMD	1955
UP	1000-1140	GP60/GP62	EMD	1987-1994
UP	1200-1216	GP39-2	EMD	1977-1984
UP	1335	GP40R	EMD	1966
UP	1337-1442	GP40-2/GP40-2N	EMD	1972-1980
UP	1441	GP40R	EMD	1966
UP	1445-1457	GP40-2	EMD	1972-1983
UP	1458	GP40-2M	EMD	1974-1980
UP	1459-1460	GP40R	EMD	1966
UP	1461-1469	GP40-2	EMD	1979-1980
UP	1470-1534	GP40M-2	EMD	1979
UP	1535-1540	GP40-2	EMD	1979-1980
UP	1550-2011	SD40-2/SD40N	EMD	1972-1985
UP	3035-3700	SD40N	EMD	1972-1985

Union Pacific classifies this GE ES44AC as an AC45CCTE. *Jeff Wilson*

Initial	Number series	Model	Builder	Dates
UP	1900-2098	GP60	EMD	1987-1994
UP	1938	SD40-2	EMD	1975
UP	1982-1996	SD70ACe	EMD	2005
UP	2001, 2002	SD70M	EMD	2001
UP	2010	C45ACCTE	GE	2009
UP	2100-2239	SD60/SD62	EMD	1986-1988
UP	2240-2519	SD60M	EMD	1989-1992
UP	2520-2569	ES44AC (T4C)	GE	2015
UP	2570-2769	ET44AC	GE	2015
UP	2965-2992	SD40-2	EMD	1973-1976
UP	3000-3099	SD70ACe-T4	EMD	2016
UP	3106-3769	SD40-2/R	EMD	1972-1985
UP	3484-3777	SD9043AC	EMD	1995-1998
UP	3778-3999	SD70M	EMD	2003-2004
UP	4000-5231	SD70M	EMD	2000-2004
UP	4141	SD70ACe	EMD	2005
UP	5245	GP40-2	EMD	1974
UP	5248-6081	C45ACCTE	GE	2001-2006
UP	6106, 6165	SD60M	EMD	1989-1992
UP	6145-6887	C44AC	GE	1995-2000
UP	6888-6935	C44/60AC	GE	1995-1998
UP	6936	DDA40X	EMD	1971
UP	6937-6968	C44/60AC	GE	1998-2000
UP	6995-7009	C44AC	GE	1997-1999

Initial	Number series	Model	Builder	Dates
UP	7010-7079	C6044AC	GE	1995-1996
UP	7080-7297	C44AC	GE	1997-1999
UP	7300-7344	C6044AC	GE	1995-1998
UP	7345-7529	C45ACCTE	GE	2009-2011
UP	7600-8051	C45ACCTE	GE	2007-2012
UP	8052-8267	C45AH	GE	2013
UP	8146-8196	SD9043AC	EMD	1995-1998
UP	8309-8823	SD70ACe	EMD	2005-2013
UP	8824-8996	SD70AH	EMD	2014
UP	8997-9061	SD70AH (T4C)	EMD	2016
UP	9101-9355	C40-8	GE	1987-1989
UP	9356-9395	C40-8W	GE	1990-1993
UP	9396-9559	C41-8W	GE	1990-1993
UP	9564-9834	C44-9W	GE	1993-1994
UP	9835-9899	SD40-2	EMD	1972-1985
UP	9900-9927	SD59MX	EMD	2010-2014
UP	9986-9992	GP40-2	EMD	1979-1980
UPY	105-175	CCRCL	GE	R2003
UPY	302	SD40N	EMD	R 2015
UPY	402	PS6B		R 2015
UPY	545-714	GP15-1/GP15N	EMD	1973-1982
UPY	715-744	GP15-1AC	EMD	1982
UPY	800-867	SD38-2/PS6B	EMD	1973-1975
UPY	887-899	RP20SD	Railpower	2008-2012
UPY	900-913	RP20GP	Railpower	2015
UPY	926	S4-B	EMD	1982
UPY	927929	S5-2B	EMD	1991
UPY	932936937	S3-2B	EMD	1981-1982
UPY	939940	S6-1B	EMD	R2003
UPY	1072-1214	SW1500	EMD	1970
UPY	1367	MP15DC	EMD	1974-1982
UPY	1401-1487	MP15AC/MP15N	EMD	1975-1980
UPY	2005	GS14B	EMD	2005
UPY	2100-2112	MP20GP	MotivePower	2006
UPY	2602-2699	RP20GE	Railpower	2006-2007
UPY	2701-2760	GS21B	NRE	2006-2007
UPY	3001	GP59ECO	EMD	R2013
UPY	3002	S3-2B	GE	R2013
UPY	3003	SD40N	EMD	2015
UPY	3004	S3-2B	UP	2015
UPY	3005	SD40N	EMD	2015
UPY	3006	S3-2B	UP	2015
UPY	3007	SD40N	EMD	2015
UPY	3008	S3-2B	UP	2015
UPY	3011	SD40N	EMD	2015
UPY	3012	S3-2B	UP	2015
UPY	3200-3207	SD40-2R	EMD	1972-1985
CNW	8646, 8701	C44-9W	GE	1993-1994

Utah Railway
1952-2002

The Utah Railway dieselized in the early 1950s with Alco's six-axle RSD-4 and RSD-5 locomotives. The first ones were purchased new, then in the 1970s the railroad bought used six-axle Alcos from several railroads. In 2002 the railroad was sold to holding company Genesee & Wyoming.

Utah RSD-4 No. 307 is a former Central of New Jersey locomotive. *Ed Fulcomer*

Road numbers	Qty.	Model	Builder	Dates built	Notes
300-305, 307	7	RSD-4	Alco	1952-53	1
306	1	RSD-5	Alco	1955	
400-403	4	RSD-15	Alco	1959-60	2
600, 601	2	RSD-12	Alco	1956	3
2000-2009	10	GP38-2	EMD	1964-65	4
3000-3002	3	GP40	EMD	1970-71	5
5001-5006	6	MK50-3	Morrison-Knudsen	1994-95	6
6060-6064	5	SD50S	EMD	1982-83	7
6606-6608, 6613	4	F45	EMD	1969	8
9001-9011	11	SD40M	EMD	1969-70	9
9012	1	SD45-2M	EMD	1972	10
9013	1	F45	EMD	1968	11
9140-9150	11	SD45	EMD	1966-70	12

Notes:
1—No. 307 is ex-Central of New Jersey 1611, acquired 1971.
2—Ex-Santa Fe 9822, 9823, 9839, 9847, acquired 1975.
3—Ex-Lake Superior & Ishpeming 2014, 2016, nee Chesapeake & Ohio 6707, 6709, acquired 1974; 601 wrecked before being repainted and renumbered.
4—Former Southern Pacific and Rio Grande GP35s rebuilt to GP38-2 standards.
5—Ex-Baltimore & Ohio 4046, 4040, ex-Western Pacific 3525.
6—Former MK5000Cs rebuilt by Boise Locomotive; 5001-5003 are ex-SP 501-503.
7—Ex-Hamersley Iron.
8—Ex-Burlington Northern 6606-6608, 6613, nee Great Northern 433-435, 440.
9—Former C&O, Clinchfield, Louisville & Nashville, and Western Maryland SD40s, rebuilt, acquired 1991.
10—Ex-Santa Fe 5855, rebuilt with Caterpillar engine, acquired 1993.
11—Ex-Santa Fe 5960.
12—Ex-SP, acquired 1985-88.

Published rosters:
Diesel Locomotive Rosters (Wayner Publications); Diesel Era, May-June 1994

Vermont Railway/Vermont Rail System
Includes Clarendon & Pittsford; Green Mountain Railroad; and New York & Ogdensburg
1964-present

The Vermont Railway began operating in 1964 when the state of Vermont acquired much of the former Rutland. Vermont purchased the Clarendon & Pittsford in 1972 and the Green Mountain in 1997 by forming a new umbrella corporation, Vermont Rail System. The system also owns the New York & Ogdensburg. Road power is typically the collection of second-hand GP38 and GP40 diesels VRS has acquired since the 1990s, but larger leased power is also used. The Alcos have all been retired or sold except for RS-1 405, an original Rutland unit that powers excursions and sees occasional freight duty.

Road numbers	Qty.	Model	Builder	Dates built	Notes
1, 10	2	44-tonner	GE	1948, 1946	1
5	1	SW1	EMC	1940	2
14 (NY&O)	1	SW900	EMD	1951	3
201, 202	2	GP38-2	EMD	1972, 1974	
203 (C&P)	1	GP38	EMD	1966	4
204 (C&P)	1	GP38-2	EMD	1973	4
205-207	3	GP38-3	EMD	1969	5
250	1	RS-1	Alco	1947	6
301	1	GP40	EMD	1967	7
302, 304, 305 (GM)	3	GP40	EMD	1970-71	7
303	1	GP40-2	EMD	1977	8
306 (C&P)	1	GP40-2	EMD	1972	9
307, 308	2	GP40-2	EMD	1984, 1977	10
310, 311	2	GP40-2LW	EMD	1976	11
312, 381	2	GP40-3	EMD	1967, 1990	12
401-404	4	RS-1	Alco	1951, 1946	13
405 (GM)	1	RS-1	Alco	1951	13
431, 432	2	SD70M-2	EMD	2006	14
501	1	SW1500	EMD	1966	
601	1	RS-3	Alco	1951	15
751	1	GP9	EMD	1954	16
801	1	GP18	EMD	1961	17
802 (C&P)	1	GP16	EMD	1950	17
803 (GM)	1	GP9	EMD	1956	17
804 (GM)	1	GP9r	EMD	1955	17

Notes:
1—No. 1 is ex-Middletown & Unionville 1; 10 is ex-Pennsylvania 9334, acquired 1964.
2—Ex-Erie Lackawanna 355 (nee Delaware, Lackawanna & Western 433), acquired 1965.
3—Ex-Rock Island.
4—No. 203 is ex-Maine Central 255, acquired 1991; 204 is ex-Seaboard Coast Line 528, acquired 1991.
5—Rebuilt GP38s, originally Penn Central and Southern; no. 205 acquired in 2005, others in 2011.
6—Ex-New York, Susquehanna & Western 250, acquired 1965.
7—No. 301 is ex-Western of Alabama 701, acquired 1993; 302 is ex-Baltimore & Ohio 4017, acquired 1997; 304 is ex-B&O 3756, acquired 1998; 305 is ex-SCL 1606, acquired 1999.
8—Ex-Boston & Maine 314, acquired 1998.
9—Ex-Texas, Oklahoma & Eastern D-15, acquired 2000.
10—No. 307 is ex-St. Louis Southwestern 7255; 308 is ex-B&M 303, acquired 2004-05.
11—Ex-Canadian National 9650, 9662, acquired 2005.
12—No. 312 is ex-Rio Grande GP40 3077, rebuilt, acquired 2009; 381 is ex-Texas-Mexican GP60 869.
13—Nos. 401-403 are ex-Rutland 401-403, acquired 1964; no. 404 is ex-Duluth, South Shore & Atlantic 102, acquired 1967; No. 405 is ex-Rutland 405, acquired 1965.
14—Ex-Florida East Coast 101, 103.
15—Ex-Lehigh & Hudson River 12, acquired 1970.
16—Ex-Conrail 7301.
17—No. 801 is ex-Toledo, Peoria & Western 600, acquired 1983; 802 is nee Atlantic Coast Line GP7 103, rebuilt by SCL in 1979, acquired 1993; 803 is ex-Chesapeake & Ohio 6181; 804 is ex-Norfolk & Western 13, rebuilt, acquired 1992.

Published rosters:
Diesel Locomotive Rosters (Wayner Publications); Trains, December 2014

Virginian
1954-1959

The Virginian dieselized late, relying on steam and heavy electric locomotives (the line included a 134-mile electrified segment) into the 1950s, with the last steam running in 1957. It became noted for dieselizing with all Fairbanks-Morse power, other than a second-hand GE 44-tonner. The Virginian rostered the largest fleets of both H-24-66 Train Masters (25) and H-16-44s (40). The Virginian merged into the Norfolk & Western in 1959.

Virginian No. 58 is an early H-24-66, with a space between the radiator fans.
Fairbanks-Morse

Road numbers	Qty.	Model	Builder	Dates built	Notes
6	1	44-tonner	GE	1941	1
10-49	40	H-16-44	F-M	1954-57	2
50-74	25	H-24-66	F-M	1954, 1957	

Notes:
1—Ex-New Haven 0806.
2—Two equipped with steam generators.

Wabash
1939-1964

Wabash began buying diesel switchers from several builders in 1939 and began dieselizing main lines with a large fleet of F7s, along with some Geeps, in 1949. Main lines were fully dieselized by 1953 and the last branch line in 1955. Wabash had just begun sampling second-generation diesels from EMD (GP35s), Alco (C-424s), and GE (U25Bs) when it was merged into Norfolk & Western in 1964.

Wabash No. 454 is a GP7 built in 1951. It's one of 34 on the Wabash. *EMD*

Original road numbers	Second numbers	Qty.	Model	Builder	Dates built	Notes
51		1	45-tonner	GE	1939	
95-97	347-349	3	NW2	EMD	1940-41	
100, 150		2	HH660	Alco	1939-40	
101-111		11	SW1	EMD	1939-49	
120-132		13	SW8	EMD, GMD	1950-53	
151-159		9	S-1	Alco	1941-48	
200		1	VO660	Baldwin	1941	
201, 202		2	DS-4-4-6	Baldwin	1947	
300-302		3	VO1000	Baldwin	1942-44	
303, 304		2	DS-4-4-10	Baldwin	1946, 1949	
305-309		5	S-12	Baldwin	1951, 1953	
310-321, 325		13	S-2	Alco	1942-49	1
322-324		3	S-4	Alco	1953	
346-353		8	NW2	EMD	1946, 1949	2
355-362		8	SW7	EMD	1950	
363-374		12	SW9	EMD	1951-53	
375-379		5	SW1200	EMD	1954, 1957	
380-383		4	H-10-44	F-M	1946, 1949	
384-386		3	H-12-44	F-M	1953	
400-411		12	LS-1200	Lima	1950	3
450-483		34	GP7	EMD	1950-53	4
484-495		12	GP9	EMD	1954-56	
500-514		16	U25B	GE	1962	5
540-547		8	GP35	EMD	1964	
550-554, 552A-554A	555-557	8	H-24-66	F-M	1954, 1956	
B900-B906		7	C-424	Alco	1964	6
1000, 1003-1015		14	E8A	EMD	1949-53	
1001A, 1002A	1016, 1017	2	E7A	EMD	1946-47	
1020, 1021, 1020A, 1021A	1050-1053	4	PA-2	Alco	1949	
1100B-1108B	600-608	9	F7B	EMD	1949	
1100-1108, 1100A-1108A, 1140-1189, 1140A-1189A	609-726	118	F7A	EMD, GMD	1949-53	
1200B-1204B	800-804	5	FB-1	Alco	1949	
1200-1204, 1200A-1204A	805-814	10	FA-1	Alco	1949	

Notes:
1—No. 325 is ex-Nickel Plate 5, acquired 1964.
2—Nos. 346-349 are ex-NKP 98, 95, 96, 97 (nee Wheeling & Lake Erie); no. 353 is ex-New Jersey, Indiana & Illinois 2 (nee Indiana Northern 100).
3—Nos. 400 and 407 are ex-Lima-Hamilton demonstrators 1002, 1003.
4—Nos. 454, 464, 474, 479-482 are steam-generator equipped.
5—No. 512 was wrecked; another U25B, no. 515, was delivered as a replacement in 1965 following the merger.
6—Built for National of Mexico, used by Wabash as boosters only.

Published rosters:
Extra 2200 South, January 1968; Wabash, by Donald J. Heimburger (Heimburger House 1984)

Western Maryland
1941-1973

The Western Maryland bought diesel switchers during World War II and Alco RS-2s and EMD BL2 after the war, but didn't begin dieselizing mainline freights until GP7s and F7s began arriving in 1950. The WM bought new, large steam locomotives (4-8-4s) as late as 1947, but the railroad was dieselized by 1954. The WM was controlled by the Baltimore & Ohio and Chesapeake & Ohio, and diesel numbering in the mid-1960s reflected a common numbering system of locomotive models with the parent railroads. This roster covers locomotives through February 26, 1973, when Western Maryland became part of Chessie System with B&O and C&O.

Number 186 is an Alco RS-3. *Western Maryland*

Road Numbers	Second road numbers	Qty.	Model	Builder	Dates built	Notes
51, 52		2	F3A	EMD	1947	3
53-66		14	F7A	EMD	1950	
53B-65B (odd)	401-407	7	F7B	EMD	1950	
75, 76		2	44-tonner	GE	1943	
81, 82		2	BL2	EMD	1948	
101		1	VO660	Baldwin	1941	
102		1	S-1	Alco	1941	
103-105		3	VO660	Baldwin	1942	
125-127, 140-144		8	S-2	Alco	1943-46	
128-132		5	VO1000	Baldwin	1943-44	
133, 134		2	DS-4-4-10	Baldwin	1946	
145, 146		2	S-4	Alco	1950	
151, 152		2	S-6	Alco	1956	
170-172		3	DRS-4-4-15	Baldwin	1947-48	
173-177		5	AS-16	Baldwin	1951	
180-184		5	RS-2	Alco	1947, 1950	
185-198		14	RS-3	Alco	1953-54	4
231-242		12	F7A	EMD	1952	
231B-243B (odd)	408-414	7	F7B	EMD	1952-53	
301-304		4	FA-1	Alco	1951	
501-505	3576-3580	5	GP35	EMD	1963	
3795-3798		4	GP40	EMD	1971	
7432-7436		5	SD35	EMD	1964	
7446-7449, 7470-7474, 7495, 7496		11	SD40	EMD	1966-69	

Notes:
1—GP7s and GP9s were rebuilt with home-shop chopped noses from 1962-1966.
2—No. 33 is former EMD demonstrator 7257.
3—Rebuilt to F7As in 1954.
4—Nos. 197, 198 steam-generator equipped.

Published rosters:
Diesel Era, January/February 2000; Extra 2200 South, January-February 1973

Western Pacific
1939-1982

Western Pacific began acquiring diesel switchers in 1939 and was an early buyer of EMD's FT, receiving 48 (12 A-B-B-A sets) during World War II. Additional F units and Geeps followed, with most steam gone by 1951 and dieselization complete in 1953. Other than some early Alco and Baldwin switchers, the railroad stuck mainly with EMD, dabbling a bit with GE (U30Bs and U23Bs) around 1970. The WP was merged into Union Pacific in December 1982.

Western Pacific FTs carried number boxes atop the cab roof. *Western Pacific*

Original road numbers	Second road numbers	Qty.	Model	Builder	Dates built	Notes
501-503		3	SW1	EMD	1939	
504-511		8	S-1	Alco	1942	
551-562, 554 (2)		12	S-2	Alco	1942-50	1
563, 564		2	S-4	Alco	1951	
581-585		5	VO-1000	Baldwin	1945	
601-606		6	SW9	EMD	1952	
607, 608		2	NW2	EMD	1940	2
701-713		13	GP7	EMD	1952-53	
725-732		8	GP9	EMD	1955	
751-771	3051-3071	9	U30B	GE	1967-71	3
801A-803A	925A, 925D	3	F3A	EMD	1947	4, 5
801B-803B, 801C-803C		6	F3B	EMD	1947	4
801D	926A	1	F3A	EMD	1948	6
804A, 805A, 804D, 805D		4	FP7	EMD	1950	
804B-806B		3	F7B	EMD	1950	4
901A-912A, 901D-912D		24	FTA	EMD	1942-44	
901B-912B, 901C-912C		24	FTB	EMD	1942-44	
913A-924A, 913D-924D		24	F7A	EMD	1950-51	
913B-924B, 913C-924C	806B	24	F7B	EMD	1950-51	7
1501-1503		3	SW1500	EMD	1973	
2001-2010		10	GP20	EMD	1959-60	
2251-2265		15	U23B	GE	1972	
3001-3022		22	GP35	EMD	1963-65	
3501-3544		44	GP40	EMD	1966-71	
3545-3559		15	GP40-2	EMD	1979-80	

Notes:
1—No. 554 (2) is ex-Tidewater Southern 745, nee Texas Pacific-Missouri Pacific Terminal 12.
2—Ex-Stockton Terminal & Eastern 1000, 1001, nee Union Pacific 1000, 1001; no. 1000 was EMC demonstrator 889.
3—Engines ride on EMD trucks from traded-in F units. No. 765 wrecked in 1971, not renumbered; 3070, 3071 are former GE demonstrators 303, 304.
4—Steam-generator equipped.
5—No. 803A not renumbered.
6—Ex-Sacramento Northern 303, nee New York, Ontario & Western 503.
7—No. 920B renumbered 806B in 1967.

Published roster:
Extra 2200 South, October 1968

Wisconsin Central Ltd.

1987-2001

The Wisconsin Central was formed in 1987 as a spinoff of the Soo Line, and included much of the original Wisconsin Central (pre-Soo merger). The WC added routes and acquired a substantial fleet of second-hand power, concentrating heavily on SD45 and GP40 family diesels.

Space precludes listing all of the predecessor owners for each locomotive; the online roster thedieselshop.us provides an excellent unit-by-unit roster summary. The WC was purchased by Canadian National in 2001.

SD45 No. 6525 is typical of WC's second-hand power. *Tom Danneman*

Original road numbers	Second road numbers	Qty.	Model	Builder	Dates built	Notes
1		1	SW1	EMD	1941	
581-590		10	SDL39	EMD	1969, 1972	
700..721, 814..840	2251..2258	24	GP30	EMD	1963	
723..731	2551-2555	5	GP35	EMD	1964-65	
900		1	SW8	GMD	1951	
1230, 1233-1235, 1237, 1278	1232	6	SW1200	EMD	1963-66	
1231		1	SW9	EMD	1951	
1501-1508		8	GP7	EMD	1951-52	1
1550..1571		15	SW1500	EMD	1968-72	
1701, 1702		2	GP9	EMD	1957-58	1
1750-1756		7	FP9	GMD	1953-57	
1760-1762		3	F9B	GMD	1954-57	
2000-2006		7	GP38-2	GMD	1981	
2287	1236	1	SW1200	EMD	1965	
2401, 2402		2	SD24	EMD	1959	
2500		1	SD35	EMD	1965	
3000..3027		24	GP40	EMD	1966-71	2
3073, 3102		2	SD40	EMD	1966, 1971	
3102 (2)		1	SD40-2	EMD	1973	
4002 (1), 4004-4010, 4012, 4013	2051..2061	10	GP35m	EMD	1963-65	
4001-4003, 4016, 4018, 4025	4013 (2)	6	SD40	EMD	1967-68	
4119..4159, 4304..4332		11	GP7r	EMD	1951, 1955	
4501..4514		7	GP9r	EMD, GMD	1951-60	
5318		1	SD45u	EMD	1966	
6001		1	SD40	GMD	1971	
6002-6006		5	SD40-2	GMD	1973	
6495-6533, 6550..6556, 6578..6655	7495-7533, 7550..7556, 7578..7655	101	SD45	EMD	1966-71	1
6634	7634	1	SDP45	EMD	1970	
6650, 6651, 6653-6656		6	F45u	EMD	1968	
6652		1	FP45u	EMD	1967	
6904..6949		6	SD40-3	GMD	1970-71	

Notes:
1—Series includes both unrebuilt and rebuilt ("u" or "r" suffix) locomotives.
2—Nos. 3026, 3027 rebuilt to GP40-2.

Appendix: Railroad abbreviations

A&R	Aberdeen & Rockfish	CUT	Cincinnati Union Terminal	L&NE	Lehigh & New England	P&N	Piedmont & Northern
AC&Y	Akron, Canton & Youngstown	CITX	CIT Financial (Leasing)	LV	Lehigh Valley	P&LE	Pittsburgh & Lake Erie
AT&N	Alabama, Tennessee & Northern	CRR	Clinchfield	L&M	Litchfield & Madison	P&WV	Pittsburgh & West Virginia
AC	Algoma Central	C&S	Colorado & Southern	LIRR	Long Island Rail Road	PC&N	Point Comfort & Northern
A&S	Alton & Southern	C&C	Columbia & Cowlitz	L&A	Louisiana & Arkansas	PTMe	Portland Terminal (Maine)
AHdeM	Altos Hornos de Mexico	C&G	Columbus & Greenville	L&N	Louisville & Nashville	PTOr	Portland Terminal (Oregon)
AA	Ann Arbor	CR	Conrail	MEC	Maine Central	P&W	Providence & Worcester
AN	Apalachicola Northern	D&H	Delaware & Hudson	MRS	Manufacturers Ry.	QNS&L	Quebec, North Shore & Labrador
A&A	Arcade & Attica	DL&W	Delaware, Lackawanna & Western	MD&S	Mason, Dublin & Savannah	RR	Raritan River
AD&N	Ashley, Drew & Northern	D&RGW	Denver & Rio Grande Western	MCR	McCloud River	RF&P	Richmond, Fredericksburg & Potomac
ATSF	Atchison, Topeka & Santa Fe	DoE	Department of Energy	MILW	Milwaukee Road (Chicago, Milwaukee, St. Paul & Pacific)	RDG	Reading
A&StAB	Atlanta & St. Andrews Bay	DOT	Department of Transportation			RM	Reserve Mining
A&WP	Atlanta & West Point	D&M	Detroit & Mackinac	M&StL	Minneapolis & St. Louis	RUT	Rutland
A&D	Atlantic & Danville	D&TSL	Detroit & Toledo Shore Line	MN&S	Minneapolis, Northfield & Southern	SN	Sacramento Northern
A&EC	Atlantic & East Carolina	DE	Detroit Edison	MT	Minnesota Transfer	StJ&LC	St. Johnsbury & Lamoille County
ACL	Atlantic Coast Line	DT&I	Detroit, Toledo & Ironton	MW	Minnesota Western	SLSF	St. Louis-San Francisco
B&O	Baltimore & Ohio	D&NE	Duluth & Northeastern	MC	Mississippi Central	SSW	St. Louis Southwestern (Cotton Belt)
B&OCT	Baltimore & Ohio Chicago Terminal	DM&IR	Duluth, Missabe & Iron Range	MEx	Mississippi Export	StM	St. Mary's
BAR	Bangor & Aroostook	DSS&A	Duluth, South Shore & Atlantic	MKT	Missouri-Kansas-Texas	S&A	Savannah & Atlanta
B&C	Barre & Chelsea	D&S	Durham & Southern	MP	Missouri Pacific	SAL	Seaboard Air Line
BCR	BC Rail	EJ&E	Elgin, Joliet & Eastern	MON	Monon	SCL	Seaboard Coast Line
B&ML	Belfast & Moosehead Lake	EL	Erie Lackawanna	MGA	Monongahela	SBD	Seaboard System
BRC	Belt Ry. of Chicago	EM	Erie Mining	MCon	Monongahela Connecting	SJG	S.J. Groves (construction company)
B&LE	Bessemer & Lake Erie	FdelE	Ferrocarril del Estado	MRL	Montana Rail Link	Soo	Soo Line
BS	Birmingham Southern	FdelP	Ferrocarril del Pacifico	M-K	Morrison-Knudsen	SOU	Southern Ry.
BdeC	Bosque de Chihuahua	FMex	Ferrocarril Mexicano	NC&StL	Nashville, Chattanooga & St. Louis	SP	Southern Pacific
B&A	Boston & Albany	FSRR	Ferrocarril del Sureste	NdeM	National of Mexico	SI	Spokane International
B&M	Boston & Maine	FerO	Ferrominera Orinoco	N&SS	Newburgh & South Shore	SP&S	Spokane, Portland & Seattle
BCK	Buffalo Creek	FvrM	Ferroviaria Mexicana	NOPB	New Orleans Public Belt	TA&G	Tennessee, Alabama & Georgia
BN	Burlington Northern	FEC	Florida East Coast	NYC	New York Central	TC	Tennessee Central
BNSF	Burlington Northern Santa Fe	FDDM&S	Fort Dodge, Des Moines & Southern	NYNH&H	New York, New Haven & Hartford	TCI&RR	Tennessee Coal, Iron & Railroad
BA&P	Butte, Anaconda & Pacific	FW&D	Fort Worth & Denver	NYO&W	New York, Ontario & Western	TVA	Tennessee Valley Authority
CW	California Western	G&W	Genesee & Wyoming	NYS&W	New York, Susquehanna & Western	TRRA	Terminal Railroad Assoc. of St. Louis
C&I	Cambria & Indiana	GRR	Georgia	NN	Nevada Northern	T&P	Texas & Pacific
CN	Canadian National	GTW	Grand Trunk Western	NKP	Nickel Plate Road	TM	Texas Mexican
CP	Canadian Pacific	GN	Great Northern	NS	Norfolk Southern	TO&E	Texas, Oklahoma & Eastern
CG	Central of Georgia	GB&W	Green Bay & Western	NL&G	North Louisiana & Gulf	TU	Texas Utilities
CNJ	Central of New Jersey	GM&O	Gulf, Mobile & Ohio	NAR	Northern Alberta	TP&W	Toledo, Peoria & Western
ChP	Chihuahua Pacific	HB&T	Houston Belt & Transfer (Terminal??)	NP	Northern Pacific	TFM	Transportacion Ferroviaria Mexicana
CI	Chattahoochee Industrial	IC	Illinois Central	OAK	Oakway Leasing	URR	Union Railroad
CV	Chattahoochee Valley	ICG	Illinois Central Gulf	OM	Oliver Mining	UP	Union Pacific
CW	Chehalis Western	IT	Illinois Terminal	O&W	Oneida & Western	USDOT	U.S. Dept. of Transportation
C&O	Chesapeake & Ohio	IHB	Indiana Harbor Belt	ON	Ontario Northland	USS	U.S. Steel
C&EI	Chicago & Eastern Illinois	IU	Indianapolis Union	O&NW	Oregon & Northwestern	VGN	Virginian
C&IM	Chicago & Illinois Midland	IRR	Interstate	PE	Pacific Electric	WAB	Wabash
C&IW	Chicago & Illinois Western	IAIS	Iowa Interstate	PGE	Pacific Great Eastern	WRT	Warrior River Terminal
C&NW	Chicago & North Western	KS	Kaiser Steel	P&BR	Patapsco & Back Rivers	WC	Wisconsin Central
C&WI	Chicago & Western Indiana	KC	Kennecott Copper	PC	Penn Central	WM	Western Maryland
CB&Q	Chicago, Burlington & Quincy	K&IT	Kentucky & Indiana Terminal	PRR	Pennsylvania Railroad	WP	Western Pacific
CGW	Chicago Great Western	KCS	Kansas City Southern	PRSL	Pennsylvania-Reading Seashore Lines	WofA	Western Ry. of Alabama
CRI&P	Chicago, Rock Island & Pacific	KCSdeM	Kansas City Southern de Mexico	PM	Pere Marquette	WRT	White River Terminal
CStPM&O	Chicago, St. Paul, Minneapolis & Omaha	KCT	Kansas City Terminal	PD	Phelps-Dodge	YD	Yankeetown Dock
		LEF&C	Lake Erie, Franklin & Clarion	PB&NE	Philadelphia, Bethlehem & New England	Y&N	Youngstown & Northern
ChP	Chihuahua Pacific	LS&I	Lake Superior & Ishpeming			YS&T	Youngstown Sheet & Tube

About the author

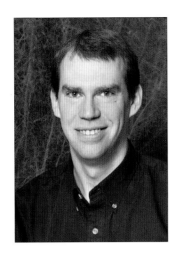

Jeff Wilson has written numerous books on railroads and model railroading. Jeff spent 10 years as an associate editor at *Model Railroader* magazine, and he currently works as a freelance writer, editor, and photographer, contributing articles to MR and other magazines. He enjoys photographing both prototype and model railroads.

Acknowledgments

I used hundreds of sources in compiling information for this book, including books on specific railroads and locomotive types; roster and spotting guides; historical society periodicals, data sheets, and books; Internet-based roster and spotting guides; promotional materials from manufacturers and railroads; and railfan, trade, and modeling magazines. Among the best resources for information on diesels are the magazines *Diesel Era* and *Extra 2200 South*. Both are devoted to diesel locomotives, with in-depth articles on specific locomotives. Back issues of each are extremely valuable reference sources. Some material in this book originally appeared in my earlier book *The Model Railroader's Guide to Diesel Locomotives* (Kalmbach, 2009). The timeline at the end of Chapter 1, written by Greg McDonnell, originally appeared in *Diesel Victory*, a 2006 special issue of *Classic Trains* magazine.

Inevitably, multiple sources on rosters don't always agree with each other. In many cases these discrepancies hinge on whether an extensively rebuilt locomotive counts as a new locomotive, which matters more to a railroad accountant than a modeler or railfan. I did my best to accurately sort these out, and any mistakes contained herein are my own.

—Jeff Wilson

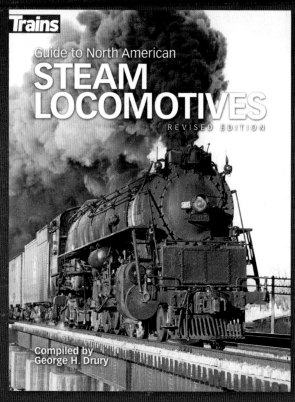